Arabian and Islamic Studies

Arabian and Islamic Studies

Articles presented to R. B. Serjeant
on the occasion of his retirement from
the Sir Thomas Adams's Chair of Arabic
at the University of Cambridge

Editors:
Dr. R. L. Bidwell, Secretary, The Middle East Centre, Cambridge.
Dr. G. R. Smith, Lecturer in Arabic in the University of Durham.

Longman London and New York

Bob and Marion Serjeant

Longman Group Limited
Longman House, Burnt Mill, Harlow
Essex CM20 2JE, England
and Associated Companies throughout the world.

First published 1983
ISBN 0 582 78308 9

Set in Lasercomp 9/10½pt Plantin

British Library Cataloguing in Publication Data
Bidwell, R. L.
Arabian and Islamic studies.
I. Islam—study and teaching
I. Title II. Smith G. R. III. Sergeant, R. B.
909'.092761 BP42
ISBN 0-582-78308-9

Library of Congress Cataloging in Publication Data
Arabian and Islamic studies.
1. Arab countries—Addresses, essays, lectures.
2. Civilization, Islamic—Addresses, essays, lectures.
3. Sergeant, R. B. (Robert Bertram)—Bibliography.
I. Bidwell, Robin Leonard. II. Smith, G. Rex (Gerald Rex) III. Serjeant, R. B. (Robert Bertram)
DS36.4.A65 1983 909'.0974927 83-12027
ISBN 0-582-78308-9

Printed in Great Britain
by Butler & Tanner Ltd,
Frome and London

Acknowledgements
We are grateful to the following for permission to reproduce copyright photographs:
The British Library for page 116; the Chester Beatty Library for page 114; Foto Mas for page 112; Museum of Islamic Art for page 115 & 117; Walter Dostal for pages 210, 211, 212, 213.

Contents

Introduction

Robert Bertram Serjeant was born in Edinburgh in March 1915 and after schooling in that city, attended its University, taking first class honours in Semitic Studies. During his years in Edinburgh he absorbed the Scottish tradition of meticulously accurate scholarship which has been so evident in all his work. He then went on to Trinity College, Cambridge, where, under the direction of the late Professor Storey, he wrote a dissertation on 'Materials for a History of Islamic Textiles' for which he was awarded a doctorate in 1939 and which has since been published in Beirut.

Thus far RBS had received a conventional training as an academic Arabist and if he had been a man of different character might well have decided, as so many of his most distinguished predecessors had done, that Arabic studies could best be pursued in the great libraries of Europe. This however was not his way, for he set out to make himself a fluent speaker of the language and to see as much of the Arab world as possible. His mastery of the spoken tongue became as remarkable as his knowledge of the classical language and he has frequently caused astonishment by this linguistic facility during his visits to the Middle East. He has often been invited to lecture in universities and to speak to wider audiences on radio and television. Wherever he goes – and he has now visited every Arab country except Iraq – he speaks to the local people and relates what he hears from them to what he has learned in the study. He has been above all an outstanding field-worker and it is to be hoped that he will now have leisure enough to write up the extensive research that he has carried out on the ground.

His first experience of the Arab world was a visit to Syria in 1935 and then the outbreak of war found him in Aden. There was in 1940 a distinct possibility that the large Italian army which had already overrun Ethiopia and British Somaliland might manage to cross the Red Sea and to cut the vital imperial communications with India. To prevent this, the youthful RBS, appointed to a commission in the Aden Government Guards, was sent off into the hinterland on a camel with a wireless set and a handful of tribal irregulars. However, during these two years he found the area which was to absorb his interest for the rest of his career and with the study of which he will always be mainly associated.

He returned home in 1942 to work for the BBC Arabic Service, editing *The Arabic Listener* and other publications in that language and their success was largely due to the high standards that he maintained. Even in wartime he insisted upon absolute accuracy in all matters.

He had already been appointed a Lecturer in the School of Oriental and African Studies and at the end of the war he took up teaching duties there.

It was not long before his scholarship and his dedication to his students came to be realised. He was particularly good with students from overseas, interesting himself in their personal, as well as their academic difficulties and many of them have remained his friends to this day.

In 1947 he was awarded a Colonial Research Fellowship for a year's work in the Wadi Hadhramawt, an area with a unique and extremely rich civilisation which had never been studied by academics, although some work had been done there by scholar-administrators, such as Harold Ingrams. In the field he had to start from scratch, compiling lists of MSS, studying the history, the language, the folklore, the legal system and the customs. He worked closely with local scholars who were delighted to find an outsider interested in their culture. His work from this period onwards gave him an insight into the traditional life of Arabia which was denied to those of his predecessors who had relied solely upon written sources.

In 1948 he was appointed Reader and in 1955 a Chair of Modern Arabic was specially created for him in SOAS. He went to the Middle East whenever he could and in 1963 he paid his first visit to North Yemen, whose new Republican government was supported by a huge Egyptian military presence. For some months he travelled with the Royalist forces, walking hundreds of miles over the mountains, sheltering in caves from Egyptian air attacks and all the while making copious notes on the dialects, agriculture, tribal customs etc., of the country. His reports, together with others who visited the Royalists, acted as a valuable corrective to the propaganda of the Egyptian media.

In 1964 in order to have more opportunity for research, in a more congenial atmosphere, he resigned his Chair at SOAS and returned to Cambridge as a Lecturer. He was soon made Reader and Director of the Middle East Centre and when A. J. Arberry died in office in 1969, he succeeded him in the Sir Thomas Adams's Chair of Arabic, the oldest in the country.

The following years were extremely busy, for in addition to continuing to publish articles of the highest scholarship and travelling whenever possible, he found time to bring into being *Arabian Studies*, the first interdisciplinary academic journal solely concerned with the Peninsula, and to become a founding-father of both the Middle East Libraries Committee and of the Arabian Seminar. Both these institutions have brought about many useful and convivial meetings of scholars who had previously only known each other on paper. He also organised the Exhibition of the City of Ṣanʿā' at the Museum of Mankind, which was one of the most successful parts of the World of Islam Festival Trust Festival of 1976; so successful was it that by popular demand it was kept open for two years beyond the scheduled closing date.

In December 1981 he retired from the Chair and it was to mark this occasion that the editors invited a number of his friends and former students to contribute the articles which make up the present volume. The response showed that he is held in affection as well as in respect by those who have been closely connected with him. The editors are extremely grateful to all those whose contributions enabled this tribute to be paid. Cerries Smith translated the article of Professor Cahen as her own contribution to this collection. The editors also wish to record their thanks to Robert Coombs of Longman and their appreciation of his kindness and courtesy. Finally they wish to report with great regret, the death of Shaykh Abd al-Aziz al-Khalifa since the receipt of his article 'Fishing in Bahrain'.

It only remains for the editors, speaking on behalf of all the contributors, to wish Bob and Marion, whose constant support through the years needs no emphasis to those who know them, a long and happy retirement.

Note on presentation

The editors gave the contributors to this volume complete freedom in the choice of subject matter, and as a result the topics chosen vary from the earliest times down to the present day. The editors wish to affirm, however, that the acceptance of contributions for inclusion in this volume does not necessarily imply that either they or Longman Group, the publishers, severally or individually concur with views and opinions expressed by authors, who must be considered primarily responsible for the content of their own chapters.

The editors have chosen to present the material in three roughly chronological sections: I Pre-Islamic Arabia; II Early and Mediaeval Islam; III Modern period. Within each section the articles are arranged in alphabetical order of the names of contributors.

As far as possible the transliteration of Arabic words in English follows the system of *Arabian Studies*. There are some exceptions to this general rule in the section on the modern period. Contributors making use of European sources in the main have frequently spelt proper names as they appear in those sources. 'An assessment of Gibran', by Dr. Samra, also for example, retains many spellings of personal names in the form in which they have become familiar to scholars of Arabic literature and which may be regarded, to all intents and purposes, as accepted forms. Again Professor Pearson in his bibliography of the publications of RBS has chosen to employ his renowned *Index Islamicus* style and presentation.

P.S. March 1983. The Editors learned with great regret of the death of Professor T. M. Johnstone. He read the galley proofs of his contribution, but did not live to see the page proofs. The Editors apologise if they have missed any errors which his expert eye would have picked up.

PART 1

Pre-Islamic Arabia

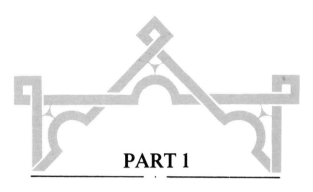

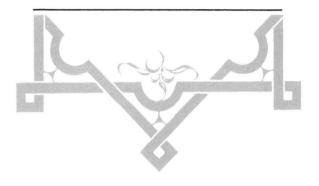

Women in Saba

A. F. L. Beeston

Our information about the status of women in ancient Sabaean society is somewhat scanty, and virtually confined to the 'middle' period (first three centuries A.D.), the age of the mass of votive inscriptions, which afford more intimate glimpses of everyday life than do the more public texts of earlier and later periods. The present note contains little that has not been said before, but I think it may be useful to collate the rather scattered notices, and to take the opportunity of adding some minor details and comments. Furthermore, an article by J. Chelhod[1] contains some remarkable data about present-day features of social life among the Ḥumūm,[2] decidedly alien to Muslim principles, which are certainly, as Chelhod remarks, survivals of ancient practices and throw valuable light on the epigraphic evidence for ancient times.

The votive texts, after describing the particular motive for the dedication, normally end with aspirations for the future. Along with petitions for deliverance from various misfortunes, the positive boons most commonly sought are the goodwill of seigneurs, fine crops, and healthy children; but in a large proportion of cases, it is specified that the desired children should be males. This suggests that in some respects females were regarded as less desirable; and this is borne out by a remarkable text recently published.[3] It is a decree made by the town of Maṭarat (modern al-Quṭrah) in Nihm, of which the third clause runs, 'It is forbidden for any member of the community of Maṭarat to kill his daughter'. One thinks immediately, of course, of the pre-Islamic bedouin practice of female infanticide (*wa'd*), prohibited by Islam. Yet it seems unlikely that in either ambience was the practice very widespread (females at least have the value of being potential mothers of male children); the *Lisān al-ʿarab* comments that the motive for the practice was 'fear of dishonour' (*ʿār*) or 'poverty' (*ḥājah*), which indicates that it was occasioned by rather special circumstances.

On the other hand, women could in Sabaean society occupy quite high positions. I remind readers that in that society the basis of social structure was the *bayt*, a village or clan community; a group of such communities constituted a *s² ʿb*; within the *s² ʿb*, it was normal for one clan, styled *qayls*,[4] to exercise a quasi-feudal[5] seigneury over 'client' or vassal groups and individuals (*ʿbd*, plural *'dm*) who gave service (*s²wʿ*) in return for protection. Now in C 95, the dedicator thanks the deity for granting him a successful career (*wfy*) 'since the time when he repaired to the town of ʿAmrān in order to do service for his *wrṯt*': evidently the lady in question had inherited the position of seigneur vis-à-vis the dedicator, either from her father (in default of male heirs) or perhaps from a deceased husband. Conversely, females could stand in a direct relationship of 'clients' or vassals (*'mt*, plural *'mh*) to a seigneur. This attests some degree of independency of status for women.

Apart from the services rendered in general by the vassals, both kings and *qayls* had personal administrative officers, comparable with a mediaeval English bailiff or steward, styled *mqtwy*; and we have one or two instances of a female occupying such a position (e.g. N 14/2). Chelhod's remark[6] that 'La femme . . . n'intervient pas, du moins directement, dans la conduite des affaires publiques' seems not to have been true in ancient society.

Polyandry is said to have been practised in Yemen, according to many external observers both ancient and mediaeval. In an exhaustive article on the subject, W. W. Müller[7] argues that there is good epigraphic evidence for this, but rightly stresses that it was certainly not the sole marital form, but coexisted with both monogamy and polygyny.

Chelhod tells us[8] that among the Ḥumūm, 'la femme jouit d'une liberté sexuelle pré et postnuptiale; les enfants nés de ces amours hors des liens du mariage appartiennent normalement au clan utérin, portent le nom de leur mère, sont élevés par leur oncle maternel . . . héritent de ses biens et lui laissent les leurs s'ils meurent sans laisser de descendance': i.e. there was in some cases a full matrilinear succession.

Two of our epigraphic texts are royal decrees issued in favour of two seigneural clans, the ʿUthkulan in Mārib, Nashq and Nashan (F 76), and the Ḥubāb in Ṣirwāh-Khawlān (F 3). The decrees assign to each of these clans, as vassals, a list of individuals both men and women, who are to constitute in each case a community (*bayt*) 'having the same status as the other [scil. vassal] communities' of the respective localities, owing service to their seigneurs.[9] In F 3/5–6 the list of individuals is summed up in the words 'all those men and women and their children, grandchildren and successors'. In F76 we have ' 'Aslam and (five more masculine names) and of individuals we have *Rbbt*, *'b'mn* and *Nʿmlt* each followed by *wbnyhw*: since the first is certainly, and the other two probably,[10] feminine, we should here interpret the common-gender pronoun *-hw* as having a feminine application, 'and her children'. On the other hand, we have *ḥqbm*/*w'wldhw* and *wlds*[1]*ʿd*/*w'wldhw* where the gender of the two names seems *prima facie* to be masculine. And at the end of the list comes 'and all their (masc.) brothers and their (masc.) children and their (masc.) successors'. In F 76 we have ' 'Aslam and five more masculine names) and their mothers and their sisters, namely Mḥyt and (four more feminine names); and all their (masc., referring to the six men) brothers and all those women and their (fem.) daughters and their (fem.) *'wld* and their (fem.) successors, descendants of Mḫbḏm Ḏḫrn, the *mqtwy* of the ʿUthkulan clan'. A summary recapitulating the list follows, 'Those men 'Aslam and [lacuna] and all his [sic, singular] brothers, and those women Mḥyt and all her sisters and her daughters and all their (fem.) children and grandchildren and successors'. All this somewhat chaotic arrangement indicates a coexistence of matrilinear and patrilinear systems of reckoning descent.

That conflict could sometimes arise out of the operation of these two opposing systems appears from J 700.[11] Here we read that a woman who belonged to a vassal group appealed to (s^1*tws*^{2}*ʿt*) a *mqtwy* of her seigneurs for the return to her (*l-'wln/lhw*) of her son by (*bʿm*) her husband; the *mqtwy* and the husband met and a fight ensued in which the husband was killed and the *mqtwy* wounded. What was evidently at stake was whether the child should be claimed by his father's or his mother's lineage. The fact that the woman's claim was sustained by the representative of her seigneurs perhaps has some relevance to Chelhod's remark[12] that, when the child's lineage was reckoned matrilineally, 'selon une information isolée, qui demande donc à être confirmée, on pourrait lui donner également le nom du chef de clan auquel appartient la mère'.

One text cited by Chelhod[13] in connection with the matrilineal principle, E 34, is however slightly less cogent than J. Ryckmans' treatment of it[14] (on which Chelhod has relied) would lead one to suppose. Three females and one male are described collectively as *bnt/'lt/grhmm*, which J. Ryckmans renders as '*bnt* de celles [sic] de Grhmm'. But the pronominal form *'lt* is not feminine: it is a common-gender plural in which the *-t* is the case-mark of the genitive/accusative, contrasting with nominative *'ly*. Hence the *'lt/grhmm* are simply 'the Gurhumites' as a whole, and not only their female members. As for *bnt*, Ryckmans comments, 'Est-ce par une simple erreur, ou en vertu d'une conception matriarcale de la descendance que la présence d'un fils . . . n'empêche pas de qualifier de *bnt* l'ensemble des enfants?'. But in the light of Wellcome Museum A 103664/11 *bnt*,[15] and YM 438/7 *'ẖt*[16] – both of them cases where a feminine interpretation is unlikely – I would be inclined to regard *bnt* as not necessarily a feminine plural (*banāt*) but in some cases as a common-gender collective (*banuwwat*). In spite of this, the text still has some significance (though it is not unique in this respect) in that it is three women and their daughter who take the initiative in making the dedication for the well-being of their four children.

One specially striking text is C 581. Though I have discussed this fully elsewhere,[17] I have had second thoughts on one or two points of it. My general view of it remains unchanged: two women who belonged to a clan who were vassals of a Kibsite seigneur were afflicted with childlessness (*btr*), but were directed by an oracle to offer (see below) a votive statuette in the event of either of them becoming pregnant; an unnamed man 'came and on the sixth day he *wgr* their *bayt*' (this verb I would interpret as a metathesis of *jāwara* and a euphemism for sexual intercourse); and so they 'accepted the gift' (*gtzḥ*) from this man'. In the event, they did dedicate the statuette, hence clearly one of them did conceive. The oracular directive (*qr'*) was to s^2*'m* the statuette: this verb normally means 'acquire', like *qny*, but in the present context it seems to me that it must have a causative sense equivalent to *hqny* 'dedicate'. The syntax of the following passage in lines 10–12 *hbrrw/lgtzḥ[n]/bʿm/'*s^1*n/wnfq/bnhw/wṣlmtn/[. .]l/lhmw* is problematical. Rhodokanakis placed a full stop after *bnhw* and rendered 'Darauf aber beschlossen sie sich beschenken zu lassen von diesem Mann und von ihm loszukommen. Die Statuette also schenkte er ihnen'.[18] In this, 'von ihm loszukommen' seems fairly meaningless, and if one adopts his punctuation I would at all events prefer to take *nfq* as a finite verb and not an infinitive, i.e. 'und er ist von ihr [scil. der Familie, *bythmw*] losgekommen'. An interpretation on these lines takes on a new potentiality of significance in the light of what Chelhod says:[19] among the Ḥumūm, a woman may, without any social discredit, have extra-marital relationships with a man; her kinsmen may then call on the man to marry her[20] but 's'il refuse, il lui est fait obligation d'assurer à la mère et à sa progéniture leur subsistence pendant un certain temps . . . l'enfant portera le nom de sa mère ou celui de son oncle utérin'. This seems to be precisely what our Sabaic text describes: the father did not marry the woman, but by the family's acceptance of the compensatory payment from him, he was discharged from further obligation. This explains the otherwise odd feature that the man is not named: the child was in any case going to be reckoned as belonging to its maternal lineage, as Chelhod observes, so that the name of the actual genitor became an irrelevancy.

A difficulty still lies in the last three words of the passage quoted, specially with the mutilation of the penultimate word. I still find it difficult to credit Rhodokanakis' notion that the man gave the statuette to the women (or the family): why should he do so, seeing that it was a thanksgiving for a child, all claim to whom he was renouncing? I fear I must leave this as an unresolved problem.[21]

It is noticeable that the dedication of C 581 is made in the name of both women, although only one of them actually bore a child. Similar instances occur elsewhere, e.g. in J 686 where two women, Ḥmlt and N'ms¹'d, both of the group Gb't, jointly offer a statuette in gratitude for a child born to the latter. Unless we envisage (as I did in my earlier treatment of C 581, though I now have doubts about it) that in each case the women were co-wives of one husband, such instances can only mean that the child was reckoned as belonging to the mother's lineage and not to the father's. This indeed seems to be suggested by the explicit of C 581 (though its phraseology is not entirely clear), running, 'and may the deity in future protect the person of her *mr'* Mhbḏ b.Wdm and her son Lḥy'ṯt and His (the deity's) female vassals the clan Tḥy'z'. Now Mhbḏ was certainly not (as Rhodokanakis wrongly supposed) her seigneur, since her seigneur has been named at the beginning of the text as S¹'ds²ms¹ the Kibsite; nor was he the father of the child, since in that case he would have been named when first mentioned; the only remaining alternative is that she was a married woman and that *mr'* here means 'husband'. Lḥy'ṯt was evidently 'her child', who as Chelhod says, 'porte le nom de sa mère'. The association of another woman of the group Tḥy'z in the dedication reflects the incorporation of the child Lḥy'ṯt into his mother's matrilineal kin group. One might even speculate that this other woman was the maternal aunt of Lḥy'ṯt, and that the modern practice of naming such a child after his maternal uncle, and the latter's mutual inheritance rights with the child (see above), is an innovation contrasting with a more rigidly matriarchal ancient system in which such rights pertained to the maternal aunt.

J 584 is a unique example of a joint dedication by a brother and sister.[22] The man expresses gratitude for protection 'in the region (read *bḫlf* for Jamme's *ḏlf*) of Dhamār'; his sister's gratitude is for 'what the deity had manifested (*hydʿ*) to her in respect of (*bʿbr*) her brother', and because the deity had granted both her and her brother some favour (the last word is mutilated, and Jamme's restoration is hardly plausible). This at least attests very close links between the two siblings, in spite of the fact that the woman was probably married: she is designated *ḏt/lnh'*, and if *lnh'* had been her natal clan one would have expected it to be mentioned earlier in the text along with the naming of the brother. In this case at least, *ḏt* is probably best regarded as expressing a marital relationship.

In E 24 a man gives thanks because he had been enabled to marry (*hkrb*) and bring home (*hkll*) a bride from a different branch of his clan into his own household. The significant verb here is *hkll*, which should be equated with Jibbālī *eklē*[23] 'bring home (a bride)'. This would hardly have been worth saying if it had been the case that the bride invariably moved into her husband's household. One must infer that there were fairly frequent cases of an uxorilocal marital arrangement, whereby the bride remained in the household into which she had been born.

Chelhod quotes[24] from Ibn Baṭṭuṭah a passage in which it is remarked that the women of Zabīd were quite willing to marry strangers, but in no case did they ever consent to leave Zabīd, no matter what inducements were offered. A somewhat parallel sentiment seems to motivate the second clause of the decree of Maṭarat mentioned above: 'It is not permitted to *ʿḏb* a woman of Maṭarat into any other place or town'. The verb *ʿḏb* is rendered by Robin as 'livrer en réparation', but this bald statement, without any explanation of what kind of reparation could be envisaged, sounds to me dubious. The passage should be compared with R 4233/9 *lʿḏb/whkrbn/ ǵlmtn*[25]. Here, with 'the girl' as object, it would seem necessary to take *hkrb* in the sense of 'marry', as in E 24; one must conclude that *ʿḏb* also has a technical sense connected with marriage, and one will then inevitably recall Genesis 2.24, 'a man shall leave (*ʿazab*) his father and his mother and shall cleave unto his wife'. It might, of course, be objected that the Arabic reflex of this Hebrew verb is *ʿazaba* and not *ʿaḏaba*, but it would surely be rash to deny the possibility of the two roots having coalesced in Sabaic, even if they were different originally. If one allows the comparison, then it looks as if *ʿḏb* is a technicality implying leaving the parental roof to enter the household of a spouse, and the second clause of the Maṭarat decree prohibits this for the womenfolk of the town, i.e. it sanctions only uxorilocal marriage arrangements.[26]

Textual References

C = Corpus Inscriptionum Semiticarum, pars quarta.
E = Motahhar Ali al-Eryani, *In Yemen History*, Sanaa, 1973.
F = A. Fakhry, *Archaeological Journey to Yemen*, II, Epigraphical Texts, by G. Ryckmans, Cairo, 1952.

J = A. Jamme, *Sabaean Inscriptions from Maḥram Bilqis*, Baltimore, 1962.
N = Y. Nami, *Našr nuqūš sāmiyah qadīmah*, Cairo, 1943.
R = Répertoire d'Epigraphie sémitique, Paris.

Notes

1 'Du Nouveau à propos du "Matriarcat" arabe', *Arabica*, Leiden, XXVIII, 76 ff.

2 A folk living in a rather out-of-the-way area, bounded on the east by the Wādī 'l-Masīlah and on the west by a line from Tarīm to the sea.

3 C. Robin, 'Mission archéologique et épigraphique française au Yémen du nord en automne 1978', *CR Acad. des Inscr.*, Paris, 1979.

4 But not so named, apparently, in Mārib, Nashq and Nashan.

5 In the past, I have been reluctant to use the term 'feudal' with reference to ancient South Arabian society, but is has to be admitted that there are at least some close resemblances between that and mediaeval European feudalism.

6 'Du Nouveau', 80.

7 'Sabäische Texte zur Polyandrie', *Neue Ephemeris für semitische Epigraphik*, II, Wiesbaden, 1974, 125 ff.

8 'Du Nouveau', 87.

9 F 3/8 *l-hy'/w-hwṣln/l-kl/hs²k/w-mwṣt/w-qht/'mr'-hmw/bny/ḏḥbb* 'to perform and carry out every bidding, ordinance and command of their seigneurs the clan Ḥubāb'. This all-embracing obligation need not be taken quite literally; almost certainly, custom set certain limits on the services which could be demanded of the vassals.

10 Names compounded with 'b- and -lt are very frequently (but not exclusively) feminine.

11 On this text see A. K. Irvine, 'Homicide in pre-Islamic South Arabia', *BSOAS*, XXX, 1967, 286–92.

12 'Du Nouveau', 83.

13 Op. cit., 100.

14 'Himyaritica 4', *Le Muséon*, Louvain, LXXXVII, 1974, 493–4.

15 Beeston, 'The South Arabian Collections of the Wellcome Museum', *Raydan*, Louvain, III, 1980, 16.

16 *Corpus des Inscriptions et Antiquités sud-arabes*, I, 1977, 75–6.

17 'Temporary Marriage in Ancient South Arabia', *Arabian Studies*, IV, 1978, 1–5.

18 cf. H. Gressmann, *Altorientalische Texte zum Alten Testament*, Berlin-Leipzig, 1926, 467–8.

19 'Du Nouveau', 83.

20 If she is already married, she can demand that her existing husband should divorce her (85).

21 My earlier attempt to circumvent the problem by taking *nfq/bnhw/wṣlmtn* as one phrase, 'to vow her [future] son and the statuette' now seems to me very dubious.

22 On this text see J. Ryckmans, 'Himyaritica 2', *Le Muséon*, LXXIX, 1966, 477–8.

[23] T. M. Johnstone, 'Gemination in the Jibbālī language of Dhofar', *Zeitschr. f. arab. Linguistik*, Wiesbaden, IV, 1980, 69. Morphologically this is a causative (*'af'ala*) stem from root *kly*.
[24] 'Du Nouveau', 93; *Riḥlah*, ed. Defrémery & Sanguinetti, Paris, 1854, II, 168.
[25] Read so with K. Mlaker, *Die Hierodulenliste von Ma'in*, 1943, 56.
[26] And, presumably, the retention of the children as members of the town's community, thus avoiding diminution of its manpower.

Addendum

Since the above was written, a new text (Wadi al-Sirr 1) of considerable relevance to the subject has been published by R. Stiegner (*Al-Hudhud, Festschrift Maria Höfner*. Graz, 1981, p. 327). This deals with a woman described as *ḏt/zwrm/wbnt/bny/ṯgrm*, who built a 'tower' (*mḥfd*) with the support (*rd'*) of 'her *b'l*, 'ZBR, and his children the Bani ZWRm'. Stiegner has assumed that 'ZBR is the name of a deity who was the patron of the clan ZWRm. Yet in the vast majority of cases, a deity is the *b'l* of his sanctuary but the *mr'* of his worshippers; in the present context it seems much more probable that *b'l* has the sense 'husband' (which it retains in present-day Arabic). This would be completely concordant with Stiegner's own, very probable, understanding of *ḏt/zwrm* as meaning that the woman, whose natal family was ṮGRm, had married into the ZWRm family.

The statement that the woman 'built' this construction can mean nothing else than that the major part of the costs were borne by her out of her private fortune, though with some financial assistance from her husband and his family. Evidently, therefore, a woman could even during the lifetime of her husband retain and control her own private fortune. This sheds a particularly clear light on the financial independence enjoyed by women in Sabaean society.

Biblical and Old South Arabian Institutions: Some Parallels

Jacques Ryckmans

Our knowledge of the pre-Islamic institutions of South Arabia in the period from the 5th century B.C. to the 6th century A.D. has been considerably augmented during the last twenty years as a result of the publication of numerous texts, the study of which has given new information on such topics as pilgrimages to central temples, with the various observances and prohibitions involved, in particular religious meals organised with the product of the tithes, or sexual prohibitions (*22*.10; *22*.16, pp. 452–453); rules and interdictions related to the notion of ritual purity (*22*.7, *22*.8; *22*.11, pp. 104–108; *22*.16, pp. 454–457); the consultation of the oracle by means of arrows (*22*.5); the ritual of supplication for rain (*22*.9), etc.

A comparative evaluation of the South Arabian data and the information on the paganism of pre-Islamic Arabia made available by the Arabian tradition (analysed by J. Wellhausen and H. Lammens, among others) as well as by the classical authors, has brought to light a remarkable general convergence (*22*.11, pp. 104–107; *22*.16): a proof of the importance of South Arabian inscriptions, as authentic documents contemporary to the events to which they are related, in gaining a better understanding of the cultural background in which Islam is born. Such findings flatly contradict a conception, still professed today by some Islamologists,[1] according to which many data on pre-Islamic religion collected by Muslim authors, are in general to be considered as mere projections by Muslim writers, into Arabia's pagan past, of early Islamic uses, which are themselves for the most part directly borrowed by Muḥammad from Jewish circles in Medina.[2]

It is quite clear that, except for such observances as fasting, the borrowing of which from the Judaeo-Christian tradition is beyond doubt, Islam has incorporated numerous features of a pre-Islamic Arabian heritage, common to the paganism of Hijaz as well as that of South Arabia.

This common Arabian pre-Islamic heritage is itself a part of a larger whole that could be termed, if not 'the' religion of the Semites, at least a basic cultural and religious patrimony with many features common to several Semitic peoples.

The present contribution aims at confronting the findings of the South Arabian epigraphical research with the data of the biblical background of the Old Testament, and even occasionally, in a more general manner, of the religion of the ancient North West Semitic world. Not included in the present study are: the analysis of the data on ritual purity, since they have been studied in detail elsewhere (*10*; *22*.7 and *22*.8); and Jewish uses of words which appear in late Sabaean inscriptions emanating from Jewish or proselyte circles, since they only demonstrate a direct influence from Judaism.

In the ancient period of South Arabian history (3rd quarter of the 1st millenium B.C.), the idea of the state was essentially expressed by the trinomial 'national god(s) – sovereign – nation' (*22*.11, pp. 101–102; *22*.16, p. 447). Thus the Sabaean state was designated as 'Almaqah (i.e. the national god of Saba), Karib'il (i.e. its sovereign at the time), and Saba' (RES 3945, 13; 3946, 2, etc.). In a similar manner 'Sīn, Ḥawl, Yada''il and Hadhramawt', and "Amm, Anbay, Waraw'il and Qatabān' are designations of Hadhramawt and Qatabān (RES 3945, 12–13). The sovereign was considered the representative both of the national god, and of his people. After his conquests in the South of Yemen, Karib'il of Saba symbolically makes over to 'Almaqah and Saba' the territories he had opened to Sabaean colonists (RES 3945, 6–7). A similar conception of the state was familiar in Mesopotamia, but also in the kingdom of Moab, a rival of ancient Israel: at line 12 of his famous stele of victory, now in the Louvre in Paris, Mesha, king of Moab, prides himself on having reconquered territories 'for Chemosh (the national god of Moab) and Moab' (*7*, p. 76). A parallel conception, less strictly expressed, however, is found in Israel, where the land is the land of the Lord (*24*.1, p. 252: Hos 9,3 f.); it is the land which the Lord has given to His people (Num 32,7). In the Israelite kingship the king is the representative both of Yahweh and of His people (*5*.1, pp. 134–136, 268 ff.; *5*.2, pp. 140–148).

In several ancient South Arabian texts (CIH 428,3, 455,2; RES 3890, no. 5) the relation 'national god – sovereign – nation' appears as the result of an 'alliance' (*'ẖwt*, 'fraternity') with the national god.[3] In the kingdom of Juda, 2 Kings 11, 17 mentions a covenant concluded by the priest Jehoiada 'between the Lord and the king and people, that they should be the Lord's people; and also between the king and the people' (cp. *17*, pp. 77–81). In a similar manner the Moabites are called in the Bible 'people of Chemosh' (Num 21,29) after the name of their national god.

The South Arabian nations called themselves, and were called 'the offspring' (*wld*) of their national god. Thus the Sabaeans could be termed *wld 'lmqh*, 'the offspring of Almaqah' (RES 3945,5), while the tribes of Qatabanian obedience were *wld 'm*, 'the offspring of 'Amm' (RES 3550,2; 4328, 2–3, etc.; and Ja 576,16, etc.). In biblical tradition, terms of kinship and filiation express – metaphorically – the ties binding together the chosen people and its God. Thus Yahweh is named 'relative' (*24*.4, 1, pp. 259–260, rather than 'fear' in the RSV) of Isaac (Gen 31,42 and 53). Compare also Ex 4,22: 'Israel is my first-born son'.

The notion of primogeniture expressed in the last quotation is an important one in the Bible (*24*.1, 1, p. 89; *3*, col. 482–491) in terms of divine rights on the male offspring of human beings and of domestic animals, (Ex 13,2, 12; 22, 29; *24*.1, p. 72; *11*.1, pp. 174–176) and in the form of a birthright in human inheritance (*24*.1, 1, pp. 72, 89–90). Remarkably enough, the notions of primogeniture and birthright did not play any significant role in pre-Islamic western Arabia (*11.1*, p. 169–170; *11.2*, col. 473), while they are well attested for ancient South Arabia (*3*, col. 483–484; *11.3*). In Qatabān, some sovereigns (called *mukarrib*) styled themselves 'priest of (the national god) ʿAmm', and 'first-born (*bkr*) (of the gods) Anbay and Ḥawkam' (RES 3540, etc.).[4] In Saba, eponymate magistrates called *kabīr* (*kbr*), belonging to a sacerdotal class, played a role in collecting the tithes, and in obtaining rain (*16.2*, p. 61; *16.3*, pp. 287, 291–292). The office was transmitted from father to son (or adoptive son), but according to an elaborate system of rotation of office distributed alternatively among three privileged clans (*16.3*, pp. 286–287; *22.6*, p. 24; *22.12*, pp. 97–98).[5] Many eponyms are called *bkr*, 'first-born' of their clan (*16.2*, pp. 73–74; *16.3*, p. 286). Their period of office was probably limited to seven years, a period comparable to the biblical sabbatical cycle (*16.2*, p. 71; *16.3*, p. 285). At the term of the function of an eponym the god ʿAṯtar frequently 'redeemed him' (*fdyhw*)[6] from all his temples', cp. the redemption of the first-born in Israel (*16.2*, p. 60; *24.1*,2, pp. 329–330: Ex 13, 12; 34,20).

As in biblical usage (*24.1*,1, pp. 165–167) the South Arabian sovereigns bore distinctive dynastic names: originally, in Saba, the choice was among six names and four epithets, which were exclusively reserved for them (*22.1*, p. 56; *2.6*, pp. 19–21). In the other kingdoms, and later on in Saba too, the range of names and epithets was broader, and only part of them were exclusively reserved. Originally the sovereigns probably assumed their regal epithet, if not also their regal name, by their accession to the throne, as in the kingdom of Juda (*24.1*,1, pp. 166–167). In the middle period, the Hadhrami kings seem to have assumed their epithet in a special ceremony of investiture, held outside the capital and in the presence of foreign envoys (RES 4852–4902; 4908–4917; *2.1*; *15.2*; *22.3*, pp. 278–282), while for some Sabaean kings the taking of an oath (?) of allegiance by various groups of the population, and an enthronization of the new (or designated) king in the royal palace are attested (Ja 562, 564, etc.; *22.4*, pp. 475–476; *16.1*, pp. 190–191; *22.13*, pp. 242–243). Similar procedures are known in the biblical kingship (*24.1*,1, pp. 163–165).

In the entourage of the kings of Maʿīn and of the ancient sovereigns of Saba, important chieftains bear the title *mwd*, plur. *mwddt*, 'friend' of one or several sovereigns or kings mentioned by name (*22.1*, pp. 35–36, 90–92). Although both institutions may be independent, the title reminds one of the Hebrew title *rēʿēh*, 'familiar' of the king, a term which merely transcribes an Egyptian title meaning 'known' to the king (*24.1*,1, p. 188).

The biblical – and common Semitic – conception of a central temple serving as a national sanctuary, was also valid in South Arabia. Among numerous temples dedicated to various deities, the sanctuary of the national god, in the capital city, enjoyed a special status as a national place of pilgrimage and as a privileged recipient of the tithes – two functions also cumulated by the sanctuary in Bethel (1 Sam 10,3; Am 4, 4; *24.1*,2, p. 118), and by the temple in Jerusalem (1 Kings 12,27; Deut 16, 13–15, etc.; *24.1*,2, p. 185). Both functions appear for the temple of Sīn in Shabwah, and that of Almaqah in Mārib (*22*.15, pp. 217–219). Yathil, a major city of Maʿīn, was also the centre of a pilgrimage (CIH 547). The place of pilgrimage of the god Ta'lab in Riyām was famous down to Islamic times. It had belonged to the kingdom of Sumʿay, incorporated at an early date into the Sabaean kingdom. A text found there (RES 4176) determines the tithes to be paid by each tribe, and states that the god will organise each year, at the time of the pilgrimage, a number of collective banquets for the tribes, by means of the product of the tithes (*22*.10, p. 37; *22*.12, pp. 330–333). The allotment of part of the product of the tithes to entertain guests is quoted for the temple of Shabwah by Pliny (*Nat. Hist.* 12,63), who states that the taxes on the aromatics paid in the temple served to meet the public expenses 'because the god entertains gratis his guests for a number of days each year' – obviously those of the local pilgrimage. The pilgrimage of Mārib took place yearly in a particular month in autumn; collective sacrifices and probably also banquets were organised on that occasion (*22*.10, pp. 36–38; *22*.12, pp. 332–333). This may be compared (*22*.16, p. 453) to biblical passages such as Deut 12, 5–12 and 14, 22–27, in which it is prescribed that the faithful bring to the temple his offerings and sacrifices and eat there with his family, in the presence of the Lord, the tithe of his grain and of his wine, and the firstling of his herd and flock.

In Maʿīn, the income of the religious tithes (*kbwdt*) was allotted to 'liturgies' of public constructions, including the erection of the surrounding wall of cities. In large inscriptions, engraved on various parts of the wall, each tribe concerned mentioned the section of the wall built under its responsibility, naming the defence towers it had erected, as well as the tribes responsible for the adjacent sections (RES 2774, 2789 etc.). This is exactly the system applied to the repairs and rebuilding of the wall of Jerusalem, on the initiative of Nehemiah (Neh 3, 1–38; *22*.2, p. 53 n.2).

The Minaean merchants had secured the control of the trade in South Arabian aromatics and were established in the South Arabian states, and in some oases of North Arabia (in Dedan in particular), as well as in Egypt and probably also in Syro-Palestinian cities. Members of this Minaean diaspora certainly were responsible for the so-called *List of Hierodules* (*18*; *22*.2), engraved on pillars near the temple of the Minaean capital. About eighty short entries are preserved, each containing the name, patronym and tribal affiliation of the author; two synonymous verbs of offering; the object of the dedication: a woman, mentioned by her first name, with her geographical provenance (*22*.2, pp. 53–61). The women originate from various parts of South Arabia, and North Arabian places, such as Dedan, and from Egypt or from Syro-Palestinian places (Moab, Ammon, etc.). It is widely agreed upon that the 'offering' of these women did not amount to a true hieroduly, the sacred prostitution practised in the pagan cults of Syria. I have suggested (*22*.2, p. 53) that it consisted in putting at the disposal of the temple, for a limited time of service, foreign women, mostly slaves, as a special substitute, imposed on the expatriate Minaean colonists, for the tithes for which they still were liable to the main temple of the motherland. An alternative and attractive explanation has been put forward by M. A.

Ghul[7]: the women 'offered' were foreign brides of Minaeans, who presented them formally to the temple, thereby obtaining the right to marry them (or the legalisation of their union). In such a case a Jewish influence is not excluded, since a Jewish colony had probably been established in Dedan during the reign of Nabonidus (cp. *6*, pp. 85–86; *22*.8, p. 11). Deut 21, 10–14, provides for a procedure for the marriage with a foreign captive woman, while in the Mishnah (*Ketūvōt*, 3,1) several kinds of fines are quoted in the event of an irregular marriage, in particular with a foreign woman. However, a Jewish influence would not explain the intervention of the temple in the case of the Minaean *Lists*. Two Sabaean texts use the same form of the verb of offering (4th form of *krb*) as in the *Lists*, with a woman as object. In one case (Ir 24; *22*.14, pp. 512–514) the rest of the text makes it clear that a woman taken as a bride is meant, while in the second text (RES 4233, reinterpreted in *18*, pp. 56–57) the 'offering' is prescribed by oracle to the dedicator as a means to free himself from an interdict he had incurred (*bn ḥrm hḥrm*). It seems quite possible that both cases concerned a marriage with a woman, foreign at least to the tribe of the dedicator, and that in the second case the interdict resulted from an irregular marriage with the woman involved, so that the action prescribed would have been intended to legalise the union, thereby suppressing the cause of the interdict. Such an interpretation (*22*.14, p. 514) would give fresh support to M. A. Ghul's suggestion, while on the other hand – since a Jewish influence on institutions in Saba during the pagan period seems materially difficult to postulate – the South Arabian use would then constitute a parallel development, independent from the Jewish institution.

In the Minaean texts from Dedan appears a class of men and women apparently presented as pledges to the temple and called *lw'*, fem. *lw't* (RES 3351, 3356, 3357, 3697, 3698). A relation has formerly been claimed by H. Grimme (*9*) between these *lw'* and the Israelite levites, on the assumption that the Minaean occupation in Dedan dated back to the 2nd millenium B.C., while we now know that it must be later than the middle of the 1st millenium. Moreover the mutilated Minaean contexts reveal an institution rather different from that of the biblical levites (*24*.3, p. 285; *24*.1,2, pp. 228–229), so that any comparison seems highly questionable.

A South Arabian interdict *ḥrm* has been mentioned above. The term occurs in other texts than the one quoted, but only twice in a context giving some idea about the crime it sanctioned. In RES 3878, it appears as a penalty for homicide (*13bis*, pp. 278–281), while the controversial text CIH 126[8] apparently makes legislation on the case of a murderer who would try to elude a sentence by unduly taking advantage of the right of asylum (cp. Num 35,11), in a temple. The ban (*ḥrm*), which is to be pronounced (in the temple) by the assembly (cp. Num 35,121) includes the death sentence. The property of the criminal falls legally to the king – a provision which may be related to the similar conclusion of the Naboth episode in 1 Kings 21,15 (*8*, p. 441; *22*.18, pp. 213–214, and n. 26).

This extreme case of a South Arabian *ḥrm* looks closely related to the biblical practice of the *ḥērĕm*, consisting in 'utterly destroying', or 'devoting (to the Lord) by extermination' (*24*.1,2, pp. 76–77). This practice, to which Jericho was submitted (Josh 6,17), was also known in Moab: the Israelite town of Nebo was 'devoted by extermination' to the Moabite god Ashtar-Chemosh by Mesha, king of Moab, according to line 17 of the Louvre stele quoted above (*7*, p. 76; *24*.1, 2, p. 77). A similar kind of anathema, but expressed by another verb, occurs in particular in the text of Karib'il of Saba already quoted. In describing his conquest of the kingdom of Awsān, Karib'il relates that after he had eliminated the Awsanite king, the latter's noblemen 'devoted (*ʿtb*) him (Karib'il) to (their goddess?) Samahat', but that he instead 'vowed (*ʿtb*) it (i.e. the people of Awsān) to killing and captivity' (RES 3945,5).

In the South Arabian cult there were several categories of hereditary priests, as well as the principal kinds of sacrifices and offerings (*24*.1,2 pp. 320–321; *24*.2) used in the Semitic world in general, and in the biblical and North Semitic sphere in particular. Even the use of birds – in the Bible, a cheap substitute for the sacrifice of other domestic animals (Lev 1, 14–17; 5,7–10; *24*.1,2, pp. 292–293; *24*.2, pp. 29–30, 83) – seems to be attested in South Arabia by reliefs showing women holding a bird (*19*.1, pp. 327–329, pl. XIV,1; *19*.2, p. 119, pl. VIII, d, IX, d). But priests so far appear only in administrative functions, while no information is available on the normal priestly functions in the temple. In a similar manner sacrifices and offerings almost exclusively appear in casual, particular circumstances, which leaves us without any information on the probable existence of a daily or regular cultic ritual in the temple, of the kind attested in the Bible.

The immolation (verb *ḏbḥ*) of numerous animal victims (*'ḏbḥ*) in the court (*ḥḏr*, cp. Hebrew *ḥāṣēr*) of the temple, is a well attested rite in the kingdom of Maʿīn, as well as (but without mention of a court) in ancient Saba, in connection with the erection of public buildings. Sacrifices of animals were also offered by communities, on the occasion of a pilgrimage, or by private people. In the text CIH 392, a man indicates that he has erected a raised stone according to an oracle of the god enjoining him to erect this monument in his property and to sacrifice on it once every year a perfect victim, female or male – a typical pagan practice, frequently met with and condemned by the Bible (*24*.1,2, pp. 107–113).

Other texts were of an expiatory nature. An example is RES 4782, which prescribes the offering of a thigh and two forequarters of an animal as an expiation, 'in order that (the dedicator) may rejoin the tribe'. In his reinterpretation of the text A. F. L. Beeston (*2*.2, pp. 193–195) convincingly argued that it related to a kind of redemption at the outcome of an ibex hunt, the ibex being the sacred game of a god. R. B. Serjeant (*23*, p. 31) has further remarked that the parts of the animal which are to be offered are just the ones which are presented to the representative of the religious authority at the outcome of the ibex hunt in modern Hadhram awt. This analogy holds also for the North Semitic and biblical world, since the same parts are due to the priest in the ritual of the sacrifice not only in Israel (Lev 7,32–34; 10,14–15) but also in Punic Carthage, according to line 4 of the famous tariff from Carthage found in Marseilles (*4*, no. 69, pp. 83–87; *22*.17, p. 266).

In his stimulating study of the hunt in South Arabia R. B. Serjeant (*23*, pp. 60–74) has shown that in modern Hadhramawt ibex hunting retains some features which allow us to trace it back to the cultic hunting of an animal devoted to a god, a ritual intended as a charm to obtain rain, and supposed to work if the hunting was successful. This general interpretation quite satisfactorily accounts for the meaning of the ritual hunt in the pre-Islamic South Arabian civilisation. In the inscription CIH 571 (*2.2*, pp. 187–189) a goddess imposes on a tribe once a year the task of executing a hunt for her, in order to obtain good crops. In CIH 547 (*2.2*, pp. 191–193) a tribe confesses its guilt for not having delivered on time to the god his hunt (or: his game), while it postponed doing so in order to attend a pilgrimage to another god in Yathil. As a result, the god avenged himself by sending only a little rain water into the irrigation system of the tribe. This close connection, in South Arabia, between hunting the symbolic animal of a god, and obtaining rains or good crops, allowed me to suggest a new interpretation of the hunt prescribed to Esau by Isaac in Gen 27, 1–29 (*22.16*, pp. 459–460; *22.17*, pp. 261–262). In spite of the expurgation to which this story certainly was submitted, a central idea stands out clearly: the successful hunt (and its corollary, the consumption of game) is a necessary and preliminary condition to the granting of the benediction which concerns, as it appears, the fecundity of the soil and of the race. 'Sit up and eat of my game, *that you may bless me*', says Jacob (v. 19). I think the text retains the trace of a hunt practised as an incantation rite: the success of the hunt (that is, the slaying of game which the holder of the benediction can consume) is a sign that the benediction to be given will be operational, so that the holder of the benediction verily could wish: 'May God give you the dew of heaven, and the fatness of the earth, and plenty of grain and wine' (v. 28).

South Arabian sacrifices were executed on altars, *mḏbḥt*, which naturally remind one of Hebrew *mizbēaḥ* (*21*, p. 254). Another analogy of the *mḏbḥt* with biblical use is that, like the *mizbēaḥ*, that kind of altar was also used for the combustion of perfumes (*21*, p. 254).[9] Similarly the term *mslm* designated a table for libations (several examples of which are known), although *mslm*-altars were also used as incense burners (*21*, p. 254). An etymological connection probably existed between the offering made on the *mslm*-altars and the biblical 'peace offerings' (*zĕbaḥ šelāmīm*) (*24.2*, p. 37), since both words originally belong to the same Semitic root.

South Arabian *mqṭr* (cp. Hebrew *miqtĕrĕt*) designates an incense burner, probably of the small domestic type, forming a parallelepiped of no more than a few centimetres, many examples of which have been recovered. Some bear on each side the name of a different aromatic (CIH 681 ff.): this indicates that a mixture was used, exactly as for the incense offerings in the temple in Jerusalem (Ex 30, 34–38; *24.1*, 2, pp. 301–302). This South Arabian type of burner has penetrated into Palestine and Mesopotamia, where it is found on various archaeological sites (Gezer, Megiddo, etc.) from the 6th century B.C. onwards.

There is no doubt that any fresh and representative inscriptional material giving a better insight into the South Arabian institutions, will also bring new points of comparison with the institutions of the Old Testament.

Notes

To my colleagues M. Gilbert and P. Bogaert I owe useful advice on biblical matters. Biblical verses are quoted as in the Revised Standard Version. Other references contain the author's name (or his number in italics in the bibliography), eventually followed by the relevant number in the list of his works.

[1] E.g. *25*, p. 16–17. A conception first expressed by A. J. Wensinck, 'Die Entstehung der muslimischen Reinheitsgesetzgebung', *Der Islam*, Strassburg, v, 1914, pp. 62–79.

[2] However, the technical vocabulary of the pagan South Arabian texts on ritual purity shows very close analogies to that of the Islamic law, cp. *22*.16, pp. 454–455.

[3] According to G. M. Bauer, *1*, p. 30 n. 82, an alliance of Saba with other states is meant.

[4] A term probably implying no more than primacy of status among the devotees of ʿAmm and Anbay, see *2*.4, p. 367. A. G. Lundin, *4*, pp. 278–281 and *5*, pp. 129–130, interprets this title in the light of Strabo, *Hist.* 16, 43 (quoting Eratosthenes on South Arabia), stating that the king is succeeded by the man who was the first male child born among the nobility after the king's accession to the throne, and he compares this to a system (analogous to the *gada* mentioned in next note) of royal succession in the mediaeval Swahili state of 'Pate'.

[5] A system similar to the age-sets systems of North East Africa, of the type of the *gada* of the Galla (see *13*, pp. 41–45) – a comparison I owe to my former pupil H. J. Stroomer.

[6] Against the widespread translation 'he redeemed himself', see *20*, pp. 61 n. 35 and 62 n. 36.

[7] Unpublished paper delivered in 1970, see *PSAS*, London, 1, 1971, p. 4. The same idea is taken up by A. F. L. Beeston, 'Two Epigraphic South Arabian Roots', in *Al-Hudhud, Festschrift Maria Höfner*, Vienna, 1981, pp. 27–29. This article also discusses the texts Ir 24 and RES 4233 mentioned below.

[8] Reinterpreted: *2*.3; *12*, pp. 20–26; in *2*.5, pp. 418–420, A. F. L. Beeston identified the crime as being that of a leper eluding his prescribed seclusion (cp. Lev 13, 45–46). However the reading of the relevant word – *tgdmm*, compared to the Arabic root *jḏm* – is not supported by W. W. Müller, who analysed the stone (oral information).

[9] See *24*.1,2, p. 286 and *21*, p. 258 on the possibility that the 'golden altar', *mizbēaḥ hazzāhāb* (1 Kings 7,48, etc.) originally was an altar for *zāhāb*-perfume, which would be the incense called (probably because of its colour) *ḏhb*, 'gold' in ESA.

Abbreviations

Initials for inscriptions:

CIH: *Corpus Inscriptionum Semiticarum*, Pars IV, Inscriptiones Himyariticas et Sabaeas continens, Paris, 1889–1929, 3 vols.

Ir, Ja: see hereunder nos. *14* and *15*.1.

RES: *Répertoire d'Epigraphie Sémitique*, Paris 1900–1968, 8 vols.

Other abbreviations:

AION: *Annali dell'Istituto Orientale di Napoli.*

Festschr. Caskel: Ed. Gräf (ed.), *Festschrift Werner Caskel*, Leiden, 1968.

LM: *Le Muséon*, Louvain.

PSAS: *Proceedings of the Seminar for Arabian Studies*, London.

SDB: *Supplément au Dictionnaire de la Bible*, Paris.

VDI: *Vestnik Drevnej Istorii*, Moscow.

Bibliography

1 G. M. Bauer
'"Mukarrib" i "Carr"', *VDI*, LXXXVIII, 1964, 2, pp. 17–36.

2 A. F. L. Beeston
1 'Appendix on the Inscriptions Discovered by Mr Philby', in H. St. J. B. Philby, *Sheba's Daughters*, London, 1939, pp. 441–454.
2 'The Ritual Hunt, A Study in Old South Arabian Religious Practice', *LM*, LXI, 1948, pp. 183–196.
3 'A Sabaean Penal Law', *LM*, LXIV, 1951, pp. 305–315.
4 'Kingship in Ancient South Arabia', *Journ. of Econ. and Soc. History of the Orient*, XV, 1972, pp. 256–268.
5 'Notes on Old South Arabian Lexicography, X', *LM*, LXXXIX, 1976, pp. 407–423.
6 'Epigraphic South Arabian Nomenclature', *Raydān*, Louvain, 1, 1978, pp. 13–21.

3 H. Cazelles
'Premiers-nés. II. Les premiers-nés dans l'Ancien Testament', in *SDB*, VIII, fasc. 43–44, 1968–1969, col. 482–491.

4 H. Donner and W. Röllig
Kanaanäische und aramäische Inschriften. II, Kommentar, Wiesbaden, 1964.

5 J. de Fraine
1 *L'aspect religieux de la royauté israélite*, Rome, 1954.
2 *Adam et son lignage*, Paris, 1959.

6 C. J. Gadd
'The Harran Inscription of Nabonidus', *Anatolian Studies*, London, VIII, 1958, pp. 35–92.

7 J. C. L. Gibson
Textbook of Syrian Semitic Inscriptions. I, Hebrew and Moabite Inscriptions, Oxford, 1971.

8 J. Gray
I & II Kings. A Commentary, London, 1970^2.

9 H. Grimme
'Der südarabische Levitismus und sein Verhältnis zum Levitismus in Israel', *LM*, XXXVII, 1924, pp. 169–199.
10 J. Halévy
'Ex-voto sabéens relatifs aux purifications', *Revue Sémitique*, Paris, VII, 1899, pp. 267–278.
11 J. Henninger
1 'Zum Erstgeborenenrecht bei den Semiten', in *Festschr. Caskel*, pp. 162–183.
2 'Premiers-nés. I. La primogéniture en ethnologie', in *SDB*, VIII, fasc. 43–44, 1968–1969, col. 462–482.
3 'Zum Erstgeborenenrecht im alten Südarabien', *Ethnologische Zeitschrift Zürich*, I, 1972, pp. 185–192.
12 M. Höfner
Sabaeica. III. Teil, Hamburg, 1966.
13 G. W. B. Huntingford
The Galla of Ethiopia. The Kingdoms of Kafa and Janjero, London, 1969[2].
13bis. A. K. Irvine
'Homicide in pre-Islamic South Arabia', *Bull. of the School of Or. and Afric. Studies*, XXX, 1967, pp. 277–292.
14 M. A. Al-Iryānī
Fī Tārīkh al-Yaman, Cairo, 1973.
15 A. Jamme
1 *Sabaean Inscriptions from Maḥram Bilqîs (Mârib)*, Baltimore, 1962.
2 *The Al-'Uqlah Texts*, Washington, 1963.
16 A. G. Loundine (Lundin)
1 'Deux inscriptions sabéennes de Mârib', *LM*, LXXXVI, 1973, pp. 179–182.
2 *Sammlung Eduard Glaser V. Die Eponymenliste von Saba (aus dem Stamme Ḫalīl)* (Österr. Akad. d. Wiss., Phil.-Hist. Kl., Sitzungsber., 242. Bd., 1. Abh.), Vienna, 1965.
3 *Gosudarstvo Mukarribov Saba' (sabejskij eponimat)*, Moscow, 1971, French summary, pp. 280–301.
4 'Principy prestolonasledija v drevnej Aravii', in *Meroe. Istorija, istorija kul'tury, jazyk drevnego Sudana*, Moscow, 1977, pp. 278–281, French summary, p. 301.
5 'Prestolonasledie v Katabane', *Sovetskaja Etnografija*, Moscow, 1978, IV, pp. 123–130.
17 D. J. McCarthy
'Berît and Covenant', in *Studies in the Religion of Ancient Israel*, Leiden, 1972, pp. 65–81.
18 K. Mlaker
Die Hierodulenlisten von Ma'īn, Leipzig, 1943.
19 J. Pirenne
1 'Notes d'archéologie sud-arabe (I)', *Syria*, Paris, XXXVII, 1960, pp. 326–347.

2 'Notes d'archéologie sud-arabe (IV)', *Syria*, XLII, 1965, pp. 109–136.

20 Chr. Robin and J. Ryckmans
'L'attribution d'un bassin à une divinité en Arabie du Sud antique', *Raydān*, Louvain, I, 1978, pp. 39–64.

21 Gonzague Ryckmans
'Sud-arabe *mḏbḥt* = hébreu *mzbḥ* et termes apparentés', in *Festschr. Caskel*, pp. 253–260.

22 Jacques Ryckmans

1 *L'institution monarchique en Arabie Méridionale avant l'Islam (Ma'în et Saba)*, Louvain, 1951.

2 'Les "Hierodulenlisten" de Ma'īn et la colonisation minéenne', in *Scrinium Lovaniense, Mélanges Historiques E. Van Cauwenbergh*, Louvain, 1961, pp. 51–61.

3 'Les rois de Ḥaḍramawt mentionnés à 'Uqla', *Bibliotheca Orientalis*, XXI, 1964, pp. 277–282.

4 'Himyaritica (2)', *LM*, LXXIX, 1966, pp. 475–500.

5 'La mancie par *ḥrb* en Arabie du Sud ancienne, L'inscription Nami NAG 12', in *Festschr. Caskel*, pp. 261–273.

6 'Some Recent Views on the Public Institutions of Saba (Ancient South Arabia)', *PSAS*, I, 1971, pp. 24–26.

7 'Dve južnoarabskie ispovedal'nye nadpisi iz Leningrada (RES 3956 i 3957)', *VDI*, CXIX, 1972, 1, pp. 112–123, French summary, p. 123.

8 'Les confessions publiques sabéennes; le code sud-arabe de pureté rituelle', *AION*, XXXII, 1972, pp. 1–15.

9 'Un rite d'*istisqâ'* au temple sabéen de Mârib', *Annuaire de l'Institut de Philologie et d'Histoire Orientales et Slaves*, XX, Brussels, 1968–1972, pp. 379–388.

10 'Ritual Meals in the South Arabian Religion', *PSAS*, iii, 1973, pp. 36–39.

11 *Les inscriptions anciennes de l'Arabie du Sud : points de vue et problèmes actuels*, Oosterse Genootschap in Nederland, 4, Leiden, 1973, pp. 75–110.

12 'Le repas rituel dans la religion sud-arabe', in M. A. Beek *et al* (eds.), *Symbolae Biblicae et Mesopotamicae F. M. Th. de Liagre Böhl Dedicatae*, Leiden, 1973, pp. 327–334.

13 'Himyaritica (3)', *LM*, LXXXVII, 1974, pp. 237–263.

14 'Himyaritica (4)', *LM*, LXXXVII, 1974, pp. 493–521.

15 'Himyaritica (5)', *LM*, LXXXVIII, 1975, pp. 199–219.

16 'Les inscriptions sud-arabes anciennes et les études arabes', *AION*, XXXV, 1975, pp. 443–463.

17 'La chasse rituelle dans l'Arabie du Sud ancienne', in *Al-Bahit, Festschrift Joseph Henninger*, St. Augustin/Bonn, 1976, pp.259–308.

18 'Un cas d'impiété dans les inscriptions sud-arabes', in *Studia Paulo Naster Oblata*, II: *Orientalia Antiqua*, Leuven, 1983, pp. 207–214.

23 R. B. Serjeant
South Arabian Hunt, London, 1976.
24 R. de Vaux
1 *Les institutions de l'Ancient Testament*, Paris, I: 1958; II: 1960.
2 *Les sacrifices de l'Ancien Testament*, Paris, 1964.
3 '"Lévites" minéens et lévites israélites', repr. in R. de Vaux, *Bible et Orient*, Paris, 1967, pp. 277–285.
4 *Histoire ancienne d'Israël*, Paris, I: 1971; II: 1973.
25 J. Wansbrough
Quranic Studies, Oxford, 1977.

PART 2

Early and Mediaeval Islam

A document concerning the sale of Ghayl al-Barmakī and al-Ghayl al-Aswad by al-Mahdī ʿAbbās, Imam of the Yemen, 1131–89/1718–75

Hussein Abdullah al-Amri

Introduction

1. *Al-Mahdī ʿAbbās (1131–89/1718–75)*

Al-Mahdī ʿAbbās succeeded his father, Imam al-Manṣūr Ḥusayn b. al-Qāsim, on the latter's death on 7th Rabīʿ I, 1161/9th March, 1748. Al-Mahdī was a young, strong and ambitious man in the prime of his life. His contemporary biographers are unanimous in their opinion that his reign was '... better than that of his father, al-Manṣūr Ḥusayn, and than that of his grandfather, al-Mutawakkil Qāsim b. Ḥusayn (d. 1139/1727). It was also better than that of his son, al-Manṣūr ʿAlī (d. 1224/1809) and his grandson, al-Mutawakkil Aḥmad (d. 1231/1816) in every respect. Indeed he had more good qualities than them and more authority, reputation and fame.[1] Shaykh al-Islām al-Shawkānī described him as '... perspicacious, just and a strong manager (*qawī 'l-tadbīr*)'.[2]

Nevertheless al-Mahdī ʿAbbās did have faults and shortcomings – as of course is the case with many rulers and indeed with mankind in general. We are concerned here with two in particular and these in fact are one single issue.

(A) His love, even greed for buying up land '... until the whole affair ended in disaster. This was his buying up of *waqf* lands and transferring them from *waqf* to private ownership'.[3] But it was also a question of his transferring or exchanging his own property and *waqf* property in the lands around Ṣanʿāʾ, like Shaʿūb to the north, al-Ṣāfiyah to the south and Biʾr al-ʿAzab to the west and in many other areas. *Waqf* land, as is well known, '... cannot be sold or exchanged' and this was expressly stated by Sayyid Muḥammad b. Ismāʿīl al-Amīr (1099–1182/1688–1768) in his letter addressed to al-Mahdī in Dhū 'l-Ḥijjah, 1180/1767. In this letter Ibn al-Amīr is giving al-Mahdī his advice and also warning him.[4] Many other ulema did the same, though it can be said that Ibn al-Amīr was in many cases urging them on.[5] If the age of Ibn al-Amīr (who was over eighty at the time) and his literary and social position brought forgiveness for him from al-Mahdī, the latter certainly did not forgive the others for their opposition to his increasing buying up of agricultural land and his removal of *waqf* land to his own private ownership, also to his transferring or exchanging his own less fertile and more distant lands for better and nearer ones. The punishment for his critics and those who opposed him in his policies proved more than once to be confiscation of land or imprisonment. This is indeed what happened to a number of prominent figures and ministers like Yaḥyā b. Ṣāliḥ al-Saḥūlī and others.[6]

(B) This is connected closely with (A) above and is what al-Mahdī did in order to gain possession of two main *ghayl*s whose ownership was supposed to be common or to be under the control of the Treasury (*Bayt al-Māl*). Al-Mahdī claimed that he had rebuilt the canals and re-excavated the two *ghayls* and that all the expenditure had been from his own private wealth, a claim we can see in the document concerning this case, which is itself the main subject of this contribution. Al-Mahdī was opposed in this by Ibn al-Amīr and others including Faqīh ʿAlī b. ʿAbd Allāh al-ʿAmri (an ancestor of the present writer), the latter of whom was responsible for the two *ghayl*s and indeed for all government constructions and the internal affairs of the city of Ṣanʿāʾ. The result of his opposition to the general question of *waqf* property and to al-Mahdī's behaviour in this particular case was nothing but distress, for his house and property in Ṣanʿāʾ were confiscated. Later in the same year, 1182/1769, in Dhū 'l-Ḥijjah, he was arrested and died in the Qalʿat al-Qaṣr prison in Ṣanʿāʾ in Shaʿbān, 1183/1770.[7]

In fact the case of the two *ghayl*s, al-Barmakī and al-Aswad, is the subject which we have prepared for this paper. The document concerning the *ghayl*s is here published for the first time. The document is the exact copy of the judgement given in this case by the Qāḍī of Ṣanʿāʾ, Ismāʿīl b. Yaḥyā al-Ṣiddīq, issued in Ramaḍān, 1180/1767. According to this judgement al-Mahdī ʿAbbās owned these two *ghayl*s as after his death did heirs of Āl al-Mahdī, until recently (in the 1960s) when their water ran out and the matter came to an end.

2. *Al-Ghayl al-Aswad and Ghayl al-Barmakī*

The two *ghayl*s have been known for a very long time. The former surfaces on the plain situated between the village of al-Jardāʾ in the west and Bayt Sabaṭān in the east, a few miles to the south of Ṣanʿāʾ. Ghayl al-Barmakī surfaces at a greater distance than the former, by two or three miles, south-east of Ṣanʿāʾ. Its source is near the village of Bayt ʿUqab and Ghaymān. Al-Aswad crosses the city to water the suburbs of the north, west and south together with al-Barmakī. As a result of negligence or wilful destruction at times when Ṣanʿāʾ has been under siege, the water channels of these two *ghayl*s have often been blocked. Also the water has on occasion dwindled and decreased from the sources themselves, so the authorities in Ṣanʿāʾ would re-excavate the water channels or carry out restoration and preservation work on them in the general interest of the population of the city. The earliest reference of which we are aware to this practice is that of al-Rāzī concerning Ghayl al-Barmakī '... that Muḥammad b. Khālid al-Barmakī, governor of Ṣanʿāʾ on behalf of Hārūn al-Rashīd it was who created the *ghayl* of Ṣanʿāʾ and he it was who gave it its name. That was in the year 183/799'. He also states 'that he assembled the people to bear witness and to swear by God that he had spent no wealth of the state and spent nothing on it which was forbidden'.[8] It seems too that negligence, the passage of time and lack of preservation work led to the filling in of al-Ghayl al-Aswad. This process was exacerbated by the actions of Sultan ʿĀmir b. ʿAbd al-Wahhāb (894–923/1489–1517) during his siege of Ṣanʿāʾ in 910/1504. He filled in a part of Ghayl al-Barmakī and this had a great effect on the strength of flow and the quantity of its water.[9]

Al-Mahdī ʿAbbās, who was concerned with agriculture and irrigation, gave orders in 1177/1764 for the re-excavation of the channels and source of both al-Ghayl al-Aswad and Ghayl al-Barmakī.[10] Supervision of the work was carried out by al-Qāḍī al-Faqīh ʿAlī b. ʿAbd Allāh al-ʿAmri, who was also responsible for government property.[11] Work continued until 1181/1766. At that time al-Mahdī decided that the two *ghayls* were his private property on the pretext that the money spent on getting the two *ghayls* flowing again had been from his own pocket, on the basis of his paying 1400 *riyāls* in silver coinage (*ḥajar fiḍḍī*). This latter amount is referred to in the document.

Al-Mahdī met with opposition, as we have seen above, for this decision. Perhaps the most important such opposition was that of Ibn al-Amīr in his above mentioned letter. He touched on the matter when he wrote, warning al-Mahdī:

> It was to be hoped for and expected from your good intentions that you bring about the gratitude of God's favour upon you by opening up a long-buried *ghayl*. Thereby you will irrigate the *waqf* properties of Shaʿūb, so that grain may become plentiful for the employees (*ahl al-waẓāʾif*) whose grain [granted as a salary] decreases for four months every year in comparison with the year before [sic]. By God! Think of your grandfather, al-Mahdī Aḥmad b. al-Ḥasan [d. 1092/1681],[12] may God have mercy upon him. He opened up his *ghayl* in al-Rawḍah and made it common property for all. Not only this, but he watered his grapes exactly like other people without any special privilege. God blessed him and the grapes which were irrigated from his *ghayl* became the best and the most expensive in al-Rawḍah.[13] That was because of his good intention and because he knew that these *ghayls* were themselves 'treasuries' (*buyūt amwāl*) and were excavated by means of money from the Treasury. He felt no right to grant himself preferential treatment in anything from it.[14]

3. *The document concerning al-Mahdī's buying the two* ghayls

The document in question is a hand-written copy of the original made in 1219/1804. About ten years after its copying two well known Qāḍīs of Ṣanʿāʾ certified to its originality with their own signatures. The first is Qāḍī Aḥmad b. Muḥammad Mashḥam whom al-Mahdī appointed Qāḍī of Ṣanʿāʾ to succeed his father who had died in 1181/1767. He remained in his position until al-Mahdī ʿAbbās died and was succeeded by his son, al-Manṣūr ʿAlī in 1189/1775. Al-Mansur 'respected him and depended upon him in some very important matters' and, al-Shawkānī adds in praise of him, '. . . he was one of the eminent and honourable *qāḍīs*'.[15]

The second signatory is Yūsuf b. Ismāʿīl b. Yaḥyā al-Ṣiddīq, the son of Qāḍī Ismāʿīl who issued the judgement (*ḥukm*) in the document. He was a disciple of al-Shawkānī and, when his father died, Imam al-Manṣūr ʿAlī appointed him his successor in the Court. Al-Manṣūr depended on him also in his private affairs and in matters of property. He died in Dhamār in 1244/1828.[16]

As for the original of the document, we no longer know where it is. About 25 years ago the Yemeni historian, the late Muḥammad b. Muḥammad Zabārah, made a copy from the original, which, when compared with the document reproduced here, was found to be exactly the same. It is probable that one of al-Mahdī's heirs might have had reason at some time to make a copy of the original. The copy under discussion here was discovered among a few other documents in the Bayt al-ʿAmrī library.[17]

Returning to the actual document, we find that it was Qāḍī Ismāʿīl b. Yaḥyā b. al-Ḥasan al-Ṣiddīq (1130–1209/1718–94) who issued the judgement. He was a *faqīh*, scholar and a figure of respectability. He held many judicial positions in different towns of the Yemen until al-Mahdī appointed him in 1172/1758 '... one of his judges (*ḥukkām*) in Ṣanʿāʾ'. He greatly respected him and depended upon him in different matters, especially that of his father's legacy which he requested him to consider. He was revered and esteemed in the hearts of men and had a profound knowledge of jurisprudence and enunciated his words with a strong guttural sound'.[18]

The judgement given in the document and made by Qāḍī al-Ṣiddīq provides us with a model for the style of the 12th/18th and 13th/19th centuries. The introduction used to preface a legal decision and to give the reasons on which the judgement is based and its style is still in use to this day.

This document also gives us the opportunity to study the style of Qāḍī al-Ṣiddīq, which would have been enunciated, according to al-Shawkānī '... with a strong guttural sound'.[19]

As for the legal reasons of his judgement of al-Mahdī's taking possession of the two *ghayl*s, they were that the cost of the excavations came from his private wealth and from a legitimate income (*maḥḍ al-ḥalāl*). In spite of this, Qāḍī al-Ṣiddīq adds, al-Mahdī took the precaution of having the Qāḍī investigate the matter. So he instructed certain fair-minded people (*ʿudūl*) and he mentions their names in the text – to estimate the cost of the two *ghayl*s. This they did and came up with the cost of 700 *riyāl*s, which the Qāḍī doubled to 1400 *riyāl*s. Al-Mahdī gave orders to Faqīh ʿAlī al-ʿAmri, who was responsible for properties (*amlāk*), to pay this sum. In his order, however, al-Mahdī stated that the sum was to be paid from the *jāmakiyat al-ajnād*, i.e. the soldiers' monthly stipend for Shaʿbān, 1180, and this was under the responsibility of Ṣāliḥ ʿIzzān, al-Mahdī's agent. This raises a problem, for we do not know really whether this was from wealth which belonged personally to al-Mahdī which he had returned to his own special account from the stipends of the month previous to the judgement, or whether it was state money. If it were the latter, to whom was it paid?

After this introduction, the document may be left to explain itself. There were a few dictation errors which have been corrected and a very few words which have been added. These latter have been put between square brackets with an explanation in the notes.

[نص الوثيقة]

بسم الله الرحمن الرحيم (١٩)

وبعد حمد الله الذي أجرى الأنهار بعظيم قدرته وسلكها ينابيعا في الأرض على وفق مشيئته ومقتضى باهر حكمته ، وصلاته وسلامه من نبع الماء النمير من بين أصابعه المشرفة فكان من أعظم آياته وباهر معجزاته ، وعلى آله الذين فجروا عيون العلوم بثواقب الأنظار فجرت جداول أنهارها في رياض قلوب العارفين الأبرار ، صلاة وسلاما دايمان ما تعاقب ليل ونهار .

فانه لما كان إلى عام [سبع] (٢٠) وسبعون ومائة وألف جرت الأيادي الرحمانية والأقدار السمطانية ، والمشيئة الربانية الهام مولآنا ومليكنا ، وولي أمرنا ونهينا ، خليفة الله في العالم سيد ملوك بني أدم ، ظل الله على العباد ، أمين الله في البلاد ، أمير المؤمنين المهدي لدين الله رب العالمين ، العباس بن أمير المؤمنين المنصور بالله الحسين بن أمير المؤمنين المتوكل على الله القاسم ، لابرح مخصوصا بالاقبال والانعام ، مؤيدا بالعز الذي لا يضام والسعادة الأبدية ، والنصر والتمكين والانعام والفوز في الدارين برضى الملك العلام . فصرف عنان العناية إلى التفتيش عن الغيلين المباركين ، المسمى أحدهما «بالغيل الأسود» والآخر «بالغيل البرمكي» الكائنا [ن] في جهة عدني (٢١) مدينة صنعاء المحمية بالله عز وجل ، بعد أن كانا قد دمرا وخربا ، ودرست أثارهما ، وعفت رسومهما ، وأحكم بالسد البليغ قرارهما ومجاريهما ، ونسيت مع طول الأزمان أسماءهما فلم يبق لهما في العالمين ذكرا ، ولا يعرف في هذه العصور عن شأنهما خبرا ولا خبرا ، بل شاهدتهما وهما من موات الأرض في حين العدم المحض، قد اتخذ الناس تلك المجاري من درعات ونضموها في سلك أراضيهم وخصائص أموالهم لا يعرفونها ولا أبائهم الا كذلك ، فبالغ حفظه الله وبارك للمسلمين في أوقاته في احياء ذلك لنفسه العزيزة المشرفة ، وبذل حفظه الله من خالص الأملاك ومحض الحلال مالا يكاد يأتي عليه الحصر حتى كملت بحمد الله فايدتهما وعظم بعون الله نفعهما .

ثم وقع منه حفظه الله لزوم طريقة الورع ، وسلوك مسلك الاحتياط لجواز أن يكون هناك حق في معلوم الله عز وجل يتعلق بهما لبيت مال المسلمين ، فرجح حفظه الله توسيط شرع الله الذي هو الحجة العظمى والعروة الوثقى ، فأمرت عدولا من المسلمين الجامعين بين كمال الخبرة والأمانة والثقة والديانة ، والمعرفة الكاملة لتلك المحلات قبل اتفاق العمل وبعده ، فمازالوا يغلبوا الظن ويبالغوا في الاحتياط بكل ممكن مع اتفاقهم على الأياس من وجدان الراغب وعجز الطالب لقطع الناظر ينادي الرأي ان احيائهما ان لم يكن مستحيل عادة فمتعذر لا محالة ، غير أن الأمر كله لله ، والفضل بيد الله يؤتيه من يشاء . فأجمع رأيهم على تقويم «الغيل الأسود» المسمى الأن «بالأخضر» بأربع مائة قرش ، و «غيل البرمكي» بثلاث مائة قرش . فرجحت بحسب نظر الشرع الشريف في المصلحة الراجحة ، الثابتة قطعا ، المحكوم لها شرعا نصب أمين شرعي لبيع ذلك . فوقع منه البيع الصحيح والايجاب باللفظ الصريح المتناول للغيلين المذكورين قرارهما ومجاريهما وما يتبعهما شرعا وعرفا بثمن قدره ومبلغه أربع عشر مائة قرش . ووقع من وكيل سيدي المولى حفظه الله قبول ذلك الايجاب في الموقف الشرعي وسلم الثمن جميعا بالمعاينة والمشاهدة ، ثم صرف باطلاع المأمون (واذن للشرع) (٢٢) ، ورای المولى حفظه الله إلى أجناد الحق المعدة لارغام أعداء الله ولاعلاء كلمة الله ، وايفاد شرع الله محسوبا من جوامكهم اللازمة في شهر شعبان سنة ١١٨٠ . وكان ذلك البيع بيعا صحيحا نافذا منبرما بعد ما تبينت المصلحة المسوغة وتقريرها لدى شرعا ، فاستقر المبيع وكل ما يتبعه في ملك مشتريه استقرارا تاما ، وانفصل عنه وعن ثمنه كل حق وعلاقة ودعوى وطلب . واستخرت الله ونعم المستخار ، وحكمت بصدور ذلك وصحته ونفوذه بعد أن تقرر أن الغرامة الواقعة في كلا الغيلين المذكورين خاصة بالمولى حفظه الله مستقرة في ملكه لصدورها من خاصة أملاكه ، فليعتمد وبالله الثقة ، وحسبنا الله وكفى ونعم الوكيل وصلى الله وسلم على سيدنا محمد وآله .

وقد أمرت من حضر موقف الشرع الشريف بالشهادة على ذلك .
حرر بشهر رمضان الكريم سنة ١١٨٠ . (فبراير ١٧٦٧ م)
والعدول المشار اليهم أولا هم :
الشيخ عبد الله الرحبي شيخ شعوب
والشيخ أحمد حسن شيخ بئر العزب
والشيخ عبد الرحمن الحواني شيخ حدة
والشيخ علي سعيد شيخ بيت بوس
بتاريخ شهر رمضان الكريم سنة ١١٨٠

اسماعيل بن يحي الصديق لطف الله به

حرر هذا في شهر رجب الفرد سنة ١٢١٩

« الحمد لله

« يا فقيه علي العمرى عافاك الله ، سلم من الخاص قيمة أبار الغيلين التي قررها الحاكم لبيت المال من جامكية الأجناد بنظر صالح عِزّان وذلك أربعة عشر مائة قرش حجر وتقرر تسليم ذلك القاضي اسماعيل منا يخص لتاريخ شهر شعبان سنة ١١٨٠

عبد الله

المهدي لدين الله « العباس وفقه الله »

« الحمد لله

هذه صورة الحوالة المهدوية بخط سيدي المولى المهدي لدين الله وهو معروف عندي معرفة محققة

احمد محمد مشحم (توقيع)

« الحمد لله

وقع الاطلاع على الأصل المذكور من الحاكم العلامة المشهور رحمه الله والتحويل الواقع من مولانا أمير المؤمنين المهدي رضوان الله عليه للقيمة المذكورة، وقوبل هذا عليها بتاريخه

« يوسف بن اسماعيل الصديق » (توقيع)

« هذا النقل صحيح من الأصل الشرعي الذي عليه علامة حاكم الشرع المعتمد القاضي العلامة اسماعيل بن يحي الصديق رحمه الله .

بتاريخه سنة سبع وعشرين ومائتين وألف

« أحمد محمد مشحم عفا الله عنه » (توقيع)

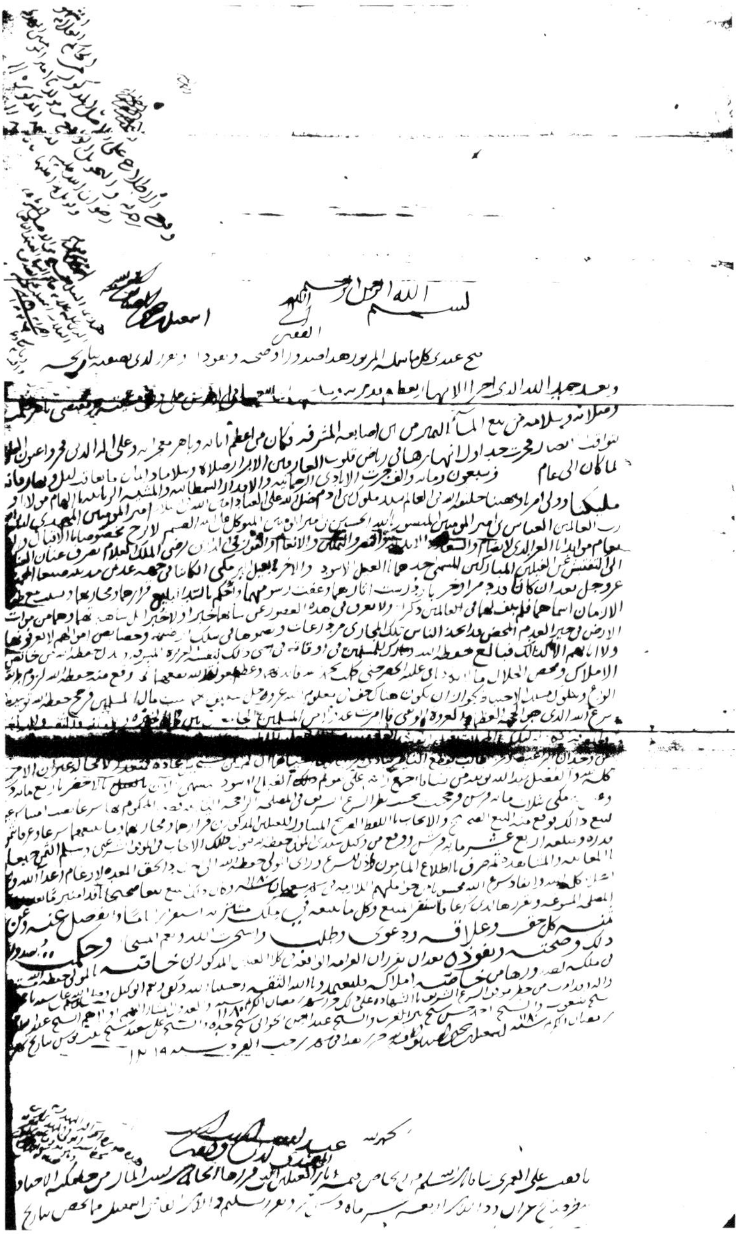

A document concerning the sale of Ghayl al-Barmakī and al-Ghayl al-Aswad by al-Mahdī ʿAbbās

Notes

[1] Muḥammad b. Muḥammad Zabārah, *Nashr al-'arf li-nubalā' al-Yaman ba'da 'l-alf*, Cairo, 1376 H, II, 12.
[2] Muḥammad b. 'Alī al-Shawkānī, *al-Badr al-ṭāli' bi-maḥāsin man ba'da 'l-qarn al-sābi'*, Beirut, n.d., 2 vols., I, 310.
[3] *Nashr*, II, 10.
[4] *Nashr*, II, 10.
[5] Qāsim Ghālib, *Ibn al-Amīr wa-'aṣruh*, Cairo, 1966, 268–70.
[6] *Al-Badr*, II, 334. See also *al-Badr*, II, 1 and *Nashr*, II, 508.
[7] *Dhayl al-Badr al-ṭāli'*, II, 168; *Nashr*, II, 248–9; *Ibn al-Amīr*, 269.
[8] Aḥmad b. 'Abd Allāh al-Rāzī, *Tārīkh madīnat Ṣan'ā'*, ed. Ḥusayn 'Abd Allāh al-'Amrī and 'Abd al-Jabbār Zakkār, Damascus, 1974, 106–7.
[9] 'Abd al-Raḥmān b. 'Alī al-Dayba', *Qurrat al-'uyūn bi-akhbār al-Yaman al-maymūn*, ed. Muḥammad b. 'Alī al-Akwa', Cairo, 1977, 2 vols., II, 207–9; *Ibn al-Amīr*, 269.
[10] *Nashr*, II, 13.
[11] See above note 7.
[12] Cf. *al-Badr*, I, 43–4; Muḥammad al-Muḥibbī, *Khulāṣat al-athar fī a'yān al-qarn al-ḥādī 'ashar*, Beirut, 1290 H, I, 180.
[13] Al-Rawḍah is situated in the grape-growing area about nine kilometres north of Ṣan'ā'. The *ghayl* still flowed until the beginning of the 1960s and the grapes of al-Rawḍah are famous to this day.
[14] *Nashr*, II, 11.
[15] *Al-Badr*, I, 95; Muḥammad Zabārah, *Nayl al-waṭar min tarājim rijāl al-Yaman fī 'l-qarn al-thālith 'ashar*, Cairo, 1348 H, V, 235–7.
[16] *Al-Badr*, I, 158.
[17] Reference has already been made to the confiscation of the wealth of Faqīh 'Alī al-'Amrī by al-Mahdī 'Abbās, when the former had bequeathed his wealth at al-Ṣāfiyah as *waqf* for Qubbat Ṭalḥah, so that it would not become al-Mahdī's private property. The situation has remained thus to the present day. The elders of al-'Amrī were responsible for looking after the *waqf* and this perhaps explains why Āl al-'Amrī retained this document, as well as other archival material, the majority of which is lost.
[18] *Al-Badr*, I, 106–8; *Nayl*, I, 116; his biography also occurs in Luṭf Allāh b. Aḥmad Jaḥḥāf, *Durar nuḥūr al-ḥūr al-'īn*, MS, Library of the Imam Yaḥyā (now in the Great Mosque Library), f. 241.
[19] After the *basmalah* the following expression of approval is given: '*ṣaḥḥa 'indī kullamā shamalahu 'l-mazbūr hādhā ṣudūran wa-ṣiḥḥatan wa-nuqūdan wa-taqarrara ladayya bi-ṣifatihi bi-tārīkhih. Al-Faqīr ilā Rabbih Ismā'īl b. Yaḥyā al-Ṣiddīq, laṭafa 'llāh bih*'.
[20] I have added this from the original which Zabārah (*Nashr*, II, 13) found. My copy of the document has a blank space at this point.
[21] ''Adanī' with the meaning of 'southern'.
[22] What is between brackets is not clear. It is perhaps a textual error.

A legal text to the aid of history: a note on the *sūqs* of Baghdad in the first century of the Abbasids

Claude Cahen

It is now being realised that Islamic law, although expressed through conceptual outlines, does meet the demands of reality.[1] This is true for all periods, but is particularly evident in the works of those who lay the foundations, and who have no predecessors to copy. Of course people have tended for practical reasons to refer to later more systematic and well-balanced treatises; but it is obvious that the historian should turn first to the earliest works,[2] even if they are less well preserved.

Quite apart from legal factors, the historian will find something more in these early works. Because they deal with real life, he will be able to extract from them material which is valid *per se*, irrespective of the legal considerations. This material is of two kinds: it alludes to events,[3] and it describes aspects of current society. It is this which we can deduce from a reading of *K. al-Aṣl*[4] by Muḥammad al-Shaybānī, younger colleague of and collaborator with the better known Abū Yūsuf. Al-Shaybānī had written methodical analyses of Ḥanafī law which was being established in Iraq under the Abbasids at that period. The works, entitled *al-Jāmiʿ al-kabīr* and *al-Jāmiʿ al-ṣaghīr*, had both been published some time earlier. These analyses, the result of an accumulation of material giving us direct insight into everyday life, make up the *K. al-Aṣl*. This feature is particularly obvious in the section on 'Sales' published by T. Chehata in 1954, when the rest was still almost completely unedited and neglected. This evidence is particularly precious because, for that period of Islam, the historiography of the Eastern World has had no documentation from archives, apart from Egyptian ones, on which to base its works of socio-economic history; and while other sources allow us to remedy this paucity of material, they give us more information about the later period than about the first century of Abbasid rule. I shall attempt below to extract from the 'Book of Sales' a brief but comprehensive portrait of the *sūqs* in the time of the author.

One feature is immediately evident: there is no mention of any international trade, or even inter-regional trade, any more than in most other treaties on *fiqh*. It is small business which is being described, or business on a moderate scale at most, such as took place in the everyday life of the *sūqs*, at a period when big business remained in the hands of non-Muslims or of Muslims who had adopted non-Muslim practices. It is true that in some later chapters there are less detailed paragraphs on *qirāḍ* which apply implicitly to big business in particular; but no link is established with the transactions dealt with in the 'Book of Sales'. Nor does our jurist appear to allude to the multiplicity or manifold variety of the *sūqs*, which no doubt existed; but presumably these did not create any different legal problems. There seems to be no mention of the official in charge of the *sūqs*, either with the title of *muḥtasib* or with the more traditional title of *ṣāḥib al-sūq*; it is not certain that the former title was yet in use in Shaybānī's time;[5] anyway, whether it existed or not, the legal problems posed remained the same. There is no mention either of the broker (*simsār*) or of the commission to which he is entitled.

However, Shaybānī does give us quite ample information on the products being sold in the *sūqs*.[6] Of course he does not claim to have given us an exhaustive list, nor does he guarantee that he has actually seen each of the goods he describes sold; but it seems reasonable to suppose that the products he mentions are in the main the ones actually for sale. Similarly when he mentions a price, he obviously did not check it in the *sūq* on that particular day; but it is unlikely that the price mentioned would be very different from the actual average.[7] With these reservations, here are the products that have been noted.

First of all, naturally, a great variety of food produce is included. Corn heads the list, indeed we are told that in current usage in Baghdad it is often referred to by the general word *ṭa'ām*, 'food', as well as by *ḥinṭah* (never by *qamḥ*, which is Mediterranean).[8] Then comes barley, though no other cereal, no rice for example.[9] Among the vegetables, which are often referred to as *baqal* without specification, melons, cucumbers and beans are mentioned in particular, though it is evident the list is incomplete.[10] As for fruit there are good quality dates (*fārisī*) and mediocre ones (*daql*),[11] raisins (*zabīb*), grenadines, quinces and nuts.[12] Oil-yielding products include sesame and olives, the animal fats and butter; cheese is mentioned, eggs, meat, fresh and dried fish, salt (though no sugar), vinegar, wine and pork for non-Muslims;[13] flour is listed, but not bread; clover, lucerne and straw are also mentioned, no doubt for animals.[14] One cooked dish is on the list, *sawiq*.[15]

Next come plants for dyeing and perfuming; saffron, henna, roses for rosewater, violets, jasmin etc., *wasmah* (the indigo dye, *nīl*).[16] Musk is also listed.[17]

Metals and other raw mineral materials follow: iron, lead, copper; assorted woods, *sāj* (teak), bricks, plaster, pitch, glass; amber, pearls and other jewels.[18] The raw materials are handed over to an artisan with an order to produce a certain article.

Then paper and various textiles are listed: sheep-, cattle- and camel-skins; cotton, linen and woollen material, clothes (see below), shoes, bags; live animals, birds, feathers, male and female slaves.[19]

As we have already stated, Shaybanī does not guarantee that the prices he mentions are exact, but they are quite remarkable. For we learn that a *kurr* of corn (about 2,800 kgs.) was worth 50 dirhams which, converted into gold, was at that time about three dinars. This price is about a tenth of what is known elsewhere in either the ninth or tenth century. This could perhaps be considered a slip on the part of the author or the copyist, were it not for the fact that the price of slaves is much more precise and is given not only as an absolute, but also in comparison with corn: one slave for ten *kurrs* of corn and barley. The price of slaves ranged from 100 to 1,000 dirhams, on average 500; barley always cost half as much as corn, therefore in this example the price of the latter per *kurr* would be about 33 dirhams, still two dinars lower than previously. It is obviously impossible to work out in the same way the price of clothes which is ill-defined; the average is around, say, five dirhams. These facts, however basic and tenuous they may be, should be taken into consideration in any discussion on the probable rise in prices in the course of the ninth century, a subject which we can only hint at here.[20]

The *K. al-Aṣl* allows us in particular to follow the successive operations of the textile and clothing industry, a field in which R. B. Serjeant has long been renowned. The chapters consulted do not mention spinning and weaving. This does not mean that they posed no problem for lawyers, but is presumably because thread and unmanufactured material were not sold in the *sūq*. It is possible that thread was made in areas which produced raw materials,[21] as Khūzistān did linen, but not in Baghdad.[22] We are not told where or how weaving was carried out though, in the case of expensive materials for commercial use at least, this must have been manufactured more in urban areas (as in Kāzirūn in Fārs).[23] Anyway unmanufactured cloth, *thawb* (the word always takes this meaning and not that of garment), was taken to the *qaṣṣār*, (fuller cum grease-remover) and then to the dyer. Red, yellow and black dyes are mentioned.[24] The dyer was held responsible if he used the wrong colour. Similarly the *qaṣṣār* had to guard against any deterioration, tearing, burning etc. . . . The tailor too took the blame if he made a garment which differed from what had been ordered or with the wrong measurements.[25] Often the customer would bring him the necessary cloth and even the thread. Everything would be weighed before manufacture and then on completion of the garment to ascertain that there had been no fraud.[26]

The main garments ordered were hats (*qalanswah*), trousers (*sarāwīl*), dresses (*jubbah*), over-garments (*burd*), jackets (*qabā*), tunics (*qams*), veils/mantles (*ṭaylasān*), cloaks/blankets (*kisā*) and *katīfah*, and belts (*manṭiqah*). Jewish materials (*yahūdī*) are also mentioned frequently and once a cloth called *zuṭṭī*. Materials were commonly sold in bales (*'idl*) of zutts (*zuṭṭī*) (one MS., however, gives *nabaṭī* which would apply to Iraqi peasants[27]) or in sacks (*jirāb harawī*) from Herat. Sarakhsī in his *Mabsūṭ* again uses the latter names[28] which according to the editor also occur at about the same time in the Muslim west in the *Mudawwanah* of Sahnūn;[29] but we do not know what they constituted exactly. In the *K. al-Aṣl* they imply bulk selling (*murābiḥatan*). Other cloths suggest to us Iranian provenance: Merv, Qūhistān[30] etc. *Sābūrī* are also mentioned.[31]

Clothes are also included among items which could be hired, for a special short-term occasion rather than for any length of time.[32]

It is not clear whether the craftsman would sometimes sell to wholesale merchants (*bazzāz*) or to state officials as well as to individual customers.[33]

The sale could take place on a cash basis or by means of barter, for future (short-term) delivery (*khiyār*), and also through work-orders (*istiṣnā'*). Terms of contracts were sometimes drawn up in Persian as well as in Arabic.[34]

The 'Book of Sales' states that not only the Muslim festivals but also Jewish and Christian ones are to be observed.[35] Coinage mentioned is in orthodox dirhams as well as in old coins or base metal which were in circulation at that time[36]. *Fulūs* must also be mentioned. The text mentions dinars only twice (76 and 205) and then only very vaguely. Baghdad was in the eastern area of the empire, inherited from the Persian Sasanian state, where coinage was silver based, but it was an empire, the Mediterranean half of which traded in gold and paid its taxes in gold. It is most unlikely therefore that its capital, Baghdad, did not use dinars, though they were used only by the Treasury and a few wealthy merchants and senior civil servants; at the time of Shaybānī silver currency was employed for the business of the *sūq*.

Notes

I would like to say that this short article begun quite a long time ago is only a draft of what I wanted to offer to R. B. Serjeant. I hope that it will be acceptable to him; it is only of value in pointing the way forward. At present the author is unable to do more, but it would have grieved him not to have contributed at all.

1 I have dealt with this in more detail at the colloquium of the Union Européenne des arabisants, Ravello 1966, and in the *Introduction à l'histoire du monde musulman* (in the press), a re-working of the book which appeared under the name of Sauvaget and myself in 1961 (English edition 1965) which is a little less clear in this respect.

2 I am thinking in particular of the use made of Islamic law in the history of North Africa by R. Brunschwig and his pupil, Idris.

3 Even in many later works there are some details which apply only to their period and, even if they are copying predecessors, a choice is made between what is useful and what is not.

4 A complete edition has been undertaken at Hyderabad. The five volumes which have appeared cover about a sixth of the whole. I have in my possession a photo-copy of the complete Cairo MS.

5 See *EI*², '*ḥisba*'.

6 Some of these goods come from fairly distant places, but it is not so much a matter of where they are imported from as, with all the others, the dealings they give rise to in the *sūq*.

7 With these reservations these data can be added to those collected by E. Ashtor in his *Histoire des prix et des salaires . . .*, Paris 1970.

8 Ashtor, *Prix*, 3 and passim.

9 Although rice was certainly to be found, cf. M. Canard, 'Le riz dans le Proche Orient', *Arabica*, VI, 1959, 113–31.

[10] Canard, 'Riz', passim.
[11] Ibid.
[12] Ibid.
[13] Ibid., 4 and 7. Pork and wine can be sold by a Muslim, providing the buyer is a non-Muslim.
[14] Ibid.
[15] Ibid., 7.
[16] Ibid., 4 and passim.
[17] Ibid., 8 and passim.
[18] Ibid., 4 and passim.
[19] Shaybānī seems to be particularly interested in the question of what lowering of price occurred for a slave when his hand had been cut off by the vendor prior to the sale. Slaves are often sold to partners, each thus having a half-share. One has in mind here the *mukātab*, the *mudabbar*; there are references to slaves used in commerce (*tijārah*).
[20] For these data, cf. Ashtor, *Histoire*, and Cl. Cahen 'Quelques problèmes ...' *Bulletin Inst. Or. Fac. Lettres*, Algiers, 1952 and 'Commercial Relations ...', *Islam and the Medieval West*, ed. Kh. Semaan, New York, 1980.
[21] It was perhaps clear to the reader of the day but it is not always so to us, whether the material mentioned was linen, wool, or on occasion some other substance. Silk and cotton are mentioned here and there, quite an expensive time for the latter.
[22] Naturally we are not discussing luxury materials made in the State *Ṭirāz*.
[23] See A. Mez, *Renaissance*, index, on Kāzirūn.
[24] To these must be added the *wasmah* of indigo mentioned above.
[25] One can imagine cases of spoiling through sword-cuts.
[26] Cairo MS, 245, f. 2.
[27] 'Sales', ed. Chehata, 5 n. 2.
[28] Ibid., 85, 106, 1.4, 1.5, 130, 134, 149–153, 159.
[29] Ibid., 5 n. 3.
[30] Ibid., 119 also wool from Hamadhān, Kurdish or Khwarizmian *ṭaylasān*.
[31] Ibid. 5 n. 4 and 18.
[32] Cairo MS. 234r ff.
[33] It may be that this was the case for bales of materials (always 50).
[34] 'Sales', 174.
[35] Ibid.
[36] Nabahardja, 325, 328 etc. Cf. my note in the volume in honour of Miles (= my *Makhzūmiyyāt*, 176); *zuyūf*, 14 (with note 1 referring to the *Mabsūṭ*, XII, 144); *zaīfa* 14, 24; *sattūq* 14 with n. 7.

The Mosque of al-Janad

Paolo M. Costa

The Great Mosque of al-Janad, nowadays a small hamlet some 20 kms. north of Ta'izz, is reputed to be one of the most important religious buildings of the Yemen, second only to the Great Mosque of Ṣan'ā' (Plate 1).

According to local tradition, the mosque of al-Janad, also popularly known as al-Janadiyyah, was founded by Mu'ādh b. Jabal al-Anṣārī, who was sent to the lower Yemen by the Prophet Muḥammad himself; Mu'ādh arrived in al-Janad on the first Friday of the month of Rajab, 9/631.[1]

This explains the passage of Najm al-Dīn 'Umārah al-Ḥakamī (fourth/tenth century), who reports the local belief that 'a visit to the mosque of al-Janad paid in the first week of the month of Rajab is equivalent to a visit to the holy places of Mecca or even to the performance of the pilgrimage' (Kay, 10).

The fifth/eleventh century Ṣan'ānī historian, Aḥmad 'Abd Allāh al-Rāzī maintains that the mosque of Ṣan'ā' is undoubtedly older than the mosque of al-Janad, and mentions 6/628 as one of the possible dates for its foundation. He concludes, however, that most probably between the building of the two mosques there was a lapse of only five months (Rāzī, 78, 79 & 212).

According to local tradition, a large town was soon built around the mosque of al-Janad, defended by a wall with several gates. This town was the capital of one of the three chief districts, in which south-western Arabia was divided: that of Ṣan'ā', in the north, the most extensive, that of al-Janad in the centre, and that of Ḥaḍramawt in the south (Daghfous, 6).

An aerial photograph of al-Janad taken by courtesy of Aeroprecisa, (Beirut), in 1971 shows clearly the possible extent of the original town; this corresponds to the roughly rectangular area which stands out as a darker colour and higher level on the cultivated land (Plate 2). It is the huge mound of debris of the ancient built-up area, today overlain by the humble and rather primitive dwellings of the few hundred inhabitants of the site.

The curious clustering of these one storey houses with broken pots as chimneys is, to my knowledge, a unique feature in the various kinds of settlement in the Yemen. It would be very interesting to carry out a socio-anthropological study of the settlement of al-Janad in order to understand why and how it took over this peculiar form. Apparently there is no relation between the settlement and the old mosque apart from the fact that they stand one beside the other.

In the centre of the aerial photo, the rectangular shape of the white mosque stands out boldly against the dark irregular ground and the ochre of the earth roofs of the houses. The building is a striking feature in the whole landscape also for its large size looking even larger in comparison to the tiny hamlet where it stands but to which it does not belong.

The aerial photo shows very clearly the last part of an old water channel. It has a straight course, A-A, then a sharp turn eastwards to B where it flows into a large cistern. This builds up the water-head needed for the final course of the channel through level ground to the mosque. The stretch C-C is still above ground. Then the water channel (*ghayl*) meets the *tell* of the ancient city and therefore it runs underground to emerge at D from where it runs open for a few metres before flowing into a beautiful scalloped cistern E, near the eastern corner of the mosque and to the ablution area F. It is possible that originally the *ghayl* was also used to supply an adjacent thermal bath G (see below page 50).

There are fortunately interesting information and comments on the mosque of al-Janad and its *ghayl* in the sixth/twelfth century historical work of Abū ʿAbd Allāh Bahā' al-Dīn al-Janadī, *Kitāb al-Sulūk fī maʿrifat al-duwal wa-'l-mulūk* (Kay, 258–260, n. 44). It will be useful to quote verbatim excerpts from Kay's translation of al-Janadī's text concerning the mosque and the *ghayl*.

'The Queen appointed al-Mufaḍḍal to replace (his brother Khālid) ... Al-Mufaḍḍal became the Queen's trusted adviser and administrator of her kingdom. The Queen decided upon nothing without his advice. He attained great power, and his word was raised on high ...

'Among the still existing memorials of al-Mufaḍḍal's rule, is the watercourse he constructed, extending from Hinwah to the city of Janad. It passes over places where its channel has been excavated in the living rock, in such wise that a description of the work is hard to be believed. Many such channels were made, and a stream of water is led through them. On reaching a spot between two mountains, the craftsmen provided for its passage by means of a wall, about two hundred cubits of the new measure in length from one mountain to the other, its height from the ground about fifty cubits and its width about ten cubits. These are the dimensions according to my own measurements and estimates. A person contemplating that great work, feels convinced that it can have been executed only by the Jinn, and but for absolute certainty of its visible existence, it were impossible to believe in it.

'Another great work of al-Mufaḍḍal was the reconstruction of the mosque of Janad. The portions he built are the front and the two aisles. The rear was built by a Ḳāḍi, one of the Jurists attached to the mosque. The portion erected by al-Mufaḍḍal may be distinguished through its being built of stone. He roofed it and it continued in existence until Mahdy son of ʿAly ibn Mahdy captured the city. He demolished the mosque and burnt it with fire, as will be related hereafter, if it please God. It remained a ruin until the *Ghuzz* (the Turkish and Northern soldiery under the Ayyūbites) arrived in Yaman. The power of the family of Mahdy did not long endure after the destruction of the mosque, nor had it been long in existence before. When Sayf al-Islam reached the city, he restored the mosque and added to its height the existing portion, built of brick. This will be mentioned hereafter, when the history of the Ayyūbite conquest is related.

'The Ḳāḍi Abu Bakr al Yāf'y mentions the story of the water channels, in the verses he composed in praise of Mansūr son of al-Mufaḍḍal, wherein he eulogised the father as well as the son, extolling al-Mufaḍḍal as the constructor of that great work. I doubted to whom it was to be rightly attributed, until I found the passage in question in the Ḳāḍi's poem. I have already, when giving an account of al-Yāf'y's life, said enough to render it unnecessary to recur to the subject here, but I desire to add the lines in which he refers to the artificial watercourse, and to its author al-Mufaḍḍal, as follows:

I say, render honour unto him and of his noble work –
in leading the waters along their rocky bed,
He cleft the lofty mountains and their streams became –
as heaven's rains, flowing over a level plain.

The words he cleft the lofty mountains are sure evidence to the truth of what we have said.'

From the air the mosque appears to be sunken in the ground. Only when looking at it from ground level one realises that it is actually surrounded by a huge *tell*, 4–5 metres high, retained by a dry stone wall, built a few metres from the mosque. The plastered floor around the mosque does not in itself mark the original level of the building: the inner floor of the eastern *riwāq* is about 50 cm. lower than the outer floor.

The mosque is a low rectangular building about 66 metres long and 43 metres wide. A lofty octagonal minaret stands in the western gallery. Its elaborate construction with ornate balcony contrasts sharply with the bare walls of the mosque. These show clear signs of various construction phases, decay, restoration and repairs.

These were the conditions of the mosque in 1971 when I visited it twice: once with my friend and colleague Muṭahhar al-Iryānī, who kindly helped to measure the mosque; a second time with photographer Ennio Vicario, who has provided most of the illustrations accompanying this article.

A complete study of al-Janad would have required more fieldwork, possibly some soundings, and a study of the several inscriptions visible in various parts of the building. For some time I was not able to carry out this work and then in 1973, the mosque became the object of the pious zeal of a merchant who unfortunately decided to use part of his wealth to 'embellish' it. The work was done without notifying the competent authorities: a horrendous new ablution area was built, towering near the old cistern like a power station; all remains of the original mosque, former steps, obsolete doors and corbels, old walls or decoration etc., were carefully removed. All the walls and ceilings were covered by a thick layer of cement render. In a word: any evidence of the long history of the mosque was obliterated.

In the western wall is clearly visible the abutment of the coursed stone construction by al-Mufaḍḍal (Plate 3, 1) and the wall of the prayer hall, originally built in bricks but not long ago reconstructed in *opus incertum* with scored cement pointing, (Plate 3, 2), a very unsatisfactory work which greatly altered the architecture of the building, employing a kind of masonry totally unknown in the Yemen. Above the wall is the brick restoration possibly done under the Rasulids after the earlier, partial destruction of the mosque at the hands of the Mahdids of Zabīd (Plate 3, 3). Plate 4 shows the doorway with a kind of pointed horse-shoe arch. The northern reveal and part of the arch above it are missing; its bottom voussoir projects slightly from the reveal. This is an interesting detail not to be regarded as casual as it occurs also in the eastern doorways of the Great Mosque of Ṣan'ā' which belong to the extension of the mosque constructed also by the Sulayhids.

In plate 4 a block is also visible above the arch with a carved star; above it a fragmentary inscription is partly visible. The door looks blocked by rather carefully set courses of masonry up to the impost block. Above this level the original opening is filled in by blocks crudely piled up without the use of mortar.

The same brick work which I called 'Rasulid restoration' appears on the top of the southern wall of the mosque, again extending in height a well-built stone coursed wall. This is preserved to an even height of 18 courses for almost all the length of the wall. On this side of the mosque, 3 doors originally gave access to the southern gallery. The western door is now blocked with reused stones crudely laid without mortar up to the blind arch above the lintel. All three doorways have the same design observed in the partly preserved door on the western wall of the mosque. Each of the 3 lintels is surmounted by a two line inscription in raised letters. The doorways are very simply framed by a flat moulding created by the recessed repetition of arches and reveals. Above the lintels and the inscribed stones, there are plain blind panels of the same coursed masonry.

The mosque of al-Janad follows the classic plan of the great mosques of the Yemen: a large courtyard surrounded by four galleries, the deepest being the one along the *qiblah* wall and the narrowest the two on either side of it. In the mosque of al-Janad the variation is that the southern gallery has the same depth of the one along the *qiblah* wall. Despite its size, the southern gallery is nothing but a vestibule giving access to the vast courtyard, the real heart of the building, (Plate 6). This gallery does not have the small subsidiary *miḥrāb* which is a common feature in almost all the large mosques of the Yemen.

Slightly off the centre of the courtyard and towards its northern corner a roughly cut stone pillar is set in the floor. Square in section, this slender pillar is 2.1 metres high from the present floor level, (Plate 7). Although on the gypsum plastered floor, there are no marks of any sort, the stone is no doubt a sundial, traditionally used to find the time for the call to prayer. To my knowledge, sundials are not common in religious buildings in the Yemen and in Arabia in general.[2] For the indication of the time of prayer, mainly noon and late afternoon, great accuracy was not required: perhaps the two positions of the shadow were never marked on the floor surface.

In the prayer hall the seven pointed arcades originally opening on the courtyard have been, perhaps long ago, filled in with masonry, with a grilled window in the middle of each arch. The only access from the courtyard is through a simple door in the middle of the southern wall. The *qiblah* wall had originally, like the Great Mosque of Ṣanʿā', the imam's door on the right hand side of the main *miḥrāb*. The door exists to this day, but gives access to a small cubic room used to store books, documents and other items, built at an unknown date behind the *miḥrāb*. The main *miḥrāb* is a very deep and narrow niche surmounted by a high pointed semidome framed by two concentric recessing arches, (Plate 10). Each of these two mouldings, square in section, rests on a pair of cylindrical engaged columns with very simple capital. The whole niche is contained in a projecting panel framed by a simple moulding, partly damaged and obscured by restorations and replastering. The *miḥrāb* displays a very fine stucco decoration on the front face of the first arch with a band of intricate pattern (and perhaps some writing) which generates from one vase on either side of the arch, (Plate 11). The lower part of the recess is plainly plastered. The semidome is decorated with formalised plant motif above 3 horizontal bands. The central one bears the *shahādah*: 'There is no god but God. Muḥammad is the Apostle of God; upon him God's blessings and peace' is legible, and the two others are decorated with floral motifs. Unfortunately the carving is obscured by many coats of whitewash. On the pair of capitals on the right hand side, I could only read '... this *miḥrāb* to the *faqīh* ʿAbd Allāh b ʿAlī al-Faraj ...'

To the right of the imam's door, there is a wooden *minbar*, (Plate 12). This splendid piece, probably the best example of its kind to be found in the Yemen, deserves thorough examination and the study of the three-line inscription in raised calligraphy, carved on the panel above the door.

The *minbar* looks well preserved although covered by several coats of paint which, obviously spoil the sharpness and clearness of the relief. Ideally the *minbar* should be properly restored and moved to a museum.

A few metres to the right of the main *miḥrāb*, there is a smaller one without any carved ornament and poorly preserved. The very simple mouldings which frame the niche are damaged and in some parts missing altogether.

The mosque has a flat roof supported by arcades. In each gallery these arcades are parallel to the perimeteral walls, (Plate 8). Each aisle is built as a long narrow room spanned by rough branches or mangrove poles covered by a cross layer of sticks and 30 cms. of clay. The roof is then finished with a layer of special water-proof plaster made of lime and crushed volcanic stone mixed together.

It is possible that the original building had carved and painted ceilings, like the Great Mosque of Ṣanʿā' and the Great Mosque of Shibām Kawkabān. When the mosque was repaired, under the Rasulids, the work was most probably limited to mere roofing, since woodwork would appear an extravagance for the mosque of a town which had lost its role of capital city.

On the roof branches appear here and there, remains of painted decoration: some crude writing and classic motifs like the 'running dog' occur. Some parts of the roof were repaired with a different building technique, using large squared beams to span the aisle and support other similar but smaller beams set parallel to the outer walls.

It is interesting to note that in the prayer hall three columns on the left hand side of the central bay and the *qiblah* wall are braced by three transverse arches, (Plate 9). Another arch ties together two columns on the opposite side of the same bay. These arches, set perpendicularly to the *qiblah* wall, an anomaly in the mosque of al-Janad, as it would be in the other early mosques of the Yemen, were probably built in order to strengthen the building when the prayer hall was reconstructed (possibly by the *qāḍī* mentioned by al-Janadī).

One can understand that for many reasons, including a certain psychological reluctance to introduce an unusual feature, the transverse arches were built only where required for static reasons. But one would nevertheless expect that transverse arches were at least built all the way from the arcade overlooking the courtyard (*ṣaḥn*) to the *qiblah* wall and on both sides of the central bay; and this, not only for a more even and logical distribution of the strengths, but also for aesthetic reasons. I believe that the eight arches were constructed when this part of the mosque was rebuilt. Four of them were destroyed when, rather recently, the *ḥaram* had a new roof built together with the north-western of its outside wall (cross-hatched, Plate 21).

The mosque of al-Janad has one minaret rising from the western gallery: its tall octagonal shaft containing one spiral staircase is probably entirely built in bricks, (Plate 1). For about four metres the lower part of the shaft is covered by thick render (Plate 15). The plain shaft ends with a band of stucco decoration with small blind arches. Above it three orders of blind arches of decreasing size support a small projecting balcony and link the shaft to the octagonal parapet. The access to the first balcony is through a door opened on the northern side of the octagonal lantern. Each of the other sides of the lantern is decorated with a blind arch. The top of the octagonal lantern forms a second smaller balcony with access through a door on the northern side of cylindrical lantern capped by a conical dome.

The lower part of the minaret below the gallery roof is a cylindrical shaft, built against the outer wall of the mosque. The access to the staircase of the minaret is through a door opened on its northern side (Plate 14). A similar cylindrical shaft is preserved up to the roof in the third bay of the eastern gallery; it is now used as a store with access through a door opened on the western side of the shaft, about three metres from the ground (Plate 13).

At some time, therefore, the mosque had two minarets, both cylindrical and both built on the inside of the external walls of the mosque in a symmetrical position in relation to the central axis of the building. If the walls of the two minarets are, as it appears, a construction independent of the outer walls of the mosque, the date of the latter cannot unfortunately help to date the minarets.

It is interesting to notice however, that the other mosque of contemporary foundation, the Great Mosque of Ṣanʿāʾ, has also two minarets, which originally, were in a position very similar to that of the minarets of al-Janad (Costa, 1974: plan). The minarets of the Great Mosque of Ṣanʿāʾ were probably built at the end of the third/ninth century. (Finster, 96). In the mosque there is epigraphic evidence of their repair in the early years of the seventh/thirteenth century. We can also assume that at least the eastern minaret existed when the Sulayhids reconstructed the eastern gallery of the mosque (Costa, 1974, 497–499). In order to enlarge the building and preserve its balanced lay-out, the courtyard was shifted eastwards and the eastern minaret remained standing on the eastern side of the new courtyard. In other words, the builders of the new eastern gallery clearly preserved the eastern minaret as an existing structure which, because of the enlargement of the mosque, acquired a new location within the modified plan of the building.

I believe that the twin minarets of the mosque of al-Janad, probably built in the fifth/eleventh century or even earlier, were in as bad a state of disrepair, as was the mosque, when al-Mufaḍḍal reconstructed part of the mosque and the *ghayl*. Most probably at the same time he reconstructed one or perhaps both minarets. They were then seriously damaged at the end of the sixth/twelfth century when the mosque was partly destroyed. Finally the western minaret was reconstructed by the Ayyubids, or more likely by the Rasulids. The building was done in bricks, like the reconstruction of the outer wall. I strongly believe that the minaret, as it is preserved today, is a construction of the Rasulid period, possibly of the time of al-Malik al-Manṣūr Nūr al-Dīn ʿUmar (626–47/1229–49) when the new dynasty had its seat at Zabīd and al-Janad. The same Rasulid king bestowed many endowments on the mosque of al-Janad.

Not surprisingly, at Zabīd, there is a minaret very similar to the one of al-Janad: the minaret of the mosque of the citadel, al-Iskandariyyah. It is a lofty cylindrical tower, entirely built in bricks, rising from a high octagonal base and marked by tapering to its narrowest diameter under the balcony. The parapet then gains a diameter almost equal to the lowest part of the cylindrical shaft. Above the balcony, the lantern is a rather heavy, tapering cylinder with a sort of ribbed decoration and capped by a conical dome with shallow *muqarnas* (stalactite ornaments). The transition between shaft and balcony is marked by two staggered rows of blind arches. The plain masonry of the balcony corbels out with the only ornament of three rows of angled bricks (Costa, 1977, Plate 199).

Although there are differences, mainly in shape and proportions, the two minarets of Zabīd and al-Janad have much in common, particularly, in the discreet and tasteful use of blind arches as decoration. This is slightly more articulated in the minaret of al-Janad where the first row of larger arches casts stronger shadows than the shallow arches of Zabīd, almost anticipating the striking play of light and shade typical of the Rasulid mosques of Taʿizz. On the other hand, on the Iskandariyyah of Zabīd, a motif appears for the first time which was going to become the most typical ornament of the Rasulid mosques of Taʿizz: a broad frieze of superimposed rows of blind arches on the outside of the *qiblah* wall and the *miḥrāb*.[3]

As we have already seen, the water for the ablutions was supplied to the mosque by the water channel (*ghayl*) which flowed into the simple attractive pool (Plate 17) and to the ablution rooms and basins (Plate 16). (There are eleven rooms in a row and one larger, separated. Each of the twelve rooms is covered by a graceful dome).

The *ghayl* of al-Janad originates at Wadi Khinwah (the Wadi Hinwa of al-Janadī) about 7 kms. north of al-Janad as the crow flies, but it develops a total length of 15 kms. in its winding course. Originally the *ghayl* supplied drinking water to 22 villages before reaching its final destination of the mosque. It does not tap a spring, but water collected in the gravel bank of the wadi. The conduit is a stone construction 40 × 60 cms. in section, which runs underground for about 300 metres, of which 40 lie under the wadi bed. Then above ground for its total length except, as we mentioned above, where it negotiates the tell of al-Janad. The channel, built with the main purpose of serving the mosque, has been traditionally regarded as a holy construction, its water used exclusively for drinking at least until it reached the town.

To the south of the large cistern mentioned above, page 44, there are traces of ancient irrigation and cultivation within a walled ground where the faded remains of a fortified building are visible. Is this site to be identified with the site where once the residence of the governor stood who, as various sources point out, during the time of the Prophet and the first caliphs administered the southern region from his seat at al-Janad? Only excavations could help to answer this question. Certainly this is the only area around the mosque which seems to have remained undisturbed at least from the time of the construction of the *ghayl*. The only other buildings of a certain importance in the area, a large ruined building near the track entering al-Janad from the west and the *qubbah* near the *qiblah* wall seem both to belong to more recent epochs.

Whether the *ghayl* of al-Janad was constructed or only restored by al-Mufaḍḍal b. Abī 'l-Barakāt *c.* 1130 is a problem which probably cannot be solved. If it looked already so to al-Janadī in the sixth/twelfth century, to find evidence to date the *ghayl* will be a difficult, if not impossible task, some 800 years later. I personally share Kay's doubts that the work of al-Mufaḍḍal was only the restoration of an ancient channel which appears to have been so strictly related to the very existence of the mosque. I believe that the *ghayl* is at least as old as the construction of the mosque. Al-Janadī says that the Sulayhid al-Mufaḍḍal rebuilt the front and side galleries of the mosque and that this work was done in stone.

On the southern side of the mosque, we observe that its outer wall, the three doorways and the construction of the front yard with the open channel and scalloped cistern, all seem to have been built together and in relation to the thresholds level. Consequently, all this work must be ascribed to al-Mufaḍḍal. There is, on the other hand, no evidence against the hypothesis that the *ghayl* might have pre-existed; the original floor level of the mosque (which I believe remained always the same throughout the centuries mainly because of the efficient drainage system existing at the centre of the court-yard) corresponds to the *ghayl* water level as can be seen today (Plate 5).

A well supplies fresh drinking water to the mosque; the well is in the last bay of the outer aisle of the eastern gallery (Plate 18). The original access to it from the mosque interior was most probably by a flight of steps still visible behind a wall which was later built to separate the well from the mosque, obviously to ensure privacy to the women who wanted to draw water from it. A small double reservoir was then built inside the mosque; it was supplied with water through a little channel starting from a trough built beside the well's mouth, (Plate 19). Users of the well willingly poured buckets of water into the reservoirs, as a pious, kind gesture towards the mosque-goers. Although the well must be as old as the mosque, its upper part and mouth appear to have been restored and altered several times during its long history. It is interesting to note the lonely decorative motif of the stylised plant (resembling a kind of schematic fleur-de-lys) above the arch surmounting the well mouth. This motif, which probably symbolises a crop in general, is not uncommon on the façades of Yemeni houses and occurs, sometimes with slight variations, in south Arabian art over a long period of time. It is interesting to find it here associated with water.

On my visit to the mosque of al-Janad in 1971, accompanied by Muṭahhar ʿAlī al-Iryānī, we discovered the remains of a thermal bath buried in the tell which surrounds the mosque: we managed to enter the bath (*hammām*) through an opening caused by a small landslide. Later other parts of the ruined building collapsed, including the top of two domes covering one chamber at the corner of the *ḥammām*, near the mosque and the ablution area, and the *calidarium* (Plate 20). This *ḥammām* is obviously very important for the history of al-Janad and should be properly excavated and studied.

Religious scholars of Radāʿ told me that it is known that ʿĀmir b. Ṭāhir, the first ruler of the Tahirid dynasty (858–923/1454–1517) built a *ḥammām* at al-Janad. I think that there are reasons to believe that our *ḥammām* is the one built by the Tahirids who continued the great building activity of their predecessors.[4]

An old *ḥammām* near the ʿĀmiriyyah mosque at Radāʿ is locally attributed to ʿAmir b. Ṭahir and should consequently date to the second half of the ninth/fifteenth century. The *ḥammām*, still in use, shows striking similarities to the one of al-Janad in the proportions and in many details of the building and in some peculiarities of plan, mainly the absence of a developed *apoditerium*. A comparison between the two *ḥammāms* will remain largely speculation without a full excavation of that of al-Janad, not only in order to have a complete plan of the building but also, it is hoped, to find some evidence for its date.

The mosque of al-Janad underwent, as we have seen, several repairs and reconstructions, retaining nevertheless its original plan and character. The various constructive phases of the building were fully documented by archaeological evidence, at least until they were recently destroyed.

The mosque of al-Janad, as I have fortunately seen, was a unique example of an ancient building preserving the hallmarks of all the events of its long life. We have seen how all the information contained in the historic sources were punctually confirmed by details of the masonry and the decoration. The long age of the mosque is also strikingly witnessed by the huge tell which surrounds it, grown throughout the centuries, after the decline of the ancient town. Al-Janad, unlike Ṣanʿāʾ did not enjoy a revival after the fall of the Tahirids. In a way the foreign yoke was a great injection of new vigour for Ṣanʿāʾ; the captial of the high Yemen found in the centralised system of the Turkish administration a new position and a new *raison d'être* which prepared its role of capital of the Zaydī kingdom, and centre of the 'Rassite renaissance' in the second half of the eighteenth century.

Al-Janad, on the contrary, after the fall of the local dynasties, experienced a decline from which it never recovered. Yet the two mosques remained virtually alike, both preserved in their original lay-out by the great sense of respect and veneration of the people: they were repaired, perhaps even slightly enlarged, as in the case of the eastern gallery of Ṣanʿāʾ, but never knocked down and rebuilt.

Notes

When asked to contribute to a book in honour of Prof. Serjeant, I immediately thought of al-Janad.

It seemed appropriate for this book to use my notes and Vicario's photographs since, by accident more than by design, they have become a unique archaeological document for the history of al-Janad.

[1] I owe this and other historical information on al-Janad to Qāḍī Ismāʿīl b. ʿAlī al-Akwaʿ, Chairman of the Organization for Antiques and Libraries of the Y.A.R., and to Dr. Rex Smith. Dr. Leonardo Costa drew the plan.

[2] Sundials are largely used in Oman to check the exact time of the water rotas supplied by the channel (*falaj*). The best example of this sun clock is the one preserved in al-Rustāq on Falaj al-Maysar. The accuracy required to define the water rotas makes it necessary to have a careful indication of the various positions of the shadow on the floor: this is done by means of pebbles set vertically in the ground.

[3] For a study of the Rasulid mosques of Taʿizz, cf. R. B. Lewcock & G. R. Smith, 1974.

[4] The most typical and impressive building of the Tahirid period is the ʿĀmiriyyah mosque of Radāʿ, perhaps one of the most beautiful buildings in the Yemen. The mosque is built on a high substructure containing warehouses, a small mosque for women and an ablution area. The pointed arcades of the loggia surrounding the prayer hall, recall the loggia of the Rasulid Muʿtabiyyah mosque of Taʿizz whereas the rows of blind arches are clearly reminiscent of the outer decoration of the other mosques of Taʿizz, built in the same period; cf. Lewcock & Smith, 1974, passim.

References

Costa, Paolo, 'La Moschea grande di Sanʿā'', *Annali Istituto Universitario Orientale di Napoli*, XXXIV, 1974.

Costa, P. Vicario, E, *Yemen, land of builders*, London, 1977.
Daghfous, Radhi, 'Pour une chronologie de l'histoire du Yémen à l'époque musulmane', *'Awrāq*, III, Madrid, 1980.
Finster, Barbara, 'Die Freitagsmoschee von Ṣan'ā' voläufiger bericht', *Baghdader Mitteilungen* Bd. IX, Teil I, 1978.
Kay, H. C., *Yaman, its early medieval history*, London, 1892.
Lewcock, R. B. & Smith, G. R., 'Three mediaeval mosques in the Yemen', *Oriental Art*, XX/1–2, 1974, 75–86, 192–203.
Rāzī, Aḥmad b. 'Abd Allāh al-, *Kitāb Ta'rīkh madīnat Ṣan'ā'*, ed. Ḥusayn 'Abd Allāh al-'Amrī and 'Abd al-Jabbār Zakkār, Damascus, 1974.

Plates

Plate 1 The Mosque of al-Janad
Plate 2 Aerial view of the mosque, showing the old watercourse
Plate 3 The western wall
Plate 4 Doorway with horse-shoe arch
Plate 5 The mosque and the *ghayl*
Plate 6 The large courtyard surrounded by galleries
Plate 7 The courtyard with sundial
Plate 8 General view of the arcades
Plate 9 The prayer hall
Plate 10 The main *miḥrāb*
Plate 11 Stucco decoration in the *miḥrāb*
Plate 12 The wooden *minbar*
Plate 13 Access to the staircase of the minaret
Plate 14 Access to the minaret through the store-room
Plate 15 The lower part of the minaret
Plate 16 The ablution rooms and basins
Plate 17 Water pool
Plate 18 The well
Plate 19 The double reservoir
Plate 20 The *calidarium*
Plate 21 Ground plan of the mosque of al-Janad
A. Main *miḥrāb*
B. *Minbar*
C. Secondary *miḥrāb*
D. Bricked-up door
E. Well
F. Access to well
G. Water reservoirs
H. Steps formerly leading to well
I. Bricked-up door
J. Sundial
K. Minaret

1

2

3

4

5

6

7

8

9

10

11

12

13

14

15

16

17

18

19

20

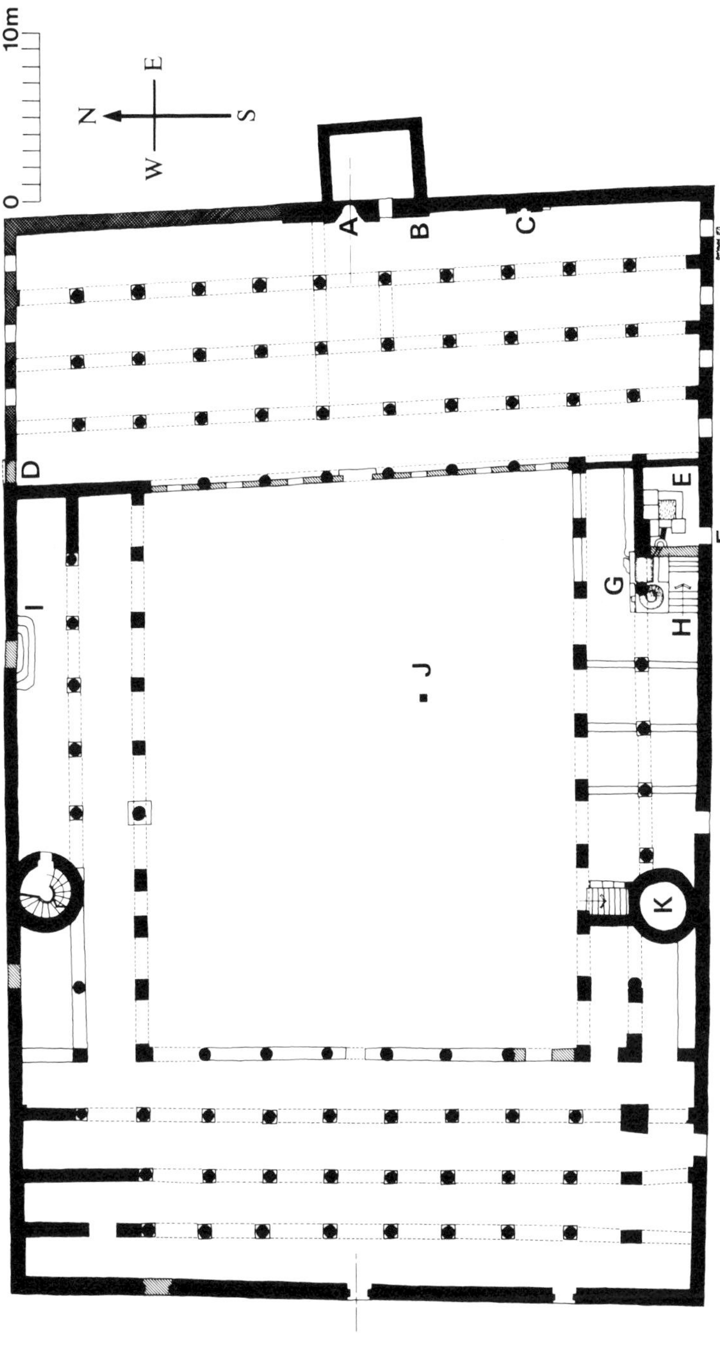

21

The Library of Muḥammad b. ʿAlī b. ʿAbd al-Shakūr, Sulṭān of Harar, 1272–92/1856–75

A. J. Drewes

In 1976 I had the opportunity to photograph a document listing the houses, landed property and the books belonging to the estate of the last ruler of Harar before the arrival of the Egyptians. I was at that time engaged in an investigation of Arabic manuscripts preserved in the city of Harar, in the main in private collections, as I had been on various occasions in earlier years. Once, after the third International Conference of Ethiopian Studies, in 1966 Professor Serjeant and I spent several days in Harar and, together we saw various manuscripts and visited the most important shrines.

The number of Arabic manuscripts from Harar, whether preserved in the city or in Dire Dawa or Addis Ababa, must be considerable. Altogether, I have seen some seven hundred, most of them not older than about three centuries. It is difficult to say how many more still exist or to assess to what extent this sample is representative of what was read and copied in Harar during the last three hundred years. But within this sample it is possible to distinguish between texts which are regularly or even frequently encountered and works which are comparatively rare. The library of Muḥammad b. ʿAlī comprised some of the more unusual titles as well as a typical collection of the popular texts. Reference will be made to the manuscripts I saw, whenever this may be useful for the identification of the books which once belonged to the Sulṭān. Among these manuscripts, there were at least four which had been part of his library, see below, entries 3, 22, 35 and 44; three were marked with his seal, dated 1273, for all practical purposes the year of his accession to power.

It will be obvious that the manuscripts constitute a major source for the study of the history of Harar and of its culture in the past. Strictly speaking, however, historical texts are rare. Since E. Cerulli's discoveries, published in a series of articles,[1] very few such items have been found. Recently, E. Wagner published a legendary history of Harar, *Fatḥ madīnat Harar*,[2] a brief chronicle of events just before and after the battle of Callanqo, which I photographed during one of my visits, has so far not been published. Important further discoveries of this kind are unlikely: historical events were apparently recorded only exceptionally.

On the other hand, surprisingly rich material of a different nature, but particularly valuable for our understanding of the economic and social history of Harar in the nineteenth century, has come to light in recent years. In 1960, Yūsuf Aḥmad published a document,[3] for the greater part consisting of a register of the income of three rulers of Harar, between 1243 (1827) and 1269 (1852), both from their real estate and from their trade activities. It is certain that similar documents may still be found in the city.[4]

An even more important source of information is a set of manuscripts, now preserved in the Institute of Ethiopian Studies in Addis Ababa, which contain a record of the division among the heirs of the estates of deceased persons, a register of marriages and divorces and, less systematically, notes on various other matters, such as transactions of sales. The period covered in the first four volumes ranges from 1242/1826 to 1292/1875; but other volumes continue the records through the time of Egyptian rule into the early years of the Ethiopian administration. The first to refer to these manuscripts and to appreciate their value, was the late V. Stitz, in a paper read at the Conference on the History and Culture of the Peoples of Harar Province, Addis Ababa, June 1975.[5]

The manuscripts represent a no doubt substantial part of the archives of the *qāḍī* court, but the collection is certainly not complete. In 1976, I photographed a number of loose sheets which had clearly belonged to yet another volume from the same archives.

The names of the *qāḍīs* are mentioned on various occasions. The first to appear in these texts is Qāḍī ʿAbd al-Raḥmān, son of the Qāḍī Muḥammad b. Idrīs. After his death, in the early fifties, his work was continued by Qāḍī ʿAbd al-Raḥmān b. ʿUmar Ḥay. Another name which appears occasionally in the middle fifties is that of Qāḍī Ibn ʿUmar b. ʿAbd al-Raḥmān. ʿAbd al-Raḥmān b. ʿUmar Ḥay may or may not be the same as Qāḍī ʿAbd al-Raḥmān Ibn al-Ḥājj ʿUmar b. Aḥmad al-'brī, who was in office at least between 1252 and 1261, but who is probably to be identified with ʿAbd al-Raḥmān Ibn al-Ḥājj ʿUmar. If so, he continued to work until the late eighties. The name of Qāḍī ʿAbd Allāh is found in 1293.

The contents of the manuscripts are arranged in sections, according to subjects. The individual entries may be quite brief, in particular in the case of marriage or divorce. But even in connection with inheritance, the accounts clearly contain, however detailed they may be, only a summary of the court's decisions rather than full documentary evidence. Thus, while an estimate of the total value of an estate is usually given in the beginning of each entry, it is often described only in terms of the portions allotted to the heirs. Obviously, these accounts must be based on other official, legal documents.

On rare occasions, I was shown examples of such documents, issued to the interested parties in the case of sale of property. Another example is the document published in these pages, a description of the estate, or part of it, of the late Sulṭān Muḥammad b. ʿAlī b. ʿAbd al-Shakūr.

Muḥammad b. ʿAlī was Sulṭān of Harar from *ʿaṣr*, Saturday, 28 Dhū 'l-Ḥijjah 1272 until his death at the hands of an Egyptian soldier, probably on Wednesday 27 Ramaḍān 1292.[6] The document in question lists his houses, landed property and his library, as they appear in his own records. The houses and landed property enumerated were acquired by gift or by sale and, in each case, the previous owners are mentioned by name. It may often still be possible to trace the actual location of these possessions, but this would require an intimate knowledge of the city.

In general, the books are easier to identify, even though their description is often too brief to be unambiguous. In such cases, however, the manuscripts preserved in the city may point to the correct identification. For instance, the short title *Irshād*, see below entries 11 and 63, undoubtedly refers to Ibn al-Muqri''s *Irshād al-ghāwī*, given the number of copies still existing of this text. Oral information confirms this conclusion: it was in fact the standard legal textbook.

At the time of his death, the library of Muḥammad b. ʿAlī comprised 99 items, according to the document under discussion; but this number is arrived at rather arbitrarily. Sometimes two volumes of the same work are listed separately, e.g. entries 12 and 13, sometimes together, e.g. entry 75, but cf. entries 77 and 83. Various copies of the same text may be mentioned in one and the same entry, e.g. 58, or in more than one, cf. entries 53 and 73. Perhaps these inconsistencies have to do with the order of acquisition of the books.

The major disciplines of Islamic scholarship were represented in the library, often by several of the standard works in the field. Not surprisingly, Islamic law is especially well covered: about one out of four entries refer to well-known textbooks of the Shāfiʿī school, such as:

1. Ibn. al-Muqri''s *Irshād al-ghāwī ilā masālik al-ḥāwī* and Ibn Ḥajar al-Haythamī's commentary on the *Irshād*. A commentary on another work by Ibn al-Muqri' is Zakariyyā' al-Anṣārī's *Asnā 'l-maṭālib*.
2. Nawawī's *Minhāj al-ṭālibīn* and various works related to it: the commentaries by Ibn Ḥajar al-Haythamī, Ramlī and, perhaps, Maḥallī, as well as Zakariyyā' al-Anṣārī's *Fatḥ al-wahhāb*.
3. Zakariyyā' al-Anṣārī's *Tuḥfat al-ṭullāb*.
4. Bā Faḍl al-Ḥaḍramī's popular introduction, the *Muqaddimah*.

The library of Muḥammad b. ʿAlī also contained a representative collection of *mawlids*, *ṣalawāt*, religious poetry and other texts for recitation. Most of the texts in this collection, whether widely known classics or local compositions, are still very popular in Harar and have been copied for centuries.

The *mawlid* text referred to in entry 8 is undoubtedly Abū 'l-Ḥasan Nūr al-Dīn's *ʿUnwān al-sharīf*. In the manuscripts, this text is usually preceded by Būṣīrī's *Burdah*, most often – as in the Egyptian edition of 1947 – by Muḥammad al-Fayyūmī's *Takhmīs* of the *Burdah*. A facsimile edition of a recent Harari copy of this text, dated A.H. 1365, was published in Addis Ababa in 1386 (1966) by ʿAbd al-Fattāḥ al-Ḥājj Yūnus. There is also an old Harari *mawlid* in verse which appears to be based on the *ʿUnwān al-sharīf* rather than on another *mawlid* text.

Al-Qayrawānī's *Tanbīh al-anām* and the poems in praise of the Prophet by Warrāq and Ṭarā'ifī were frequently copied in Harar. In 1386 (1966), Ḥajj Yūsuf ʿAbd al-Raḥmān published, in Addis Ababa, a facsimile edition of a manuscript copy of Warrāq's and Ṭarā'ifī's poems by the hand of Abū ʿAbd Allāh Hāshim b. ʿAbd al-ʿAzīz al-Hararī, dated A.H. 1150.

Shaykh Hāshim, as he is usually called in Harar, was himself the author of several texts. Two of these were included in the Sulṭān's library. The

Fatḥ al-raḥmānī is still recited regularly; the oldest manuscript copy I saw was dated 1133, the second oldest 1142. Around 1970, a facsimile edition of a recent copy, A.H. 1386, of a manuscript written by the author himself and completed on Thursday 19 Shaʿbān 1171 was published in Addis Ababa, again by Ḥājj Yūsuf ʿAbd al-Raḥmān. An Egyptian edition, by Muṣṭafā ʾl-Bābī ʾl-Ḥalabī, appeared in 1949.

Shaykh Hāshim lived in the twelfth century A.H. and must therefore be distinguished from the tenth century saint of that name.[7] In two copies of the *Fatḥ al-raḥmānī* it is stated that he died *bi-taʾrīkh sabaqat kalimatunā li-walī*, i.e. in 1179, but this may not be correct. Another work by the same author, the *Rasāʾil al-yaqīniyyah fī bayān ḥaqq al-rabbiyyah wa-ʾl-ʿabdiyyah*, was completed only in 1181, according to the colophon of a copy made in 1261.

Shaykh Hāshim composed at least two more texts in Arabic: the *Ḥizb al-abrār*, published in the Addis Ababa edition of the *Fatḥ al-raḥmānī*, and the *Yanābīʿ al-ḥukm*, of which Muḥammad b. ʿAlī owned a copy, see below, entry 16.

It is likely that Muḥammad b. ʿAlī acquired most of his books by purchase or by gift, just as in the case of his real estate. But he inherited part of his library from his father and from his aunt, Gīsti (Lady) Amat Allāh bint al-Sulṭān ʿAbd al-Shakūr. One of the manuscripts in the Institute of Ethiopian Studies contains a record of the division of the estates of his father ʿAlī and his father's sister Amat Allāh, dated Monday 28 Muḥarram 1275 and Monday 28 Muḥarram 1274 respectively.

The court's records show that Muḥammad b. ʿAlī inherited from his aunt the following books, enumerated in this order:

1. *Muṣḥaf* (cf. below entries 1, 56, 89),
2. *ʿUmdat al-murīd* (cf. entries 32, 45),
3. *Bukhārī* (cf. entry 2),
4. *Taʾrīkh al-khulafāʾ* (cf. entries 3, 88),
5. *Mawlīd* (cf. entries 4, 19, 67),
6. *Fatḥ al-mubīn* (cf. entry 5),
7. *Iqnāʿ* (cf. entry 6),
8. *Dalāʾil* (cf. entry 7),
9. *ʿUnwān al-sharaf* (cf. entry 8),
10. *Jawharat al-tawḥīd* (cf.) entries 9, 34),
11. *Nasafī* (cf. entry 10),
12. *Irshād* (cf. entries 11, 63).

It is curious that, with the exception of the *ʿUmdat al-murīd*, these books are listed in the same order as in the document describing the library belonging to the estate of Muḥammad b. ʿAlī. This can hardly be accidental. But if this document, which is based on the Sulṭān's own records, in some way reflects the order of acquisition of the manuscripts, the reasons for this coincidence are clear. It may, in that case, be inferred that the manuscripts Muḥammad b. ʿAlī inherited from his aunt constituted the beginnings of his library.[8]

To some extent, the list of the books left to Muḥammad b. ʿAlī by his father also agrees, as to the order of the entries, with the document in question. According to the Qāḍī's records, they were, in this order:

1. *al-Juz' al-awwal min Ḥayāt al-ḥayawān* (cf. entry 35).
2. *Mīzān* (cf. entries 33, 71, 87),
3. *Fatḥ al-wahhāb* (cf. entries 12, 13),
4. *Muṣḥaf* (cf. entries 1, 56, 89),
5. *Fatḥ al-jalīl* (cf. entry 36),
6. *Siyar maqṭū'* (cf. entry 37),
7. *Ṭarrāf* (*sic*) (cf. entries 52, 58, 81, 94),
8. *al-Manẓūm*
9. *Siyar ṣaghīr*(cf. entry 38),
10. *Manāsik al-ḥajj*,
11. *Multaqaṭ durr al-manḍūd* (cf. entry 39),
12. *Rawḍah*(cf. entry 40),
13. *Bahjah* (cf. entry 41),
14. *Sharḥ qaṭr* (cf. entry 42),
15. *Ṭarrāf ayḍan* (cf. entries 52, 58, 81, 94),
16. *Fatḥ al-raḥmān* (cf. entry 57),
17. *Tanbīh al-anām ṣalawāt* (cf. entry 93),
18. *Tuḥfat al-ṭullāb* (cf. entry 43).

At the time of his death, the library of Muḥammad b. 'Alī b. 'Abd al-Shakūr, as itemised in the description of his estate, consisted of the following books:

1. *Muṣḥaf qā'im*, i.e. a copy of the Qur'ān; see also entries 56 and 89. This copy probably once belonged to his aunt, cf. Amat Allāh's legacy no. 1.

2. *Bukhārī awwal*, the first volume of Bukhārī's *al-Jāmi' al-ṣaḥīḥ*, cf. Amat Allāh's legacy no. 3. Two other, complete, copies of the *Ṣaḥīḥ* are mentioned below, entries 51 and 60.

3. *Ta'rīkh al-khulafā'*, i.e. Jalāl al-Dīn al-Suyūṭī's *Ta'rīkh al-khulafā'*, *GAL*, II, 157. This was probably the copy Muḥammad inherited from his aunt, cf. her legacy no. 4. For another copy of this text, see below, entry 88. In 1975, I saw one of the two copies of this text owned by the Sulṭān, marked with his seal.

4. *Mawlid*, unidentified. Probably a manuscript inherited from his aunt, cf. Amat Allāh's legacy no. 5.

5. *Fatḥ al-mubīn*, perhaps to be identified with Ibn Ḥajar al-Haythamī's commentary on Nawawī's *Kitāb al-Arba'īn*, *GAL*, I, 399. I have seen only one manuscript copy of this text in Harar. See also Amat Allāh's legacy no. 6.

6. *Iqnā'*, perhaps a reference to Shirbīnī's commentary on Abū Shujā' al-Iṣfahānī's *al-Mukhtaṣar fī 'l-fiqh*, *GAL*, I, 392. Cf. Amat Allāh's legacy no. 7. Copies of the *Mukhtaṣar* itself and of Ibn Qāsim al-Ghazzī's commentary, the *Fatḥ al-qarīb*, are more frequently encountered in Harar than the *Iqnā'*.

7. *Dalā'il al-khayrāt*, i.e. Jazūlī's well-known text. Cf. Amat Allāh's legacy no. 8.

8. *'Unwān al-sharaf*, a manuscript containing, no doubt, Būṣīrī's *Burdah*

as well as Abū 'l-Ḥasan Nūr al-Dīn's *'Unwān al-sharīf*. Cf. Amat Allāh's legacy no. 9.

9. *Jawharah*, i.e. Ibrāhīm al-Laqānī's *Jawharat al-tawḥīd*, *GAL*, II, 316. The Sulṭān probably inherited this copy from his aunt, cf. Amat Allāh's legacy no. 10. For a second copy, see below, entry 34. The commentary on this text by the author himself, the *'Umdat al-murīd*, is found in entries 32 and 45.

10. *Tafsīr Naṣaf*[*ī*] (*sic*), presumably Abū 'l-Barakāt al-Nasafī's commentary on the Qur'ān, *GAL*, II, 197. I did not come across a copy of this work. Confusion between *ṣād* and *sīn* is not unusual in Arabic manuscripts from Ethiopia; the name of the author is spelled correctly in the list of books Muḥammad b. 'Alī inherited from his aunt, see above no. 11, where undoubtedly the same manuscript is mentioned, just as here, between the *Jawharah* and the *Irshād*.

11. *Irshād*, i.e. Ibn al-Muqri''s *Irshād al-ghāwī*, a compendium of Qazwīnī's *al-Ḥāwī 'l-ṣaghīr fī'l-fatāwī*, *GAL*, I, 394. This must have been the copy the Sulṭān inherited from his aunt, cf. Amat Allāh's legacy no. 12. Two other copies of this text are mentioned below, entry 63. For commentaries on the *Irshād* in the library of the Sulṭān, see entries 21, 23, 28 and 97.

12. *Fatḥ al-wahhāb awwal*, the first volume of Zakariyyā' al-Anṣārī's commentary on his own *Manhaj al-ṭullāb*, a compendium of Nawawī's *Minhāj al-ṭālibīn*, *GAL*, I, 395 f.; cf. entry 61. For the second volume, see entry 13. Muḥammad inherited a copy of the *Fatḥ al-wahhāb* from his father, see above, 'Alī's legacy no. 3.

13. *Fatḥ al-wahhāb thānī*, the second volume of Zakariyyā' al-Anṣārī's work, cf. entry 12.

14. *Anwār*, probably a reference to Bayḍāwī's commentary on the Qur'ān, *Anwār al-tanzīl wa-asrār al-ta'wīl*, *GAL*, I, 417; see also entry 76. But the identification is not entirely certain: elsewhere in this list, entries 27, 29 and 96, this commentary is indicated by the name of the author. The designation *Anwār* may therefore refer to some other text, e.g. Ardabīlī's *Kitāb al-Anwār li-a'māl al-abrār*, *GAL*, II, 199. In 1976, I saw two copies of this text.

15. *Ḍiyā' al-shamsī*, i.e. Muṣṭafā al-Bakrī's commentary on his own *al-Fatḥ al-qudsī wa-'l-kashf al-unsī*, or the *Wird al-saḥar*, *GAL*, II, 350; cf. entry 44.

16. *Yanābī' al-ḥukm*, undoubtedly to be identified with Abū 'Abd Allāh Hāshim b. 'Abd al-'Azīz al-Qādirī al-Hararī's *Yanābī' al-ḥukm al-qudsī al-'irfānī fī manāqib al-shaykh Muḥyī 'l-Dīn 'Abd al-Qādir al-Jīlānī*. For another text by this author, see entry 57. I have seen only one copy of the *Yanābī' al-ḥukm*.

17. *Tuḥfah thālith*, i.e. the third volume of Ibn Ḥajar al-Haythamī's commentary on Nawawī's *Minhāj al-ṭālibīn*, the *Tuḥfat al-muḥtāj*, *GAL*, I, 395; cf. entry 61, see also entries 75, 77, 83 and 95. The manuscripts still extant indicate that a complete copy of this work consisted of four volumes, while Zakariyyā' al-Anṣārī's *Tuḥfat al-ṭullāb* consisted of one volume only.

18. *Mishkāt awwal*, no doubt the first volume of al-Khaṭīb al-Tibrīzī's version of Baghawī's *Maṣābīḥ al-sunnah* the *Mishkāt al-maṣābīḥ*, *GAL*, I, 364. For the second volume, see entry 65. On various occasions, I have seen copies of the second volume of this work.
19. *Mawlid* ---, an unidentified *mawlid* text.
20. *Taṣrīḥ*, probably to be identified with Khālid al-Azharī's *al-Taṣrīḥ bi-maḍmūn al-tawḍīḥ*, a commentary on Ibn Hishām's *Awḍaḥ al-masālik ilā alfiyyat Ibn Mālik*, *GAL*, I, 298; cf. entry 80. Copies of both the *Taṣrīḥ* and the *Tawḍīḥ* can be found in Harar.
21. *Fatḥ al-jawād min nikāḥ ilā ākhir*, i.e. the last volume of Ibn Ḥajar al-Haythamī's commentary on Ibn al-Muqri''s *Irshād al-ghāwī ilā masālik al-ḥāwī*; cf. entry 11, see also entries 28 and 97.
22. *Asnā 'l-maṭālib thānī*, the second volume of Zakariyyā' al-Anṣārī's commentary on Ibn al-Muqri''s *Rawḍ al-ṭālib fī 'l-fiqh*, *GAL*, II, 191. In 1976, I saw this volume, marked with the seal of Muḥammad b. ʿAlī. It is a comparatively early manuscript finished, according to the colophon, 11 Shawwāl 973 by the scribe ʿAlī b. ʿAbd al-Khāliq Ibn al-Faqī (*sic*) ʿAlī al-Khaṭīb al-Ṭayyib al-ʿIbādī *baladan* al-Shāfiʿī *madhaban*.
23. *Iʿānat sharḥ al-Irshād*, an unidentified text related to Ibn al-Muqri''s *Irshād al-ghāwī*; cf. entry 11.
24. *Tafsīr Bakrī*, an unidentified commentary on the Qur'ān.
25. *Nihāyah thānī Ramlī*, the second volume of Ramlī's commentary on Nawawī's *Minhāj al-ṭālibīn*, the *Nihāyat al-muḥtāj*; cf. entry 61.
26. *Zawājir*, perhaps a reference to Ibn Ḥajar al-Haythamī's *al-Zawājir ʿan iqtirāf al-kabā'ir*, *GAL*, II, 388. For other works by this author in the library of the Sulṭān, cf. entries 5, 17, 21, 30, 75, 77, 83 and 95.
27. *Bayḍāwī mujalladān*, a probably complete set of Bayḍāwī's commentary on the Qur'ān, the *Anwār al-tanzīl wa-asrār al-ta'wīl*; see also entries 29 and 96; cf. entries 14 and 76. The manuscript copies I saw of this text usually consisted of two volumes, the second beginning with the Sūrat Maryam.
28. *Fatḥ al-jawād awwal*, the first volume of Ibn Ḥajar al-Haythamī's commentary on the *Irshād al-ghawī*; see also entries 21 and 97.
29. *Ḥāshiyat Bayḍāwī*, an unidentified commentary on Bayḍāwī's commentary on the Qur'ān; cf entries 27 and 96.
30. *Sharḥ Shamā'il*, probably to be identified with Ibn Ḥajar al-Haythamī's commentary on Tirmidhī's *Kitāb al-Shamā'il*, the *Ashraf al-wasā'il*, *GAL*, S. II, 529. In 1976, I saw a manuscript copy of a *Kitāb Sharḥ al-Shamā'il*, by Ibn Ḥajar, dated 27 Rajab 1186.
31. *Talbīs Iblīs*, Ibn al-Jawzī's well-known work.
32. *ʿUmdat al-murīd*, i.e. Ibrāhīm al-Laqānī's commentary on his own *Jawharat al-tawḥīd*; cf. entry 9; for another copy of this text in the library of Muḥammad b. ʿAlī, see entry 45. One of these two copies may have belonged to his aunt, see above, Amat Allāh's legacy no. 2.
33. *Mīzān thānī*, the second volume of an unidentified work; cf. entries 71 and 87. This was perhaps the copy Muḥammad inherited from his father ʿAlī, see above, ʿAlī's legacy no. 2.

34. *Jawharah*, another copy of Ibrāhīm al-Laqānī's *Jawharat al-tawḥīd*; cf. entry 9.
35. *Ḥayāt al-ḥayawān awwal*, i.e. the first volume of Damīrī's famous work; a manuscript which the Sulṭān undoubtedly inherited from his father, see above, ʿAlī's legacy no. 1. In 1975, I saw this manuscript, which was marked with the seal of the Sulṭān. Muḥammad b. ʿAlī also possessed a complete copy and an abbreviated version of Damīrī's text, see below, entries 64 and 68.
36. *Fatḥ al-jalīl*, unidentified; cf. ʿAlī's legacy no. 5.
37. *Siyar maqṭūʿ*, unidentified; cf. ʿAlī's legacy no. 6.
38. *Siyar ṣaghīr*, unidentified; cf. ʿAlī's legacy no. 9.
39. *Durr al-manḍūd*, unidentified; cf. ʿAlī's legacy no. 11.
40. *Rawḍah*, perhaps a reference to Nawawī's *Rawḍat al-ṭālibīn*, *GAL*, I, 396. Cf. ʿAlī's legacy no. 12. In 1976, I saw two copies of the third volume of Nawawī's *Rawḍat al-ṭālibīn*.
41. *Bahjah* perhaps to be identified with Ibn al-Wardī's poetry version of Qazwīnī's *al-Ḥāwī al-ṣaghīr*, *GAL*, I, 394; cf. entry 70. But the identification is uncertain: in the course of my investigations, I also came across Suyūṭī's commentary on Ibn Mālik's *Alfiyyah*, the *al-Bahjah al-marḍiyyah*, as well as the *Bahjat al-ṭarf fī ʿilm al-ḥarf*, by Ibn --- (illegible). Undoubtedly, this manuscript once belonged to Muḥammad's father, cf. ʿAlī's legacy no. 13.
42. *Sharḥ al-Qaṭr*, most probably to be identified with Fākihī's *Mujīb al-nidā ilā sharḥ Qaṭr al-nadā*, a commentary on Ibn Hishām's *Qaṭr al-nadā wa-ball al-ṣadā*, *GAL*, II, 23. Cf. ʿAlī's legacy no. 14. Both Fākihī's commentary, the *Mujīb al-nidā*, and the *Nukat* by Ibn Hishām himself are well represented among the manuscripts still preserved in Harar.
43. *Tuḥfat al-ṭullāb*, undoubtedly a reference to Zakariyyā' al-Anṣārī's commentary on his own *Taḥrīr*, a work based on Abū Zurʿah al-ʿIrāqī's *Tanqīḥ al-lubāb* which, in turn, was based on Maḥāmilī's *Lubāb al-fiqh*, *GAL*, I, 181. Cf. ʿAlī's legacy no. 18. Zakariyyā' al-Anṣārī's *Tuḥfat al-ṭullāb* and especially his *Taḥrīr tanqīḥ al-lubāb* must have been popular in Harar, given the number of copies extant. In 1974, I saw one copy of another text with the title *Tuḥfat al-ṭullāb*: Ibn al-Madhḥijī's *Tuḥfat al-ṭullāb fī 'l-fiqh naẓm al-Irshād*, *GAL*, II, 404.
44. *Sharḥ Wird al-saḥar*, i.e. *al-Ḍiyā' al-shamsī*, a commentary by Muṣṭafā 'al-Bakrī on his own *al-Fatḥ al-qudsī wa-'l-kashf al-unsī*. This manuscript is still preserved in Harar; the full title of the text is *Sharḥ Wird al-saḥar al-kabīr al-musammā bi-'l-Ḍiyā' al-shamsī ʿalā 'l-Fatḥ al-qudsī*. There is a note stating that the ownership of the manuscript was transferred from Mahdī b. al-Sayyid ʿAla[w]ī (?) to Sulṭān Muḥammad b. ʿAlī b. ʿAbd al-Shakūr in 1273. For another copy of this text in the Sulṭān's library, see entry 15.
45. *ʿUmdat al-murīd*, another copy of Ibrāhīm al-Laqānī's text; see entry 32.
46. *Shinshawrī*, most probably a reference to Shinshawrī's well-known commentary on Raḥbī's *al-Urjūzah al-raḥbiyyah*, *GAL*, I, 391. In 1976, I came across one copy of this text.

47. *I'ānat Nawawī*, an unidentified text most probably related to Nawawī's *Minhāj al-ṭālibīn*; cf. entry 61.
48. *Muqaddimah*, undoubtedly to be identified with Bā Faḍl al-Ḥaḍramī's *al-Mukhtaṣar fī 'l-fiqh*, i.e. *al-Muqaddimah al-ḥaḍramiyyah*. During my visits, I have come across several manuscripts containing Bā Faḍl's popular and still widely used introduction, with or without Ibn Ḥajar al-Haythamī's commentary, *al-Manhaj al-qawīm*.
49. *Sharḥ al-Kāfiyah*, an unidentified commentary, presumably on Ibn al-Ḥājib's grammatical treatise.
50. *Ibn 'Aqīl*, most probably a reference to Ibn 'Aqīl's *Sharḥ al-Masālik li-Alfiyyat Ibn Mālik*. Among the manuscripts I saw, there were several copies of this commentary on Ibn Mālik's *Alfiyyah*, but no other work by Ibn 'Aqīl.
51. *Bukhārī kāmil ṭābi'*, a complete, printed, copy of Bukhārī's *al-Jāmi' al-ṣaḥīḥ*; see also entries 2 and 60. According to Brockelmann, *GAL*, S. I, 261, the earliest edition of this text is dated 1279, printed at Būlāq, early enough to be included in the Sulṭān's library.
52. *Malqūṭ min Ṭarrāf wa-Warrāq*, an unidentified selection from Ṭarā'ifī's *Abkār al-afkār fī madḥ al-nabī al-mukhtār* and Warrāq's *Takhmīs* of al-Wā'iẓ al-Baghdādī al-Witrī's *al-Qaṣīdah al-witriyyah fī madḥ khayr al-bariyyah*; see also entries 58, 62, 81 and 94.
53. *Jalālayn kāmil*, a complete copy of the well-known commentary on the Qur'ān by Jalāl al-Dīn al-Maḥallī and Jalāl al-Dīn al-Suyūṭī; for a second copy of this work, see entry 73.
54. *Nujūm*, unidentified.
55. *Khuṭbah* unidentified.
56. 3 *Muṣḥaf*, presumably three copies of the Qur'ān rather than one copy in three volumes; see also entries 1 and 89.
57. *Fatḥ al-raḥmānī*, i.e. Abū 'Abd Allāh Hāshim b. 'Abd al-'Azīz al-Qādirī al-Hararī's text of that title; for another text by the same author, see entry 16. Cf. 'Alī's legacy no. 16.
58. 3 *Warrāq ma'a Ṭarrāf*, i.e. three volumes, each containing Warrāq's *Takhmīs* of al-Witrī's *al-Qaṣīdah al-witriyyah fī madḥ khayr al-bariyyah*, followed by Ṭarā'ifī's *Abkār al-afkār fī madḥ al-nabī al-mukhtār*; cf. entries 52, 62, 81 and 94.
59. *Lubāb thānī*, the second volume of an unidentified work.
60. *Bukhārī kāmil mujallad* 4, a complete copy in four volumes of Bukhārī's *al-Jāmi' al-ṣaḥīḥ*; see also entries 2 and 51.
61. 2 *Minhāj al-ṭālibīn*, i.e. two copies of Nawawī's version of Rāfi'ī's *Muḥarrar*, *GAL*, I, 395. For other works in the library of the Sulṭān connected with this text, see entries 12, 13, 17, 25, 75, 77, 83, 95 and perhaps 47 and 72.
62. *Warrāq*, Warrāq's *Takhmīs* of al-Witrī's *al-Qaṣīdah al-witriyyah fī madḥ khayr al-bariyyah*; see also entries 52, 58 and 81.
63. 2 *Irshād*, two more copies of Ibn al-Muqri''s *Irshād al-ghāwī ilā masālik al-ḥāwī*; see entry 11.
64. *Ḥayāt al-ḥayawān kāmil*, a complete copy of Damīrī's text; cf. entries 35 and 68.

65. *Mishkāt thānī*, presumably the second volume of Tibrīzī's *Mishkāt al-maṣābīḥ*; for the first volume, see entry 18.
66. *Baghawī kāmil ṭābi'*, a complete, printed, copy of one of Baghawī's works, presumably his commentary on the Qur'ān, the *Ma'ālim al-tanzīl*. This commentary on the Qur'ān was printed in Bombay as early as 1269, according to Brockelmann, *GAL*, S. I, 622. The earliest edition of Baghawī's *Maṣābīḥ al-sunnah*, Būlāq, 1294, is too late to be taken into consideration.
67. *Mawlid*, unidentified.
68. *Multaqaṭ min Ḥayāt al-ḥayawān*, an unidentified, abbreviated version of Damīrī's *Ḥayāt al-ḥayawān*. In 1974, I saw a manuscript with the title *Multaqaṭ min Ḥayāt al-ḥayawān al-kubrā*, dated 3 Muḥarram 1289; according to the colophon, the text was completed in Rajab 773. Cf. entries 35 and 64.
69. *Awfāq*, unidentified.
70. *Sharḥ al-Bahjah*, an unidentified commentary, possibly on Ibn al-Wardī's version of Qazwīnī's *Ḥāwī*; cf. entry 41.
71. *Mīzān*, unidentified; cf. entries 33 and 87.
72. *Maḥall*[*ī*] *awwal wa-ākhir mujalladayn*, perhaps Jalāl al-Dīn al-Maḥallī's commentary on Nawawī's *Minhāj al-ṭālibīn*, cf. entry 61, rather than his commentary on Subkī's *Jam' al-jawāmi' fī uṣūl al-fiqh*. But manuscript copies of both works can be found in Harar.
73. *Jalālayn kāmil*, another complete copy of the commentary on the Qur'ān by Maḥallī and Suyūṭī; cf. entry 53.
74. *Qāmūs*, i.e. Fīrūzābādī's *al-Qāmūs al-muḥīṭ* or, perhaps, 'Īsā b. 'Abd al-Raḥīm's commentary, *al-Mazj al-ma'nūs bi-dībājat al-qāmūs*. Various copies of both works are preserved in the city.
75. 3 *Tuḥfat al-muḥtāj awwal wa-thānī wa-thālith*, the first three volumes of Ibn Ḥajar al-Haythamī's commentary on the *Minhāj al-ṭālibīn*; see also entries 17, 77, 83 and 95.
76. *Anwār kāmil*, presumably a complete copy of Bayḍāwī's commentary on the Qur'ān; but see entry 14.
77. *Tuḥfah ākhir*, the fourth and last volume of Ibn Ḥajar al-Haythamī's *Tuḥfat al-muḥtāj*; cf. entries 17, 75, 83 and 95.
78. *Fatḥ al-Sha'm*, legendary early Islamic history.
79. *Kutub ahl al-riddah*, unidentified.
80. *Awḍaḥ ma'a sharḥ F'LL*, no doubt Ibn Hishām's *Awḍaḥ al-masālik ilā Alfiyyat Ibn Mālik*, with commentary, cf. entry 20.
81. *Warrāq ma'a Ṭarrāf*, i.e. Warrāq's *Takhmīs* of Witrī's *al-Qaṣīdah al-witriyyah*, followed by Ṭarā'ifī's *Abkār al-afkār*; cf. entries 52, 58, 62 and 94.
82. *Alfiyyah wa-Sullam*, Ibn Mālik's *Alfiyyah* followed, no doubt, by Akhḍarī's *al-Sullam al-murawniq fī 'ilm al-manṭiq*, *GAL*, II, 463. Among the manuscripts I saw, there were two which contained both Ibn Mālik's *Alfiyyah* and Akhḍarī's *Sullam*.
83. *Tuḥfah ākhir*, the fourth and last volume of Ibn Ḥajar al-Haythamī's *Tuḥfat al-muḥtāj*; see also entries 17, 75, 77 and 95.

84. *Sharḥ Talkhīṣ*, perhaps to be identified with Taftāzānī's shorter commentary on Qazwīnī's *Talkhīṣ al-miftāḥ* a compendium of the third part of Sakkākī's *Miftāḥ al-'ulūm*, *GAL*, I, 295. In 1976, I saw a copy of Qazwīnī's *Talkhīṣ* as well as a manuscript beginning with Taftāzānī's *Mukhtaṣar min sharḥ al-Talkhīṣ fī 'ilm al-ma'ānī wa-'l-bayān wa-'l-badī'*; but I also saw a copy of Ibn Ḥajar al-'Asqalānī's *Talkhīṣ al-badr al-munīr fī takhrīj aḥādīth sharḥ al-Yāfi'ī*.
85. *Alfiyyat al-'Irāq[ī] ma'a riyāḍ al-mustaṭāb*, i.e. 'Abd al-Raḥīm al-'Irāqī's *al-Alfiyyah fī uṣūl al-ḥadīth*, a versification of Shahrazūrī's *'Ulūm al-ḥadīth*, *GAL*, I, 359, no doubt followed by 'Āmirī's *al-Riyāḍ al-mustaṭābah*, *GAL*, S. II, 226.
86. *Ma'ūnat ḥisāb*, unidentified.
87. *Mīzān awwal*, the first volume of an unidentified work; cf. entries 33 and 71.
88. *Ta'rīkh al-khulafā*, another copy of Suyūṭī's text, cf. entry 3.
89. *Muṣḥaf qā'im*, another copy of the Qur'ān; cf. entries 1 and 56.
90. *Fawākih al-janiyyah*, undoubtedly to be identified with Fākihī's, *al-Fawākih al-janiyyah*, a commentary on Ru'aynī's *Mutammimat al-ājurrūmiyyah*, *GAL*, II, 238. Both the *Mutammimah* and Fākihī's commentary were read and copied in Harar.
91. *Sharḥ Burdah majmū'*, a volume containing, among other texts, an unidentified commentary on Būṣīrī's *Burdah*.
92. *Mashra' awwal*, the first volume of an unidentified work.
93. *Tanbīh al-anām*, i.e. al-Qayrawānī's *Tanbīh al-anām fī bayān 'uluww maqām nabiyyinā Muḥammad*. Many copies of this text can be found among the manuscripts in Harar. This copy may have belonged to the Sulṭān's father, see above, 'Alī's legacy no. 17.
94. *Sharḥ Ṭarrāf*, an unidentified commentary on Ṭarā'ifī's *Abkār al-'afkār*; cf. entries 52, 58 and 81. See also 'Alī's legacy nos. 7 and 15.
95. *Tuḥfah awwal*, the first volume of Ibn Ḥajar al-Haythamī's *Tuḥfat al-muḥtāj*; cf. entries 17, 75, 77 and 83.
96. *Bayḍāwī awwal wa-thānī*, a probably complete copy of Bayḍāwī's commentary on the Qur'ān; cf. entries 27 and 29, 14 and 76.
97. *Fatḥ al-jawād 'awwal*, another copy of the first volume of Ibn Ḥajar al-Haythamī's commentary on the *Irshād*; cf. entry 28.
98. *Tanbīh al-ghāfil*, unidentified.
99. *Qiṣṣat madīnat Bahnasā*, legendary early Islamic history.

Notes

[1] Most of them reprinted in his *L'Islam di ieri e di oggi*, Rome, 1971.
[2] E. Wagner, *Legende und Geschichte, der Fatḥ madīnat Harar von Yaḥyā Naṣrallāh*, Wiesbaden, 1978.
[3] Yūsuf Aḥmad, 'An Inquiry into some Aspects of the Economy of Harar and the Records of the Household Economy of the Amirs of Harar', *Bulletin of the Ethnological Society, University College of Addis Ababa*, X.
[4] In 1975, I saw one such document; unfortunately, I was not allowed to photograph it.

[5] 'Arabic Town Records and the Economic and Population History of Harar during the 19th Century'; as far as I know, this paper has never been published.
[6] Cf. S. Tedeschi, 'L'Emirato di Harar secondo un documento inedito', in Accademia Nazionale dei Lincei, *Problemi attuali di scienza e di cultura*, Quaderno N. 191, IV Congresso Internazionale di Studi Etiopici, I, Rome, 1974, 497 ff.
[7] Cf. E. Wagner, 'Eine Liste der Heiligen von Harar', *ZDMG*, CXXIII, 1973, 284 f.
[8] It is certain, however, that at least one other manuscript had already come into his hands by 1273; see entry 44.

The Apostasy of ʿAlī b. al-Faḍl

C. L. Geddes

It is interesting to note that in the history of the spread of Ismaʿilism prior to the establishment of the Fatimid Caliphate in North Africa in the early eighth/fourteenth century, we should have more detailed information about the first *dāʿīs* appointed to the Yemen than those in any other part of the Islamic empire. As a result, we are able to examine surprisingly closely the apostasy of one of these trusted propagandists in a period during which the movement was plagued with internal dissension. The desertion of ʿAlī b. al-Faḍl from the cause at a time when three separate groups were vying for power – the Ismaʿīlīs, the Zaydīs, and the ʿAbbasids (the latter represented in the local rule by the Yuʿfirids) – did irreparable damage to the Ismaʿīlī *daʿwah* in the Yemen from which it never fully recovered. A surprising modern result of his apostasy has been the adoption of ʿAlī b. al-Faḍl by the current régime of the People's Democratic Republic of Yemen as a national hero to serve as an example for those 'fighting against imperialism'.

During the period of expansion of the Ismaʿīlī movement outwards from the secret residence of the Imam in Salamiyyah, Syria, in the last decades of the third/ninth century, in the interest of safety and with the lack of easy communication, it was necessary for the leaders of the sect responsible for its propagation to rely completely upon the judgement of those appointed as *dāʿīs* as to the methods to be employed within their respective *jazīrah*. Because of the need for missionaries and the inherent dangers involved in working amongst often hostile populations in areas controlled by enemies, it was sometimes necessary for the leaders to appoint individuals newly converted to Ismaʿilism and poorly prepared, with the result that this reliance was occasionally ill-placed. Thus, while the *Dāʿī 'l-duʿāh* might be responsible for the selection, training and appointment of those to be sent to selected regions (often at the outskirts of the empire), he had little opportunity to supervise them and so the *dāʿī*, once he had arrived at his station, was alone accountable for how he carried out his mission. As we may read in the various sources for the period, there were a surprising number of instances in which this independence resulted in rebellion against the teachings and authority of the Ismaʿīlī Imams. On at least two occasions it was the Dāʿī *'l-duʿāh* who himself apostasised thereby setting unfortunate precedents for the lesser *dāʿīs* should they have the inclination or self-serving interest to do so, often, however, resulting in their untimely demise.[1] It is one such case which it is my purpose to examine here.

In the early summer of 267/881 the first two *dāʿīs* to be sent to the Yemen departed from Kufa with the pilgrim caravan. The one, variously known in history as Abū 'l-Qāsim, Ibn Ḥawshab, or Manṣūr al-Yaman, was Abū 'l-

Qāsim al-Ḥasan b. Faraj b. Ḥawshab, a native of Kufa. The other, Abū 'l-Ḥusayn 'Alī b. al-Faḍl al-Khanfarī, was a native Yemenite from the southern town of Jayshān. Both had been but recently converted and recruited for their posts. Each was assigned to his own district – Abū 'l-Qāsim to the village of 'Adan Lā'ah, two days journey to the west of the capital of Ṣan'ā' and on the upper reaches of the Wadi Lā'ah, and 'Alī b. al-Faḍl to return to his own town.[2] Although Abū 'l-Qāsim appears to have been designated as the *Dā'ī 'l-du'āh* and was responsible for recruiting and despatching from the Yemen *dā'īs* to such diverse places as Yamāmah, Bahrain, India, Egypt and the Maghrib, he apparently had, or was unable to exert, little authority over Ibn al-Faḍl.

While Abū 'l-Qāsim, with the assistance of the inhabitants of 'Adan Lā'ah, was able to undertake his missionary activity through both preaching and military conquest shortly after his arrival, 'Alī b. al-Faḍl's movements were more circumspect. Instead of returning to his home in Jayshān as ordered by the Imam in Kufa he remained in Aden, where they had both first gone. From Aden he shortly established himself, without prior authorisation, in the country of Yāfi', north-east of the city, where he slowly gained a reputation for himself amongst the tribesmen for his piety and asceticism. Through the years which followed he so acquired their trust and confidence that he was able to use them to overcome the rulers of the surrounding countryside. By the end of 291/904 Ibn al-Faḍl, in slightly over twenty years, had obtained virtual mastery over most of southern Yemen which he ruled from the fortress of al-Mudhaykhirah on one of the upland arms of the Wadi Zabīd.[3]

Approximately five years prior to this significant success his master, the Imam, found it expedient to leave Salamiyyah to escape capture by his enemies or arrest by the 'Abbasid governor. According to a long-term servant of the family the Imam explicity stated that the Yemen was their possible destination.[4] After several years on the road eluding their pursuers the Imam and his party arrived safely in Egypt towards the middle of the year 292/905. There they remained for but a short time, and on the eve of their expected departure for the Yemen the Imam announced that they were going instead to the Maghrib. According to Ja'far al-Ḥājib, it was at this time that the chief *dā'ī*, Fīrūz, deserted and made his own way to the Yemen to meet Abū 'l-Qāsim.[5] The reason for Fīrūz abandoning the Imam at this vitally important time is not at all made clear in the various Isma'īlī sources. For whatever the reason his stay with the *Dā'ī 'l-du'āh* of the Yemen was comparatively brief, only indeed, until a letter from the Imam could reach Abū 'l-Qāsim ordering the execution of the apostate. When this did arrive Fīrūz was informed of its contents by a servant of the *dā'ī* and escaped to join 'Alī b. al-Faḍl. Ja'far continues his narration in the following manner:

> The *dā'ī* searched for him everywhere until he found that Fīrūz had joined 'Alī b. al-Faḍl al-Jayshānī, stirring him up to rebellion and treason. The *dā'ī* Abū 'l-Qāsim, learning of all this and of the efforts of Fīrūz to proclaim himself an Imām, helped by the shaykh and the

peoples of that place, attacked them with a force and, after a long struggle, ultimately suppressed them, and executed both of them.[6]

The story as thus recounted contains many discrepancies which are impossible to reconcile with the more detailed Yemenite sources for the history of the activities of Ibn al-Faḍl. None of these mention the name of Fīrūz in any manner, nor do they indicate that Ibn al-Faḍl had any outside influence upon him to apostatise. Further, Ja'far gives the impression that the period between the departure of Fīrūz from Egypt and the apostasy of the Yemenite *dā'ī* was comparatively short; even if we accept Ivanow's date of 292/905 (presumably the latest possible) for the arrival of the Imam in Egypt it cannot coincide with the known date of 297/910 for Ibn al-Faḍl's abandonment of the Isma'īlī cause. Finally, the statement that Abū 'l-Qāsim was responsible for the death of his former co-*dā'ī* is patently erroneous. Abū 'l-Qāsim died of natural causes on 11 Jumādā II 302/1 January 915. Ibn al-Faḍl succumbed to poison on 15 Rabī' II 303/28 October 915.[7] Thus, the role of this Fīrūz in seriously damaging the Isma'īlī movement in the Yemen must be viewed, if not with outright rejection, at least with serious suspicion. The cause for Ibn al-Faḍl's apostasy must certainly have come from his own character rather than from influence from another.

In the year following his extraordinary successes in subduing the south of the Yemen Ibn al-Faḍl was determined to conquer the capital of Ṣan'ā' and the north from Yu'firid rule. With the taking and sacking of the city on 15 Muḥarram 292/16 November 905 Ibn al-Faḍl must have appeared as nearly invincible. By this time the two *dā'īs*, who, apparently, had not met personally since their first arrival in the country in 267/881, were now operating independently within the same geographical area. This could lead only to disaster. At a meeting of the two, extending from Muḥarram through Rabī' I (November-December) it is reported that Abū 'l-Qāsim attempted to convince his subordinate that they should co-operate in consolidating their respective conquests into a more cohesive state in which the Isma'īlī *da'wah* would be supreme.[8] However, with 'Alī b. al-Faḍl's invasion of the low-land coastal region of Tihāmah shortly after this meeting we may see the beginnings of the *dā'ī*'s refusal to accept direction from a superior which could only lead to his eventual apostasy. In his absence from the capital Ṣan'ā' was retaken by its Yu'firid ruler, but only for a short period before its recapture by Ibn al-Faḍl. Following his successes in Tihāmah, crowned by the taking of the important city of Zabīd at the end of Jumādā II 293/April 906 and his reconquest of Ṣan'ā' the Isma'īlī propagandist was the master of most of southern and western Yemen and without a doubt the most powerful man within the entire country.[9]

It was upon his return to his fortress capital of al-Mudhaykhirah from the coast in Ṣafar 297/October-November 910 that 'Alī b. al-Faḍl not only repudiated his allegiance to the *da'wah*, but, if we are to believe our sources, apostasised from Islam as well. According to all of the Yemeni historians for this period Ibn al-Faḍl's public pronouncements included the denial of the Prophet and his revelations, a claim to the lordship of the worlds, the ordering of incestuous relations, and generally forbidding the lawful and permitting the unlawful.[10] It would be tempting to dismiss out-of-hand the numerous accusations laid against Ibn al-Faḍl regarding his denial of Islam if they were related by Isma'īlī sources, but such is not the case. Rather, they are related, some, it is true, with more lurid details than others, by Sunnī *faqīhs* such as 'Abd al-Jabbār b. Muḥammad and al-Janadī, and by Zaydī jurists (al-'Abbāsī and Ibn Mālik), among others. Al-Janadī states categorically:

> 'Such practices are most shameful and pernicious, and they are repudiated by all who follow the doctrines of Ismaīlism. They are things that cannot be proved against anyone but Ibn Faḍl. I have inquired of many persons, from whom correct information can be obtained respecting the doctrines of the sect. They condemned these misdeeds, and I found all agreed in regarding 'Aly ibn Faḍl as an atheist, whilst upholding Manṣūr al-Yaman as one of the most distinguished and most worthy of men of their sect.'[11]

Thus, it is probably necessary to accept the basic statement that Ibn al-Faḍl was an apostate from Islam as well as from the Isma'īlī *da'wah*. In order to understand these actions, which irreparably damaged the cause of the Isma'īlīs in the Yemen, it is necessary for us to examine the possible reasons and state of mind of Ibn al-Faḍl.

With regard to his faithlessness to the *da'wah* it must be acknowledged that there were precedents in apostasy from the tenets of Isma'īlism by earlier *dā'īs*, some from the highest order, of whom he may have had some knowledge, e.g., Ḥamdān Qarmaṭ, 'Abdān, the 'Qarmatian' brothers,[12] *possibly* Fīrūz, and a number of others. Secondly, he had been a great deal more successful in carrying out his mission in the Yemen than had Abū 'l-Qāsim, his supposed superior; therefore, why should his extraordinary efforts over a quarter of a century rebound to one less able than himself who would thereby gain the glory? Thirdly, it is known that by 293/906 'Ubayd Allāh, the Isma'īlī Imam, had reached the Maghrib and, furthermore, was either in prison or under house arrest. We may presume that these facts were known in the Yemen through the interchange of letters. To Ibn al-Faḍl certainly it would appear that it was most unlikely that the Imam, or his descendants, would ever be willing or able to assume political and spiritual authority in person over the territories which he himself had conquered. Rather than place these dominions under the suzerainty of a ruler so far distant, and apparently in disgrace, why should he not claim them for himself? Finally, it would appear that his soldiers gave him absolute obedience, particularly as he permitted them to sack and pillage the towns they captured to their hearts' content. Furthermore, he had seldom met with defeat. To some of the uneducated tribesmen, upon whom Islam sat very lightly, 'Alī b. al-Faḍl may have appeared more than human. In none of the sources are we informed that following his apostasy did he lose any of his following. On the contrary, his army appears to have increased in size and his successes continued, including the surrender and submission of Abū 'l-Qāsim, his former superior, and of Asʿad b. Ibrāhīm al-Yuʿfirī, the legitimate ruler of the highlands of the Yemen and once greatest opponent.[13]

What was it within his character which led him to forsake his allegiance to Ismaʿīlī doctrine and abandon his inherited faith? Al-Khazrajī, in writing of his conversion to Ismaʿilism at Kufa states that '. . . he was a failure when young, not famous though learned, sagacious, courageous, daring, and eloquent'.[14] The traits required to be a successful *dāʿī* were also those required to be a successful renegade. He was not born to be a follower, but rather a leader of men and the history of his actions in the Yemen well illustrates this assessment. Many of his military exploits do indeed show courage and daring. The result was that he soon felt himself to be invincible, and both his followers and his opponents must have believed this as well. In addition, he was able to bring over to his side a number of the political leaders of the time who originally fought against him, even though they were not themselves followers of Ismaʿilism. He was able to convince them that his was the winning side. Ibn al-Faḍl was incapable of following orders, as witnessed by his failure to return to his home in Jayshān to begin his mission and by his unwillingness to obey Abū 'l-Qāsim when told to return to Ṣanʿā' so that they could consolidate their conquests. His own estimation of the situation was nearly always the correct one. Finally, it does not appear that, although born into a Shiʿite home, Islam was held strongly in his heart, particularly when material considerations could have a greater appeal. In this he was not alone amongst his countrymen at the time. His overweening ambition and self-assuredness did indeed bring him fame, fortune and power, but it also brought about his death.

Al-Mahdī, the Ismaʿīlī Imam, by now living in Sijilmāsah with a state now beginning to take form, was undoubtedly kept informed by Abū 'l-Qāsim of the developments within the Yemen, including the apostasy of Ibn al-Faḍl. Realising the danger to the continuance of his *daʿwah* in the country by the rebel the Imam was determined that this threat be eliminated. The best solution of course was to bring about his death. Towards the beginning of 303/915 al-Mahdī is reported to have ordered two of his agents, whether living within or outside the country we are not informed, to assassinate the apostate. One of the two, posing as a physician, was able to gain admittance to Ibn al-Faḍl in his home at al-Mudhaykhirah and administer a poison. While the two fled from the wrath of his followers, Ibn al-Faḍl succumbed to the effects of the drug on Thursday, 15 Rabīʿ II/28 October.[15]

Notes

1 W. Ivanow, *Ismaili tradition concerning the rise of the Fatimids*, Calcutta, 1942, 47–48.

2 Qāḍī al-Nuʿmān, *Iftitāḥ al-daʿwah wa-'btidā' al-dawlah* MS, Muḥam-

madiyyah Hamdāniyyah Library, ff. 11–13. (Published, ed. Wadād al-Qāḍī, Beirut, 1970).

[3] Ibn Mālik, *Kashf asrār al-Bāṭiniyyah wa-akhbār al-Qarāmiṭah* ed. Muḥammad Zāhid b. al-Ḥasan al-Kawtharī, Cairo, 1939, 28–30; Abū Muḥammad Idrīs b. 'Alī, *Kitāb Kanz al-akhyār fī ma'rifat al-siyar wa-'l-akhbār* MS, British Library, Or. 4581, f. 179a; Abū 'l-Ḥasan 'Alī b. al-Ḥasan al-Khazrajī, *Kitāb Ta'rīkh al-Kifāyah wa-'l-i'lām fī-man waliya 'l-Yaman wa-sakanaha min ahl al-Islām*, MS British Library, Or. 6941, ff. 25b–26a.

[4] *Sīrat Ja'far al-Ḥājib*, ed. W. Ivanow, *et. al.*, *Bulletin of the Faculty of Arts of the Egyptian University*, Cairo, 1939, 110. Trans. W. Ivanow, *Ismaili Tradition*, 189. M. Canard states that the year of arrival in Egypt was probably 291/903, cf. *EI*², 'Fāṭimids'.

[5] *Sīrat*, text, 116, Ivanow trans., 197.

[6] *Sīrat*, text, 116, trans., 197. (Ivanow's translation).

[7] 'Alī b. Muḥammad al-'Abbāsī, *Sīrat al-Hādī*, MS British Library, Or. 3901), fol. 164a. (Published, ed. Suhayl Zakkār, Damascus, 1972).

[8] 'Abbāsī, f. 159b.

[9] 'Abbāsī, f. 159b.

[10] 'Abbāsī, ff. 160b–161a.

[11] Abū 'Abd Allāh Bahā' al-Dīn Yūsuf b. Ya'qūb al-Janadī, *Kitāb al-Sulūk fī ṭabaqāt al-'ulamā' wa-'l-mulūk*, in H. C. Kay, *Yaman, its early mediaeval history*, London, 1892, text 147, trans. 204 (Kay's translation).

[12] Ivanow, *Ismaili Tradition*, 47–48.

[13] 'Abbāsī, f. 163a.

[14] *Kifāyah*, f. 25a.

[15] 'Abbāsī, f. 164a.

The Prosody of an Andalusian *muwashshaḥ* re-examined

J. Derek Latham

Given Professor Serjeant's interest in Arabic literature in general and South Arabian poetry in particular, he may, for reasons we shall see later, find my observations on the prosody of a mediaeval Andalusian *muwashshaḥ* a suitable subject for a contribution to his *Festschrift*.

In *Edebiyât* I (1976) J. T. Monroe has an article entitled 'The Structure of an Arabic *Muwashshaḥ* with a Bilingual *Kharja*' (113–23). In it he examines a *muwashshaḥ* contained in Ibn al-Khaṭīb's *Jaysh al-tawshīḥ* and attributed to Abū Yaḥyā al-Saraqusṭī ('of Zaragoza') al-Jazzār (*fl.* 11th century A.D.). His aim is clearly to establish a norm, for he expresses the hope that his prosodic, thematic and structural analysis will provide 'a model for the study of *muwashshaḥ* esthetics'.[1] Of these three analytical aspects of his examination it is the first that is of primary importance if only because it is on Professor Monroe's prosodic interpretation of al-Jazzār's *muwashshaḥ* that a potentially weighty submission is based, namely this, that 'On the prosodic level we . . . find in this poem, as in many others from Andalus, substantial evidence for a Romance influence upon Arabic poetry'.[2] Taken in its context, the expression 'substantial evidence' suggests a standard of proof higher than that of the mere preponderance of probability: it invites the conclusion that the case is proved beyond reasonable doubt. To show that this is not so is the purpose of all that now follows.

I will begin by reproducing part of the text of the *muwashshaḥ* as it is transcribed and arranged in *Edebiyât*, leaving till later the complete text set out in an arrangement acceptable to me. The parts I select here are:[3]

[0] *wáyḥa l-mústahā́m*
ṣā́ra l-jísmu fī́yā
bi-'áydī s-saqā́m

[1] lam yúbqi l-hawā́
min jísmi siwā́
habā́'an hawā́
bi-ṭáyfi l-manā́m
fa-'dhíri sh-shajī́yā
wa-khálli l-malā́m

[2] wa-hí́m bi-ftiḍā́ḥ
fī l-ghī́di l-milā́ḥ
wa-qúm li-ṣṭibā́ḥ
bi-ká'si l-mudā́m

thummá shrab hanīyā
wa-[']ásqi n-nidấm
... ...

[5] fa-káyfa s-sabīl
an yúshfā l-ghalīl
idh ẓállat taqū́l

[*kharjah*] *MÁMMÁ SHŪ́ l-ghulām*
lā búdd kullū lī́yā
ḥalāl [*a*]*w harấm* (read *ḥalấl*?)

Starting with the *kharjah*, Monroe's view of its scansion is that 'exact stress-syllabic parallels can be discovered in the Spanish folk tradition of the *villancico*'.[4] For him, Arabic prosody is out of the question. The nearest he comes to entertaining any thought of it is an admission that 'when scanned quantitatively according to the Arabic rules, [the *kharjah*] does in fact display a certain patterning which is more or less regular'.[5] However, he immediately banishes the thought on the ground that the patterning 'cannot be interpreted as any one of the classical meters of the Arabic inventory'.[6] In a footnote he expands on this point by observing: 'The quantitative sequence obtained would be: – – – ∪ – (–) (thrice)'.[7] In this same note he then throws caution to the wind and confidently declares: '*Since there is no such Arabic meter* [my italics], whereas the stress-syllabic pattern that results is well known to Spanish prosody, *the conclusion is inevitable that Arabic quantity is being adapted to fit a pre-existent Romance stress-syllabic pattern* [my italics] and not the reverse'.[8]

The Romance prosody applicable to the *kharjah* is explained by Professor Monroe as follows: 'From the stress-syllabic angle, the *kharjah* is a tercet of hexasyllabic lines rhymed *m n m*, exhibiting a rhythm that is predominantly dactyllic, but which in one segment is trochaic'.[9] To justify this hexasyllabic interpretation of the first and last lines of the *kharjah*, he then invokes a law of Spanish prosody, 'namely the so-called "law of compensation", according to which lines with end-stress require the addition of an extra syllable which is included in the metric count though it need not be pronounced'.[10] 'This conventional prosodic syllable,' he goes on, 'in effect reduces our *kharja* to a regular hexasyllabic tercet'.[11]

So utterly Spanish does the *kharjah* seem to Monroe by this stage that he classifies all else as 'the Arabic part of the *muwashshaḥ*',[12] though there appears to be no justifiable reason for so doing. For, even if, for the sake of argument, we accept that *shū* is Romance (i.e. 'su'), there are no more than two Romance words in the whole of the 'bilingual' *kharjah*.[13] But can we in fact be sure that *shū is* Romance? Could it not be colloquial Arabic? Such a possibility certainly cannot be dismissed out of hand if we accept, as we must, that *shū* for the commonplace Arabic *shūf* is known to certain dialects in countries as far apart as Morocco and Iraq.[14] If then, as I myself suspect, *shū* is colloquial Arabic, we are left with *mammā* as the one and only lexical item in the *kharjah* that seems to be Romance.

But let us now leave the *kharjah* and see how, according to Monroe, 'the Arabic part' of our *muwashshaḥ* is to be viewed from the point of view of prosody. Quite simply, the 'Arabic part ... reproduces the prosody of the *kharjah* with two exceptions: the middle lines of the *ghuṣn*s bear a final rather than a penultimate stress, and their rhyme scheme is *a a a* rather than *m n m*. Both these features are perfectly permissible in Spanish prosody'.[15] At this juncture and with these words Monroe rests his case on the subject of prosody and thus, in effect, invites us to accept as fact that al-Jazzār's *muwashshaḥ* is cast in a Romance prosodic mould. It is, however, a case to which there are some disconcerting aspects. For one thing, the notion of an 'Arabic part' of the *muwashshaḥ* with its 'middle lines' of *ghuṣn*s can scarcely be accounted felicitous. For another, the case relies on plain assertion: not only does its proponent offer no quotations from Spanish poetry to illustrate the metric parallels of which he speaks; he does not even furnish a single reference to a source that would enable his reader to seek out for himself examples for comparison. But these are not the only, or even the main, points to be made: there are others of more fundamental importance, and it is to these that we may now turn our attention.

In the first place, it is important to note that Monroe is firmly persuaded of the validity of the thesis propounded by the well-known Spanish Arabist Emilio García Gómez in *Las jarchas romances de la serie árabe en su marco* (Madrid, 1965; 2nd ed. Barcelona, 1975) that the prosody of Romance *kharjahs* is stress-syllabic[16] and, accordingly, that 'the prosody of the *muwashshaḥ* must also be based upon the same principles'.[17] Here it must be said immediately that to rely, as does Monroe, on García Gómez's texts of the *muwashshaḥāt* as presented in *Las jarchas romances* is to rely on the unreliable. That the texts *are* unreliable is an assertion grounded in evidence of the kind adduced in a recent article by Alan Jones entitled 'Romance Scansion and the *Muwaššaḥāt*' (*Journal of Arabic Literature*, Leiden, XI, 1980, 36–55).

Since the evidence raised by the author of this paper is there for all to read, I will neither reproduce it in its fine detail nor add to it evidence of my own of a similar kind. All that need concern us here is the answer to the question: Do García Gómez's texts provide solid evidence for the Romance scansion theory? Regrettably, Jones finds himself obliged to reply in the negative. His conclusions, solidly based on the weight of the evidence set out in his paper – evidence drawn, be it noted, from the Oxford corpus of *muwashshaḥāt* assembled in computerised form from available Arabic manuscripts[18] – are (a) that García Gómez's texts are 'seriously misleading' in that what we are offered by this noted Spanish Arabist is 'a virtuoso synthesis of text and interpretation, in which, for whatever reason, he has decided to ignore detailed textual points',[19] and (b) that in the poems in question 'the difficulties about the proposed Hispano-Romance scansion are not merely far greater than those connected with the Arabic scansion. They are insuperable in terms of the theory as it is now propounded'.[20] In short, García Gómez, contrary to Monroe's belief, has proved no case at all for the use of Romance prosody in Andalusian *muwashshaḥāt*. Put quite bluntly, the most he has done is to raise the suspicion of 'a desire to regulate the lines [of the lyrics] to conform with an imposed hypothetical norm'.[21] It follows, then, that if Monroe has drawn inspiration or encouragement for his view of al-Jazzār's prosody from García Gómez and his *Jarchas romances*, he has followed a false lead.

The second point to be made bears on what can justly be described as the outright rejection of an Arabic origin for al-Jazzār's metre simply because his *kharjah* 'cannot be interpreted as any one of the classical meters of the Arabic inventory', despite the fact that 'when scanned quantitatively according to Arabic rules, [it] does in fact display a certain patterning which is more or less regular'.[22] But whence Monroe's authority for the tacit formulation of such an exclusionary rule? For my part, I know of none. My own work on the prosody of the *muwashshaḥāt*, carried out independently of that done by Alan Jones, but along similar lines with much the same material, has forcibly brought home to me, as his work has to him, that proponents of the theory of Romance origins are increasingly inclined 'to dismiss Arabic as the likely source simply because most of the metrical patterns in the *muwaššaḥāt* are not Xalīlian'.[23] Rightly, he goes on to observe that 'this is to adduce and demolish an argument that has never been propounded by those who think that the source of the metres is most probably Arabic. Arab writers have always stated that extensions to the Xalīlian system were involved . . .'[24]

At this point it seems to me appropriate to introduce a note of caution. While Jones's observations on the views of Arab writers seem to me entirely justified in the context in which they appear, it behoves us to subject Arab analyses of metre to the most careful scrutiny when the prosody of *strictly classical Arabic* poetry is not in issue. No one, perhaps, has more strikingly demonstrated the need for such scrutiny than Laurence Elwell-Sutton, whose percipient and painstaking examination of Persian verse has revealed as an ill-fitting garment the garb of Khalīlian metrics in which the theorists see the work of Persian poets clothed. The opening paragraph of Elwell-Sutton's introduction to *The Persian Metres* (Cambridge, 1976) puts the matter plainly:[25]

> For more than one thousand years the study of the metres of Persian verse has been dominated by the theories and principles devised by the analysts of Arabic poetry, and thereafter applied without discrimination to the classification of the compositions of the Persian poets. So complete has this domination been that this use of the traditional Arabic terminology has actually misled many scholars, both eastern and western, into assuming an intimate relation between the two systems, and even into asserting that Persian verse is derived from Arabic. In fact ... there is no support for such a belief. It is true that the Arabic terminology may (with some stretching of its legitimate use) be employed to describe the Persian metres; but this does not mean that the latter, as used by the poets, were copied from Arabic poetry – any more than the fact that Shakespeare wrote in what we choose to call iambic pentameters means that he copied this metre from the Greeks.

It would be naive not to foresee proponents of the Romance scansion theory seizing upon this very same passage to support the notion that the scansion of the *muwashshaḥāt* had its origins in that of Romance verse and that, like Persian prosody, it has been forced to masquerade in Arab clothing. But, before such proponents think me hoist with my own petard, I will apprise them of at least one fact that must give them pause: one of the earliest extant *muwashshaḥāt* – it dates from the late tenth or early eleventh century A.D. – presents a composite prosodic scheme with component sections cast in metres which Elwell-Sutton has shown to be Persian. I refer to 'Ubādah b. Mā' al-Samā''s *Ḥubbu 'l-mahā 'ibādah//min kulli bassāmi 'l-sarārī*, whose metrical scheme clearly presented Samuel Stern with problems.[26] Nor, I hasten to add, is this particular *muwashshaḥ* an isolated instance of the phenomenon to which it draws attention. But that is a matter which I hope to take up elsewhere. *Retournons à nos moutons.*

Before we take leave of the findings of Alan Jones which prompted the foregoing digression, there is one finding of his which remains to be brought to the fore and to be impressed on the minds of all who are either committed to or inclined to accept Romance scansion theories. It is namely this, that *muwashshaḥāt* with Romance or bilingual *kharjah*s amount to *less than ten per cent* of the extant corpus.[27]

Now from *muwashshaḥāt* in general to the particular *muwashshaḥ* of al-Jazzār which concerns us here. Because, to Monroe's way of thinking, the prosody of its *kharjah* is of the stress-syllabic type, 'it follows . . . that the prosody of the *muwashshaḥ* must also be based upon the same principles.'[28] Central to this stress-syllabic view is Monroe's belief that, when scanned quantitatively 'according to the Arabic rules', the three lines that make up the *kharjah* produce the quantitative sequence ‒ ‒ ‒ ∪ ‒ (‒) (thrice).[29] The fact that such a sequence *thrice* is to be found neither in the *kharjah* nor elsewhere in al-Jazzār's composition is a point worth noting, but far less important than the question: Is Monroe right in his belief that there is no such Arabic metre as ‒ ‒ ‒ ∪ ‒ (‒)?[30] The straight answer is that he certainly is, *if* he allows his Arabic prosodic horizons to be bounded, as in fact he does, by the strictly classical metres of the Khalīlian system. That much said, it is essential to make a point that evidently eludes him, namely that, even where it seems wholly legitimate to look to Arabic scansion (as opposed to Persian, say) for guidance on the prosody of the strophic genre, there can be no valid case for confining oneself within the straitjacket of the classical system. The reason is not far to seek: as Jones so rightly observes, 'expansion of the Xalīlian system would have been inevitable once the poets began splitting up lines and hemistichs'.[31]

Having asked and answered the most basic question of all, we are now in a position to proceed to the one that logically follows, which is: Does there exist, *outside the Khalīlian system and beyond the bounds of the Iberian Peninsula* an Arabic quantitative metre of the pattern ‒ ‒ ‒ ∪ ‒ (‒)? The question can be answered in the affirmative: the metre ‒ ‒ ‒ / ∪ ‒ ‒, styled *mustaṭīl*, is to be found in the Yemen in a form of strophic, or stanzaic verse used in that category of song which is described as Ṣan'ānī ('of Ṣan'ā'').

The genre of verse in question is known as *mubayyat*, and, like the Yemeni *muwashshaḥ*, it is classified as *ḥumaynī*, a term applied to verse in which the rules of classical Arabic grammar, vocabulary and prosody may be, 'and are in practice, relaxed'.[32]

In the corpus of odes of Ṣanʿānī songs collected and studied by Muḥammad ʿAbduh Ghānim in *al-Abḥāth* there are two *mubayyat*s in which the use of *mustaṭīl* is encountered. The more recent of the two, dating in all probability from the second half of the eighteenth century, is the work of one ʿAlī b. Aḥmad,[33] who died in 1220/1805. Its metre is the dimetric-trimetric variety of *mustaṭīl*, i.e. – – –/∪ – –//– – –/∪ – –/∪ –, and the first line of the opening stanza runs as follows:[34]

ḥāwī khay/r ilaykum // *ṣādir min* / *asīr al-/hawà*

The second of the two poems antedates the first by two centuries or so. Composed by Ibn Sharaf al-Dīn Yaḥyā al-Kawkabānī (d.1106/1607), it could well date – and most probably does – from the second half of the sixteenth century. It opens with the following stanza:[35]

maʿshūq al-/jamāl // *nahab fu'ā/dī jamāluh*
fī hijrī / aṭāl // *wa-[a]dhāba qal/bī maṭāluh*
lā kān al-/miṭāl // *limah taqū/lū aṭāluh*
abdā lī l-/malāl // *waylāh man / dhā amāluh*

It will be immediately apparent to anyone with a basic knowledge of Arabic prosody that this stanza is cast not in one metre, but in two. Both hemistichs of each line are dimetric, but, whereas the first is in *mustaṭīl manhūk* (– – –/∪ –),[36] the second is in *mujtath majzū'* (∪ – ∪ –/– ∪ – –).[37]

Now to al-Jazzār's *muwashshaḥ*. First, let us abandon Monroe's re-arrangement of the lines and reproduce the arrangement to be found in all the three manuscripts in which the *muwashshaḥ* is extant:[38]

[0]
wayḥa 'l-mustahām //*ṣāra 'l-jismu fiyyā* //*bi-'aydī 'l-saqām*

[1]
lam yubqi 'l-hawà
min jismī siwà
habā'an hawà
bi-ṭayfi 'l-manām //*fa-ʿdhiri 'l-shajiyyā* //*wa-khalli 'l-malām*

[2]
wa-him bi-ftiḍāḥ
fī 'l-ghīdi 'l-milāḥ
wa-qum li-ṣṭibāḥ
bi-ka'si 'l-mudām //*thumma shrab haniyyā* //*wa-'asqi 'l-nidām*

[3]
li-nafsī 'l-latī
qalbī ṣallat[ī]
fa-ʿan ḍallatī
lā 'aslu 'l-gharām //*mā lāḥa l-thurayyā* //*wa-ghannà 'l-ḥamām*

[4]
fatātun ka'āb
na'īmu 'l-shabāb
'alayhā 'l-madhāb
ka-rawḍi 'l-ghamām || *la-hā 'l-misku rayyā* || *wa-'l-durru btisām*

[5]
fa-kayfa 'l-sabīl
an yushfà 'l-ghalīl
idh ẓallat taqūl
Mammā shū 'l-ghulām || *lā bud kullu liyyā*[39] || *ḥalāl* [*a*]*w ḥarām*

To take the *maṭla'* and the *kharjah* first, the metrical pattern in each case is –––/∪–//–––/∪––//∪––/∪–.[40] As in al-Kawkabānī's *mubayyat*, there is here a combination of two metres. Of these, one is instantly recognisable as *mustaṭīl*, while the other may safely be categorised as a *mutaqārib* since ∪––/∪– is found in the last two feet of the orthodox *mutaqārib* tetrameter catalectic.[41] Our combination, then, is one of *mustaṭīl* and *mutaqārib* dimeters.

In the entire *muwashshaḥ* there are only two points at which straightforward scansion does not reveal either –––/∪–(–) or ∪––/∪–. One is to be found in the middle section of the *simṭ* of stanza [1], and the other in the corresponding section of the *simṭ* of stanza [4]. In the first case the scansion *required by the Arabic orthography* is –∪–/∪––, while in the second it is ∪––/∪––. In both cases it is the short vowel in the first foot that strikes a discordant note, for elsewhere the corresponding vowel is long.

To see these two variations as permissible anomalies is one view that could be taken of them, but, since there is nowhere any evidence to suggest, much less support, such a view, I see nothing to commend it. A more justifiable approach is to suggest that the anomalous short vowels are to be treated as long in accordance with the classically acceptable licence, known as *ishbā'*, which permits the lengthening of a short vowel within a word (e.g. *'āmūd-un* for *'amūd-un*, *anẓūr-u* for *anẓur-u*).[42]

It may, of course, be objected that there is nothing in the Arabic orthography to justify the assumption of the licence I suggest. True, but it must be borne in mind that what may be an accurate indicator of the quantities required of a reciter of classical poetry, subject to the strict and well-defined rules of the Khalīlian system, may well be a less than faithful guide to the articulation of the old Andalusian *muwashshaḥ*. For, the plain fact is that, for all its markedly classical features which set it apart from the *zajal*, the *muwashshaḥ* is *not* classical poetry, and it has never been regarded as such.[43] We must not, then, assume that the *washshāḥ* could avail himself only of such licences as were sanctioned by classical prosodists. On the contrary, we must recognise, as does Jones, the existence of evidence, within the corpus of extant Andalusian *muwashshaḥāt*, pointing to the admissibility, in the genre, of certain classically unacceptable licences.[44]

For my own part, I am prompted, after careful consideration of metrical variations, anomalous by Khalīlian norms, to comment that some at least could certainly be seen as resulting from the intrusion of vernacular quantities. Arabists should need no reminding that, in the case of words common to both written and spoken Arabic, the quantity required of the articulator of a word in its literary context may, and often does, differ from that current in popular speech.[45] There is no reason to think that in this respect the situation in Muslim Spain differed from that prevailing in the modern Arab world. And, indeed, of one thing we can be quite sure: as far as phonemic length is concerned, the vowels of Spanish Arabic were one thing and those of Classical Arabic another. The vowels of the former had quantities and qualities quite their own, and for this fact we have the evidence of data drawn, not only from works intentionally dialectal in character, but also from texts whose authors expressed themselves in what we may take to be the standard written Arabic of their day.[46] The subject of Sp.A vowels, complicated as it is by the Andalusian use of *matres lectionis* as orthographical devices to indicate phonetic phenomena other than phonemic length,[47] cannot be treated here in any detail, but some useful purpose will be served by illustrating, with the following examples, the way in which the phonemic length of Sp.A vowels could differ from those of CA: *fāʿāl* (*ādhān*, *āmān*) < CA *faʿāl*;[48] *fāʿīl* (*qārīb*, *wāzīr* / *dākhīl*, *shāhīd*) < CA *faʿīl*/*fāʿil*;[49] *fāʿūl* (*qātūl*, *qādūm*, *bāʿūḍ(a)* < CA *faʿūl*;[50] *fīʿāl* (*ṭīḥāl*, *ṭīrāz*, *qīṭāʿ*) < CA *fiʿāl*.[51]

Since the short vowel with which the middle section of the *simṭ* in stanza [4] opens occurs in *la-hā*, it would be remiss of me not to bear in mind the *possibility* of its articulation as *lī-ha*, for in certain parts of the Maghrib today the vernacular *lī-ha* for CA *la-hā* is not at all uncommon. Here I need only single out the use of the former in the dialect of the Algerian coastal town of Cherchell, whose population around the middle of the sixteenth century is known to have been predominantly Andalusian and whose modern vernacular has preserved words and usages that are close to, if not identical with, Arabic words and usages known to have been current in the Hispano-Arabic dialects.[52]

If *washshāḥ*s did in fact make any concessions to such non-classical quantities as were current in the spoken language, why, it may be asked, did they – or at least those who committed their work to paper – not make use of orthographical resources available to them to apprise readers of the Arabic text of the quantities required? One very simple answer could be that they and such of their fellow-countrymen as were conversant with the genre needed no such device.[53] From what is known of the old *muwashshaḥāt* their composers were also writers of classical poetry[54] and, as such, were well versed in prosody. They were, moreover, Andalusians whose compositions were intended for the entertainment of other Andalusians of comparable education, culture, literary tastes and talent.[55] It almost goes without saying, then, that any need to allow a vernacular quantity to prevail over one required by standard orthography would not pass unrecognised. One further point on orthography: if, in a genre with such pronounced classical features as those characterising the *muwashshaḥ*, the resources of standard orthography *had* been used, it is almost certain that, in the course of transmission, deviations from the norms of CA morphology would have been regularised by copyists or scholars, or both.[56]

Hand in hand with acceptance of the fact that the *muwashshaḥ* is not CA poetry must go recognition that it is a genre of verse composed for expression in song. Today, whether in North Africa or the Yemen, *muwashshaḥāt* are *sung*, not recited, and there is no evidence that the case was otherwise at any stage in the history of the genre.[57] Now, singing is an interpretative art, and it is the experience both of myself and others familiar with the singing of non-classical verse as it is heard today that a singer's treatment of such verse, even when in a recognisably classical metre, is not necessarily that which the Khalīlian prosodist would demand of the reciter of CA poetry.[58] The singer takes liberties with words and metre, and, of all such liberties none are more common – and, in the case of blatantly popular genres, more extreme – than those taken with vowels.[59] Where the music is not markedly subordinate to the words the discriminating listener cannot fail to note that the length of vowels, no matter what their apparent quantity on paper, is often determined by the correlation between words and melody. Whether the mediaeval singer of the near-classical Andalusian *muwashshaḥ* was, to any significant extent, influenced by the music to vary the quantity of his vowels is a question as tantalising as it is pertinent; for, our present position vis-à-vis a genre in which 'melody and text formed a close unit'[60] is not unlike that of a people of alien culture inheriting the lyrics of Gilbert without the music of Sullivan.[61]

To recapitulate, in the matter of vowels if nothing else, we cannot rule out the possibility that composers of Andalusian *muwashshaḥāt* were prepared to make certain concessions either to vernacular articulation or to musical interpretation, or both. Consequently, it behoves us not to assume that the orthography in which extant compositions have come down to us *necessarily* reflects the actual quantity to be assigned to a vowel.

Apart from the two apparently short vowels in the *asmāṭ* which it may be legitimate to treat as long, there is only one other in al-Jazzār's *muwashshaḥ* to which the same treatment may be applicable, and that is the /*a*/ of *na'īm* in the second *ghuṣn* of stanza [4]. The thought is prompted not by any anomaly it generates in the foot of which it is part, but by the metrical pattern set, not only by the *aghṣān* of stanzas [2] and [3], but also by the second *ghuṣn* of all other stanzas in the composition, which scans as ‒‒‒/∪‒. With this modification of quantity – which may not in fact be essential, but which can clearly be justified if the notion of concessions to vernacular articulation is accepted[62] – there emerges for the *aghṣān* as a whole a prosodic scheme in which there is a harmonious combination of unity and diversity. Of these two qualities, the first seems to me to be represented by stanzas [2], [3] and [4], and the second by stanzas [1] and [5], which are distinguished from the rest and from each other by metrical pattern. As is plain to be seen from the notation below, the pattern presented by the *aghṣān* of stanza [5] is a mirror image of those of stanza [1], in the sense that the former are reversely arranged in comparison with the latter. Such an arrangement, whether intended or not, points a neat contrast between the opening and closing stanzas.

Let us now look at the metrical patterns of the *aghṣān* as they emerge from the application of Arabic scansion to them. Nothing, be it noted, is presupposed beyond the reasoned lengthening of the *one vowel* last considered. They are:

Aghṣān

– – –/∪ –	(Stanza [1])
– – –/∪ –	
∪ – –/∪ –	
∪ – –/∪ –	(Stanzas [2], [3], [4])
– – –/∪ –	
∪ – –/∪ –	
∪ – –/∪ –	(Stanza [5])
– – –/∪ –	
– – –/∪ –	

Applying the same scansion to the *maṭla'*, *kharjah* and *asmāṭ* and presupposing no more than the reasoned lengthening of the *two vowels* discussed earlier, we find:

Maṭla', kharjah, asmāṭ

– – –/∪ –//– – –/∪ – –//∪ – –/∪ –	*Kharjah, maṭla'*,[3]
∪ – –/∪ –//– – –/∪ – –//∪ – –/∪ –	[1], [2]
∪ – –/∪ –//– – –/∪ – –//– – –/∪ –	[4]

It is perhaps worth commenting, first, that if the /*ā*/ of *lā* in the first foot of the *simṭ* of stanza [3] is to be treated as short,[63] the *simṭ* pattern of [3] is exactly as in [1] and [2]; and secondly that, had account been taken of an observable Sp.A tendency towards the elimination (*takhfīf*) of gemination,[64] the scansion of the last section of the *simṭ* of [4] would also have put the latter into the same category.[65]

To sum up, Professor Monroe's theory of a Romance stress-syllabic pattern for al-Jazzār's *muwashshaḥ* is far from watertight. It is rooted in his belief that there is no such Arabic metre as – – – ∪ –(–), but, as we have seen, we have clear proof of the use of just such a metre in non-classical Arabic poetry – which, when all is said and done, is what the *muwashshaḥ* is. His riposte may well be that the Andalusian *muwashshaḥ* is known to have found its way into the Yemenite poetic repertoire[66] and that therein lies the explanation for the existence, in the Yemen, of a stress-syllabic pattern derived from the Spanish folk tradition of the *villancico*. But, in the event of his making such a riposte, it is for him to discharge the burden of proof. It is also for him to prove the truth of his observation: 'It is the lack of familiarity with the stress-syllabic nature of *muwashshaḥ* prosody that leads some scholars into serious pitfalls when editing or reading the texts'.[67] There may be some profit to be derived from a closer acquaintance with

Persian metres, on the one hand, and with the peculiarities of Sp.A, on the other.

(Since writing this paper, I have in fact encountered, in *Classical Arabic Poetry*, several instances of concessions to the peculiarities of Sp.A).

Notes

[1] Op. cit., 113.
[2] Ibid., 114.
[3] Ibid., 120.
[4] Ibid., 114.
[5] Ibid.
[6] Ibid.
[7] Ibid., 121, n.11.
[8] Ibid.
[9] Ibid., 114.
[10] Ibid.
[11] Ibid.
[12] Ibid.
[13] This is not denied by Monroe. He writes of 'a colloquial *kharja* including two words in Romance, which has been overlooked by past *kharja* scholars' (ibid., 113).
[14] The apparently masculine gender of *shū* is no obstacle. Apart from other reasons that could be cited in justification of the form, the use of masculine for feminine, when the reference is in fact to a woman, is not uncommon in Arabic poetry. On the currency of *shū*<*shūf* in Iraq, see R. J. McCarthy and F. Raffouli, *Spoken Arabic of Baghdad*, I, Beirut, 1964, 362 (cf. 360: 'shū shlōn ...' 'see how ...'). For Morocco see H. Mercier, *Méthode moderne d'arabe parlé marocain*, IV: *Dictionnaire arabe-français*, 2nd edn., Rabat, 1951, s.v. *šušu* ('... pour šuf šuf'). (From personal experience, I can say that the same form serves both genders.) It is perhaps worth noting that in Morocco the verb *shāf* is often used with the preposition *l*(= *li*) to mean 'to look for (s.th.) for (s.o.).' See, e.g., R.S.Harrell (ed.), *A Dictionary of Moroccan Arabic: Arabic-English*, Georgetown, 1966, 150, s.v. *šaf*: '*šuf-li ši-xedma* ... find some work for me'. Consequently, in our *kharjah*, the imperative *shū* could be taken as having the sense 'Go and get [me] the lad ...' as well as 'Just look at ...' or 'Go and see ...' i.e. 'Visit' (cf. Mercier, loc. cit.).
[15] Op. cit., 114.
[16] Ibid.
[17] Ibid.
[18] On this corpus see A. Jones, 'The Oxford Corpus of Andalusian *Muwashshaḥāt*', *Bull. of the British Society for Middle Studies*, IV, 1977, 42f.
[19] 'Romance Scansion', 54.
[20] Ibid.
[21] Ibid., 51.
[22] Op. cit., 114.

23 'Romance Scansion', 54 f.
24 Ibid., 55.
25 vii.
26 See *Hispano-Arabic Strophic Poetry: Studies by Samuel Miklos Stern* (ed. L. P. Harvey), Oxford, 1974, 32. For the four metres involved in the stanza given by Stern see the following references in Elwell-Sutton's *Persian Metres*: 4.7.07, p. 106; 2.3.09, p. 93; 2.4.05 (2), p. 95; 5.4.07 (2), p. 112. I should explain that I believe the metrical anomaly presented by *qamarun yaṭla'* in this stanza to be more apparent than real, for, in Andalusian Arabic the shifts *fa'al>fa'l* and *fa'l>fā'.l* are not rare (cf. Corriente, op. cit. infra in n. 47, 77 (5.1.6) and 62, n. 87). But, in any case, see Elwell-Sutton, op. cit., 4.5.05 (4), 188.
27 'Romance Scansion', 54.
28 Op. cit., 114.
29 Ibid., 121, n. 11.
30 Ibid.
31 'Romance Scansion', 55.
32 M.'A. Ghānim, 'Verse Used in Ṣan'ānī Songs', *Al-Abḥāth*, xxv, 1972, 20.
33 Ibid., 266.
34 Ibid., 47, 168.
35 Ibid., 49, 117 f.
36 Ibid., 34 f. Cf. 36.
37 Ibid., 36.
38 Monroe, who relies on the printed text of Nājī and Maḍur (Tunis, 1967), seems not to have consulted the manuscripts.
39 The consonant cluster /dd k/ in Monroe's *lā búdd kullū* is quite inadmissible. We must either supply an anaptyctic vowel to give the colloquial *buddı* or eliminate the gemination so as to give the equally colloquial *bud*, which we find in Ibn Quzmān, for example. (Cf. also Pers. *lā bud*.) Prosody, whether syllabic or quantitative, demands the latter. Secondly, the 3rd. masc. sing. pronoun suffixed to *kull* and represented in the Arabic text as *ḍammah* is clearly intended to derive its quantity from the colloquial and not from its classical counterpart as scanned according to Khalīlian rules, viz. *kulluhū*. I read it as *kullŭ*.
40 On the assumption, of course, that the middle section of the *kharjah* is to be scanned on the basis of the suggestions made in the preceding note.
41 Cf. W. Wright, *A Grammar of the Arabic Language*, Cambridge, 1951, II, 364 B.
42 Ibid., 382 D, 383 A.
43 Cf. Jones, 'Romance Scansion', 37: 'Ibn Bassām's decision to exclude *muwaššaḥāt* from his work [because most of the metres were not based on the rules of Classical Arabic metre] set a trend that is still current in the Arab world today. Hence many Arab specialists in Arabic poetry still ignore the *muwaššaḥ*.' Just how misleading classical features in non-classical verse can be is clearly illustrated by Pierre Cachia in 'The Egyptian *Mawwāl*', *J. of Arabic Literature* VIII, 1977, 84. Students of the

muwashshah would do well to note his comment: '... choice diction and unvocalised script can sometimes combine to conceal most of the differences between an uninflected *mawāliyā* and classical verse.' (The example he analyses dates from the fourteenth century.)

44 'Romance Scansion', 50 (penultimate paragraph).

45 A good example is provided by the negative *lā*, the quantity and quality of which are highly variable in popular pronunciations. One of the most interesting comments on this fact is to be found in McCarthy and Raffouli, I, 25: 'A keen ear will detect six [Baghdadi] pronunciations of this negative: *la*, *lā*, *la'*, *lā'*, *la'*, *lā'*. The pronunciation varies according to circumstances, emotion, etc.'

46 In this respect treatises on *ḥisbah* are particularly interesting as can be seen from, for example, al-Saqaṭī's work on the subject, written around the beginning of the thirteenth century. See 'Notes linguistiques' in G. S. Colin and E. Lévi-Provençal (edd.), *Un manuel hispanique de ḥisba*, Paris, 1931, 1–9.

47 On this crucial but complex question see F. Corriente, *A Grammatical Sketch of the Spanish Arabic Dialect Bundle*, Madrid, 1977, 60 ff. It is my view, based on first-hand knowledge of certain Moroccan dialects known for their affinities with Sp.A, that Corriente attaches far too much importance to the function of *matres lectionis* as orthographical devices to convey stress. In this and other areas the *Grammatical Sketch*, though in many respects a worthy manual, should be used with caution (see my review in *JSS*, XXV, 1980, 141–47).

48 Corriente, op. cit., p. 62, n. 87. Both the examples I cite derive from Al-Zubaydī, *Laḥn al-'awāmm*, ed. 'Abd al-Tawwāb, Cairo, 1964, 49, 251.

49 The sources are indicated by Corriente, loc. cit. The shift *fa'īl*>*fā'īl* still characterises pronunciations to be heard in certain parts of Morocco. (I am indebted to Dr M. Ben Madani for confirming my recollection on this point.)

50 The sources are indicated by Corriente, loc.cit. On *qādūm* see al-Zubaydī, 100.

51 See Corriente, loc. cit. On *ṭīḥāl* and *ṭīrāz* see al-Zubaydī, 76. On *ṭīḥāl* see Colin and Lévi-Provençal, (see n. 46), 3. Al-Zubaydī also notes *qiṭā'*< *qiṭa'*, 287.

52 See J. Grand'Henry, *Le parler arabe de Cherchell*, Louvain, 1972, 144; also my review *JSS*, XX, 1975, 136, 138 f.

53 No more than a moderately educated native speaker from the north of England would need any written indication of his need to abandon his short vowel in the articulation of 'pass', say, if it were in a rhyming position with 'farce'.

54 Cf. Jones, 'Romance Scansion', 37.

55 Cf. Stern, 43.

56 As, indeed, they are only too often regularised today by Middle Eastern editors of mediaeval Arabic texts, who feel no need to record the actual manuscript readings in the critical apparatus.

57 This is not to say that the writers of lyrical compositions never recited

them. However, on the modifications required in the event of recitation, see Stern, 18. Add to which that recitation does not necessarily exclude adjustment of quantity, stress, etc. to achieve dramatic effect.

[58] In addition to Cachia's observations (op. cit.), see for example, those of S. Fanjul in 'The Erotic Popular Mawwa:l in Egypt', *J. of Arabic Literature* VIII, 1977, 104–22.

[59] Cf. Cachia, 89.

[60] Stern, 45. Cf. 171.

[61] The importance of the correlation between the words and music of the mediaeval Andalusian *muwashshaḥ* seems to me to be implicit in Ibn Khaldūn's account of an incident in which we see the philosopher Ibn Bājjah (Avempace) as panegyrist of the governor of Zaragoza – by curious coincidence, the very city of which our al-Jazzār had been a native. Describing Ibn Bājjah as 'the composer of well-known melodies' (*ṣāḥib al-talāḥīn al-ma'rūfah*), Ibn Khaldūn clearly portrays him teaching a singing-girl, or singing-girls, a eulogistic *muwashshaḥ* of his own composition. The subsequent rendering leaves no doubt as to the nature of the performance: it was a *talḥīn*, according to Ibn Khaldūn (*Muqaddima*, ed. Quatremère, III, 393). Be that as it may, the character of the music of the mediaeval *muwashshaḥ* escapes us entirely (cf. Stern, 16). No one would dream of suggesting that any conclusions could be drawn from the music to which even the oldest *muwashshaḥ* is sung today. See F. Valderrama Martínez, *El cancionero de al-Hā'ik*, Tetuan, 1954, 35. Cf. P. García Barriuso, *La música hispano-musulmana en Marruecos*, Madrid, 1950, 31.

[62] See above p. 98, n. 49. Corriente, it should be noted, is prepared to accept that we might have *ghāyīb* for *ghāyib*, but he attributes the phenomenon to stress shift justified by poetic licence (p. 64, n. 91). On the possible influence of *'ayn* on the lengthening of a preceding vowel /a/ see Colin and Lévi-Provençal, 2 ff.

[63] See n. 45 above.

[64] Cf. Corriente, 6 (3.2.2.).

[65] Here I have in mind a gemination produced by the assimilation of /*dh*/ in *idh* to the /*ẓ*/ in *ẓallat*. On *takhfīf* in Persian scansion see Elwell-Sutton, op. cit., 5.

[66] See Stern, 19, 73, 76.

[67] Op. cit., 122, n. 18 (from 121).

Postscript

If we accept the recent argument that *mammā* may, in fact, not be a Spanish ('Mozarabic') word at all (see K. Whinnom, 'The *mamma* of the Kharjas', in *La Corónica* XI, 1, (autumn 1982), 11–17), al-Jazzar's *kharjah* contains no Romance elements at all.

The painted dome of the Ashrafiyyah in Ta'izz, Yemen

Ronald Lewcock

Foreword

In 1972 Professor Serjeant organised an expedition of Cambridge scholars to begin detailed research in the Yemen. I was asked to join and, through the generosity of the T. E. Lawrence Fund, I began architectural studies. One of the early results of this first journey was the publication, with Dr. G. R. Smith, of two preliminary reports on the mosques of Ta'izz.[1]

Since then, I have often returned to admire these buildings and, in particular, the beauty of the paintings in the domes. From the perspective of almost a decade, and a far wider knowledge of much of the two Yemens, it now seems to me that they are among the greatest works of man in South Arabia – a country extraordinarily rich in fine art and architecture – and of unique importance in the wider realm of Islamic art.

History and General Description

The Jāmi' al-Muẓaffar was built, at least in substantial part, by Sultan al-Muẓaffar Yūsuf (647–694/1249–1295). The Ashrafiyyah was built either by al-Ashraf I (694–697/1295–1297) or by al-Ashraf II (778–803/1376–1400) or by the two in succession.

The prayerhall of the mosque of Muẓaffar is covered with three large domes, and twelve smaller ones. That of the Ashrafiyyah by one large dome, flanked by eight small domes.

While it seems likely that all the domes were originally decorated internally, partly with bas-relief ornament (in the niches under the squinch arches and in the blind openings simulating window openings in the drums) and partly by painted decorations, only the largest domes and a few of the smaller ones have preserved a substantial amount of the painted decoration. The reason for this seems to have been the enthusiasm of zealots in repainting the interiors of the prayerhalls with whitewash as far as it could be painted or thrown – the larger dome decorations have been preserved mainly because they were out of reach.

There is therefore an intriguing possibility that the original paintings of some of the lower domes, and of the lower sections of the large domes, may be preserved beneath the layers of whitewash. Only careful analysis will establish whether this is so, and then only the most skilful conservation by professional experts will enable them to be revealed again, if, indeed, it can be done at all. Even more tragic is the deterioration of the condition of the external surfaces of the domes during the last ten years, since the photographs published here were taken in 1972. The resulting penetration of water has severely damaged many of the paintings, so that the possibility of preserving and restoring them completely is now a matter of some doubt.

The decoration of the main dome of the Ashrafiyyah

(The numbers in brackets identify design elements for later discussion)

The bowl of the dome is decorated with a central rosette of 24 lobes (1). A monumental *naskhī* inscription of a verse from the Qur'ān surrounds it.

A similar monumental *naskhī* inscription of verses from the Qur'ān forms the lower border of the dome; it is divided into four sections by large 8-lobed rosettes, each containing two concentric circles within which is a smaller rosette of irregular lobing (2).

A third Quranic inscription stands above the lowest one, executed this time in eastern kufic, divided into twelve panels by doubled vertical shafts (3) which rise up through the lettering to support a decorative painted arcade of five-cusped arches (4), the centre of each of which is linked in turn to a ring encircling the central inscription of the dome by a double shaft (5).

A number of features of the shafting deserve special attention. Alternate double-shafts rise above the kufic inscription only a short distance before they divide to encircle, again alternately, spiralling rosettes, which might almost be attempts to represent fireworks ('Catherine-wheels') (6) and twelve-pointed stars in three concentric rings, which are also made to appear to be spiralling by the way they are coloured and shaded (7).

The double shafts then move up together again until they divide to form the cusped arches. But at the top of each of these they divide again and proceed towards the central ring, interrupted only by a tiny knot near the top (8).

Between these knots, small fleur-de-lis shaped arrow heads grow out from the central ring, each with a smaller fleur-de-lis in its centre (9).

The other main double-shafts rise above the kufic lettering to large four-looped knots (10) with adze or axe forms outlined between the shafts above them (11).

Finally, in the space between every pair of main double shafts, there rises above the kufic lettering a second, minor, double-shaft motif. Linked to the main shafts by horizontals which form a frame above the letters, this motif leaves the inscription after forming a semi-circle around a palmette motif (12). It then moves upwards to terminate in another fleur-de-lis arrow head (13). But, before it reaches this, the shaft is studded in the centre with spiralling rosettes not unlike swastikas. They also give the illusion – perhaps this is intentional – of spiralling fireworks (14). In colour, the eastern kufic, the shafts, bands and cusped arches are all gold; the *naskhī* inscriptions and most of the decorative features are white.

Running uniformly behind all these motifs is a spiralling vine decoration with leaves and flowers, creating a rich floral field on a blue background (15).

The circular drum of the dome is alternately pierced by windows and niches. Both have shell scallopping of ancient Umayyad type which was in widespread use over a long period. The rear walls of the niches are pierced in a variety of overall geometric patterns made up of straight lines radiating from star-shaped openings evenly spaced across the surfaces (16). A similarly patterned bas-relief covers the wall of the drum between the arches, with the difference that the patterns radiate from large half-rosettes (17).

Below the circular drum, an octagonal drum has a painted chevron ornament in a band (18) below which the surface of the drum is painted in an extremely beautiful pattern with alternate triangles framing hexagons (containing three open triangles fitted together) and star-rosettes of geometrical construction (19). This decoration is highlighted in lime-green and dark pink.

The squinch arches contain domes which are decorated in a radiating arabesque ornament (20). Between them, blind rectangular windows are crowned with circular blind recesses, and these contain star patterns based on triangles (21). The surface in front of them had a bold, free lily pattern (21A).

The cusped arches over the latter, and the squinch arches themselves, have narrow painted bands of alternately red and white voussoirs (22).

Finally, one range below the main squinch arches there are small squinch arches containing plaster bas-reliefs, now whitewashed over, with elaborately intertwining arabesques in different styles, with superimposed bands of trilobed arches overlaying them (23). Intermediate panels have rich intertwining arabesques in a different design (24) and the central feature is a circular, deeply recessed shell boss (25).

The decorations on one of the Muẓaffar mosque domes

These will be only briefly considered for comparison purposes. The dome chosen is the eastern one. Here a floral arabesque (26) surrounded the central boss, itself already obscured by damp penetration in 1972 when the photograph reproduced here was taken (Plate 4). Outside of this a free monumental Quranic inscription is divided into four sections by rondels, each again containing a floral arabesque pattern (27). A further floral arabesque pattern encircles the dome to frame the central pattern (28).

The main surface of the dome outside of the central area is filled with eight large waterpot-shaped medallions outlined in broad dark ornamented bands. Alternate waterpots have geometrical overall patterns of the type referred to in one of the areas of the Ashrafiyyah – no. 16 (29). An additional feature is that the central stars are filled with 4-vaned spirals of the swastika type identified as (14) above. The other medallions have complex overall patterns of arabesques intertwined with straight lines (30). The surface between the medallions has a further complex arabesque pattern (31) and the dome surface is completed with a continuous band of inscription.

The circular string course below the dome is decorated with a row of curious, almost semicircular arches standing on a horizontal step on top of columns, all against a floral arabesque background (32). Below, the rows of window and niche arches have chevron patterns and stripes of various types (33). The niches below have bold floral patterns, such as found on plates, and indeed some of them are set in circles, with a central floral star (34). The main squinch arches have patterns extremely close to those of the Ashrafiyyah (35), and the surface in between has an ingenious overall pattern of overlapping and intertwining floral rosettes (36).

Decorative Style

In the articles published in 1974 we identified the decorations of the domes as related to Egyptian work at the end of the 7th/13th century and the beginning of the 8th/14th century.[2] The possibility that the decorations may be later merits a more detailed examination of the evidence. This is an important issue in ascertaining the dates of work on the building, which are in dispute between the reigns of the two Sultans al-Ashraf.[3] Detailed examination is particularly desirable in view of the increased evidence that is available as a result of the growing number of studies on the development of the Mamluk styles that have been made in recent years.[4]

In the paragraphs that follow I have examined the decorative elements one by one in an attempt to date the fashionable period when each motif was in use in the Islamic art of other areas and determine, if possible, the date of its original appearance and its provenance. I hope in this way to build up a general body of evidence which will suggest the main source of the style of the design, and even the approximate date of work of executing the painting and reliefs.

Considering the decorations on the main dome of the Ashrafiyyah first, with the numbers below referring to the decorative elements already identified:

Of the large *rosettes*, that in the centre of the dome (1) is sufficiently general in type to be difficult to date to any particular place or period. But the large 8-lobed rosettes on the lower edges of the dome (2) are more specific in form, and resemble elements of Mamluk art in Egypt and Syria in the 8th/14th century in evidence in metalwork and book decoration (Plates 5 and 6).[5]

The division of the dome surface with *double-shafts carrying cusped arches* (3), (4), (10) etc., is paralleled in much decoration in the Islamic world in the 7th/13th and 8th/14th century, notably in Hispano-Moorish, Anatolian and Indian examples. An important example cited by Creswell is a panel at the base of the minaret of Sayyidnā al-Ḥusayn which is assumed by him to be contemporary with the inscription on the gate of the minaret, which is dated 634/1237.[6] That panel is, however, almost exactly similar, in its particular combination of forms, to two important examples of a century later – first, the courtyard panels of the Bū ʿInāniyyah Madrasah in Fez (751–756/1350–3),[7] and second, the main central tympanums and other decorations of the Mirador and the Court of the Lions of the Alhambra, Granada (Plate 3, 755–794/1354–91).[8] This combination of forms was therefore apparently the height of fashion around 750/1350 in western

Islamic architecture; it seems unlikely that it could have been executed over a century earlier in Cairo.

It is worth noting at this point that the extremely beautiful monumental *naskhī* inscriptions are in a style very similar to that of the celebrated calligraphy of the Great Mosque in Ashtarjān, Persia (715/1315),[9] as well as, of course, resembling closely the calligraphy of a series of Mamluk metalwork pieces actually made for the Rasulid court in Taʿizz, and other celebrated pieces of Mamluk metalwork, which are all datable to the period 689–751/1290–1350.[10] Many of these pieces also have double-shaft ornament of types (3), (10), etc.[11]

The large *knots* appearing on the doubled shafts (10), (8) are already evident in eastern kufic inscriptions in the 7th/13th century.[12] More elaborate forms of the knotting are to be found in Anatolian Seljuk architecture.[13] *Cusped arches* (4) are also found in the 7th/13th century in many areas of Islam.[14] Finally, *eastern kufic* (3) sometimes carrying knotting in its vertical shafts, was a common feature of 8th/14th century Mamluk art.[15]

Spiralling rosettes, both large (6) and small (14) are a feature of Mamluk art in the early 8th/14th century. But while the latter can be paralleled exactly (in cloth), that example is assumed to be from the 9th/15th century,[16] whereas the generic type, similar except that it has six or eight vanes instead of four, is common in examples of metalwork of the period from 689/1290 to 731/1330, some of them made for the Sultan in Yemen.[17] An example of the spiralling rosette on a building is that on the Madrasah-Mausoleum of Zayn al-Dīn Yūsuf in Cairo (697/1298) where it is carved in stone over some of the windows.[18] Exact precedent for the dotting and rainbow colouring of the spirals in the Ashrafiyyah (6) is not yet established.

The equivalent motifs of the *12-pointed stars* looking rather like concentric chevron rosettes (7) have similar models in the central stars of some pages of calligraphy (e.g. Plate 7).[19] Their use in isolation is unusual, except in Indian Islamic, where concentric floral rosettes are sometimes found on buildings (e.g. Jamaat Khana Masjid, Delhi, c. 720/1320 (?)).[20] Ettinghausen has, however, noted the appearance of these rosettes in a Qur'ān otherwise Mamluk in style.[21] But the latter are far removed from the simple geometry of the rosettes in the Ashrafiyyah.

The use of fleur-de-lis shapes as terminals (9) is common throughout Islamic art, and particularly so in the Yemen.[22] Not surprisingly, it was a frequent ornament in 8th/14th century Mamluk art (e.g. background floral ornament of the monumental kufic in the Sultan Ḥasan Madrasah, Cairo, 758–764/1356–1362).[23] Similarly, *axehead forms* (11) occur in Mamluk art (cf. ceramic strainer in Museum of Islamic art, Item no. 1288),[24] as do *palmette* forms (12), the latter on metalwork of the period of al-Nāṣir Muḥammad and his successors (*c.* 689–751/1290–1350).[25]

The peculiar combination of *arrow on a shaft* pointing up into the centre of a cusped arch (13) is evident in the examples referred to above, from Cairo (Minaret of Sayyidnā al-Ḥusayn), Fez (Madrasah of Bū ʿInāniyyah) and the Alhambra – cf. Plate 3.

The overall background of *spiralling vines and leaves* across the dome (15), has, of course, an ancient tradition; but close parallels in detailed character may be seen in the background to the monumental kufic of the Madrasah of Sultan Ḥasan, Cairo, 758–764/1356–1362. Other fine examples may be seen in the Quranic illuminations of the period around 735/1334.[26]

Bands of *chevron* ornament (18) were used in Anatolian Seljuk architecture before being adopted in Mamluk architecture for the north-east portal of the Mosque of Baybars (665–8/1266–9).[27]

Star-rosettes of the type used in the pattern of the circular drum (19) are another common feature of 8th/14th century Mamluk decoration, both in carpentry, in inlaid doors and shutters, and in the illumination of Qur'āns.[28] A similar precedent exists for overall star patterns of straight lines (16) and (29),[29] although these can be taken back further in time to Anatolian Seljuk architectural decorations.

The beautiful *radiating arabesque patterns* of the squinch domes (20) and (35) likewise have close parallels with both Mamluk book illuminations of the 8th/14th century (Plate 7, centre), and, in their lower part, with decorations on metalwork (e.g. Plate 6).[30]

Star patterns based on triangles are again widespread, but close parallels to the types found here (21) are observable in Mamluk art (Plate 5, centre and Plate 8) not only in crafts but in architecture (Cairo, Ṭaybarsiyyah Madrasah, *miḥrāb*, 709/1309–10).[31]

Bold free *arabesque* patterns (21A), (26), (27), (28), (31), are characteristic of all the best work of Mamluk craftsmen in many different materials (Plates 6 and 8). Superimposed and intertwining arabesques are a feature of Andalusian and Moorish Islamic in particular, but were in widespread use in other parts of the Islamic world by the end of the 7th/13th century (Lājīn's pulpit, once in the Mosque of Ibn Ṭūlūn, 696/1296,[32] Madrasah-Mausoleum of Qarāsunqur, 700/1300–1, Cairo).[33]

The *striped stone work arch* patterns (22) first became popular in Cairo after al-Nāṣir Muḥammad built the Qaṣr al-Ablaq in the Citadel (713/1313), probably copied from the palace of the same name in Damascus (665/1266–7).[34] In red and white, this technique was used in the arches flanking the interior door of the portico of the Mosque of Sultan Ḥasan, Cairo (758–64/1356–62), apparently modelled on Hispano-Moorish examples.[35]

The large eastern dome of the Muẓaffar mosque is clearly designed by a different hand, and while many features suggest that it is, at least in part, almost contemporary, there is not sufficient space here to do more than draw attention to the provenance and style of some of the elements not already dealt with above. (It is hoped to publish a more detailed and systematic study of the decoration of the Muẓaffar mosque at a later date.)

The most striking features of this dome are the large *waterpot-shaped medallions* (29) and (30). Similar motifs were in widespread use over a long period in Quranic illumination.[36] In architectural decoration they appeared in Cairo on the Madrasah and Mausoleum of the Emir Sunqur Saʿdī

(715/1315)[37] and the Mosque of the Emir Ḥusayn (719/1319),[38] and continued in occasional use thereafter. On wall decorations, both internally and externally, their appearance was quite similar to those on the Muẓaffar dome, except that they were usually free of a supporting moulding, and had fleur-de-lis ornaments both top and bottom. Arabesque ornaments of a type extremely close to those between the medallions (31) likewise appeared in Cairo in the dome decoration of the Madrasah-Mausoleum of Zayn al-Dīn Yūsuf (697/1298) and the Madrasah-Mausoleum of Sultan al-Nāṣir Muḥammad (695–703/1295–6 – 1303–4).[39]

The use of bold *chevron* and striped patterning framing arches and niches (33) was a fashion in Cairo from the period of at least the Mausoleum of Qalā'ūn (684/1285) onwards.[40] The precedent for plain striped patterning of arches is discussed above.

As has already been mentioned, the decoration of the semidome niches within large squinch arches (35) is almost identical with that of the Ashrafiyyah, an indication that the work above may be almost contemporary in date.

The walls of the corner niches in the octagonal drum (34) seem to be decorated in imitation of precious plates of Mesopotamian and Fatimid, and possibly Persian, provenance. No precedent for such a practice in decorative painting is known, but it seems to reflect a fashion for setting precious ceramic plates into walls as ornamentation, a practice that has survived down to the present day in many parts of the Islamic world.[41]

Conclusion

The consistently fine quality of design and execution of these ceilings, particularly that of the Ashrafiyyah, argue that each was conceived and executed on a coherent scheme over a short period under the direction of a leading master. Who that master may have been we have as yet no way of knowing, although it is possible that cleaning may yet reveal his signature. In the meantime, among the mass of evidence discussed above, there is a clear indication that the painted domes were executed in the style current in the period between 715/1315 and 762/1360, and probably still fashionable in the 770s/1370s and 780s/1380s.

The dome decoration of the Ashrafiyyah was, in its general design and many of its features, unlike any other such decoration of which we have knowledge. It was, interestingly enough, apparently derived in part from sources other than purely architectural decoration. While much of the 8th/14th century was marked by internationalism, by a tendency for artists and craftsmen to travel and for ideas to be interchanged between many different parts of the Islamic world, we have no reason to suppose that the designer of these decorations came from further afield than the Mamluk realms of Egypt and Syria – whose art we already know the Rasulids to have admired.[42]

In overall pattern the Ashrafiyyah dome follows the arrangement typical in much metalwork (cf. Plate 6) but it involves a richness of imagination and a diversity of motifs far in excess of anything normally demanded of a craftsman working in a small compass. That it has been achieved so masterfully, and with such subtleties of colour and form, is an indication of the outstanding calibre of the artists and craftsmen who accomplished it. They achieve a level of artistic design, colouring and execution equal to work of the highest quality in the Islamic world at that period – which also saw the construction of the Mosque-Madrasah-Mausoleum of Sultan Ḥasan in Cairo, the Madrasah of Bū ʿInāniyyah in Fez, and the two great courts of the Alhambra at Granada.

It is to be hoped that the Yemeni government will ensure that these dome paintings, which were recently severely damaged by water, will be safely protected against further deterioration. Their interest is not limited by national boundaries. They are singular in their type and quality; until a decade ago they were in an extraordinarily perfect state of preservation; and they are surely unique in their beauty and magnificence among dome paintings in the Mamluk style.

Notes

[1] R. B. Lewcock and G. R. Smith, 'Three Medieval Mosques in the Yemen', Parts I and II, in *Oriental Art*, xx, 1, 1–12 and xx, 2, 192–203.

[2] Op. cit., 2, 200–2.

[3] Op. cit., 2, 192 and 200.

[4] For an extensive recent bibliography the reader is referred to the catalogue of the exhibition *Art of the Mamluks* prepared by Esin Atil, published by the Smithsonian Institution Press, Washington, D.C., 1981, and the forthcoming proceedings of the symposium 'Art of the Mamluks', May, 1981, to be published in a special volume of *Muqarnas*.

[5] Discussed in G. Bosch, J. Carswell and G. Petherbridge, *Islamic Bindings and Bookmaking*, Catalogue of an Exhibition at The Oriental Institute, University of Chicago, May–August 1981, 161.

[6] K. A. C. Creswell, *Muslim Architecture of Egypt*, II, 83–4, Plate 29b.

[7] Cf. D. Hill and L. Golvin, *Islamic Architecture in North Africa*, Plate 313.

[8] Cf. T. Burchkhardt, *Art of Islam*, London, 1976, Plate 57 and O. Grabar, *The Alhambra*, London, 1978, Plate 51, 61, 115.

[9] M. Rogers, *The Spread of Islam*, London, 1976, 78 top right.

[10] E. Atil, op. cit., 64–5, 81–4, 86–99, etc.

[11] e.g. Item Catalogue No. 80, Museum of Islamic Art, Cairo, Penbox in the name of Sultan al-Nāṣir Muḥammad, c. 731/1330.

[12] e.g. Delhi, Tomb of Iltutmish (633/1235), v. P. Brown, *Indian Architecture, Islamic Period*, Bombay, 1956, Plate VIII.

[13] E.g. Sivas, Turbe of Izzuddin Kaikaus (617/1220), v. R. A. Jairazbhoy, *Outline of Islamic Architecture*, London 1972, Plate 99.

[14] See note 12 above.

[15] E.g. Nazi Zain-al-Din, *Atlas of Arabic Calligraphy*, Plates 312, 323, etc. and M. Lings, *The Quranic Art of Calligraphy and Illumination*, London, 1976, plates 42, 43 and 44.

[16] E. Atil, op. cit., 238.
[17] Ibid, 62–3, 67, 86–7, etc.
[18] K. A. C. Cresswell, op. cit., Plate 82, d.
[19] M. Lings, op. cit., 78, Plate 37.
[20] P. Brown, op. cit., Plate C1.
[21] R. Ettinghausen, *Arab Painting*, Lausanne, 1962, 173 and M. Lings, op. cit., Plate 65.
[22] Cf. R. B. Serjeant and Ronald Lewcock, *Ṣan'ā', an Arabian Islamic City*, London, 1983.
[23] T. Burckhardt, op. cit., Fig. 26.
[24] Guide to the Museum of Islamic Art, Cairo, 1373/1953, Fig. 10.
[25] Wafiyya 'Izzī, 'Objects bearing the name of an-Nāṣir Muḥammad and his successors' in *Colloque International sur l'Histoire du Caire*, Cairo, 1969–72, 235–241; and E. Atil, op. cit., 87.
[26] M. Lings, op. cit., Plate 63.
[27] R. A. Jairazbhoy, op. cit., Plate 82. K. A. C. Creswell, op. cit., Plate 50 b and c.
[28] M. Lings, op. cit., Plates 59 and 65, dating respectively from 713/1313 and 766–778/1363–1376.
[29] M. Lings, op. cit., Plate 105, dating from 703/1303, probably Andalusian.
[30] E. Atil, op. cit., 99.
[31] K. A. C. Creswell, op. cit., ii, 253–4, Plate 99 b.
[32] Victoria and Albert Museum, v. S. Lane-Poole, *Art of the Saracens in Egypt*, London, 1886, Figs. 35–8.
[33] K. A. C. Creswell, op. cit., ii, Plate 89 c.
[34] Ibid. 171–2, 260–4, Fig. 144.
[35] Burckhardt, op. cit. Plate 129.
[36] M. Lings, op. cit., Plates 11, 12, 14, 15, 16, 23, 42, 43, 44, 67, 98, etc.
[37] K. A. C. Creswell, op. cit., ii, Plates 101 c, 102 d, etc.
[38] Ibid, Plate 104 a.
[39] Ibid, Plates 84 c and 86 b.
[40] Ibid, Plates 108 b, 112 a, 114 c.
[41] Notably in Oman, East Africa and Nigeria.
[42] E. Atil, op. cit., 62.

Plates

Plate 1. The painted great dome of the Ashrafiyyah
Plate 2. The springing and drum of the great dome of the Ashrafiyyah
Plate 3. Part of the decoration of the Mirador de la Daraxa, Court of the Myrtles, Alhambra, Spain (c. 755–794/1354–91 (?))
Plate 4. The painted decoration on the large eastern dome of the Muẓaffar mosque, Ta'izz
Plate 5. Leather book cover, Egypt/Syria, 8th/14th century. Chester Beatty Library Moritz Collection 20. (cf. note 5)
Plate 6. Lamp made in brass inlaid with silver and gold. Mamluk, second half of 8th/14th century

Plate 7. End page of a Qur'ān in a style typical of 8th/14th century Mamluk illumination (cf. note 19)
Plate 8. Brass plated *kursī* in the name of Sultan al-Nāṣir Muḥammad (c. 720/1320). Cairo, Museum of Islamic Art, Cat. No. 61

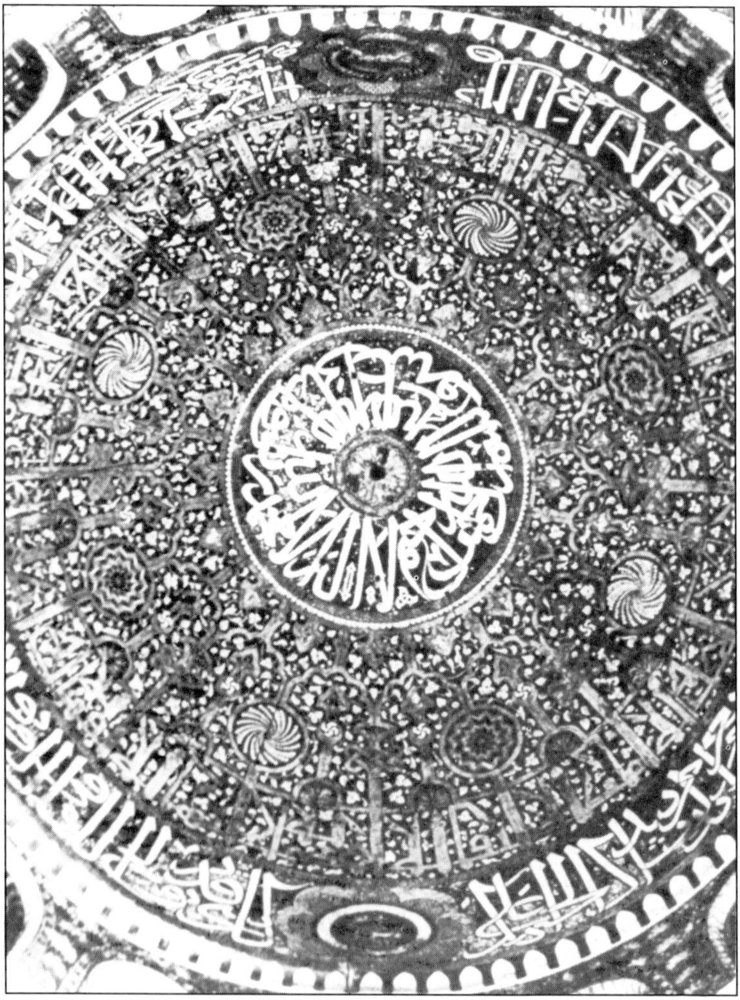

1

2

5

6

7

8

The Mustanṣiriyyah *Madrasah* and its role in Islamic education

Sami al-Sakkar

When asked to contribute to a collection of papers in honour of Professor Serjeant, I thought that the above subject would be a suitable one, remembering that Professor Serjeant has spent most of his life as a teacher and educationist. But the topic of the Mustanṣiriyyah *madrasah* is a wide one and deserves a long study. I shall confine myself here to some aspects only of this subject.

Teaching and education in Islam

Before dealing with the main topic of my paper a few words should be said about teaching and education in Islam. It is a well-known fact that Islam from the first moment of its existence, ordered Muslims to learn the arts of reading and writing, as it is clear from the first *sūrah* of the Qur'ān. '*Iqra' bi-'smi rabbika*' and '*Iqra' wa-rabbuka 'l-akram, alladhī 'allama bi-'l-qalam, 'allama 'l-insāna mā lam ya'lam.*' In these verses the pen and teaching are mentioned and God himself is described as the teacher who teaches human beings important facts about life. It was also made clear in these verses that the means for teaching are reading and writing. And so it was not strange to see the Prophet offering the prisoners at Badr the opportunity to buy their freedom by teaching reading and writing to the Muslim children in Medina.

Also, it is not strange to find so many of the Prophet's Traditions praising knowledge and scholars. From here commenced the interest of Muslims in teaching and learning, an interest which continued throughout the ages and in the whole of the Islamic World. As a matter of fact, the impact of this attitude was not limited to Muslim countries, it crossed the borders into Europe, in particular via Muslim Spain.

Indeed it is clear that one factor which led to the establishment of universities in Europe in the Middle Ages was the rich literature of many kinds which arrived there from the Arab World. There, especially in Muslim Spain, many works were translated from Arabic into Latin, or from Hebrew translations of Arabic. The latter were carried out by the Jews of the Iberian peninsula.

Moreover, as Sa'īd Nafīsī, President of the Iranian Academy, has indicated, Europeans followed the example of Muslim colleges like the Niẓāmiyyah of Baghdad in such matters as professors and instructors, the wearing of a black gown and sitting on a platform.

Establishment of *madrasahs* in Islam

It is an accepted fact among scholars of Islamic history that the mosque was the centre of all communal activities. In addition to being a place of worship, it was a sort of assembly hall where Muslims met to discuss common issues and take decisions connected with politics and war. It was also a courthouse where disputes and conflicts were resolved, as well as a club where Muslims could meet and exchange views about matters concerning their daily life. At the same time, it was a school where they could study and learn things connected with their religious and worldly affairs, including the reading of literature and especially poetry which they used to recite there, as happened during the time of the Prophet, when the poet Kaʿb b. Zuhayr recited his poem known as *Bānat Suʿād* in the Prophet's mosque in Medina. So it is possible to say that the mosque was the first Muslim school and continued to function as such throughout Islamic history, even down to the present time. But from the early days of their history, the Muslims felt the need for another place besides the mosque to be dedicated to teaching, especially since the Prophet did not confine himself to the mosque when teaching the Muslims; he used many other places as well. This tradition was followed by several scholars even in the first/seventh century like ʿAbd Allāh b. ʿAbbās, who used an ordinary house in al-Ṭā'if as a teaching centre. There are many similar references to scholars who taught in various places, during the first three centuries of Islam.

However, the earliest official attempt to establish a multi-purpose educational institute can be traced back to the time of the Abbasid caliph al-Muʿtaḍid who, it is related, planned to build a complex of buildings within his palace containing dormitories and departments for scholars of various disciplines and sciences, theoretical and practical, and to grant those schemes generous stipends. Anyone who chose to study one of those sciences could go there and become a student. However the authorities who transmitted this information did not say whether this institute was called *madrasah*. We are even uncertain whether or not this institute actually saw the light of day.

The word *madrasah* (plur. *madāris*) was known to the traditionalist Muslim, as it was mentioned in the Prophet's Traditions; the Muslims were ordered to study the Qur'ān. Also the word *madrasah* was mentioned in a poem of Diʿbil al-Khuzāʿī as a place for studying the Qur'ān.

However, the *madrasah* in its conventional sense was the product of the fourth/tenth century, although Ghunaymah thinks that it did not come into existence until the beginning of the fifth/eleventh century. But we have firm information about a *madrasah* establishment in Bust, a city in the eastern region of the Islamic world in the middle of the fourth/tenth century, and still more *madrasahs* were built in the second half of this century. But the most important *madrasashs* were established in the middle of the fifth/eleventh century, when the Seljuq minister Niẓām al-Mulk began to establish his colleges in many different regions of the Islamic world, among which the most important was that of Baghdad. This college attracted the attention of scholars from all over the Islamic world. Many books and papers have been written on it and there is no need to elaborate on this subject, but it is necessary to touch one controversial point connected with this college, namely that, with its establishment, the Islamic world witnessed the birth of 'official' institutions for teaching. One can claim on the one hand that *madrasahs* were official institutions, because they were established by persons who occupied high positions in the Islamic state. On the other hand, one can also claim that they were private institutions, because those colleges were financed by private funds, as *waqf* documents show.

Also it is noteworthy to say that those colleges became an example followed by Muslims in many parts of the Islamic world, especially by the Zangids in Syria and the Ayyubids in Egypt, and later by the Mamluks and Ottomans in the regions they ruled.

It should also be mentioned what the motives behind the establishment of those colleges were. Many scholars believe that they were established to check the expansion of Shiʿism in the provinces ruled by the Buwayhids in the east and the Fatimids in the west. But there is another opinion which says that the establishment of such colleges was a result of the strong competition which took place in the fifth/eleventh century between the different Sunnī schools of thought represented by the Seljuq sultans who adhered to the Ḥanafī *madhhab* and the Abbasid caliphs who followed the Shāfiʿī school which was also the *madhhab* of the famous minister Niẓām al-Mulk. Although this is a very important point, it need not be discussed further in this article. It is enough to say that this competition led to the establishment of colleges in which more than one single *madhhab* was taught. The most famous example of this kind of college is the Mustanṣiriyyah which set the example for many other colleges of this sort, like the Ṣāliḥiyyah and that of Sultan Ḥasan in Cairo and the Sulaymāniyyah in Mecca.

The Mustanṣiriyyah

Before the end of the sixth/twelfth century, the tradition of founding colleges had become established among rulers, scholars and the rich, men and women alike. The number of colleges increased in the main cities of the Islamic world. The Abbasid capital, Baghdad, had the lion's share of those colleges, their number exceeding 34 in certain periods.

The famous traveller Ibn Jubayr alone saw 30 of them in the eastern sector of Baghdad during his visit to the city, which took place 580/1184, but the most important college in the Abbasid capital was built later by the caliph al-Munṣtansir, which is the main subject of this paper.

The Establishment of the Mustanṣiriyyah

The end of the sixth/twelfth century and the beginning of the seventh/thirteenth witnessed the revival of the Abbasid caliphate during the reign of the two caliphs al-Naṣīr and al Mustanṣir; the first was able to secure power from the Seljuqs and to consolidate his position in Baghdad and the Iraqi regions, as well as in the neighbouring provinces. Those achievements had helped a great deal to create a new movement of cultural and architectural progress which continued until the days of al-Munstanṣir who became caliph in 623/1226. Our college could, therefore, be considered one of the fruits of that movement. As a matter of fact, the cultural atmosphere in Baghdad was such as to encourage the establishment of more cultural institutions. The caliph was aware of this fact, and so he decided to establish a new college, or rather a university, different from those colleges previously established.

The old colleges were usually dedicated to one school of *fiqh* (or two schools in some exceptional cases, e.g. the Fāḍiliyyah, established in Cairo in 580/1184, for the Shāfiʿī and Mālikī schools). He wanted his university to be opened to all Sunnī schools of thought, which enjoyed, at that time, almost equivalent positions in Baghdad. Furthermore, he was aware that the establishment of single-school colleges had instigated acute competition between the *madhhabs* which resulted in the fragmentation of Muslim unity. It was his duty as guardian of all Muslims – differences of *madhhab* notwithstanding – to take care of all of them, and to give them equal chances of learning, as well as to regain their intellectual unity in order to secure for Baghdad its position as the centre of the Islamic world.

The foundations of this university were laid in 625/1227, but the building was not finished until 631/1234. It was one of the finest buildings to be seen in the capital and it was even suggested that no other building on earth was better than the Mustanṣiriyyah! As a matter of fact the main building still stands to prove to our generation the grand conception and elegance of the Islamic architecture it represented, in spite of the suffering and destruction that the building sustained (it was once used for a long time as a warehouse). Fortunately, the Iraqi government was able in 1944 to save this building and restore it to its original function, and it is now used as a library of Arabic manuscripts.

The location of this university overlooking the Tigris, together with its beautiful Abbasid style gives it a character unique among Islamic monuments. The two-storey building contains big lecture rooms and *īwāns* which were used as classrooms, as well as many smaller rooms for student dormitories. It also contains a mosque which was sometimes used as a *jāmiʿ* for the public. The whole compound was protected by a strong dike built on the bank of the river to keep it safe from the flooding of the Tigris. There was also a water wheel to carry river water to the university tanks, which was then piped into a special tank for ablution (*mazammalah*). The outer walls of the main building were finely decorated with inscriptions engraved on bricks commemorating the foundation of the university. Fortunately this inscription is still intact.

The Mustanṣiriyyah was a residential institution, equipped with bathrooms for the students and a barber to take care of them. There was also a big kitchen and storerooms for all sorts of materials needed in the university, including cooking utensils, foodstuffs, soap, clothing, lamps, oil, ink and writing paper. A beautiful garden was annexed to the compound, with windows from where the caliph could observe what happened inside the university, as he was so much attached to that institution.

A special clock was erected for this university, which was described by historians as a wonder of its time. In the year 633/1235, a large *īwān* was built opposite the clock and a seat for a professor of medicine was placed there, so that patients could call on him for medical treatment. Also, this *īwān* served as a lecture hall for medical students.

The opening ceremony and reading of the charter

It is of interest to describe the opening ceremony of this university, because it shows the importance which the caliph had given it. He was anxious to attend the ceremony personally along with senior government officials, scholars, Ṣūfīs and other notables. As part of the official ceremonies, the *waqf* documents and the charter of the basic regulations of the university were read and made public. Also, robes of honours and gifts were awarded to the professors, building supervisors and various high-ranking officials. This occasion was colourfully described by poets who also praised the founder of the university.

The charter contained guidelines concerning university affairs, including the number of students to be admitted, which was fixed at sixty-two students for each school (*madhhab*), plus one professor, four instructors (*mu'īd*) and one imam for prayer for each school. The charter also stipulated the establishment of a Qu'rān school or department (Dār al-Qur'ān) which admitted 30 orphan boys to be taught Qur'ān recitation by a shaykh and instructor whose duty was to help them to memorise the Holy Book. The charter also contained provisions for the establishment of a school or department of prophetic Traditions (Dār al-Ḥadīth), which admitted ten students to read *Ḥadīth* under a highly qualified shaykh assisted by two readers (sing. *qārī'*). Moreover, it was stipulated that a professor of Arabic grammar would be appointed to teach all those students Arabic. As for medicine to which we have referred elsewhere, the charter fixed the number of students of this discipline at ten, which made the total number of students in the Mustanṣiriyyah 298, and the number of the teaching staff, 30.

In addition to that, the charter included provisions for a librarian to be assisted by two officials. There was also an administrative body composed of a director (*nāẓir*), supervisor (*mushrif*), clerk and a number of storekeepers, builders, bathroom workers, cooks and porters. The director and the supervisor were usually chosen from among high-ranking personalities (one *nāẓir* was a judge). It seems that the *nāẓir* was in charge of running the university, while the supervisor was to take care of student affairs.

The university also had its *khaṭīb* for the Friday prayer, a Qur'ān reader qualified in the seven different recitations, a preacher and a muezzin, plus the four imams mentioned above. The university professors had the privilege of being furnished with a well-equipped mule for their transport.

The university building was divided, for the purpose of accommodation, into four quarters, and each quarter was given to one *madhhab*, while the inner halls were used for lectures. The caliph had a window other than the one already mentioned, overlooking one of those lecture halls, through which to watch and listen to the lectures delivered.

The outer *īwāns* overlooking the courtyard were used for different purposes, including receptions held in honour of kings and important personalities.

Faculties and Departments

Needless to say, the Faculty of *Fiqh* was the dominant institution in the Mustanṣiriyyah and constituted its main body. Sufficient reference has been made to this discipline above, so we may pass on to say a few words about the other departments which were established within the Mustanṣiriyyah campus.

1. *Qur'ān Department (Dār al-Qur'ān)*

We have mentioned this department above, but it is necessary to mention here that the students of the Qur'ān had a ration of three *raṭls* of bread and a plateful of cooked meal a day, plus a monthly grant of thirteen carats and one grain of gold. The chairman of this department had a ration of seven *raṭls* of bread and two platefuls of cooked meal a day, plus three dinars a month, while the instructor was given four *raṭls* of bread and a plateful of cooked meal a day, plus a monthly salary of one dinar and twenty carats of gold. Although this department was part of the university, its building was separate from the rest of the campus because of the difference in age between the students of *fiqh* and those of the Qur'ān. We know the names of a few highly qualified scholars who chaired this department.

2. *Ḥadīth Department (Dār al-Ḥadīth)*

As mentioned above, this department, which was devoted to the *Ḥadīth* sciences, was headed by a highly qualified traditionist assisted by two readers. We add here that the chairman's ration was six *raṭls* of bread and two *raṭls* of meat a day, plus three dinars a month,[1] while the readers and the students used to get four *raṭls* of bread and a plateful of cooked meal a day, plus three dinars a month. Lessons of this department were given in the library hall three days a week. We know the names of seven prominent traditionists who chaired this department, and most of them were Ḥanbalīs.

3. *Departments of Medicine and Pharmacy*

We have already referred to this department which was established for two purposes: firstly to take care of university personnel and secondly to teach medicine to those interested in reading this discipline. The number of students was ten, who were supplied with all the facilities necessary for pursuing their studies, including a well-equipped pharmacy which was placed at their disposal. The chairman of this department was chosen from among the most qualified physicians. Besides teaching, he was authorised to grant licenses to all doctors and pharmacists willing to practice their business in Iraq. We know the names of some of those who occupied that high position.[2] However, we have no information about the length of the period which a medical student was required to spend in this department before being able to sit for the final examinations which enabled him to practice medicine.

4. *The Library*

The library of this university deserves our attention, since the founder, al-Mustanṣir, was anxious to supply his university with a rich library. He ordered that a great number of finely written and decorated Qur'āns and rare books on different subjects be supplied to this library. It was said that 290 porter-loads of books were sent from his palace to the university as a first instalment. The books were classified and arranged according to their subjects in order to make it easy for the readers to have access to them. Needless to say, those books and all other books supplied to this library were made *waqf*. Their total number exceeded 80,000 volumes. This library was also supplied with pens, ink and writing paper to be used by those who wish to copy the books in which they were interested.

The administrative body of the library consisted of a librarian (*khāzin*), a supervisor (*mushrif*) and a number of assistants (sing. *munāwil*), who were usually chosen from among the scholars. It is enough to mention in this respect two librarians: the famous historian Ibn al-Sā'ī who had compiled several books in *tafsīr*, *Ḥadīth*, *fiqh* and history. His best known book was *al-Jāmi' al-mukhtaṣar fī 'unwān al-tārīkh wa-'l-siyar* in 26 volumes. The second was Ibn al-Sā'ī's student, the well known historian Ibn al-Fuwaṭ, who was the author of several books (it is said 400!), the most important of them being *Talkhīṣ majma' al-adāb fī muj'am al-alqāb*. Ibn al-Fuwaṭ was captured by the Mongols who took him to Marāghah, where the vizier Naṣīr al-Din al-Ṭūsī established with the help of other scholars taken from Baghdad an observatory along with a great library. Ibn al-Fuwaṭ was appointed librarian, a position he held for 15 years. We know the names of a few supervisors of the Mustanṣiriyyah library, one of whom was a prominent person called Muḥammad b. Jamāl al-Dīn al-'Aqūlī.

Unfortunately, most of the books were destroyed or dispersed in many different places as a result of the fall of Baghdad at the hands of the Mongols in 656/1258. As a matter of fact, the famous scholar Nāsir al-Dīn al-Ṭūsī, who was minister to Hulagu Khan, transferred a large portion of these books to Marāghah, where he established a library attached to his observatory.

None of the Mustanṣiriyyah books can be traced with the exception of one copy of *Rabī' al-abrār* of al-Zamakhsharī which is now kept in the

Bibliothèque Nationale in Paris. So thousands of rare books in different subjects, including *tafsīr*, *Ḥadīth*, *fiqh*, Arabic literature and language, medicine, zoology, botany and mathematics were lost forever. Some of those books were original autograph copies, e.g. *Tārīkh Baghdād* of al-Khaṭīb al-Baghdādī and *Kitāb al-Adab* by Abū Bakr, Ṭāhā al-Bukhārī, and many similar books which were originally transferred from the library of al-Mustanṣir.

It is noteworthy to mention that al-Mustanṣir himself used to inspect this library from time to time. It was also said that during the Mongol invasion of Baghdad, the books of the library were either burned or looted, to be sold later for a few pence or to be used in building horse-mangers!

5. *Teaching Staff and Students*

Needless to say, the caliph showed a great interest in this university, as is clear from the generous professional salaries, twelve dinars a month, plus foodstuffs, daily rations given in kind (it was composed of 20 *raṭls* of bread, 5 *raṭls* of meat with vegetables and other items necessary for cooking), plus firewood.

Moreover, the first group of professors appointed by the caliph were chosen from among outstanding personalities of the time like Muḥyī 'l-Dīn Ibn al-Jawzī, who also occupied the high position of the *Ustādh al-Dār* (the chief of the cabinet of al-Mustanṣir), as well as ambassador. It may be interesting to note in this respect that, when the caliph could not find a suitable Mālikī scholar to occupy the professorship, he left it vacant with a temporary lecturer in charge until he was able to invite a Moroccan scholar from Alexandria. Another sign of his interest is shown by the appointment of four instructors to each professor, in order to demonstrate to the students in more detail the points to which the professor only alluded in his lectures. So we can safely say that the social status of the professor was quite high. As a matter of fact, some of them, as we have seen in the case of Ibn al-Jawzī, occupied high state positions. We also have Jamāl al-Dīn al-ʿĀqūlī who occupied the position of chief judge (*qāḍī 'l-quḍāh*) and Kamāl al-Lumghānī who was appointed as high ranking judge (*aqḍā 'l-quḍāh*). Many of the professors were highly qualified scholars in their respective fields of knowledge.

So far as the students were concerned, the charter of the university secured for them all their needs and the means of comfort, so that they could devote their efforts completely to their studies. They were given all that they needed in the way of money and food which even included sweets and fruit, plus soap, oil, paper, ink and comfortable accommodation. We have also to remember that this university was open to adherents of the four *madhhabs*, unlike the Niẓāmiyyah which was reserved for Shāfiʿīs alone. Students were attracted to this university from different regions. Among its students and *faqīhs*, we find persons coming from Marāghah and other remote cities. This enabled the students to get to know one another and to cement the existing ties of Islam with those of learning.

6. *Curriculum and Methods of Teaching*

Certainly the goal behind establishing this university was to educate the Muslim in accordance with true Islamic teachings, and to train good physicians who would be able to serve their society without regard to differences of jurisprudential rite (*madhhab*).

The Mustanṣiriyyah was placed under the personal supervision of the caliph himself in order to boost its position. Careful examination of its curriculum clearly shows its attitude towards specialisation.

It was stipulated that each student must specialise in the *fiqh* of one particular jurisprudential school or in *Ḥadīth* or medicine. It was also possible for students to specialize in grammar, literature, *farā'iḍ*, arithmetic, or zoology. This constituted a great step forward on the path of progress. The length of study is not known, although some historians think that the period during which a student could acquire what is necessary for his specialisation, may have reached ten years. If the professor was satisfied with his student at the end of this period, he granted him a license (*ijāzah*), but we know nothing about the number of hours the students should spend in the course of their studies, nor about their vacations.

The method of teaching described by Ibn Baṭṭūṭah, who visited the Mustanṣiriyyah in the first half of the eighth/fourteenth century, was based on dictation. The professor used to sit on a chair covered with a rug and placed in a wooden dome-shaped kiosk, wearing a black garment and a turban, with two instructors standing on both sides of the chair to repeat the professor's dictation. It seems to me that the lecture described by Ibn Baṭṭūṭah was a lecture of *Ḥadīth* and the instructors are *mustamlīs*.

Such a method of teaching was normal in those days, because it was not possible to secure enough copies of text books sufficient for all students. However, many students used to copy text books for themselves, in order to use them during the discussion. In the meantime, the professor used to encourage his students to discuss points raised in the lecture which may have helped to make the acquired knowledge clearer in their minds.

In this respect, we have a lively description by Ibn Jubayr of a lecture delivered in the *Niẓāmiyyah* which he visited in the second half of the sixth/twelfth century. That lecture was not very much different from the lectures delivered later in the university of the Mustanṣiriyyah. The method of teaching in both institutions appears to have been the same, as many professors of the former were appointed later in the new university (Shaykh Muḥammad b. Faḍlān was one of those who served in both). Also, it seems that freedom of discussion was guaranteed and the students were free to put any questions (written or oral) to their professors, who were supposed to give their answers at the end of the lecture. But about the end of the reign of the caliph al-Musta'ṣim, he and his ministers interfered in the methods of teaching, banned the Mustanṣiriyyah professors from using their own books and obliged them to restrict themselves to using the traditional books written by famous scholars to seek blessing and as a sign of respect (*tabarrukan wa-ta'adduban*). This measure upset the Shāfi'ī and

Ḥanafī scholars who protested saying, *Inna 'l-mashāyikh kānū rijālan wa-naḥnu rijāl* ('The shaykhs were men and we too are men'), but their protest did not change the situation in the least. Teaching, therefore, became completely based on certain books which the students had to memorise, and the duties of the professor concentrated on the abridgement of those books. This method was severely criticised by Ibn Khaldūn in his *Muqaddimah* because such concentrated abridgement made the books very difficult for the students to understand. But information exists which shows that the students were encouraged by their professors to write a sort of short thesis.

However, we are certain that the teaching of the Qur'ān was always based on recitation and memorising, because the young age of the pupils did not help them to understand the deeper meaning of the Qur'ān and its commentaries. But the opportunity always existed for those students who so desired, after learning the Qur'ān by heart, to follow a course of reading *Ḥadīth* or *fiqh*. On the other hand, the teaching of *Ḥadīth* was based on dictation. In certain cases the professor needed an assistant who was recruited from among the traditionists, to repeat each word he said with the utmost accuracy. Usually *Ḥadīth* lectures began with the recitation of some verses from the Qur'ān, followed by a reading from the *Ḥadīth* done by the professor himself, who usually started with an introduction in which he praised his professor after mentioning his name. During the reading he was supposed to draw the attention of his students to the strength of the chain of transmitters (*isnād*) and whatever characteristics it may contain. He was also supposed to be accurate when reporting the text and its *isnād*. Besides, he was to avoid discussing anything which might not be readily understood by his students. The lecture usually ended with the narration of a few stories connected with piety and good behaviour.

Nevertheless, some students were not satisfied with what they heard from their professor alone, and they tried to meet other professors, even if the latter lived in different cities or remote countries. There were many cases of students who travelled extensively, aiming to meet high ranking scholars and learn from them. One of those students was 'Umar b. 'Alī al-Baghdādī who studied in the Mustanṣiriyyah and also travelled to Damascus to read the *Ṣaḥīḥ* of al-Bukhārī with 'Alī al-Ḥajjār. He also studied there under the famous scholar Ibn Taymiyyah. It is noteworthy that this sort of travel (*riḥlah*) was not confined to students alone, since we know that some of the Mustanṣiriyyah professors themselves travelled for the same purpose. For example, one professor, Taqī 'l-Dīn al-Zarīrānī travelled to Damascus and Muḥammad b. Faḍlān went to Khurāsān to meet the scholars of those places, to enter into discussion with and to learn from them.

In this respect, we have to remember that their travels were made easier because of the establishment of *rabāṭs* and *khanqāhs* all over the Islamic world which admitted both students and professors free of charge. Ibn Jubayr saw several of them in Alexandria, where Saladin ordered that special bathrooms be constructed for the convenience of those visitors and a special hospital be established for their treatment.

Ibn Khaldūn described this kind of travel in search of knowledge as an ideal means of learning, because knowledge cannot be gained by mere listening to a lecture, but rather it needs direct contact with the professors as well.

7. *The diploma* (ijāzah)

Muslim students, whether they studied individually with a professor, or were members in an educational institution, were entitled to receive a diploma or a licence called *ijāzah*, which was granted by the professor to his students after their finishing the study of a book or a branch of knowledge with him. This diploma certified that the student had become capable of teaching the book he had read and that he was eligible to teach the subject he had studied. This licence was a necessity for every student in order to prove to other people that he had reached the status of scholarship.

The students of the Mustanṣiriyyah were not an exception, but this university like other Islamic universities and colleges did not follow the tradition of granting diplomas or licences. Rather, the licence was issued by a particular professor in response to an application submitted by a student. Sometimes seekers of licences could send their applications by correspondence if they were well-known personalities.

In the *ijāzah* which he granted, the professor would authorise the student to transmit, on his authority, a particular book or a collection of books, whether written by him or by somebody else, or he could give him the permission to teach a particular branch, or several branches, of knowledge.

This licence usually contained the student's name, the professor's name and the name of the writer, if it was written by someone other than the professor himself, together with the date of writing. Sometimes the licence was written on a sheet of paper, but in many cases the licence was written at the end of a book. An example of a licence written by a professor of the Mustanṣiriyyah is to be found in the book *al-Jawāhir al-muḍiyyah* by al-Qurashī which was granted by Aḥmad Ibn al-Saʿātī in the year 690/1291 to Zakī 'l-Dīn al-Samarqandī. This licence was written in the Mustanṣiriyyah itself and included some instructions and advice from the professor to his student.

It is very interesting to know that there were persons who adopted the profession of carrying applications for licences (*istijāzāt*) and the licences themselves between different Islamic cities. So one could send an application to a certain scholar seeking his licence and the courier would bring back the licence itself.

8. *University administration*

As we have seen, the Mustanṣiriyyah had an administrative body separate from the teaching staff. It is enough to mention here that the number of administrative employees was sufficiently large to meet the needs of the university and keep its affairs running properly. Also, it is useful to mention that the financial resources allocated were sufficient to cover the university expenses. It is said that the straw produced on the university *waqf* farms was enough, when sold, to cover those expenses. It is said also that the value of its *waqf* real estate exceeded one million dinars, which gave an annual income of more than seventy thousand *mithqāls* of gold (about 280,000 grammes). Certainly, this is a large amount of money, especially if we remember how low the prices were at that time. This income made it possible to spend lavishly on the university, especially on religious occasions, as for example Ramaḍān. In that month, the salaries and rations of the members of the Mustanṣiriyyah (professors, staff and students alike) were usually doubled.

9. *The fate of the Mustanṣiriyyah*

This university, which had attracted the admiration of those who had the chance to see or visit it, suffered burning and looting and some destruction at the hands of the Mongols after the fall of Baghdad. This also resulted in the killing of the caliph and his family, as well as a number of university professors like Muḥyī 'l-Dīn Ibn al-Jawzī and his son Jamāl al-Dīn and the head of the Shāfi'īs in Baghdad, Shihāb al-Dīn al-Zinjānī. So it was natural that studies were interrupted for a while, but the Mongols quickly realised the importance of this university, and Hulagu himself ordered it to be re-opened and convened all those scholars whose lives he spared in order to ask their opinion (*fatwā*) about the legitimacy of his rule. Soon thereafter, studies were resumed in the buildings saved from destruction, by order of the governor of Iraq, 'Alā' al-Dīn 'Aṭā Mulk, who was himself a distinguished scholar. Also one of the Mongol sultans Ghāzān Maḥmūd, a Muslim, visited the university in 696/1296 including what was left of its library.

The Mustanṣiriyyah was always an attraction to visitors; one of them whom we might mention was Nūr al-Din Arslān Shāh the ruler of Shahrazōr who paid his visit in 634/1296. The famous traveller Ibn Baṭṭūṭah, as mentioned above, visited the university in 727/1326 and described a lecture he attended there. Another traveller from Persia was Ḥamd Allāh al-Mustawfī who visited it during the reign of the Jalā'irī sultans, under whom Iraq had become independent. But since Tamurlane's invasion of Iraq, which led to anarchy and the disruption and deterioration of cultural life, we hear no more about the university. This silence continued during the rule of the Turkmen dynasties, and also during the Safavid occupation (912–939/1508–1534), with the exception of the name of one professor who taught there, al-Muḥibb ibn Naṣr Allāh al-Baghdādī. As a matter of fact, all the Sunnī institutions in Iraq had suffered a great deal of damage and humiliation during the Safavid rule, and the Mustanṣiriyyah was no exception. But the Ottoman conquest of Baghdad in 939/1534 did not restore the university to its previous favoured status. It was used during their rule as a monastery (*zāwiyah*) for dervishes, a depot for goods, a military barracks and later as a customs warehouse. After the First World War, the newly established government of Iraq under King

Fayṣal I, who visited the university in 1921, tried to restore what had been a warehouse to its original purpose, but the legal procedure took more than twenty years to complete. The Iraqi Department of Antiquities took over the building of the Mustanṣiriyyah in 1944 and did its best to repair the damage and bring the building back to its original shape. It was then made a library of Arabic manuscripts.

Conclusion

There is no doubt that the Mustanṣiriyyah played an important role in the development of learning. The institution, however, played this role within the framework of the prevailing circumstances. It left a big impact on the Islamic cultural life of the Middle Ages. As we have seen, many studies were established in this university, like *fiqh*, *Ḥadīth*, medicine, grammar, etc. So the Mustanṣiriyyah offered great opportunities for students, coming from Baghdad and elsewhere, to learn whatever they desired. It gave students of different *madhhabs* the chance to come together and live under the same roof, which helped to eliminate factors of disagreement which may have existed among them and thus made them closer to one another.

The caliph al-Mustanṣir, when founding this university, was probably aiming to achieve this goal. His action certainly had a strong impact on other Islamic countries. As we have mentioned previously, colleges in Egypt, for example, continued till 641/1243 to be dedicated to one *madhhab*, or two, but the Ayyubid sultan, al-Ṣāliḥ Najm al-Dīn Ayyūb established in that year (11 years after the foundation of the Mustanṣir-iyyah) his own college for the four Sunnī *madhhabs*. Undoubtedly he was following the example set by the caliph of his own time. Later the Mamluk sultan, Ḥasan, built a similar college in Cairo. We have another example founded by Lājīn, the Mamluk Sultan of Egypt, who repaired the Ibn Ṭūlūn mosque in 696/1296, increased its *waqf* and turned it into a university, where the *fiqh* of the four *madhhabs* was taught along with *tafsīr*, *Ḥadīth* and medicine. In the same compound he established a school for teaching the Qur'ān. Also the Sultan of Bengal, ʿAẓām Shāh, established a similar institution in 813/1410 in Mecca and the Ottoman Sultan Suleyman established a similar institution there. The impact of the Mustanṣiriyyah continued during the succeeding centuries. As a matter of fact, the Mosque of Sayyidah Zaynab in Cairo was turned at the end of the 13th/19th century into a university for the four *madhhabs* and for the teaching of *Ḥadīth* and ethics as well. Besides, we must remember that several of the scholars of the Mustanṣiriyyah played an important role in the establishment of the observatory of Marāghah and its library.

The establishment of the Mustanṣiriyyah as a residential institution put the students under strict discipline and training, so that they had to abide by the university regulations and prepare themselves to bear their responsibilities when they graduated as professors, judges, imams, etc.

There were many students who came from remote countries and who carried with them to their own countries many ideas which they had learned during their stay in Baghdad. They also carried with them details of the methods followed in the Mustanṣiriyyah and tried to apply them in their own countries.

We know the names of some of those students who studied at the Mustanṣiriyyah and assumed teaching positions in their own countries. At the same time, works compiled by professors of the Mustanṣiriyyah such as Ibn Faḍlān, Ibn al-ʿĀqūlī, Ibn al-Jawzī, Ibn al-Saʿātī, Ibn al-Faṣīḥ, etc., were carried to many Islamic countries and left a deep impact on the scholars of those lands.

The Mustanṣiriyyah also served as congregational mosque for the people of Baghdad and for the Friday Prayer and for the prayer of the two feasts, ʿĪd al-Fiṭr and ʿĪd al-Aḍḥā. Because of the importance of this mosque, the caliph stipulated that only a member of the Abbasid family could be appointed as its *khaṭīb*. In addition to all this, the Mustanṣiriyyah is a marvellous example of Islamic architecture and Islamic decorative bas-relief arts embellished with beautiful Arabic calligraphy. It can be said too that the Mustanṣiriyyah was a real university. This term has been called into question by some European scholars who argue that none of the Muslim *madrasahs* can be called universities in the European sense, because the licences were granted by the professor and not by the institutions themselves. They also said that the lectures were based on text books and not on subjects. Besides, the licences were not classified according to established degrees (bachelor, doctorate etc.). Personally, I think that what makes an educational institution a university is not the criteria used by these European scholars, but rather the number of sciences taught in that institution and the number of departments it contains. Thus we can safely say that the Mustanṣiriyyah was a real university not only in the European sense, but in any other sense.

Notes

[1] Naṣīr al-Dīn al-Ṭūsī established a Dār Ḥadīth in Marāghah where the daily payment for the traditionist was just half a dirham! Scholars of philosopy there were paid three dirhams a day! cf. al-Suyūṭī, *Ṣawn al-manṭiq*, 13–14.

[2] We have no information about the salaries paid to them, but Naṣīr al-Dīn al-Ṭūsī used to pay two dirhams a day to the *ḥakīm* of his medical school in Marāghah. (Ibid. 13–14).

Bibliography of major sources used

Al-Ālūsī, Maḥmūd Shukrī, *Masājid Baghdād*, Baghdad, 1927.
Amīn, Ḥusayn, *Al-Madrasah al-Mustanṣiriyyah*, Baghdad, 1960.
Anān, Muḥd. ʿAbd Allāh: *Tārīkh al-jāmiʿ al-Azhar*, Cairo, 1942.
ʿAwwād, Gūrgīs, 'Al-Madrasah al-Mustanṣiriyyah', *Sumer*, I, 1945.
Ibn Baṭṭūṭah, Muḥammad b. ʿAbd Allāh, *Tuḥfat al-nuẓẓār*, Cairo, 1938.
Dodge, Bayard, *Muslim Education in Medieval Times*, Washington, 1962.

Fahmī, Asmā', *Mabādi' al-tarbiyah al-islamiyyah*, Cairo, 1947.
Ibn al-Fuwatī, 'Abd al-Razzāq b. Aḥmad, *Al-Ḥawādith al-jāmi'ah*, Baghdad, 1351.
—— *Mu'jam al-alqāb*, Damascus, 1962–1967.
Ghunaymah, Muḥammad 'Abd al-Raḥīm, *al-Jāmi'āt al-islāmiyyah al-kubrā*, Ṭutwān, 19.
Al-Irbilī, 'Abd al-Raḥmān b. Ibrāhīm, *Khulāṣat al-dhahab al-masbūk*, Baghdad, 1964.
Jawād, Muṣṭafā, 'al-Madrasah al-Niẓāmiyyah fī Baghdād', *Sumer*, IX, 1953.
Ibn al-Jawzī, 'Abd al-Raḥmān b. 'Alī, *al-Muntaẓam*, Hyderabad, 1355 H.
Ibn Jubayr, Muḥammad b. Aḥmad al-Kinānī, *al-Riḥlah*, Beirut, 1959.
Ibn Khaldūn, 'Abd al-Raḥmān b. Muḥammad, *al-Muqaddimah*, Cairo, 1957.
Ibn Sa'd, Muḥammad, *al-Ṭabaqāt al-Kubrā*, Beirut, 1957–8, 8 vols.
Al-Khalīlī, Ja'far, *Mu'jam aṭibbā' al-'Iraq*, Najaf, 1946.
Ibn Khallikān, Aḥmad b. Muḥammad, *Wafayāt al-'ayān*, Cairo, 1948.
Khan, M. A. M., 'The Muslim Theories of Education', *IC*, XVIII, 1944.
Al-Khaṭīb al-Baghdādī, Aḥmad b. 'Alī, *Tārīkh Baghdād*, Cairo, 1931.
Khuda Bukhsh, S. 'The Educational System of the Muslims', *IC*, I, 1927.
Le Strange, G., *Baghdad during the Abbasid Caliphate*, Oxford, 1924.
Makdisi, George, 'Muslim Institutions of Learning', *BSOAS*, XXIV, 1961.
Ma'rūf, Nājī, *'Ulamā' al-Mustanṣiriyyah*, Baghdad, 1959.
—— *al-Madāris al-sharābiyyah*, Baghdad, 1965.
Nafīsī, Sa'īd, 'al-Madrasah al-Niẓāmiyyah fī Baghdād', *Majallat al-Majma'al-'Irāqī*, III, 1954.
Nashabi, Hishām, 'Educational Institutions', *The Islamic City*, UNESCO, Paris, 1980.
Al-Nu'aymī, 'Abd al-Qādir b. Muḥammad, *al-Dāris fī tārīkh al-madāris*, Damascus, 1948.
Pedersen, J. 'Some Aspects of the history of Madrasa', *IC*, III, 1929.
—— 'Masjid', *EI*[1]
Al-Qurashī, 'Abd al-Qādir b. Muḥammad, *al-Jawāhir al-muḍiyyah*, Hyderabad, 1332.
Al-Rāwī, Ṭāhā: *Baghdād Madīnat al-Salām*, Cairo, n.d.
Al-Sakkar, Sami, 'Lectures on the History of Islamic Education', (unpublished).
—— 'Irbil in the Middle Ages', (unpublished).
Shalabī, Aḥmad: *Tārīkh al-tarbiyah al-islāmiyyah*, Beirut, 1954.
Al-Ṭabbākh, Rāghib, 'Niẓām al-madrasah', *Majallat al-Majma' al-'Arabī*, I/4, Damascus, 1924.
Ṭalas, Muḥammad As'ad, *al-Tarbiyah wa-'l-ta'līm fī 'l-Islām*, Beirut, 1956.
Ṭībāwī, A. L., Muslim Education in the Golden Age, *IC*, XXVIII, 1954.
—— 'Origin and Character of Al-Madrasa'. *BSOAS*, XXV, 1962.
—— *Islamic Education*, London 1972.

Tritton, A., *Materials on Muslim Education in the Middle Ages*, London 1954.
Yāqūt b. ʿAbd Allāh al-Ḥamawī, *Muʿjam al-buldān*, Liepzig 1866.
—— *Muʿjam al-udabāʾ*, Cairo, 1923.
Al-Zayyātī, Sulaymān Raṣad, *Kanz al-jawāhir fī tārīkh al-Azhar*, Cairo, n.d.

Al-Birrah fī ḥubb al-hirrah – a 10th/16th century Arabic text on pussy cats

G. Rex Smith

The author of the *Birrah* and the text

The correct form of the name of the author of the *Birrah* is difficult to assess, though it might be possible to settle for Nūr al-Dīn ʿAlī b. Sulṭān b. Muḥammad al-Harawī. He was certainly also known as al-Qāri' and I have chosen to refer to him as ʿAlī al-Qāri'. Some of those writers supplying biographical information concerning our author[1] call him al-Ḥanafī and he was indeed a Ḥanafī *faqīh*. He was born in Herat, hence his *nisbah*, but moved to Mecca where he lived. He died there in 1014/1606. He was a prolific writer and Brockelmann's *GAL*[2] lists no fewer than 182 products of his pen, covering the fields of *fiqh*, *tafsīr*, *ḥadīth* and *tawḥīd*. More particularly on the subject of *fiqh* and the *fuqahā'*, he wrote biographies of prominent Ḥanafīs and refutations of both the works of al-Shāfiʿī and Mālik b. Anas. He clearly had an interest in Sufism too, as some of his terminology in the text indicates, and he composed a biography of ʿAbd al-Qādir al-Jīlānī and a critique of Ibn ʿArabī's *Fuṣūṣ*. ʿAlī al-Qāri' was responsible for a commentary on the famous pre-Islamic *qaṣīdah* which begins with the words '*Bānat Suʿād* . . .' by Kaʿb b. Zuhayr al-Muzanī. Our author is also credited with a work on Arabic grammar.[3]

It is predominantly the *muḥaddith* whom we see here at work and the opening paragraphs in particular are replete with quotations from *Ḥadīth* literature, though some of it, as our author freely admits, far from 'sound'. Indeed it is clear that it was the tradition – not found, however, in *Ḥadīth* literature – 'love of the cat is a part of the Faith' and the discussion on it between al-Jurjānī and al-Taftāzānī which led ʿAlī al-Qāri' to put together this text.[4] Such a quotation and others like it are treated entirely seriously by our author, steeped as he is in all the religious sciences. But the text is not all of a serious religious nature and the whole is neatly balanced by the narration of some pleasing anecdotes, one of which[5] appears almost heretical in the Islamic context. In it al-Shiblī tells of his meeting with his Creator and the Latter, after a fairly long drawn-out guessing game, explains why He forgave him his sins and allowed him into paradise. The story is reminiscent of a certain genre of humour in European culture in which the main character of the story stands 'before the pearly gates' and is questioned by his Maker, or possibly by His deputy, St. Peter. The author's love of the anecdote is highlighted by that on page 3, from line 15 in the Arabic text below. It is only when the story has been told, concerning the Prophet and the cat sleeping on his robe, that ʿAlī al-Qāri' informs his reader that it has no basis of truth whatsoever! He is not averse also to quoting an apposite verse of poetry. The text ends with a brief, though delightful paragraph containing definitions of the words *hirrah* and *birrah* which show clearly our author's penchant for Arabic lexicographical problems. The language, as one would expect from a scholar with the background of our author, is a correct classical Arabic. The style and presentation are clear and uncomplicated.

The MSS

Brockelmann lists four MSS containing the text of the *Birrah*,[6] those of Berlin, Munich and two of Cairo. It has only been possible to make use of the first two and my efforts to acquire microfilms of the third and fourth have failed.[7] It is, however, doubtful that the text would have been improved by their use in this edition.

The Munich MS[8] contains a collection of more than 50 of ʿAlī al-Qāri''s works and the *Birrah* occupies folios 78v–80r. The MS is undated and the folios which concern us here are written in a generally neat, if slightly square *naskhī* hand, 25 lines to the page. It is on the whole a complete and correct text. Vowels are extremely rare, though the *shaddah* is written in frequently. It was this completeness of the text and, to an extent, the neatness and general legibility which led me to use this MS as the basis of the edition.

As for the Berlin MS,[9] this is also a collection of our author's briefer works and the *Birrah* can be found on folios 61–2. The date at the end of the *Birrah* reads 1175 (1761–2). The hand is an untidy, spidery *naskhī*, with frequent marginal additions. It differs here and there from the Munich MS, as can be clearly seen in the *apparatus criticus*, and is generally inferior to it. The reader will, however, note one or two useful additons from the Berlin MS.

Editorial method

As mentioned above, the Munich MS has been used as the basis of the edition and is referred to as *al-aṣl* in the notes at the end of the text. All variant readings in the Berlin MS (abbreviated as *bā'*) have been listed in these notes. Any additions from the Berlin MS in the final text appear in brackets. I have enclosed references to the folio numbers of both MSS in square brackets in the text. I have permitted no other material in the notes at the end of the text other than a complete documentation of the differences between the two MSS used in the edition. The notes, therefore, form, purely and simply, an *apparatus criticus*. All other references, e.g. Quranic, *Ḥadīth*, poetic etc., comments and notes on the text have been confined to the introductory section which follows this, entitled 'Notes on the Arabic text'. The text has been divided up into sentences and paragraphs with the necessary punctuation. This, it is hoped, will render the text more easily readable. In the absence of any broadly accepted system of indicating titles of literary works in Arabic, I have used inverted commas in the text, as I have also for Quranic quotations. Direct speech and other quotations have been left without inverted commas after a colon.

Notes on the Arabic text

Page 1, lines 4 and 5
Both terms, *muḥibb* and *maḥbūb*, smack strongly of Sufism. The author's interest in this has already been mentioned above, 'The author of the *Birrah* and the text'. R. Dozy, *Supplément aux dictionnaires arabes*, Leyde & Paris, 1967, *ḥ-b-b*, says of *muḥibb*, 'C'est surtout aux Soufis qu'on donne ce titre'.

1, 5
'Love of the cat is a part of the Faith'. This tradition is not to be found in the major *Ḥadīth* collections.

1, 6
'Alī b. Muḥammad al-Jurjānī, called al-Sayyid al-Sharīf, was born in 740/1339. He studied in Herat, the birth place of 'Alī al-Qāri', and died in 838/1434. For his biography, cf. *EI*².

1, 7
Mas'ūd b. 'Umar al-Taftāzānī, from Taftāzān in Khurāsān, wrote primarily on logic and grammar. He died in 793/1390. It seems clear that al-Jurjānī and al-Taftāzānī would have had the opportunity to meet and discuss in person.

1, 8 and 9
A *ḥadīth marfū'* is in the strict technical sense the record of the word or deed of the Prophet reported by a Companion who heard or saw it. *Mawḍū'* means 'false'. Cf. A. Guillaume, *The Traditions of Islam*, Oxford, 1924, glossary.

1, 16
This interesting anecdote has its parallels elsewhere. *Alf laylah wa-laylah*, Beirut, 1889–1914, I, 27–8, tells basically the same tale with a hawk as the hero. Ibn al-Marzubān, *The Superiority of dogs* etc., translated and edited by G.R. Smith and M.A.S. Abdel Haleem, Warminster, 1978, trans. 18–20, text, 33–5, also has much the same story where the hero is a dog.

2, 1
Muḥammad b. 'Abd al-Raḥmān al-Sakhāwī, the famous Egyptian *muḥaddith*, biographer and historian, author of *al-Ḍaw' al-lāmi'*, died in 902/1497. He is notorious for his criticisms of the many scholars, including al-Suyūṭī, who found a place in his biographical works. Cf. Ziriklī, *A'lām*, VII, 67–8; also E.M. Sartain, *Jalāl al-Dīn al-Suyūṭī*, London, 1975, I, 77–8 and passim. Sakhāwī's 'love of one's native land is a part of the Faith' is not an accepted prophetic Tradition.

2, 2
'Alī b. Muḥammad al-Manūfī was a *faqīh* and *muḥaddith* who died in 939/1532. Cf. Ziriklī, *A'lām*, V, 164.

2, 3
Qur'ān, IV, 66.

2, 7
Qur'ān, II, 246.

2, 13
'To love the Arabs is an act of Faith'; 'to love Abū Bakr and 'Umar is an act of Faith'. Neither tradition appears in the major *Ḥadīth* collections. 'Love of the Anṣār is a sign of the Faith', cf. Muslim, *Ṣaḥīḥ*, 128; Bukhārī, *Ṣaḥīḥ*, 'al-Īmān', 10; 'Manāqib al-Anṣār', 4; al-Nasā'ī, *Sunan*, 'al-Īmān', 19.

2, 15
'He who loves the Arabs, . . .'. Cf. Abū Dāwud, *Sunan*, 'al-Sunnah', 15.

2, 18
'Uḥud is a mountain which loves us and we love it'. This is not to be found in the major *Ḥadīth* collections.

2, 26
Qur'ān, II, 177.

2, 28
Qur'ān, LXXVI, 8.

2, 29
Qur'ān, XXVIII, 32.

2, 30
Qur'ān, C, 8.

3, 1
Cf. al-Tirmidhī, *Ṣaḥīḥ*, 'al-Da'awāt', 72.

3, 3
Cf. *Dīwān Majnūn Laylā*, ed. 'Abd al-Muta'āl al-Sa'īdī, Cairo, n.d., 169. These verses do not appear in the main part of the *Dīwān*, but are attributed to Majnūn by Shaykh 'Abd al-Qādir b. 'Umar al-Baghdādī. Majnūn was Qays b. al-Mulawwaḥ who died in 68/677. Cf. Ziriklī, *A'lām*, VI, 60.

3, 6
Cf. *Dīwān al-Shāfi'ī*, ed. Zakī Yakan, Beirut, 1961, 118, which, however, there reads '*in kāna* . . . etc.'.

3, 7
Al-thaqalān means either 'men and jinn' or 'Arabs and non-Arabs'. Perhaps it is best rendered here 'all and sundry'. Cf. E. W. Lane, *Arabic-English Lexicon*, *th-q-l*. Rāfiḍī is here perhaps to be taken in the general

sense of 'heretic', though the word is particularly associated with those who deserted Zayd b. ʿAlī b. al-Ḥusayn b. ʿAlī b. Abī Ṭālib. It was also used as a general term of abuse for the Shīʿah. Cf. R. B. Serjeant, 'The Yemeni poet al-Zubayrī etc.', *Arabian Studies*, V, 1979, 115, who also comments on Nāṣibī, *3, 9* below.

3, 9
Nāṣibī was applied to an opponent of ʿAlī b. Abī Ṭālib.

3, 12
ʿAbd Allāh b. ʿAdī Ibn al-Qaṭṭān, who died in 360/971, was the author of *al-Kāmil fī maʿrifat ḍuʿafā' al-mutaḥaddithīn*, a work which would seem to be as yet unpublished. Cf. Brockelmann, *GAL*, S II, 280. The *ḥadīth* in any case finds a place in Abū Dāwud, *Sunan*, 'al-Ṭahārah', 38, al-Nasā'ī, *Sunan*, 'al-Miyāh', etc. etc. Abū Ḥanīfah al-Nuʿmān b. Thābit, who died in 150/767, was the eponym of the Ḥanafī *madhhab*. Cf. *EI*².

3, 15
This tradition finds no place in the major *Ḥadīth* collections, as the author himself freely admits in his final remark.

3, 17
Aḥmad would appear to be Aḥmad Ibn Ḥanbal.
Al-Bazzār is clear in both MSS, 'the dealer in *bizr*, "linseed oil"'. This is perhaps Aḥmad b. ʿAmr al-Bazzār, the *muḥaddith* who died in 292/905. He was a Basran and travelled widely. He died in al-Ramlah. Cf. *Aʿlām*, I, 182.
Al-Dārquṭnī, ʿAlī b. ʿUmar, was a Shāfiʿī *muḥaddith* who died in 385/995. The *nisbah* is from Dār al-Quṭn, a quarter of Baghdad.
Al-Ḥākim might be one of three *Ḥadīth* scholars as follows: 1) Muḥammad b. ʿAbd Allāh al-Naysābūrī, d. 405/1014; 2) Muḥammad b. Muḥammad, d. 334/945; or 3) Muḥammad b. Muḥammad al-Ḥākim al-Kabīr, d. 378/988. Cf. *Aʿlām*, VII, 101, VII, 242, VII, 244.
Al-Bayhaqī. Could this be Aḥmad b. al-Ḥusayn, the *muḥaddith* who died in 458/1066? Cf. *Aʿlām*, I, 113.
Abū Hurayrah was the famous Companion who died about 58/678. Perhaps it is inevitable that his name should appear in a work on cats!
The *ḥadīth* can also be found in Abū Dāwud, *Sunan*, 'al-Ṭahārah', 38; al-Tirmidhī, *Ṣaḥīḥ*, 'al-Ṭahārah', 29, etc. etc.

4,1 ff.
I have left this paragraph exactly as my MSS have it, but the following comments should be noted. Ibn Khaythamah would seem to be Ibn Abī Khaythamah, the historian and *Ḥadīth* scholar who died in 279/892. Cf. al-Dhahabī, *Mīzān al-iʿtidāl*, Cairo, n.d., I, 669; *Ṭabaqāt Khalīfah*, ed. Suhayl Zakkār, Damascus, 1972, II, 862; *Aʿlām*, I, 123. Maymūnah was the daughter of Saʿd and Ibn ʿAbd al-Barr's *Istīʿāb*, Cairo, n.d., IV, 1918, reports the *ḥadīth*.on the authority of Salmā (not Sulaymān), the Prophet's servant. Here the text has *khishāsh* (insects) in place of *ḥasharāt*.

4, 4
Cf. Bukhārī, *Ṣaḥīḥ*, 'al-Anbiyā'', 54; Muslim, *Ṣaḥīḥ*, 'al-Salām', 151 etc. etc.

4, 4
For Aḥmad Ibn Ḥanbal's *Zuhd*, cf. Brockelmann, *GAL*, I, 182. Aḥmad died in 241/855.

4, 5
'Iyāḍ b. Mūsā al-Yaḥṣubī, who died in 544/1149, entitled his commentary *Ikmāl al-mu'lim sharḥ Ṣaḥīḥ Muslim*. Cf. Brockelmann, *GAL*, S I, 265. Al-Nawawī, Yaḥyā b. Sharaf, the famous *faqīh* and *muḥaddith* who died in 676/1277.

4, 6
'Abd Allāh b. al-Ḥasan Ibn 'Asākir, who died in 571/1176, was the author of *Tārīkh madīnat Dimashq*. This work has not been published in its entirety and I have been unable to track down this story in those volumes available to me. Cf. Brockelmann, *GAL*, I, 331. I therefore cannot say also for sure which al-Shiblī is meant here. Was it Dulaf b. Jaḥdar, the disciple of al-Junayd, who died in 334/996?

4, 17
Ibn Sīdah was 'Alī b. Ismā'īl, the Andalusian littérateur who died in 458/1066. Cf. *A'lām*, V, 69.

4, 18
For *birr* in this meaning, cf. al-Fīrūzābādī, *al-Qāmūs al-muḥīṭ*, Cairo, 1330H, I, 370.

4, 19
barra, *yabarru*/*yabirru* in the sense of 'treat kindly', 'be well disposed to' here. The quotation from the *Qāmūs* is on I, 371.

4, 20
Harharah and *barbarah* are 'the call of the sheep' and 'the call of the goat' respectively. Cf. *Qāmūs*, I, 371 and *Tāj al-'arūs*, *b-r-r* and *h-r-r*.

Notes

[1] E.g. Muḥammad b. 'Alī al-Shawkānī, *Al-Badr al-ṭāli' bi-maḥāsin man ba'd al-qarn al-sābi'*, Beirut, n.d., I, 445–6.
[2] II, 394–8; the *Birrah* is listed at item 12.
[3] Apart from Brockelmann's *GAL*, see also Khayr al-Dīn al-Ziriklī, *al-A'lām* etc., 2nd edit., V, 1955, 166–7, with full references.
[4] Text 1, from line 7.
[5] Text 4, from line 6.
[6] *GAL*, II, 394.

[7] The MS containing the text is listed in *Fihrist al-kutub al-ʿarabiyyah al-maḥfūẓah bi-ʾl-kutubkhānah al-khadīwiyyah al-miṣriyyah*, Cairo, 1308H, VII, 26, no. 53. There appears to be another version listed in the same catalogue, 132, no. 23.
[8] Cf. J. Aumer, *Die arabischen Handschriften der K. Hof- und Staatsbibliothek in Muenchen*, Munich, 1866, 393, no. 886. I am extremely grateful to the Bayerische Staatsbibliothek in Munich for supplying me with photographs of the text and for giving permission for me to publish it.
[9] Cf. W. Ahlwardt, *Die Handschriften-Verzeichnisse der Königlichen Bibliothek zu Berlin*, Berlin, 1889, II, 282, no. 1639. I am similarly grateful for the same favours to the Staatsbibliothek, Preussischer Kulturbesitz, Berlin.

١

البرة في حب الهرة

للعلامة نور الدين علي بن سلطان بن محمد الهروي القارىء المتوفى
١٦٠٥/١٠١٤

[الأصل ٧٨ ب] [ب ٦١١ ب] بسم الله الرحمن الرحيم . الحمد لله الذي حبب الينا الايمان ، وكرّه الينا الكفر والعصيان ، والصلاة والسلام على من أظهر الآيات ، وبيّن العلامات ، وعلى آله وأصحابه الذين وجب حبهم ومودتهم وحرم بغضهم وعداوتهم .

وبعد . فيقول أفقر عباد الله البارىء علي بن سلطان محمد القارىء : قد[١] ساءلني بعض المحبين ـ بل الواصل إلى درجة المحبوبين ـ عن الحديث المشهور على ألسنة الأعيان : حب الهرة من الايمان ، وعن ترجيح (ما)[٢] وقع من البحث (المعروف)[٣] بين السيد الشريف الجرجاني والشيخ المعتمد المعتقد السعد التفتازاني . فأجبت بما بدا لي فيما هنالك ، وان كنت معترفا بأني لست أهلا لذلك ، فقلت : أما لفظ الحديث، فاتّفق الحفاظ على أنه[٤] ليس له أصل مرفوع ، بل صرّح بعضهم بأنه موضوع . فان قيل : فهل معناه صحيح لأنّ أصفى[٥] الأنباء لها الثابت في المدّعي صريح ، قلت : فيه ايماء إلى[٥-١] أنه لا ينافي الايمان . وأما كونه دالاّ على أنه من علاماته[٦] ، فلا عند أرباب الايمان[٧] ، لأنّ حب الهرة أمر مشترك بين المؤمن والكافر . فلا يصلح أن يكون [الأصل ١٧٩] علامة دالّة مميّزة بين الصالح والفاجر الاّ أن تعتبر الحيثيّة الفارقة عن الأمور العادية . كما حكي أنّ هرة كانت في مطبخ بعض المشايخ العظام ، فأراد الطباخ يوما من الأيام أن يغرف الطعام من البرمة للشيخ وأصحابه الكرام . فجاءته الهرة فدفعته، فدفعها ، فما اندفعت ، وتكرر منها ذلك . فلما غلب الهرة ودفعها دفعا عنيفا رمت نفسها في البرمة وماتت فيها . فكبّوا ما فيها ، فظهرت حيّة ، فتبيّن منه[٨] على خرق العادة أنها كانت تحب الشيخ والفقراء ورأت الحية فيها وأنها فدت نفسها عنهم .

٢

هذا وقد قال العلامة السخاوي في حديث : حب الوطن من الايمان ، لم أقف عليه ومعناه صحيح . فنازعه المنوفي ، وقال : ما ادّعاه من صحة معناه عجيب اذ لا ملازمة بين حب الوطن والايمان[٩] ، ويرده قوله تعالى : ﴿ وَلَوْ أَنَّا كَتَبْنَا عَلَيْهِمْ أَنِ ٱقْتُلُوا أَنْفُسَكُمْ أَوِ ٱخْرُجُوا مِنْ دِيَارِكُمْ ﴾ ، فانه دالّ على حبهم وطنهم مع عدم تلبّسهم بالايمان[١٠] اذ ضمير «عليهم» للمنافقين . وأغرب الخطاب وتكلّف في الجواب وقال : ليس في كلامه أنه لا يحب الوطن الاّ مؤمن ، وانما فيه أنّ حب الوطن لا ينافي الايمان ، فتأمّله[١١] . انتهى . وأنت تعرف أنّ هذا الكلام مدخول ، وفي النظر الصريح معلول . فانّ السخاوي أراد أنّه جاء في القرآن حكاية عن أهل الايمان [ب ٦١٢] ﴿ وَمَا لَنَا أَلاَّ[١٢] نُقَاتِلَ فِي سَبِيلِ ٱللهِ وَقَدْ أُخْرِجْنَا مِنْ دِيَارِنَا ﴾ . فعارضه المنوفي بقوله تعالى : ﴿ وَلَوْ أَنَّا كَتَبْنَا عَلَيْهِمْ أَنِ ٱقْتُلُوا أَنْفُسَكُمْ أَوِ ٱخْرُجُوا مِنْ دِيَارِكُمْ مَا فَعَلُوهُ اِلاَّ قَلِيلٌ مِنْهُمْ ﴾ . فدلت الآيتان على أنّ حب الوطن من جبلّة الانسان ولا خصوصية له بأهل الايمان . فلا يصلح أن يكون علامة عليه ولا دلالة مشيرة اليه . هذا ولا يبعد أن يكون مراده بقوله : صحيح أن يقصد بالوطن الجنة ، فانّـهـا المسكن الأول لأبينا آدم ـ[١٣] عليه السلام[١٣] ـ أو مكة ، فانّـهـا [١٤] أم القرى[١٤] .

ثم اعلم أنه ورد في الأحاديث النبوية على صاحبها ـ أفضل[١٥] الصلاة والتحية ـ حب العرب ايمان ، وحب أبي بكر وعمر ايمان ، وحب الأنصار آية الايمان . ولا شكّ في هذه الأحاديث اضافة المصدر إلى فاعله لما ورد : فمن أحب العرب فقد أحبني ، ومن أبغض العرب فقد أبغضني . والأصل في النظائر أن يكون على طبق واحد ، فهذا أحد المرجحات لكلام السعد .

ومنها أنّ نسبة المحبة إلى الهرة مجازيّة ، فالأولى حمل الكلام على الارادة الحقيقية . وكذا[١٦] أشكل على[١٦] العلماء قوله ـ صلى الله عليه وسلم :- أُحُد جبل يحبنا ونحبه . فقالوا : محبة الحي للجماد اعجابه به وسكون النفس اليه والمؤانسة به لما يرى فيه من نفع، ومحبة الجماد للحي مجاز عن كونه نافعا ايّاه سادّا[١٧] بينه وبين ما يؤذيه[١٨] . ومنها أنّ محبة الهرة غيرها جارية بطبعها لمن يطعمها ولا فرق عندها بين المؤمن والكافر ، فلا يصلح أن يكون علامة [الأصل ٧٩ ب] للايمان . ومنها أنّ فعل شخص لا يكون علامة لعمل شخص آخر . فيكون ، (فكيف)[١٩] يصح أن[٢٠] يكون حب الهرة لأحد علامة لايمانه[٢٠] ، لا يقال انه يجوز أن يجعله الشارع علامة ودليلا ، فانّا نقول : يحتاج اثباته بدليل خارج لأنّه خلاف الأصل . ومنها أنّ لام الايمان بدل من المضاف اليه ، والظاهر[٢١] أنّه المحب فالتقدير حب الهرة من ايمان المحب ، ولا يصح أن يكون المراد بالمحب الهرة ، فتعيّـن أن تكون الاضافة من باب اضافة المصدر إلى مفعوله . ثم مما يؤيّد هذا المبنى[٢٢] ويؤكّد هذا المعنى قوله تعالى : ﴿ وَآتَى ٱلْمَالَ عَلَىٰ حُبِّهِ ﴾ ، سواء كان الضمير راجعا إلى الله تعالى[٢٣] أو إلى المال . وكذا قوله سبحانه[٢٤] : ﴿ وَيُطْعِمُونَ ٱلطَّعَامَ عَلَىٰ حُبِّهِ ﴾ ، أي حب الله[٢٥] أو حب الطعام[٢٥] . ومنه قوله تعالى[٢٦] : ﴿ إِنِّي أَحْبَبْتُ حُبَّ ٱلْخَيْرِ عَنْ ذِكْرِ رَبِّي ﴾ ، أي حب الخير[٢٧] عن صلاة ربي . ومنه قوله تعالى[٢٨]: ﴿ وَإِنَّهُ ﴾ ـ أي الانسان ـ ﴿ لِحُبِّ ٱلْخَيْرِ ﴾ ـ أي لحب المال ـ ﴿ لَشَدِيدٌ ﴾ .

٣

ومنه الحديث الصحيح : اللهمّ انّـي أسألك[٢٩] ، حبك وحب (من يحبك وحب)[٣٠] عمل يقرّبني إلى حبك ، اللهمّ اجعل حبك أحب إليّ من الماء البارد .

ومنه قول مجنون بني[٣١] عامر شعر[٣٢] [وافر] :

أمـرُّ على الـديارِ ديارِ ليلى   أُقبِّـلُ ذا الجـدارَ وذا الجدارا[٣٣]
ومـا حب الـديارِ شغفـن[٣٤] قلبي   ولـكنْ حب من سكن الديارا

ومنه قول الشافعي ـ[٣٥] رضي الله تعالى عنه[٣٥] [كامل] :

لو كان رفضـا حبُّ آلِ محمد   فليشهَـدِ الثَّقَـلانِ أنّـي رافضي

[٣٦] وقال آخر[٣٦] [كامل] :

لو كان نصبـا حبُّ صحـبِ محمد   فليشهَـدِ الثَّقَـلانِ أنّـي ناصبي

[٣٧]وقال آخر[٣٧] [رمل] :

كلُّ من لم ير فرضـا حبَّهم   فهْـو مردود وان صلّى وصاما

[٦١٢ ب] ومما يوضح هذا المعنى ويبيّن هذا المبنى ما في « كامل » ابن عدي في ترجمة أبي يوسف صاحب أبي حنيفة[٣٨] ـ رحمهما الله تعالى ـ أنه روى عن عائشة ـ رضي الله عنها ـ أنّ النبي ـ صلى الله عليه وسلم ـ كان يصفي لها الاناء فتشرب ، ثم يتوضأ بفضلها ، (والحديث انتهى)[٣٩] .

وأما ما اشتهر على ألسنة العوام من[٤٠] أنّ هرة رقدت على ثوبه ـ صلى الله عليه وسلم ـ فأراد القيام للصلاة ، فقطع ثوبه مخافة انتباهها ، فكلام باطل[٤١] لا أصل له أصلا .

نعم روى أحمد والبزّار والدارقطني والحاكم والبيهقي من حديث أبي هريرة ـ [٤٢]رضي الله عنه[٤٢] ـ أنّ النبي ـ صلى الله عليه وسلم ـ دعي إلى دار قوم ، فأجاب ، ودعي إلى دار آخرين ، فلم يجب . فقيل له في ذلك ، فقال : انّ في دار فلان كلبا . فقيل له : انّ في دار فلان هرة ، فقال : الهرة ليست بنجس ، انما هي من الطوّافين عليكم والطوّافات !

٤

وروى ابن خيثمة عن ميمونة بنت سعيد مولاة رسول الله ـ صلى الله عليه وسلم ـ وهو في «الاستيعاب» ، عن سليمان خادم رسول الله ـ صلى الله عليه وسلم ـ أنه أوصى بالهرة ، وقال : ان امرأة عُذِّبت في هرة ربطتها ، ولم تطعمها ولم تتركها تأكل من حشرات الأرض ـ الحديث . وفي[٤٣] «الصحيحين» وفي [الأصل ٨٠ ب] « الزهد » لأحمد : رأيتها في النار تلمس قبلها ودبرها . قال القاضي عياض في شرح مسلم : يحتمل أن تكون[٤٤] كافرة ، ونفى النووي هذا الاحتمال .

وروى ابن عساكر في « تاريخه » عن بعض[٤٥] أصحاب الشبلي ، قال: رأيت الشبلي في النوم بعد موته ، فقلت : ما فعل الله بك ؟ قال : أوقفني بين يديه ، فقال : يا أبا بكر ، أتدري بماذا غفرت لك ؟ فقلت : بصالح[٤٦] عملي ؟ فقال : لا . فقلت : باخلاصي في عبوديتي ؟ قال[٤٧] : لا . قلت : بهجرتي إلى الصالحين ؟ فقال : لا . فقلت : باقامة أسفاري في طلب العلم ؟ فقال : لا . فقلت : يا ربِّ هذه المنجيات التي كنت أعقد عليها ضميري بظني[٤٨] أنك بها تعفو عني . قال : كل هذه لم أغفر لك بها . فقلت : فماذا ؟ قال : أتذكر حين كنت تمشي في درب بغداد ، فوجدتّ هرة صغيرة قد أضعفها البرد ، وهي تنزوى من جدار إلى جدار من شدة الثلج والبرد ، فأخذتّها رحمة لها ، فأدخلتها في فرو كان عليك وقاية لها من أليم البرد ؟ فقلت : نعم . قال : برحمتك لتلك الهرة رحمتك .

ومن الأمثال قالوا : أبرّ من هرة ، أرادوا بذلك أنها تأكل أولادها من شدة الحب لها . قال الشاعر [سريع] :

أما ترى الدهرَ وهذا الورى　　　كهرة تأكل أولادها

وقالوا : فلان لا يعرف هرا من بِر . قال ابن سيدة : معناه لا يعرف الهر من الفار ، يعني فانّ البر من معانيه الفأر . وقال الزمخشري : لا يعرف من يكرهه ممن يبره . وفي «القاموس» : أي[٤٩] ما يهره مما يبره ، أو القط من الفأر ، أو دعاء الغنم من[٥٠] سوقها ، أو دعاؤها إلى الماء من دعائها إلى العلف ، أو العقوق من اللطف ، أو الكراهية من الالزام ، أو الهرهرة من البربرة .

فهذا الذي سنح لي في هذا المقام ، والله أعلم بحقيقة المرام . والصلاة والسلام على سيد الأنام ، وعلى آله الكرام ، وصحبه العظام ، وتابعيه إلى يوم القيام ، والحمد لله الذي به البداء والختام .

٥

اصطلاحات وبعض تعليقات للمحقق

الأرقام التي بين هاتين الحاصرتين ([ ]) هي أرقام صفحات النسختين . وما بين هذين القوسين « » ساقط من الأصل ومكمل من النسخة الأخرى . والرموز الواردة في الحواشي هي كالآتي :
الأصل = المخطوطة المحفوظة في ميونيخ في ألمانيا ،
ب = المخطوطة المحفوظة في برلين .

١) ب : فقد/ ٢) اضافة من ب/ ٣) اضافة من ب/ ٤) الأصل : ان/ ٥) في النسختين: اصفا ، ولعل الصواب كذا/ ٥-أ) سقط من ب/ ٦) ب : علامته/ ٧) ب : الايقان/ ٨) ب : منها/ ٩) ب : وبين الايمان/ ١٠) ب : من الايمان/ ١١) سقط من ب/ ١٢) الأصل : ان لا/ ١٣) سقط من ب/ ١٤) ب : قرى العالم/ ١٥) سقط من ب/ ١٦) الأصل : اشتكل/ ١٧) لعل الأصل : سار ، ولكن الكلمة غير واضحة/ ١٨) لعل الأصل : ماءلوفه/ ١٩) اضافة من ب/ ٢٠) في النسختين : يكون حب الهرة لاحد يكون علامة لايمانه/ ٢١) ب : والظ/ ٢٢) الصواب من ب ، والأصل : المعنى/ ٢٣) ب : المتعال/ ٢٤) سقط من نص ب ولا توجد الكلمة الا في الهامش/ ٢٥) مكرر في ب/ ٢٦) سقط من ب/ ٢٧) ب : الخير/ ٢٨) سقط من ب/ ٢٩) في النسختين : اسئلك/ ٣٠) اضافة من ب/ ٣١) ب : بن/ ٣٢) سقط من ب/ ٣٣) ب : الجدار/ ٣٤) كذا في النسختين ، ولكن في «ديوان» مجنون : شغفن/ ٣٥) سقط من ب/ ٣٦) سقط من ب/ ٣٧) سقط من ب/ ٣٨) ب : ح/ ٣٩) اضافة من ب/ ٤٠) سقط من ب/ ٤١) ب : بط/ ٤٢) سقط من ب/ ٤٣) ب : وهي في/ ٤٤) الصواب من ب ، والأصل : يكون/ ٤٥) سقط من ب/ ٤٦) الأصل : باصالح ، والتصحيح في ب/ ٤٧) ب : فقال/ ٤٨) سقط من ب/ ٤٩) سقط من ب/ ٥٠) الصواب من ب ، والأصل : أمن .

The political significance of the Constitution of Medina

Al-Tayib Zein al-Abdin

I had the privilege of studying the Constitution of Medina, for a full academic year, under the knowledgeable guidance of Professor R. B. Serjeant in the congenial environment of the Faculty of Oriental Studies, at the University of Cambridge. It was Professor Serjeant who made me fully aware of the importance of this valuable document which has been rather neglected by Muslim scholars. Thus it suits the purpose of this publication, especially presented to Professor Serjeant at the occasion of his retirement, to make my modest contribution on a subject in which he stirred my deep interest. Being the original scholar, Professor Serjeant would, I know, appreciate that one of his students is trying his own wings in the wide horizon of academic research, making his independent assessment of a complexity of evidence and interpretations.

There is no need to discuss the historical authenticity of this document which has been proved beyond any reasonable doubt by a number of distinguished scholars.[1] We do not have to go into a detailed discussion about the exact date of the document, nor about how many treaties it originally comprised. The conclusion reached by Wellhausen, Caetani, Watt, Serjeant and Hamidullah that the first part of the Constitution was agreed upon in the first year of Hijrah, before the battle of Badr, is a logical one.[2] It was a political necessity that, before the Prophet Muḥammad became involved in any conflict, especially with a strong power such as the Quraysh of Mecca, he should make sure of the unity of his own internal front, the Muhājirūn (emigrants) of Mecca and the Anṣār (supporters) of Medina. There are good arguments to suppose that the Constitution was written in parts and over a period of time; nevertheless, any exact number for these parts or any definite date for them remains an unverifiable hypothesis. No wonder the historians who discussed these points have derived different conclusions.[3]

The problem which this paper attempts to discuss is the political implications of the Constitution as a whole: what were the objectives behind its design and how did it help the Prophet Muḥammad gradually to create a central government in the Hijaz. To see the Constitution as a typical agreement, known to the Arab tribes long before Islam, fails to explain the emergence of the political power of Muḥammad and its systematic build up.[4] This great achievement could not have been possible without the inter-relation framework set in the Constitution. All the political consequences might not have been clear to Muḥammad in his first year of the Hijrah, when the Constitution was partly written, but it would be a grotesque understatement of his genius to suppose that the political developments taking place after the Hijrah were never conceived by him. This article hopes to explain that the agreements embodied in the Constitution set the pattern for the political developments which occurred at later stages.

The purpose of the Hijrah

Muḥammad did not emigrate to Medina simply to flee from the persecution he suffered at the hands of Quraysh. After propagating Islam for thirteen years among his Meccan kinsmen Muḥammad realised that no future awaited his message in Mecca, and that a breakthrough had to come from another quarter. That was why the Prophet began to approach the Arab tribes living in the neighbourhood of Mecca and others from elsewhere when they came there for pilgrimage. He addressed himself to the tribes of Kindah, Kalb, Banū ʿĀmir and Thaqīf. He used to tell them: I am the Messenger of God to you, obey God alone and get rid of those idols whom you worship, believe me and have trust in me till I explain what God sent me to convey.[5] Thus he was asking for an abode from which he could deliver the Message of God rather than for personal protection. None of those tribes responded to his plea. A hopeful sign came when six men from Yathrib accepted the call of the Prophet and started to spread it among their people. This incident is known in Islamic annals as the First Pledge of ʿAqabah. It was a spiritual and moral pledge by which the pioneer Yathribites promised the Prophet: not to associate anything with God, not to steal, not to commit fornication, not to kill their children, not to slander their neighbours and not to disobey the Messenger of God in what was right. Nevertheless, a member of the group conceived an objective of a political nature. They told the Prophet that they had left their people (the Aws and Khazraj) divided by hatred and rancour, and hoped that God might unite them under His Messenger. Muḥammad, anxious to make the best out of this opportunity, sent to Yathrib (Medina) one of his devoted companions Muṣʿab b. ʿUmayr, to educate the new converts about Islam and to persuade new followers from among the populace of Yathrib. His mission was a complete success. In the next year seventy-three men and two women came on pilgrimage and took, before the Prophet, the famous Second Pledge of ʿAqabah.

The Second Pledge of ʿAqabah was clearly a political commitment which, later, led to the Hijrah of the Prophet. The group of men and women, who promised to protect the Messenger of God as they protected their own selves, had no illusion about the possible consequences of that promise. Before taking the pledge, a leading member in the group warned his comrades that they were giving protection to Muḥammad at a dear price: they would have to make war against all kinds of people which could lead to the loss of their property and the death of their chiefs.[6] Another member, Abū 'l-Haytham b. al-Tayyihān, said, '"O apostle, we have ties with other men (he meant the Jews) and if we sever them perhaps when we have done that and God will have given you victory, you will return to your people and leave us?" The apostle smiled and said: "Nay, blood is blood and blood not to be paid for is blood not to be paid for. I am of you and you are of me. I will war against them that war against you and be at peace with those at peace with you."'[7] A practical step followed this firm pact. Twelve *nuqabā'* (chiefs) were selected, representing all who attended the meeting, in order to be guarantors of the Pledge and to disseminate the message of Islam in Medina on behalf of the Prophet. Although the *nuqabā'* were chosen according to the strength of their clans, it was nevertheless a pointer to a new organisation based on religious commitment.

At last Muḥammad had found the refuge from which he could spread his message to the rest of Arabia. He and his Medinan supporters realised that the destiny of Islam and Medina became inseparable. Those who attended the Second 'Aqabah could not have given their promise to protect the Prophet unless they knew that Islam had entered almost every Arab household in Medina, and that no significant opposition would be expected to the Messenger of God's settling among them.[8] Being weary of their internal conflicts and rancour, the Medinans had every reason to welcome the Hijrah of the Prophet to their town. Even if that Hijrah led to fighting with other people it would be better than fighting among themselves.

The objectives of the Constitution

What Muḥammad and the Medinans needed most was peaceful coexistence in Medina, for he could not hope to achieve much for his message without internal unity. Al-Wāqidī summarised appropriately the purpose of the Constitution as follows: 'When the Messenger of God came to Medina its inhabitants were a mixed lot, consisting of Muslims whom the call of Islam had united, part being owners of mail coats and forts and part allies of both tribes, the Aws and Khazraj. After arriving at Medina, the Messenger of God wished to make concord among all the groups, and to establish peace with them. A man would be a Muslim and his father a polytheist. From among the inhabitants of Medina, the polytheists and the Jews caused most hurt to the Messenger of God and his Companions, but God – the Honourable and Glorious – ordered His Prophet and the Muslims to be patient with them and to forgive them'.[9] No doubt the primary objective of the Prophet in writing the Constitution was to establish peace in Medina. This can be clearly seen in the following pages.

Naturally enough the first part of the Constitution was written between the followers of Muḥammad themselves, the Muslims from Quraysh (Muhājirūn) on the one hand and Yathrib (Anṣār) on the other. A significant point was that the Agreement included those who would follow the Muslims and strive with them (clause 1); later this was applied to the Jews as well who would accept the Agreement (clause 16).[10] This shows how Muḥammad, from the beginning visualised an open citizenship for the Medinan community. Clause 39 made Wadi Yathrib sacred so that no conflict should arise between the different groups in Medina. Muḥammad considered the various reasons which might generate discord in Medina or might cause a limited dispute to flare up into a wider conflict and he attempted to find solutions for these eventualities in the Agreement. The Prophet did not try to impose Islam as the only religion in Medina; he stated that the Jews had their own religion and the Muslims theirs and both enjoyed the security of their populace and clients except the unjust and the criminal among them (clause 25). The difference in the customs of paying blood-money or ransoming captives between the Muhājirūn and Anṣār could cause problems among the Muslims themselves. That was why the Prophet specified for every group and clan that in paying blood-money or freeing captives they should follow their old customs (clauses 2–10). The paying of blood-money and ransom for freeing captives was a problematic issue in Arabia, as it was done according to the status of the men involved and the stature of their clans or tribes. However, these considerations were not always agreed upon by the parties to the dispute and this would often lead to bloodshed among them.

Similarly, other potential sources of conflict were spelt out: that no woman should be given protection without the consent of her people (clause 41); that no believer should take as an ally a freedman of another believer without his permission (clause 12); and that no man would be responsible for a crime committed by his ally (clause 37). The last point had stirred up many a fight among the Arab tribes because it was considered shameful not to give support to one's ally whether he were in the right or not.

The Constitution obliged the believers not to help or give shelter to a wrong-doer (clause 22), but none would be prevented from taking revenge for wounds (clause 36). A major source of conflict was dealt with appropriately by asking the believers to stand together against whosoever rebelled or committed sin or aggression, even though he was one of their own sons (clause 13). All parties to the Constitution agreed to refer to Muḥammad any dispute or quarrel that might cause dissension in Medina (clause 42). None of them was allowed to go out to war without the permission of Muḥammad (clause 36), and whoever of the groups of Medina was summoned to make peace should agree to that summons (clause 45).

It is obvious that all these clauses mentioned above were meant to preserve peace among the various groups of Medina. Had it not been for the patience and statemanship of the Prophet, these agreements alone would not have led to the internal peace enjoyed by the Medinans. After realising that the peace in Medina was most beneficial to Muḥammad's cause, the Hypocrites (*munāfiqūn*) and the Jews attempted to stir up the Medinan tribes against the 'Qurashīs' (i.e. the Muhājirūn), but without avail.[11]

The second objective of Muḥammad was to bring together all the groups in Medina to defend their town against a likely attack from Quraysh. Whatever their real feelings, no group could become party to the Constitution without accepting its share of responsibility in defending Medina against external aggression. Clause 37 stated that the Jews and the

Muslims should help each other against whoever attacked the people of the Document, and that each party should bear its share of the expenses of war. The Jews were specifically mentioned in three clauses (24, 37, 38) in relation to the defence of Medina, probably, because the Prophet was not sure that they would keep their promise. The area which each group had to defend was named as the side of the town closest to their homes (clause 45). That should make them more earnest in the fighting as they would be defending their houses and properties. However, subsequent events showed that the Jews did not abide by this agreement. In the two cases when Medina was attacked by Quraysh (the battles of Uḥud and al-Khandaq), instead of coming to the assistance of the Muslims, the Jews leant towards the enemy. There is no wonder that, after each of the two battles, a major Jewish tribe was punished by the Prophet for its betrayal.[12]

A further political objective envisaged by the Prophet was to isolate Quraysh from any alignment with a group in Medina. It was not enough for him that the different groups in Medina agreed to defend the town against Quraysh. The Prophet knew that the real obstacle that hindered the spread of Islam in Arabia was the opposition of Quraysh; thus it had to be overcome by force. The Muhājirūn, who had suffered a great deal at the hands of the Quraysh in Mecca, would not hesitate to follow the Prophet in a war against their former oppressors. That was why all the Muslim raids against Quraysh, prior to the battle of Badr, were wholly constituted from the Muhājirūn. The Anṣār, who pledged themselves to protect the Prophet inside Medina, might not welcome the idea of attacking Mecca but there was no question of allying themselves with the Quraysh if the Messenger of God attacked them. Therefore, the two clauses (20 and 43), which forbade anyone to protect Quraysh, their property or allies from a Muslim attack, were mainly intended to win over the neutrality of the Jews in an inevitable confrontation with Quraysh. Clause 20 plainly stated that no polytheist (*mushrik*) should grant protection to a person or property belonging to Quraysh against the interest of a believer. Clause 43 stressed the same point in a general manner stipulating that Quraysh and their allies, should be given neither help nor neighbourly protection. The Prophet also prepared the way for the confrontation with Quraysh by making peace with the tribes living between Mecca and Medina, such as Banū Ḍamrah and Banū Mudlij.[13]

The Prophet also aimed that all the groups in Medina should recognise him as the ultimate arbiter in matters of dispute. This would help in the process of a peaceful coexistence for all the inhabitants in Medina but it would also help in building up the leadership of the Prophet over the different groups. Clause 23 stated that any matter in which they differed, was to be referred to God and to Muḥammad. It is most likely that the people addressed here were the believers themselves, for they should be more ready than others to bring their differences before the Prophet: in fact a number of Quranic verses obliged them to do so.[14] The non-believers were asked to refer a dispute to Muḥammad only when a disaster was feared because of that quarrel (clause 42). Furthermore, the Prophet gave himself the right to decide about any fighting by any group outside Medina, as clause 36 said that no group in the city should go to war without the permission of Muḥammad.

If the Prophet was to decide about the serious disputes arising between the various groups of Medina and about making war, or not making war, these in themselves were no 'slight powers' as Watt claims.[15] However, these powers were gradually enhanced to make the Prophet in few years the undisputed ruler of all Arabia. How the Prophet managed to transfer that fragmented tribal society into a united state based on religion can be partly explained by the agreements embodied in this Constitution.

It must have been an important objective in the mind of the Prophet to strengthen the religious brotherhood among the believers vis-à-vis the tribal bond. It was not possible for him to ignore the blood ties between the different groups; that was why he wrote the Constitution between groups and not between individuals. However, the tribal grouping recognised in the Constitution was given a positive social role: that was to follow their traditions in paying blood-money and in freeing captives (clauses 2–10). At the same time the Constitution attempted to mitigate the clanship association. The second clause in the Constitution stated that the believers from Quraysh and Yathrib were a single community standing apart from other people. In other words, the religious relationship was put higher than any other form of relationship. Despite the fact that the social solidarity of paying ransom or blood-money was handed to the clan, the believers should be the second resort for the poor among them (clause 12). The believer was distinguished from the non-believer and, thus, he could not be killed in retaliation for a non-believer or a non-believer be supported against him (clause 14). In the case of a believer being unjustly killed his murderer should be slain unless his next of kin were satisfied with the payment of blood-money. All the believers should stand together against that murderer (clause 21). Furthermore, the believers were called upon to oppose any wrongdoer, even if he were the son of one of themselves (clause 13); they should give him neither refuge nor support and whoever did so deserved the curse of God and His wrath on the Day of Resurrection (clause 22). These two clauses were directed at the heart of tribal values, the support given to the next of kin against any outsider no matter who had been the aggressor. By agreeing to stand against the aggressor, even if he were a dear relative, the Muslims gave their first loyalty to their religion. Clause 17 committed the believers to make peace or war together. They also should exact vengeance for one another where a man gave his blood in the way of God (clause 19). In effect, these clauses made the Muslims, despite their different tribal grouping, a close community distinct from all other people.

It is clear that the Prophet in this Constitution, managed to found a framework of relations for the different groups of Medina in order to establish peace among them, to propagate his message among the tribes and to face at the time of his choice his old enemy, Quraysh of Mecca. He strengthened the religious brotherhood of his followers to the extent that they were ready to oppose their nearest relatives at his demand. Muslims and non-Muslims in Medina accepted his authority in arbitrating in their disputes and in deciding the question of war and peace. In that simple tribal society there were no more important issues than arbitration and the making of war. It is difficult to accept the notion that the Constitution of Medina was no more than a typical tribal agreement common at the time of the Prophet and still is among certain tribes in South Arabia.[16] The set of rules stated in the Agreement were the natural beginning for the centralised administration which emerged in Arabia. That is why it may not be a wild exaggeration to call it 'The First Written Constitution in the World'.

Notes

[1] J. Wellhausen, 'Gemeindeordnung von Medina', in *Skizzen und Vorarbeiten*, Berlin, 1899, IV, 74–86; R. B. Serjeant, 'The Constitution of Medina', in *Islamic Quarterly*, London, 1964, VIII/1–2; L. Caetani, *Annali dell'Islam*, I; M. Hamidullah, *Le Prophète de l'Islam*, Paris, 1959, I, 133–137; M. Watt, *Muḥammad at Medina*, Oxford, 1956, 221–228.

[2] Ibid.

[3] Hamidullah in *The First Written Constitution in the World* (3rd ed., Lahore, 1975, 19) suggests that it was two parts, the first written before Badr and the second immediately after; Serjeant argues that the Constitution comprised eight separate treaties, the first written during the first year of Hijrah and the last was added in the 7th year, 'The Sunnah Jāmiʿah, pacts with the Yathrib Jews, and the *taḥrīm* of Yathrib:', in the *Bulletin of the School of Oriental and African Studies*, XLI, 1, 1978, 9, 39. Professor Serjeant does not always state who were the parties to each separate treaty. He depends completely on a recurring phrase as marking the end of each separate treaty.

[4] See Serjeant, ibid., 1, 2.

[5] Cf. A. Guillaume, *The life of Muhammad*, Oxford, 1955, 194 ff.

[6] Guillaume, 203.

[7] Guillaume, 203–4. This promise explains why the Prophet remained in Medina, making it the capital of his government, even after the conquest of Mecca.

[8] See *Muḥammad at Medina*, 174–78.

[9] *Kitāb al-Maghāzī*, (*ed.*) Marsden Jones, Oxford, 1966, I, 184.

[10] The numbering of clauses used here is that of Watt in *Medina*, 221–25.

[11] See Ibn Hishām.

[12] It is surprising that European Arabists who attempted to explain the expulsion of the Jews from Medina never mention this point.

[13] Ibn Saʿd, *al-Ṭabaqāt al-Kubrā*, II, 6, 10.

[14] *Al-Nisā'*: 65, *al-Shūrā*: 10.

[15] *Medina*, 228.

[16] See Serjeant 'The Sunnah Jāmi ʿah', *BSOAS*, 1–2.

PART 3

The Modern Period

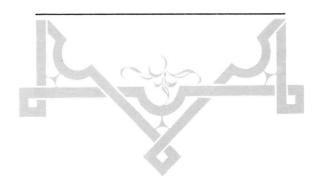

Feminism and feminist Movements in the Middle East; a preliminary Exploration: Turkey, Egypt, Algeria, People's Democratic Republic of Yemen.

Leila Ahmed

In her article on Egyptian women in the early nineteenth century Naḍa Tomiche draws attention to a curious and terrible story. Following Napoleon's invasion of Egypt and during the brief French occupation General Menou married a woman from Rosetta, becoming a Muslim and calling himself ʿAbd Allāh Menou in order to do so. He treated her 'in the French manner':

> ... led her by the hand into the dining-room, offered her the best seat at the table and the tastiest pieces of food. If her handkerchief fell to the ground he would hurriedly pick it up. When this woman had narrated these things at the Rosetta bathouse, the others began to hope for change and signed a petition to the Sultan Kabir (Bonaparte) to have their husbands treat them in the same manner. (Tomiche, 1966, 180, citing Clot-Bey, 1840)

It was probably this petition and similar audacities on the part of the women which, Tomiche speculates, led to the carnage which was to follow – again as reported by a French contemporary: 'I have heard Franks who were in Egypt when the French army left this country. They described to me horrible deeds which occurred in harems at the time. Up to several thousands of women were massacred, poisoned, or drowned in the Nile', (1966, 180). Not least curious about this story is how almost wholly it has been allowed to drop out of history. A shadow of it though appears in the pages of al-Jabarti (1754–1825) who so voluminously chronicled the Egypt of his day. The last great historian in the ancient tradition, he laments the 'pernicious innovations' and the 'corruption of women' that the French occupation brought about, and he records that the daughter of one of the greatest religious notables, Shaykh al-Bakrī, was killed after the French departed because she had mingled with them and dressed like a French woman (Jabarti, 1322 A.H. iii, 202).

Despite this bloody beginning change in the status of women in the Muslim world following upon increased contact with and openness to the West most often in fact proceeded smoothly and relatively rapidly. Far and away ahead of other Middle Eastern societies in reforms relating to women was Turkey, although they were once also responsible for developing furthest the institution of the harem until it was almost militaristically organised around the notion of woman purely as sex-object and reproduction machine. Thus, in addition to 'a multitude of female slaves and eunuch-guards' the Turkish harem contained 'a group of women chosen for their beauty and destined for the pleasure and service of the Sultan. They were organised in pyramidical form, at base of which was the Sagrideler (Novices), from which class, after wholesale eliminations, the most talented in arts and beauty were promoted to Gedikliler (Privileged Ones). It was at this stage that they first came into direct personal contact with the Sultan and in accordance with his desires, he chose those who were to share his bed. A girl thus honoured was known as Gozde (In Favour) and if the relationship showed any sign of permanence, she was promoted to the rank of Ikbal ... (Fortunate)' (Alderson, 1956, 79–80). Aside from the imperial harem, city women rarely left the house and were hemmed in even when they did by imperial decrees as to where they might go, and precisely prescribing their dress and comportment in public places – and even specifying the days of the week on which they might leave the house. But even during the most repressive pre-reform periods, some women were privately educated and a few became famous as writers, composers, calligraphers – and one as an astronomer. It was not they however, nor indeed women at all, who first called for reforms regarding women's condition.

The first moves in that direction came about as an undesigned consequence of the Ottomans' attempts to modernise Turkey. Already in the eighteenth century as the scientific revolution in Europe and advances in military technology placed Europe clearly in the lead, the need for reform and for adopting Western methods, began to be voiced. The influence of Western embassies in the imperial capital now increased, European advisers were sought and Turkish men sent to newly opened embassies abroad, so by the 1820s there existed a group who were familiar with the European heritage of ideas. In 1826, as a preliminary step to re-organising the army the Janissaries were disbanded and suppressed – a year taken now as marking the beginning of the *Tanzimat* or period of reform. In the following year male student missions were sent to various European countries; in the same year a medical school staffed by Europeans was opened in Istanbul to train doctors for the army; in 1831–2 two military schools were opened, and in 1838 primary and secondary schools for male civilians, and then in 1842 a school for midwives. Midwives presumably were thus singled out because they constituted a group practising what even males had agreed to recognise as a profession: courses were offered, Taskiran informs us, by a European specialist, and 'the government made all practising midwives attend' (1974, 32). Midwives moreover were evidently of a class of women that even at that early date could be taught by men without any concern for their 'honour'.

Not so other Turkish females. An attempt was made to start a girls' primary school in the 1850s – but failed because there were no women teachers and the school had had to be staffed by elderly males. In 1870 a teachers' college for women was opened, staffed, as its regulations stipulated, 'only by elderly men of good character', and in addition elaborate precautions were taken to insure that student and teacher were always chaperoned and never met face to face (Taskiran, 1974, 38). Fifty places were offered, and thirty-two women enrolled. In the same year a girls' primary school was also opened.

In the last decades of the nineteenth century and early in the next the emancipation of women and their education became issues much discussed, particularly by the Young Turks and their reformist and nationalist sympathisers, many of whom were graduates of the new schools. Numerous newspapers were established in which, for the first time in Turkey, a wide range of political and social reforms were freely demanded. The new graduates, including those of the teachers' college for women, published articles on the need for reform. In 1895 the first Turkish women's weekly began to be published and its contributors, almost all women, emphasised the need for education and stressed 'the three major aims of how to become a good mother, a good wife, and a good Moslem' (Taskiran, 1974: 35). Eminent male writers took up the issue. Ziya Gokalp wrote: 'In the future, Turkish ethics must be founded upon democracy and feminism, as well as nationalism, patriotism, work, and the strength of the family'; Ahmed Agaogly stressed that progress in the Islamic world depended on two factors: literacy and the emancipation of women, and Tevfik Fikret, that 'When women are debased, humanity is degraded' – and this last was adopted by the feminist movement as its slogan (Taskiran, 45, 43).

The emancipation and education of women thus became one of the reforms agitated for by the nationalist revolutionary movement and so linked with its success. Until the end of the first world war and the dissolution of empire the reformers were involved in power struggles with the sultanate but were still able to put through a number of reforms and to make important advances particularly in education. More girls' schools were opened, as were lycées (which allowed for the more extended period of study of ten years) and more women's teacher training colleges. In 1912 the nationalists opened community centres which offered lectures and cultural events which women as well as men were encouraged to attend leading to complaints that they 'were being corrupted and incited to revolt, and that they were playing the violin and reading poetry'. (Taskiran, 44). In 1914 some lectures at the University of Istanbul were opened to women: and in September of that year a university for women, affiliated to the teacher training college, was established. In 1920 women were transferred to Istanbul University proper, and the following year segregation was formally ended. Over the same years the scope of women's lives dramatically changed, because of the war – women worked in government offices, in the post-office, and as factory workers, nurses and street-cleaners, replacing men. At the end of the war the Sultan signed a peace treaty agreeing to the dismemberment of Turkey, and this led to a rebellion in which Anatolian women played an important part. (Halide Edib Adivar one of Turkey's leading women writers and feminists, served as corporal, sergeant and sergeant-major).

Kamal Ataturk, the country's new President, argued strongly for women's equality and full participation in labour on the grounds that only thus could Turkey progress. 'A country which seeks development and modernisation must accept the need for change', he said in a speech in Izmir in 1923, 'the weakness of our society lies in our indifference to the status of women'. One of Turkey's major needs he declared, was 'the enlightenment of our women in every field. They shall become educated in science and the arts; they shall have the opportunity to attend any school and attain every level of education'. At first Ataturk argued for change in the status of women – as also with other of his government's modernising secularist objectives – while seeking to conciliate and even to exploit the values of Muslim orthodoxy (Turkey was the first Muslim nation to broach feminist issues on a national political level, and the attitudes and formulations he used were to be repeatedly resorted to this century by other modernising Muslim states, for instance Iran before the recent revolution, and Tunisia). Thus, the education of women was legitimised within a Muslim framework by stressing its importance if women were to fulfil their 'highest duty' as mothers: ('paradise', runs a much-quoted *ḥadīth* 'lies under the feet of mothers'.) Furthermore, Ataturk declared in this same speech at Izmir, not Islam but 'distorting customs' originating in corrupt palaces had been responsible for the oppression of women: 'our enemies accuse us of being under the influence of religion, and they attribute our stagnation and decay to this factor. That is a great mistake, for nothing in our religion requires women to be inferior to men'. On the contrary he continued – referring here to another popular *ḥadīth* (plaques inscribed with it adorn many an Arab office now, particularly in Ministries of Education) 'the pursuit of knowledge is a duty enjoined upon every soul'. (Taskiran, 55–6.)

This conciliatory line however he soon abandoned, for on the issue of women the conservatives were proving too entrenched. A committee appointed in 1923 to review Islamic family law and to suggest ways of making it more equitable to women, came up with no significant proposals – so that their review constituted in effect an endorsement of the law as it stood. In the same year the National Assembly plunged into angry debate as to whether a law permitting men and women to sit in the same compartments on public transport (and not as previously required in separate compartments) would be violating the principles of a Muslim republic. Radical reform therefore within the old framework, particularly in relation to women, was evidently highly unlikely: and the old framework was consequently summarily jettisoned. Turkey was declared a laic state, the veil outlawed, and the Islamic family laws replaced by a civil code (1926) modelled on that of Neuchâtel, Switzerland. In 1930 women were given the vote.

Thus by 1930 Turkish women had achieved legal and civil status equal to that of women in the more advanced of European countries – and against how different a background, how different a reality. Details such as the debate over sex-segregation on public transport, or the warning issued to women in 1911 by Sheykh-ul-Islam not to wear European dress, or the arrest in 1920 of the first Turkish actress to appear on stage – simply for appearing – give some notion of how oppressively interfering and restrictive the state had been towards women. And other records of moments in women's lives more sombrely make evident how ordinary and 'natural' a part of the fabric of living was the pain of women, the deprivation of women – and how shot through that reality was with, reduced to its essence, contempt for women, for women's pain, women's lives. The debate on sex-segregation on public transport for instance translates thus into the reality of lived experience: the law requiring segregation meant that on boats sailing the Bosphorus, women were obliged to stay in closed cabins below deck. 'When women were finally permitted to remain on deck, a female author described her feelings at being able to watch the sea in the open air during the one-hour boat trip with such zest that one would think she was crossing the ocean for the first time' (Afetinan, 1962, 42). To cite only one more such record – a description of the deposed Sultan Abdel Hamid's harem – the last imperial harem – in 1909:

> One of the most mournful processions of the many mournful processions of fallen grandeur that passed through the streets during these days was one composed of the ladies of the ex-Sultan's Harem on their way from Yildiz to the Top-Kapu Palace ... These unfortunate ladies were of all ages between fifteen and fifty and so numerous that it took thirty-one carriages to convey them ... Some of them were sent to the Old Seraglio in Stamboul, but his old palace of the early Sultans had fallen into such a state of disrepair that it was found to be unsuitable for them and they were sent back to Yildiz. Finally they were collected in the Top-Kapu Palace in connection with one of the strangest ceremonies that ever took place there. It is well-known that most of the ladies of the harems of Turkish sultans were Circassians, the Circassian girls being very much esteemed on account of their beauty and being consequently very expensive ... The Turkish government telegraphed to the different Circassian villages in Anatolia, notifying them that every family which happened to have any of its female members in the ex-Sultan's Harem were at liberty to take them home, no matter whether the girls had been originally sold by their families or had (as was the case in some instances) been torn from their homes by force.
>
> In consequence of this, a large number of Circassian mountaineers came in their picturesque garb into Constantinople, and on a certain fixed day they were conducted in a body to the Old Palace of Top-Kapu, where, in the presence of the Turkish Commission, they were ushered into a long hall filled with the ex-Sultan's concubines ... all of whom were then allowed to unveil themselves for the occasion ... (McCullagh, 1910: 276, quoted in Penzer, 1936; 20–21.)

This passage, it should be stressed, records a moment in the lives of the women of Abdel Hamid's harem – but also a moment in the lives of all women who witnessed it and all women who heard of it: just as simply the very existence of harems as a 'natural' part of their social environment must inescapably form part of and inerasably scar the consciousness of every woman and child.

The new laws were to be slow in their impact on rural, as distinct from urban, Turkey. For instance the law abolishing polygamy gave property rights only to children of marriages performed by the secular authorities: despite this, and despite the fact that their children would be considered illegitimate as well as disinherited according to the civil code, men in the rural areas continued to marry more than one wife, performing only the religious ceremony. By 1950 the Turkish authorities had granted legal status to eight million children (at a time when the population was about 21 million), which gives some idea of the prevalence of the habit (Coşar 1978: 127). In urban Turkey however the old patterns swiftly disappeared and women entered and since have been freely entering the professions (one third of university professors for instance now are women): for the urban Turkish woman the battle for equality is therefore essentially now no different from and probably no greater than that of her Western sisters.

In Egypt as in Turkey the advocates of feminist notions were initially men. As in Turkey these ideas grew out of not a new concern for women *per se* or a new pressing sense of the wrongs done to women but rather out of the conviction that educating women and raising their status was part and even perhaps the chief part of a necessary process of regeneration and transformation that society must undergo for the sake of progress and the advancement of the whole nation. In the centuries immediately preceding the emergence of these ideas, European travellers had regularly commented on what they were alternately fascinated or appalled by, or envious of: the undisguised male control of women in Muslim societies, and the explicit and unequivocal ways in which women were regarded and treated as inferior. It was in this respect that Muslim societies most visibly and glaringly differed from Western societies: and as the Muslim world declined in power Westerners contemplating the 'degenerateness' 'despotism', 'vice' and general 'backwardness' of the Muslim East came up with some unanimity with the idea that at the root of these lay its degradation of women. In perceiving the status of women as perhaps the single most important aspect of their society in need of reform, Middle Eastern thinkers were therefore to some extent endorsing the diagnosis reached by Westerners. Ataturk for instance declared: 'In some places I have seen women who put a piece of cloth or a towel or something like that over their heads to hide their faces, and who turn their backs or huddle themselves on the ground when a man passes by. What are the meaning and sense of this behaviour? Gentlemen, can the mothers and daughters of a civilised nation adopt this strange manner, this barbarous posture? It is a spectacle that makes the nation an object of ridicule. It must be remedied at once. (Ataturk, speech at Kastamonu, 1925, quoted in Lewis, 1961, 165).

Nevertheless it would be erroneous to conclude that in endorsing Westerners' diagnosis, Muslim thinkers were simply uncritically echoing their ideas: on the contrary their conclusions notably Qāsim Amīn's in

Egypt were often developed from a comprehensive and rigorous analysis of their societies and a perfectly lucid sense of the various oppressions operating within them.

Ideas of reform and feminist notions emerged in Egypt out of a process that closely paralleled that which occurred in Turkey. Egypt was of course at least nominally part of the Ottoman empire, and their societies were sufficiently linked for their rulers and thinkers to be acting out a shared societal experience and a commonality of ideas. In some ways even, it was Egypt, under the more dynamic Muḥammad ʿAlī, who led the way. Muḥammad ʿAlī had for instance sent student missions to Europe the year before Turkey decided to do so. Similarly the medical school in Egypt was established just before that of Turkey. And in Egypt also, as already implied, it was among those open to Western thought, and who set themselves to explore the Western heritage, that reformist and feminist notions were born. And such ideas here even found a champion in a leading Azhar-trained, religious figure – Shaykh Muḥammad ʿAbduh, eventually (1899) Grand Mufti and one of the most prominent Egyptian reformists. Their more secular exponent, Qāsim Amīn (1865–1908) published his work on the emancipation of women (*Taḥrīr al-mara'ah*) in 1899 – arousing a storm of protest: in the few months after its publication a series of books and pamphlets were published attacking it – and a very few supporting it. In reply Amīn published a second book in 1900, on the 'new woman' (*al-Mar'ah al-jadīdah*): these two books are still looked upon in the Arab world as the seminal works on feminism – and can still, so liberal are they seen to be, rouse considerable hostility among conservative and religious elements.

But while the issue of women and the improvement of their condition was thus as live among Egyptian intellectuals as it was among Turkish, no government, party, or individual with access to power was to adopt it as a central issue – and this was to make a crucial difference to the evolution of the women's movement in Egypt. On education for instance, the government in Egypt made some moves towards making it available for women, but stopped well short of what was done in Turkey over the corresponding period. Thus a school was founded in 1873 which in 1874 admitted 400 girls – but by 1920 there were still only five government primary schools for girls, and the government made no attempt to provide more advanced schooling until 1925, when it opened the first secondary school. Private education by contrast seems to have been thriving (Bohdanowicz, 1951) so that when the Egyptian university opened its doors to women in 1928, six women were in a position to enrol in the medical faculty, and a number of others in the faculty of arts and science. Privately educated women contributed in the first decades of the century to journals established in Cairo mainly by Levantine women (who were predominantly Christian, and possibly in one or two cases, Jewish).

Women in Egypt were to be much more actively involved in the fight for their rights than they had been in Turkey: whereas in the latter the inception of feminist ideas to the granting of new rights to women had in fact been a remarkably swift process, in Egypt many of the rights granted their Turkish sisters in the 1920s have still not been granted. In the twenties a committee was set up in Egypt just as one had been in Turkey, to review Islamic family law with a view to revising it towards a more equitable treatment of women but as in Turkey the committee essentially endorsed the law as it stood. But unlike Turkey (and in different degrees, later, Tunisia) the government did not see fit, nor has any government since, to set aside the inevitably conservative findings of religious committees and sever women's civil and marital status from the heritage of Islamic received ideas.

The first political action in which women became involved in Egypt was in 1919, when hundreds of women marched through the streets of Cairo in support of the nationalists against the British, led by the wives of prominent nationalist politicians – among them Hudā Sha 'rāwī. Although the issue had been nationalist and in no way feminist, nevertheless the women's very participation seems to have enpowered them, henceforth, to take a stand on issues relating to their own status. In 1922 Hudā Sha 'rāwī formed, with her friends, the Egyptian Feminist Union – and was from then on through the twenties and thirties to be a central figure in the women's movement. In 1923 she led the Egyptian women's delegation to an international women's conference in Rome. It was at this time that she cast off her veil and thus inspired Egyptian women of the middle and upper classes to do the same. Much is made at the moment in literature on women in the Middle East of the fact that it was mainly women of the middle and upper classes who wore the veil, and of the fact that the necessities of work meant that working women did not in fact much wear it: therefore, the argument runs, the issue of wearing or not wearing the veil is really of very little significance since only a very small number anyway were affected. It consequently seems necessary here briefly to state the obvious. It is the idea of the veil much more than the veil's material presence that is the powerful symbol of their non-participation, passivity and even invisibility, in the public domain.

During the 1920s and 1930s Sha 'rāwī and her group were active in seeking to increase education for women and in urging the government, with some success, to provide free public education for girls. They campaigned too for reforms in Islamic family law – though unfortunately without any significant success (and to this day reforms in this area have been minimal). Thus Sha 'rāwī delivered a lecture in 1935 at the American University in Cairo, in which she called for 'the restriction or abolition of polygamy'. At this point in her speech, Woodsmall has reported, two white-turbaned shaykhs from al-Azhar, of whom there were many in the audience, rose up and shouted: 'Long live polygamy!' (Woodsmall, 1936, 121).

Sha 'rāwī's call for 'the restriction or abolition' of polygamy is typical in its cautious conservatism. As Woodsmall observed, Sha 'rāwī 'carefully based her demands for social reform on the spirit of the Koran and has not promoted reforms which do not have Islamic sanction. For example her claims for equality of education for girls have been based on the teachings of the Koran'; similarly when protesting against polygamy, she 'recognised the exceptions for polygamy which are granted by the Koran' (adultery, childlessness, and incompatability). 'One has the feeling', continues Woodsmall, 'that this policy of maintaining a careful balance between Islamic teaching and social reform, which is followed by Madame Sharawi and the Feminist Union is dictated more by political expediency than by religious conservatism'. (Woodsmall, 1936, 404).

No doubt this conservatism, even decorousness to women's demands, and the style in which women's demands were made was essential to some at least of these demands being granted: and no doubt Woodsmall was to some extent right in seeing it as a matter of political expediency. However this zeal in wishing to be seen to be observing the proprieties, even to be emphasising them, and to be seen to be absolutely and irreproachably respectful of Islam/Arabness is a fundamental trait not only of Sha 'rāwī but of feminists in the Arab world generally. Far from being a matter simply of diplomacy, of astute women practising 'the art of the possible', it is rather, I would argue, a position imposed upon feminism and feminists by the internal needs of Islamic civilisation – and it is an imposition that has had the consequence that feminism in the Arab world has never (never, until at least the last few years) seriously challenged that civilisation's conception of the role of women, and has been a matter – when all is said and done – of requesting merely (and often deferentially) that injustice be trimmed a little here and there, and oppression perhaps sugared over a little here, curbed slightly there.

Malak Ḥifnī Nāṣif's famous 'ten points' document beautifully exemplifies both the qualities mentioned above as typical of the history of Arab feminism, and of how feminism then becomes merely an instrument by which the fundamental assumptions of the culture are re-inforced. Nāsif, honoured as one of the pioneers of Egyptian and Arab feminism, drew up and presented to the Legislative Assembly in the 1910's ten points that she considered should form the basis of reforms for women: and the document, ostensibly in support of women's rights, in fact overwhelmingly endorses the Arabic civilisation's traditional conception of women. Thus its points include: teaching of true religion for girls – the Qur'ān and the true Sunnah; teaching domestic science, theoretical and practical health laws, training of children, etc. She asked for a certain number of girls to be trained in medicine and education, sufficient to meet the needs of women in Egypt (arguing that it was more suitable for women to be treated by women doctors), the maintenance of the welfare of the country and the refusal, as far as possible, to adopt that which is foreign; and the appointment of men to see the above carried out. (Adams, 1933, 236–7).

Similarly, in more recent times the feminist Doria Shafīq, a protegée of Sha 'rāwī, advocates in her numerous writings, quite as carefully as her mentor, a balance between Islamic teaching and feminist reform, and like Sha 'rāwī and Nāṣif, she remains scrupulously correct and loyal in her attitude to Islam. (Shafīq is associated most with the demonstrations she led in the early fifties demanding the vote: at one time provoking al-Azhar to respond (1952) by issuing a declaration prepared by a committee of shaykhs – including, for all one knows, the two who had cheered for polygamy when Sha'rāwī spoke in 1935 – stating that women were unfit for the vote on the grounds that they 'are swayed by emotion and are of unstable judgement. Whereas men are impartial and balanced, women stray from the path of wisdom even when they have the advantage of a good education'. (*Muslim World*, xlii, 1952, 307).

A Middle Eastern historian of the women's movement wrote in 1951, in praise of Sha'rāwī, that 'it was extremely pleasant and important' to be able to record that 'this outstanding woman, although profoundly imbued with European culture, never tried to separate her feminist activity from the principles of Muslim religion', (Bohdanowicz, 1951, 29). And this, together with the Nāṣif points quoted above regarding the importance of the refusal to adopt anything foreign, indicates an element that is very much at the heart of the matter: the issue of remaining loyal to one's culture and not betraying one's society's (and one's own) cultural identity: construed as a matter of remaining loyal to what is seen as being its symbolic core, 'Islam' (and in Arab societies also 'Arabness') however 'modern' and 'European' is one's outlook. The stance adopted by the Egyptian women feminists – that feminism was essentially in tune with an Islam properly understood – was (as we saw also with regard to Turkey) a stance adopted early on by Muslim reformers such as 'Abduh and Amīn. However Islam and feminism are naturally incompatible (as Ataturk found) and the literalism of Islamic civilisation and the complete enmeshing of the legal tradition with this literalism means that this incompatibility can only be resolved by the complete severance of Islamic tradition from the issue of the position and rights of women. To say that Islam and feminism are incompatible, represent ideologies with irreconcilably conflicting interests, is not to say anything extraordinary. Feminism is irreconcilably in conflict with all or nearly all currently entrenched ideologies. It is in conflict with the dominant ideologies in the West to more or less the same extent as in Islam although Western women can be critical and radically critical of their cultures and prevalent ideologies which, as elsewhere, also exert pressure towards conformity and acceptance. However, a further pressure, arising from the relationship between Islamic society and the West, bears down on the Muslim woman, and urges her to silence her criticism, remain loyal, reconcile herself to, and even find virtue in those central formations of her culture that she would normally rebel against.

As Islamic civilisation stands in a very special, even unique relation to the West, the issue of cultural loyalty and betrayal is experienced with unique force and intensity within it. For centuries it was a mutually confrontational stance in which first Islam and then the West was in the ascendant with each afraid that the power of the Infidel would triumph. Well in our case the Infidel has taken over: first, gallingly, as a coloniser and now, pervasively, in the flood of ideas, abstract and material appurtenances of Western civilisation. Islamic civilisation now finds itself emphasising and re-affirming old values the more intransigently and dogmatically because it sees itself re-affirming them against an old enemy. Against this background, the issue of cultural betrayal for the Islamic and Arab individual has a particularly disturbing quality which accounts for the persistence with which reformers and feminists repeatedly try to affirm that the reforms they seek involve no disloyalty to Islam, and are in fact in conformity with it, in spirit if not in substance.

It is only when one considers that one's sexual identity alone is arguably more inextricably 'oneself' than one's cultural identity, that one can begin to appreciate how excruciating is the plight of the Middle Eastern feminist caught between those two opposing loyalties, forced almost to choose between betrayal and betrayal. Except that the choice is not in fact between betrayals: the onus and responsibility is now on us to make a personal choice and commitment, between ways of perception, and systems of analysis drawn from different cultures because culture is no longer simply a birthright. Perhaps the issue for Middle Eastern feminists based in the West is interesting but, in a sense, academic: in terms of our personal lives and our daily existence the issue is distinctly 'cool'. But considering the matter more generally I believe only one woman to date – Fatima Mernissi, in for instance her book *Beyond the Veil* – has succeeded, while based in the Middle East, in surveying, considering, analysing, and debating the implications of a feminist perspective from a position that is cool and culturally assured, undistracted and unworried by issues of cultural rivalry.

Algeria, exceptional among Arab countries in the protracted duration of its colonisation, in the numerical size of the European presence, and in, generally, the harshness and brutality of its rulers, was to be where the confrontation between the Arab world (or one distinctive sub-culture within it) and the West was to emerge at its fiercest and most explicit. Women and the status of women there were to become openly and blatantly merely counters (and it is difficult to credit that for *either* side they were anything more than counters) in the cultural, moral and military battle between the French and the men of Algeria.

As noted earlier, the introduction of education for girls in Turkey and Egypt in the nineteenth century did not mean that education for girls therefore quickly became widespread or was instantly and easily embraced by the population. The experience in Algeria was similar, although resistence to the education of girls seems to have been considerably greater. An element in this may well have been that those who established schools and tried to persuade parents (even bribing them) to send their daughters to them were foreigners and colonisers. Thus the French established four primary schools in 1850 – and they were failures. In 1886 French law made primary education for both sexes compulsory, and an attempt was made to extend this to Algeria – again with little success. However by 1908 there were 2,667 girls in school – primary and kindergarten (compared to 30,661 boys). And although the French throughout this period did make efforts to spread the education of women, by 1954 there were only 952 girls in secondary school, and 24 in university (Gordon, 1968, 45).

This continued resistence to the education of women distinguished the experience of Algeria from that of Turkey and Egypt. Another way in which developments in Algeria differed, as a result of the specificity of the Algerian experience both as a colonised people and in Algeria's different local cultural heritage, was in the different concerns of its nationalist and reformist movements. Thus although Muhammad ʿAbduh was to be an important influence on Algerian reformists, his views on the status of women and the importance of their education were, significantly, not emphasised. A small element among the Algerian nationalists did, in vague general terms, favour women's emancipation, but they were also insistent that women must continue in their traditional role. Algerian women had had scarcely any contact with the French and therefore were not much gallicised: they were seen consequently by Algerian men as guardians of their authentic traditions and identity, traditions which they felt women must continue to preserve and uphold – and which included of course woman in her 'traditional' and inferior role. An Algerian woman novelist described men's attitude thus: 'the woman traditionally the guardian of the past, became (increasingly) passive in her role. The Algerian man, at this time, was colonised in the street, in his work, obliged to speak a language that was not his own outside, he found his real life at home, in his house, with his wife. The house was still the sacred place, which the foreigner never entered'. (Djebar, 1962, in an interview, quoted in Gordon, 1968, 47).

The inherent incompatability between the emancipation of women on the one hand and their continuing in their traditional role on the other was to become fully evident after independence. Meanwhile the French, partly at least because they too perceived the women as the repositories of traditional culture and sought (as Fanon argued) to erode it and so undermine Algerian men's resistance, tried actively to persuade Algerian women to abandon the veil. For the reasons just given, the unveiling of women was stubbornly opposed, as was also to a great extent any increase in their education. However as the struggle for independence continued, Algerian men found that they needed to use women, that when they had to go underground or flee the country, they had to turn over to women tasks they could no longer perform. So, as they had used women in their cultural battle with the French, insisting that they continue in their traditional role and remain veiled, they now proceeded to use women in their military battle. Few women it appears – although they performed heroically – entered the battle on their own initiative: 'their involvement', writes Minces, although 'sincere and courageous, occurred ... essentially on the basis of replacement ... in the capacity of wife, sister or daughter of this or that man'. Women's traditional role was now set aside, their veiling no longer respected, nor their tradition of not moving freely among men: they went, unveiled when their mission required it, veiled when their mission required it, wherever Algerian men judged it useful for them to go. Women were thus freed, indeed thrust, in the service of the struggle against the French, into abandoning their traditional role. This fact, the 'liberation' of women resulting from the struggle, was itself used as propaganda to gain the much-needed support of for instance the left in France: women who were arrested, imprisoned, tortured, were made into 'national heroines' to prove to international and especially French opinion that the struggle was 'progressive' even regarding women (Minces, 1978, 163). So eager were spokesmen for the Algerian resistance to believe this, and so profoundly irrelevant to them at root was the real interest of women that Fanon, in his famous exposition of how the French meant to undermine Algerian men by luring the women from their traditional role, actually managed to represent the actions of teachers and nuns exercising 'a truly exceptional activity' among parents to persuade them to send their daughters to school, as clearly and unmistakably diabolical and malicious, and he scoffingly reported that they would hint 'non too subtly . . . that it would be criminal if the child's schooling were interrupted' – without it occurring to him apparently that this educational deprivation of girls was indeed criminal. (Fanon, 1959/80, 17).

After independence an attempt was made to live up to the promises and declarations of the resistance leaders: women it was declared, had paid for their right to equality by their participation and suffering in the struggle. Ben Bella, the country's first president stated: 'the Algerian woman, who played an important role in the revolution, must play the same role in the construction of our country. We oppose those who, in the name of religion, wish to leave our women outside of this construction'. (Gordon, 1968, 62). From the start however, traditionalists were resistant to the idea of women's equality, and Ben Bella got little further than verbal support, and after his deposition even such declarations were no longer forthcoming. Instead the tone was to be that set by Boumédienne when, in 1966, he declared that the emancipation of women 'does not signify in any way the imitation of Western woman. We say "no" to this type of evolution, for our society is an Islamic and a socialist society. A problem exists here. It involves respect for morality. We are in favour of the evolution and the progress of women . . . But this evolution must not be the cause of the corruption of our society . . . For we have seen among several peoples, who have been recently liberated, that the woman, once free, hastens to think of things which one need not cite here . . . the evolution of the Algerian woman and the enjoyment of her rights must be in the framework of the morality of our society'. (Gordon, 1969, 77–8). On the practical as well as the 'ideal' plane women did not fare well. Freedoms gained during their participation in the struggle were on the whole to prove to have been temporary, granted for the duration of the struggle only; thus unveiled women for instance were to come increasingly under pressure and were subjected to verbal and other attacks. Economically, the country's continuing unemployment problem and the priority given to men has meant that the figure for women at work is very low – and far behind the percentage of women employed in either Tunisia or Morocco (Minces, 1978, 166–8). Altogether it is clear that Algerian men are using the power that women helped place in their hands to subjugate women and control them, and to re-institute traditions that give them, in relation to women, all the rights and more, of colonisers.

South Yemen's war of independence ending in 1967, was also against colonialists – and differed from the Algerian in at least one respect that has proved so far to be crucial to women. The Algerian struggle was paramountly and almost exclusively a war of liberation with at best only vaguely formulated ideological aims that remained essentially of peripheral concern. The South Yemen war in addition to being a war of liberation was committed to socialist goals: by 1968 the ruling National Liberation Front had declared itself committed to the goals of Marxist-Leninism, and among them the full emancipation of women.

This has meant to begin with, on the level of political declarations, statements refreshingly free from justification of oppression by reference to 'tradition', or slurs on women. Thus, denouncing women's 'humiliation, degradation, oppression and exploitation', and the denying of their right to work and to equality, President Sālim Rubayah 'Alī declared in 1974 that women's freedom was now possible under socialism, and lay 'in the education and in inculcating new traditions that lie in the secret of their love of work and production,' ('Alī, cited in Molyneux, 1979, 7). After independence the juridical powers of religious leaders were transferred to the state, and a new Family Code (1974) passed: abolishing divorce by repudiation, limiting polygamy to exceptional circumstances, giving divorced women custody rights over children, laws modifying, though not abolishing the Islamic code. 'Paralleling these changes in the law,' writes Molyneux (and her first-hand account of women in South Yemen since the revolution, including a number of interviews, must be consulted for a fuller picture) 'there has been a major effort to erode the purdah restrictions and to encourage women to enter all areas of public life including the militia, politics, the legal profession and other areas of activities formerly closed to women. The state places great emphasis on two processes which it considers fundamental for bringing about women's emancipation: education and the entry into social production'. (Molyneux, 1979, 8).

The Women's Union, tied into the party and state structures, set up technical training centres for women, to train them, in the words of a former president of the Union, to be mechanics 'for cars, tractors, refrigerators, air-conditioners ... In 1975 there were some 1,500 women involved in training centres and most ... have taken up jobs in the same projects where they were trained. The centres were residential and the courses would run for periods of up to a year. The training would generally take place in the mornings; the afternoons would be given over to activities such as military training, literacy classes, handicrafts, political education, cultural education and the like'. ('Ā'ishah Muḥsin, in an interview with Molyneux, Molyneux, 1979, 14–15). The Women's Union also has factory projects – including factories where the employees are all women. (It should be noted that aiding and probably giving special added thrust to this programme for the employment of women is the fact that, due to the departure of many men to work in oil-rich states, the labour-shortage in South Yemen is severe). On the matter of the veil fairly soon after independence a campaign against it had been mounted and had had popular support (according to Nūr Bā 'Abbād, Head of Cultural and Information Affairs), now however the veil is no longer an issue, and the view is that with education and social change the habit will die of itself. (Molyneux, 17).

Molyneux writes that 'as in all socialist countries, it is often extremely difficult to discern what is really happening behind the official claims', but concludes that nevertheless 'it is evident both that there have been substantial changes in the position of women as a result of the revolution, and that there are major areas which state policy has left untouched'. (Molyneux, 6).

From the point of view of the concerns of this article, there are a number of ways in which the experience in Yemen differs strikingly from anything so far considered. One is the degree and manner of women's involvement. Thus it is striking that, although as in Algeria their involvement initially was because of the men in their families, there seems swiftly to have developed among the women in South Yemen an active collaborativeness, an involvement on their own account. 'A'idah Yāfi'ī in connection with the women's section of the NLF founded in 1963, stated: 'political work for women was difficult. We had two fronts of struggle, one against the family and tradition, the other to wage the armed struggle against the British colonialists. The Imams of the mosque here in Aden used to make speeches against women leaving their houses and breaking purdah rules. We women went to the mosque and tried to argue with them. We also tried to convince our own families that it was right for us to struggle. They wouldn't accept that their daughters came home at midnight after political meetings and they would lock us out if we came home too late'. In Aden women's involvement remained political rather than military – 'in the country though', in the words of 'A'idah Yāfi'ī, 'they did participate in the fighting, which was natural given the social conditions of women there. Unlike the women of the towns, they don't wear the veil or the black covering known as the sheidor so they are more free and they are used to hard work in the fields. Even though traditionally women didn't have guns, they took them up during the revolutionary struggle and many were killed in the fighting. Women often carried food to their guerilla husbands and when fighting broke out they were caught up into it, so they took up guns and fought back'. (Molyneux, 11). The women heroes of the Yemeni revolution were leaders and fighters, Daara from the Radfān, and Khadījah al-Hawshabī. While in Algeria, the women heroes, Djamila Bouhired and Djamila Boupacha, were captured and tortured by the French: as if tragically figuring forth in their heroism the only role their society permitted them, their heroism is the heroism of woman as victim.

It is clear from Yāfi'ī's account that the form which women's involvement took was not a matter of the revolutionary struggle mysteriously transforming women but rather a matter of the revolution tapping an indigenous tradition of active and independent women. This is a tradition, demonstrable in history, of the women of the Arabian Peninsula. Long after such a tradition had died out in other areas of the Middle East (and died, the evidence suggests, before the spread of Islam) – the women of Arabia and the Arabian peninsula continued, and indeed continue to this day, to act out of what is clearly still a living tradition of strong independent women and of women as actors. (So far it has been implied in this contribution that feminism in the Middle East is always a result of Western influence: I am here suggesting that there is an indigenous tradition of 'feminism' in the Middle East, or rather specifically in the Arabian Peninsula: and that it is an empowering tradition enabling women I met there [not surprisingly perhaps it is not well documented in histories and studies of the area], illiterate women not exposed to Western thought, to show an awareness of patriarchy and its oppressions and even of Islam as being for the most part an ideology developed to control women, quite as shrewd and acute as that of their Western sisters).

It is this tradition I believe that is observable in the nature of women's involvement in the revolution in South Yemen, merely surfacing in and not created by the revolution. And it is this which has led their involvement to differ so markedly from that of women in other Middle Eastern feminist movements, in other ways as well as those already mentioned. For instance in the years immediately preceding changes in the family law, the matter was debated in 'public meetings all over the country', ʿĀ'ishah Muḥsin explains, and the women, she adds, 'were always more extreme – more radical – than the men, by the way!' (Molyneux, 14). In no other country we have considered does there seem to have been even the possibility of women 'all over the country', becoming or wanting to become involved in such debates, let alone of their being the more radical and 'extreme'. ʿĀ'idah Yāfiʿī, politically active since the 1960s and now a member of the Central Committee and Director of the Secretary General's office, says of women's oppression that it has 'a historical origin. It began with private ownership of the means of production. Before this women were the heads of their families, but then men took over ... When we declare we want to be equal with men, we want to be equal in rights but we don't want to be equal if men are trapped in underdeveloped thoughts. In an underdeveloped society men have underdeveloped thoughts and ideas and we don't want equality in this. We have to fight with men to eradicate these backward social relations ... They have inherited the way they are from thousands of years of backwardness and this is why they reject any demands for equality between men and women'. (Molyneux, 12). This is of course accepted socialist analysis: but it is close enough too to what was once said to me by a woman on the other side of the Peninsula, in the Arab Emirates, a woman with no conceivable contact with either Marxism or Western thought, to suggest to me that the vitality with which Yāfiʿī expresses herself on the issue in part derives from socialist analysis of the oppression of women having encountered an indigenous tradition of thoughts on the matter tending very much the same way.

Bibliography of works cited:

Adams, Charles C., *Islam and Modernism in Egypt*, New York, 1968.
Afetinan, A., *The Emancipation of the Turkish Woman*, Unesco, 1962.
Alderson, A. D., *The Structure of the Ottoman Dynasty*, Oxford, 1956.
Bohdanowicz, Arslan, 'The Feminist Movement in Egypt', *The Islamic Review*, Aug. 1951.
Coşar, Fatma Mansur, 'Women in Turkish Society', *Women in the Muslim World, ed.* Lois Beck and Nikki Keddie, Cambridge, Mass., 1978.
Fanon, Frantz, A Dying Colonialism, [1959] London, 1980.
Gordon, David C., *Women of Algeria, An Essay on Change*, Harvard Middle Eastern Monographs, XIX, 1968.
al-Jabarti, Abd al-Rahman, *Aja'ib al-athar fi'l-tarajim wa'l-akhbar*, Cairo, 1322 [1904–5] 4 vols.
Lewis, Bernard, *The Emergence of Modern Turkey*, London, 1961.
Mernissi, Fatima, *Beyond the Veil*, New York, 1975.
Minces, Juliette, 'Women in Algeria', *Women in the Muslim World, ed.* Lois Beck and Nikki Keddie, Cambridge, Mass., 1978.
Molyneux, Maxine, 'Women and Revolution in the People's Democratic Republic of Yemen', *Feminist Review*, London, I, 1979.
Penzer, N. N. *The Harem*, London, 1936.
Taskiran, Tezer, *Women in Turkey*, Istanbul, 1976.
Tomiche, Nada, 'The Situation of Egyptian Women in the First Half of the Nineteenth Century', *Beginnings of Modernisation in the Middle East, ed.* W. R. Polk & R. L. Chambers, Chicago, 1966.
Woodsmall, Ruth F., *Moslem Women Enter a New World*, New York, 1936.

Some notes on the history of Socotra

C. F. Beckingham

To R.B.S.

Piacciavi . . . aggradir questo che vuole
E darvi sol può l'umil servo vostro.
Quel ch'io vi debbo, posso di parole
Pagare in parte e d'opera d'inchiostro:
Nè che poco io vi dia da imputar sono;
Chè quanto io posso dar, tutto vi dono.

ARIOSTO

Nearly forty years ago Professor Serjeant remarked to me that it was strange how little information was to be found in Ḥaḍramī chronicles about the history of the Mahrī sultanate of Qishn and Socotra. This was a subject on which he already spoke with unique authority; I need hardly say that I have never had reason to doubt the accuracy of his statement. In this brief paper, offered as an inadequate token of admiration, gratitude and friendship, I propose to summarise and comment on a few of the scattered sources of information about the island in the two centuries that followed its incorporation in the Mahrī sultanate. Its history has yet to be written, and must be compiled from references dispersed in a multiplicity of books and records, not so much in Arabic as in Greek, Latin, Syriac, Portuguese, Dutch, English, French, and even Danish. This is no more than a tentative contribution to this formidable undertaking. It will be long before all significant allusions have been collected from chronicles, travel narratives, and the archives of European trading companies.[1]

In mediaeval Europe Socotra was probably more famous, even if not better known, than it is now. It was famous for several things, for its aloes, its dragon's blood, its ambergris, the proficiency of its inhabitants in witchcraft, and, perhaps above all, for the fact that they were Christians. Marco Polo refers to three of these factors, though not to aloes or dragon's blood, but he locates Socotra 500 miles south of the legendary Male and Female Islands, which suggests that his personal acquaintance with the western Indian Ocean was at least superficial. Over 200 years later the Rhenish pilgrim Arnold von Harff gives a fanciful description, accompanied by a most implausible illustration of the costume of the inhabitants. In fact, it is as certain as such things can be that his journeys in Africa and Asia did not extend beyond Lower Egypt and Palestine. There were, however, Europeans who did visit Socotra during the Middle Ages. Conti's account, dating from the mid-fifteenth century and preserved by Poggio Bracciolini, is well known. It is not so well known that William Adam, the Dominican Archbishop of Sultanieh and later of Antivari (Bar), spent nine months there with other friars early in the fourteenth century, when trying to reach Ethiopia. In his tractate *De modo Sarracenos extirpandi*[2] he writes: *fui in dictis insulis novem mensibus commoratus, quando volebam, causa predicandi fidei, cum quibusdam aliis ordinis mei, meis sociis, in Ethiopiam proficisci.* There is no reason to question the truth of this, especially as William's presentation of the physical and political geography of western Asia is correct and wholly free from legendary accretions. The use of the plural *insulis* is justified by the fact that Socotra is by far the largest of a group which includes 'Abd al-Kūrī and a number of islets. He regarded it, with its Christian population, as a suitable base from which the ships he wanted to have built at Baghdad could intercept the oceanic trade and so destroy the prosperity of Egypt.

I know of no evidence that the Portuguese were aware of William's proposals, but they adopted the same strategy. It is, of course, possible that Pero da Covilhã visited Socotra about 1490 during his voyages in the Indian Ocean. Though we have no explicit statement to this effect, it is inconceivable that he should not have obtained some information about the island and have transmitted it in the celebrated letter which may or may not have reached the King of Portugal. So far as we know the first Portuguese to report on the island was Diogo Fernandes Pereira. He commanded a ship from Setúbal which returned to Lisbon about the end of July 1505. After taking a number of prizes off the African coast he had gone to winter, *foi invernar*, at Socotra. By this is meant that he spent there the time when the S.W. monsoon made navigation dangerous, i.e. from late May till early August. Barros says that he *novamente descobriu* the island,[3] and it was because of what he told King Manoel that the latter gave the orders he did to Tristão da Cunha and Afonso de Albuquerque when sending them to the East in the spring of 1506. Having learnt from Pereira that the Socotrans were Christians in subjection to Muslim Arabs from the mainland who held a fort on the island, he instructed the fleet to capture the fort and install a garrison, so as to provide a refuge where ships could 'winter' safely and a base from which to close the Gulf of Aden to Muslim commerce. Lest the Arab fort should prove unsuitable for their purpose they were to take with them a prefabricated wooden structure. It is evident that the King attached great importance to Socotra, for the man designated to become its Captain was Albuquerque's nephew, Dom Afonso de Noronha, who held the 'succession', that is to say, he was to become Governor of the Estado da India should his uncle die before completing his term of office.

Barros, who did not himself go to the East, collected information from those who did, and placed on record an important description of Socotra.[4] According to this it had been subject to the Sultan of Qishn for twenty-six years when da Cunha arrived, which was in April 1507. In 1480 ten ships and a force of 1000 men had been sent under the command of the Sultan's nephew. The Socotrans had withdrawn to the mountains, where they could not be pursued, and to keep control the Arabs had built a fort at 'Soco' (Sūq), which was where trading ships called. A garrison of a hundred men was usually stationed there and tribute was imposed.

The Portuguese naturally hoped that, as Christians, the Socotrans would readily assist them against Muslims, and Barros was concerned to discover what he could about their religion. He says that they were all Jacobites of the same sect as the Abyssinians, though not following many of their practices. Most of the men bore apostolic names; most of the women were called Maria. They revered the Cross, and they all wore crosses on their chests. They usually held three services daily, more or less corresponding to Matins, Vespers and Compline; the service was antiphonal and was in Chaldaean (*caldeu*).[5] Those who had heard it thought they could distinguish the word *Alleluia*. The Socotrans practised circumcision, fasting and monogamy, and they paid tithes to the churches. The authority of Barros and the relative proximity of Ethiopia have persuaded some scholars that the Socotrans were Monophysites. Dr Sebastian Brock informs me[6] that the details supplied by Barros would be applicable to all the Syriac and Ethiopian churches, and are insufficient for identification, but that the Syriac sources afford evidence for a Nestorian hierarchy only, the latest of such sources being a reference to the presence of Cyriacus, Bishop of Socotra, at the consecration of the Patriarch Yahballaha III in 1283. It will be remembered that Polo says that they had an Archbishop subject, not to the Pope, but to a great Archbishop at 'Baudas'. Conti too described Socotra as inhabited mostly by Nestorians. However, to judge by the Portuguese accounts, by the sixteenth century Christianity on the island must have been so degenerate that neither the people themselves nor foreign observers are likely to have been able to say with precision what they believed about the Divine and Human Natures.

Four Portuguese authorities have left detailed descriptions of the capture of the fort, three of them, Barros, Castanheda, and the *Commentarios* written by the younger Albuquerque, being in substantial agreement; the fourth, Correa, as so often, differs considerably and is somewhat confused.[7] The fort was not what the attackers had been led to expect, and it was obvious that their prefabricated tower would not be needed; the wood was eventually used to build a foist. The fort is described as a compact building, on level ground about a crossbow shot from the sea, with a mountain on its eastern side. It had a courtyard, at least two towers, turrets, and a barbican in the wall which included the main gate, which itself had a postern. It was held by 120 to 130 men under the son of the Sultan of Qishn, Shaykh Ibrāhīm. They were armed with swords, small shields, lances, spears, arrows, and stones, wore corselets of mail, and had some bombards, though there was no artillery in the fort. The authorities agree that they refused to surrender and fought with courage and skill. Little now remains of the building, which was systematically demolished when the Portuguese abandoned it four years later.

The assault began just before dawn and lasted for several hours. Portuguese casualties were one man killed and about fifty wounded, of whom six or seven died afterwards. About eighty Arabs were killed, including Ibrāhīm, but some who did not get into the fort before the gate was shut contrived to escape into the interior. Only one prisoner was taken, an experienced pilot called ʿUmar, who was very useful to Albuquerque in his voyage along the Arabian coast later in the year.

Not much booty was found in the fort, only some provisions and weapons, including some swords of European make on which were inscribed in Latin words meaning 'God helps me'. The fort was restored and the usual complement of officials was installed, implying that permanent occupation was envisaged. Dom Afonso de Noronha had already been designated Captain; his brother-in-law Fernão Jacome became Alcaide Mor, and a Factor and two clerks were appointed. The fort was renamed São Miguel, and the mosque was converted to a church as Nossa Senhora da Vitória. Correa, however, says that both the fort and the church were dedicated to St Thomas, who was considered to be the founder of Socotran Christianity.

Over twenty years later Nuno da Cunha, who had taken part in the capture of the fort and was now Governor of Portuguese India, sent Ambrosio do Rego to Coromandel to collect information about the mission of St Thomas, but he spent his time making money on his own account. The work was done by Miguel Ferreira, once Albuquerque's envoy to Shāh Ismāʿīl Ṣafavī. He reported that an Ethiopian bishop named Abuna (*sic*) had come to Malabar and had said that Ethiopian and Armenian books recorded that SS. Thomas, Bartholomew and Jude had gone from Jerusalem to Basra (a city founded after the Arab conquest) and had parted there. Thomas had gone to Socotra and to Cape Gardafui, where he had converted many 'as is alleged by the people of Çacatora, where he had also been'. He then went to China with one Abaneus, who had been ordered by his lord in China to find the best builder in the world. Thomas met this requirement, constructed a palace for the King of China, and later went to India, finally dying in Coromandel.[8]

The Portuguese occupied Socotra for only four years. Their high expectations were soon disappointed, and had it not been for the King's explicit orders, they would have abandoned it even sooner. For one thing the people did not behave as they had thought newly liberated Christians would do. When the fort had been taken the houses of the Arabs were plundered, and the population fled. Da Cunha sent messengers to explain that the invaders were Christians who had come to free them from the Muslims, and would establish a garrison to protect them; they were free to trade and would only be required to supply food for the soldiers. Barros says that they came forward, prostrating themselves before the Captain Major, thanking him and asking for his protection in the name of Christ.[9]

These good relations did not last long. The Arabs who had escaped into the interior, numbering thirty or forty, incited the inhabitants against the Portuguese, alleging that they intended to seize the island as they had done India. Many of the Arabs were married to Socotran women, and they persuaded the people not to send food to the fort. Because of the monsoon the ships stayed till August. Da Cunha always slept on board for fear that the Socotrans would set fire to his ships.[10] The population soon became hostile; Barros says that the Portuguese did not often need to fight, but the difficulty of procuring food was serious. Albuquerque had left soon after da Cunha and had proceeded on his famous voyage along the Omani coast culminating in the siege of Ormuz. He learnt of the distress of the garrison and decided to send a ship with supplies. The commander, however, went to India instead and took the supplies with him.[11] It was not till the end of the year that Albuquerque himself was able to leave for Socotra. He found conditions desperate. The troops had been subsisting on dates, jujube apples, a few goats, and palm-cabbage; they had cut down half the palm grove near the fort for food; Noronha himself was ill. The provisions Albuquerque had brought with him were insufficient, so he sent a ship to Malindi to obtain more. These too were not adequate and he ordered the seizure of all the dates procurable on the island. This naturally did not improve relations with the people, but he defeated the rebels easily and imposed on them an undertaking to supply annually to the garrison 600 sheep or goats, twenty cows, and forty loads of dates.[12] It was evidently not fulfilled and was probably unenforceable.

Socotra was to have three Portuguese Captains. In 1509 Duarte de Lemos arrived in the East with orders to transfer the Captain of Kilwa, Pero Ferreira Fogaça, to Socotra; Noronha was to become Captain of the important fort of Cananor. Bad weather prevented the fleet from reaching the island at the first attempt, and it was not till about the end of October that it was able to do so. The new Captain was then installed and his nephew Antonio Ferreira was made Alcaide Mor. Noronha and Jacome were to have left for India but the ship intended for them was wrecked by a storm that hit the coast. Meanwhile Albuquerque sent Antão Nogueira from Cochin to give de Lemos the news of the serious defeat which he and the Marshal Coutinho had suffered at Calicut, and to urge his nephew to come to India as soon as possible. Noronha, accompanied by Jacome and Fr Antonio de Loureiro, a Franciscan who had been sent with other friars to instruct the Socotrans in the Catholic faith, embarked on Nogueira's ship. A rich Gujerati prize was taken and, there being no harbour in the island where it could spend the monsoon safely, Nogueira decided to risk trying to reach India. Both ships were lost off the coast of Gujerat, most of those on board, including the friar and Jacome, becoming prisoners of Maḥmūd Shāh, though Noronha perished.[13]

In May 1510 Duarte de Lemos returned to Socotra to find that the Captain had died. The Alcaide Mor, who had the right to succeed him, was ill, and Pero Correa was appointed. Next year Albuquerque, having obtained the King's authorisation, sent Diogo Fernandes de Beja to dismantle the fort and bring off the garrison and any of the population who might prefer to leave with it. According to Correa over 200 men and as many women, who were mistresses of Portuguese soldiers, chose to come. They were taken to Goa where many of the women married honourably, Socotran women being, he says, respectable and robust.[14]

The reasons for the failure of the occupation are clear. The people had intermarried with the Arabs and were easily induced to take their side. Even if armed resistance was easily quelled, it was not possible to compel them to deliver adequate supplies. The garrison suffered severely from hunger and malnutrition. As we have seen, supplies had to be sought on occasion from Africa and India. It was therefore not practicable to maintain on the island enough troops to serve a useful purpose. Above all, as was stated by Dom João de Castro, there was no harbour where ships of any size could ride out the 'winter' in safety, though 'Calacea' (Qalansiyyah) was suitable for foists and small craft.[15] Several examples of the dangers of 'wintering' at Socotra have been mentioned; the chronicles contain many more.

The Portuguese did not attempt another occupation, though they often called to take in water, to seek temporary shelter, or to enquire about shipping movements. Albuquerque called there in 1513 on his way to make his famous attack on Aden. He found about fifty Arabs, who were building houses, making gardens, and apparently preparing to reoccupy the place. When they saw the Portuguese they fled into the interior. Some Christians came to the Governor and begged him to return, rebuild the fort, and save them from Muslim oppression. Albuquerque destroyed the Arab buildings and gave the people cloth, rice and other necessaries.[16] It was still worth while to try to conciliate them and relations even with the 'King', that is, the representative of the Sultan of Qishn, were sometimes friendly. In 1529, for example, Nuno da Cunha, on his way from Malindi to Qalhāt, spent three days at Socotra, where he watered. He gave provisions to the Shaykh 'because he was a faithful friend of the Portuguese'.[17] Indeed the Sultan of Qishn himself, and even some other Arabian princes, sometimes gave help to the Portuguese, especially after the advent of the Ottomans in Arabia. When Manuel de Vasconcellos was sent to the Red Sea to try to discover what had happened to the force that had been landed in Ethiopia under Dom Cristovão da Gama, he called at Socotra, where the Shaykh warned him of the presence of Turkish galleys in the Red Sea and at Aden.[18] In 1548 a fleet was ordered to assemble at the island under the Viceroy's son, Dom Alvaro de Castro. With him was the son of the Sultan of Qishn who came every year to ask for help against the Turks, who had built a fort at Qishn and imposed tribute on his father.[19] It was at this time that the Shaykh of Khanfar sought Portuguese help in holding Aden against the Ottomans. Arab rulers sometimes regarded the Portuguese as a lesser, no doubt because a remoter, evil than the Turks, or at least as a useful counterweight to them.

When the English began their voyages to the East they too found Socotra useful for taking in water and as a rendezvous, and they too often had cause to deplore the storms they encountered in its vicinity. They never tried to occupy it and their commercial interest was principally in aloes, the Socotran variety being in demand as a purgative. The records of the East India Company contain many references to brief visits to the island. The more important can readily be traced in the well indexed six volumes of *Letters received by the East India Company from its servants in the East* (1896–1902) and the thirteen volumes of *The English Factories in India* (1906–1927). They met with a friendly reception but were sometimes disappointed with the supplies obtainable and with the price of aloes. During the Company's third voyage Anthony Marlowe wrote from the *Hector* 'at anchor at Delisha' on 22 June 1608: 'The king and people of this Island are well persuaded of our Nation, so that this Island will be a good refuge at all times for our shipping bound for these parts. Our general was invited to the king's house to dinner, and bought aloes at 20 pieces of eight the kintal. . . . This Island is very barren, yieldeth no commodity but aloes, nor any victuals, but a few kine and goats, and is not as the report was given of it'.[20] This friendliness made it possible for the English to use Socotra as a depot where ships could leave letters for each other. So, on the eighth voyage, 'the General, Captain Towerson, merchants &c went ashore and were very well received by the king and his people, and from him the General received a letter left there by Sir Henry Middleton after his escape from Moha', i.e. Mocha, where Middleton and his companions had been detained by the Turks.[21] In a letter received on 2 December 1615 William Edwards reported that he and his companions had 'bought of Mulliamer Benzaid, the king of the island, 27 kintals of aloes at 30 rials of eight per kintal, who entertained us with all love and courtesy, and showed us divers letters of Sir Henry Middleton and Captain Saris'.[22] As with the Portuguese the ruler hoped for English assistance against his enemies. On 15 February 1619 the Surat factors instructed Salbank and others bound for the Red Sea to deliver a letter from King James and a present to the ruler of Socotra.[23] A letter from 'Amer ben Said', King of Socotra, to James I, dated 6 Rajab 1032, has been calendared by W. N. Sainsbury in the *Calendar of State Papers*.[24] On 9 February 1624 Rastell, President of the Council at Surat, wrote thanking the ruler for his favour to the English, and replying to what must have been a request for help against 'the King of Share', i.e. the Kathīrī Sultan of al-Shiḥr. The English, Rastell said, were willing to do him service, but could not help that year because of shortage of shipping; besides, such important business needed consideration 'and conditions on both sides'. The Sultan was asked not to receive on his ships the enemies of the English, 'the Dabulliers and Chaulemen'.[25]

The demand for aloes was not insatiable, and as a commodity they were not always sufficiently profitable. On 21 December 1628 the Surat factors undertook to send no more until further notice.[26] On 9 March 1630 they were told that no more were wanted,[27] but they were still bought from time to time, and there was once a suggestion that arrangements should be made for a regular annual supply.[28] On 25 August 1662 Surat was instructed to buy them but only if the price did not exceed twelve pence a pound.[29] There were difficulties about packing them satisfactorily and they were sometimes damaged in transit. In 1665 the factors were asked to arrange them in layers in chests, and to take care not to include any broken bladders, the contents of which would run out and congeal; they were to be packed in the upper part of the hold so that the heat would not melt them.[30] It was also possible to buy them as cheaply without the trouble of going to Socotra. On 14 February 1625 Rastell and others reported from Swally that aloes belonging to the Sultan had been bought at 'Kishem' (Qishn, not Kishm) at the price they would have cost on the island.[31] Before the end of the century trade even with the Red Sea was ceasing to be worth while. 'Trade with Mokha was discontinued, as it was held that goods like coffee, myrrh, and aloes could be got cheaper at Surat having regard to the charges and risk involved in procuring them from Mokha'.[32] English ships had less reason even to approach Socotra.

Dutch and French experience was not dissimilar from English, but it is not always realised that the Danes too made contact with the Socotrans at least once. Their voyage was connected with the activities of the Dutch adventurer Marcelis Boschouwer, self-styled prince of Negombo and much else. He had been sent by the Dutch East India Company as an envoy to the King of Ceylon at Kandy, and had entered his service. In 1617 he arrived in Denmark as an ambassador and in March of the following year concluded a treaty with Christian IV in which he grossly exceeded any powers he may have had. As a result a fleet intended for south India was also directed to Ceylon. It comprised five ships under the command of Ove Giedde. He set sail on 29 November, 1618 but the fleet did not sight Socotra till 30 March, 1620. The pilots were in confusion over their whereabouts. Next day the *Kiøbenhavn*, captain Erich Grubbe, disappeared till evening, when Grubbe reported that he had landed and spoken with the people, that good provisions could be obtained, and that he had claimed that the ships were English. This falsehood alarmed Giedde who believed that English merchants resided on the island, which they did not. On 1 April, against his orders, Grubbe again left the fleet and went to Socotra. He did not rejoin it till 26 May, when it was off Ceylon. He had acquired some aloes. He claimed to have procured good supplies and to have concluded a treaty with the ruler. Giedde, whose own diary of the voyage has been published, came to doubt whether a written treaty existed. Grubbe, to whom he often spoke about it, always averred that it did, but excused himself from showing it at the time, and Giedde had no pretext for opening the sealed chest in which it was supposed to be.[33] Johann Heinrich Schlegel, the Historiographer Royal who edited the diary, found no evidence that the Danish East India Company ever tried to make use of the treaty.[34]

By the end of the seventeenth century European trading ships were visiting the Red Sea and the Gulf of Aden less frequently, and there began an obscure period in the history of Socotra. With the revival of interest in the Red Sea route in the early nineteenth century, and the British occupation of Aden in 1839, the island began to attract attention again, not so much now from missionaries and traders as from travellers, surveyors, and natural scientists. Aloes, ambergris and dragon's blood were no longer of such commercial importance as they had once been, and Christianity had long been extinct. The witchcraft celebrated by Marco Polo, however, survived to the present day, as Professor Serjeant and his companions found when they visited Socotra shortly before the British Protectorate was withdrawn.

Notes

[1] References will be found in H. Yule *The Book of Ser Marco Polo*, II, London, 1921, 406–410, and in Georg Schurhammer *Franz Xaver: sein Leben und seine Zeit.*, Freiburg, Bd II i, 1963, Bd II ii, 1971, *passim*; English translation *Francis Xavier: his Life, his Times*, by M. J. Costelloe, Rome, vol. II, 1977, vol. III, 1980. Tkatsch's article in *EI*[1] is valuable but refers to no Portuguese source except the *Commentarios* of Albuquerque.

[2] Printed, improbably, in *Recueil des historiens des Croisades, Documents arméniens*. Paris, II, 1906, 521–555.

[3] Barros dec. I liv.vii cap.2, and II i 1.

[4] Barros II i 3.

[5] This would normally mean Syriac, but the word is sometimes used by the Portuguese for Geʿez. Dom João de Castro also says he was told that the Socotrans worshipped in *caldeo*, *Roteiro do Mar Roxo* in *Obras completas de D. João de Castro*, edd. A. Cortesão, L. de Albuquerque, vol. II, Coimbra, 1971, 200.

[6] In a letter dated 6 December 1980.

[7] Barros II i 3; Castanheda liv.II capp.40, 41; *Commentarios* pt I capp.15, 16; Correa tom.I pp. 678–688. The last named tells a curious story of the Portuguese sending cabin boys to do washing on the beach and spreading it out to dry, in order to entice the Arabs from the fort in the hope of stealing it.

[8] Correa III, 424. This does not correspond with the Ethiopian synaxary. According to this Thomas went to India with a merchant called Abnes, professed to be a carpenter and architect, undertook to build a palace for King Gondophares, and gave away the money allocated in alms to the poor, Budge, *The Book of the Saints of the Ethiopian Church*, I, London, 1928, 134–5.

[9] Barros *loc. cit.*

[10] Castanheda II 42.

[11] Castanheda II 72; Correa I 857, 869.

[12] Barros II iii 1; Castanheda II 74, 85; *Commentarios* I 53, 54; Correa I 872.

[13] Barros II iv 1; Castanheda II 105, 116; III 5, 14; *Commentarios* II 14, 24; Correa II 11, 12, 26–29.

[14] Barros II v 11; Castanheda III 48, 71; Correa II 177, 199.

[15] João de Castro op. cit. 199, 202.

[16] Barros II vii 7; Castanheda III 103; *Commentarios* IV 1; Correa II 336.

[17] Barros IV iii 9.

[18] Correa IV 232–241.

[19] Correa IV 635.

[20] *Letters received*, London, I, 1896, 14.

[21] Idem doc. 99, 225–6.

[22] *Letters received*, II, 1897, doc. 177, 148.

[23] *The English Factories in India, 1618–1621*, London, 1906, 66.

[24] *Colonial Series, East Indies, China and Japan, 1622–1624*, 1878, no. 286.

[25] *English Factories, 1624–1629*, London, 1909, 3.
[26] *Idem*, 309.
[27] *English Factories, 1630–1633*, 1910, 9.
[28] *English Factories, 1655–1660*, 1921, 205–6.
[29] *English Factories, 1661–1664*, 1923, 187.
[30] *English Factories, 1665–1667*, 1925, 21.
[31] *English Factories, 1624–1629*, 1909, 63.
[32] Sir Charles Fawcett, *The English Factories in India, 1670–1677*, new series, I, 1936, 216.
[33] The Danish text was published by J.H. Schlegel in *Samlung zur Dänischen Geschichte, Münzkenntnis, Ökonomie und Sprache*, Copenhagen, Bd I, Stück 2, 1772, 36–117, with introductory and editorial matter in German. He supplied a German translation in *Dänische Reisebeschreibungen*, Copenhagen, 1776, 1–103. There is an English account of the voyage by P.E. Pieris, 'The Danes in Ceylon', in *Journal of the Ceylon Branch of the Royal Asiatic Society*, Colombo, XXX no. 79, 1926, 169–180, but he does not refer to Socotra. The portion of Giedde's narrative relating to Ceylon and some of the German editorial matter were translated by Mary Mackenzie in 'Ove Giedde in Ceylon' in the same journal, XXXVII, pt 2, 1946, 49–118. Pieris wrongly gives the date of setting sail of Giedde's flagship *Elephanten* as 29 December 1618; the correct date, 29 November, is given on p. 3 of the Danish text.
[34] *Samlung*, Bd I, Stück 4, 1773, 10.

Postscript

After this contribution had been submitted Professor C. R. Boxer drew my attention to José Pereira da Costa's *Socotorá e o Domínio Português no Oriente*, Coimbra, 1973, which includes a transcription, from a MS in the Torre do Tombo, of the *Livro de receita da feitoria de S. Miguel de Sacotorá, anno de 1510*. The editor describes it as 'pràticamente um inventário de quanto havia na fortaleza, revestindo-se de particular interesse os registos da descarga da nau "Omeryo", certamente a "Meri", aprisionada por Francisco Pantoja'. His preliminary remarks cite many Portuguese references to the island. One remark may give rise to a misunderstanding. He claims that in 1786–7 'ainda se fala dos cristãos de S. Tomé' whose Bishop of 'Angamali' (Cranganor, Kodungullur) had a suffragan bishop of Socotra. He cites as his authority P. António da Silva Rego, *Documentação para a História das Missões do Padroado Português no Oriente*, vol. XI, p. 855. If there were evidence that Socotran Christianity had survived until the late eighteenth century it would be surprising and of very great interest. In fact, the reference should be to vol. XII, not XI. The document in question (pp. 851–875), dated conjecturally by Silva Rego to 1786 or 1787, is entitled *História verdadeira da Christiandade de S. Thomé Apostolo no Malabar*. The passage adduced relates to the ecclesiastical organisation as it existed not later than the early seventeenth century.

The Brémond mission in the Hijaz, 1916–17: A Study in inter-allied co-operation

Robin Bidwell

In September 1914 Lord Kitchener instructed British officials in Cairo to explore the possibility of instigating an Arab uprising against the Turks, but it was not until the following July that there began the famous exchange of letters between Sharif Hussein of Mecca and the High Commissioner, Sir Henry McMahon. There were indications that the French learned of this through their own sources, but in October the Foreign Secretary, Sir Edward Grey, officially informed Paul Cambon, the Ambassador in London and suggested that the Allies discuss their interests in any future Arab state. Sir Mark Sykes and M. Georges-Picot were designated to work out the details.

The actual revolt of the Sharif on 10 June 1916 seems, however, to have caught Paris without any plans and it was not until 18 July that the Quai d'Orsay proposed to take advantage of the Pilgrimage, due at the end of September, to get some of its people close to the Sharif. Seven religious notables, led by Khaddour ben Ghabrit, who had played a very important role in helping the French to establish the protectorate in Morocco and was now Director of Protocol to the Sultan, were selected to go to the Hijaz with gifts and congratulations and to arrange for a permanent French presence in Mecca through the purchase of a hostel for future pilgrims. The Governor General of Algeria and the Residents General of Morocco and Tunisia were instructed each to nominate 200 politically reliable Muslims who would make the Hajj at the expense of the French Government.

In the meanwhile it was evident that militarily the revolt was far from a complete success, for, although Mecca and Jedda had been liberated, the attempt on Medina had failed, leaving open the possibility of Turkish reinforcements and counter-attack. On 26 July McMahon reported that the Sharif was asking for aircraft and 10,000 men and it was understood that, owing to the sacred character of the Hijaz, these would have to be Muslims. The British sent 20,000 rifles, 15 officers and 250 Muslim troops but they could provide neither suitable artillery nor Muslim gunners and they lacked experience of training bedouins to become soldiers. The War Office asked for help and on 5 August the Chief of the Africa Section of the Ministère de la Guerre recommended that this should be given, as it would open the way for subsequent French action in Palestine, Syria and Armenia. It was therefore decided to send a Military Mission which would display the armed might of France and provide training and equipment. Under a French Colonel it consisted of a French subaltern, two French interpreters, the Kabyle Colonel Cadi who had commanded two Brigades of artillery at Verdun and three other Muslim officers as instructors. It was to be followed by a 'Mission Militaire en Egypte' which eventually comprised 42 officers and 983 men, of whom all but the most senior and some of the technicians were Muslim. The 'teeth' were eight machine-gun sections, a Field Battery and a Mountain Battery both of six 80 mm. guns. Originally Colonel Touchard was designated as commander, but it was discovered that, although he had been Chief of a Bureau Arabe in Algeria for 13 years, he knew hardly any Arabic and little about Islam, so the choice fell instead upon Colonel Edouard Brémond, who had spent the previous decade with Moroccan troops and spoke and wrote the language.

On 15 August Brémond was given his instructions by the Chief of the General Staff. Under the orders of the French Minister in Cairo he was to co-ordinate the activities of the political and military missions, work with the British accepting their predominance and to establish a base through which men and supplies could be forwarded to the Hijaz. Brémond printed these orders in his book but significantly he does not recount further instructions which he received on 20 August from the Premier and Foreign Minister, Aristide Briand: these were that it was essential to act with the British, even when they were unreasonable and, by showing that France was not trying to gain influence in Arabia, to gain the confidence of Colonel Wilson who was stationed at Jedda as the main link between Cairo and the Sharifian government. Grey told Cambon on 13 September that he was glad that Brémond had been told to interfere neither in the politics, nor the administration of the new Arab state.

News of the proposed Mission reached Cairo on 14 August through Defrance, the French Minister there and McMahon reacted with alarm, telegraphing to the Foreign Office that he did not think that it was possible to oppose the idea but that any French attempt 'to have any say in the Hijaz ... should be discouraged from the outset'. London considered that an allied presence would remove the charge that the Sharif was merely a British puppet and on 28 August ordered McMahon to 'give the French Mission every assistance'.

Early in September Brémond arrived in Cairo and Clayton, head of the Arab Bureau, reported to Wingate in Khartoum that 'McMahon seems to view the Mission with disfavour and to be afraid that the French want to get their oar. I do not share his apprehensiveness as the Arabs do not like the French and never will'. A few days later he wrote that Brémond 'is an exceedingly nice man and must be a good soldier ... I must say that I welcome the arrival of this Mission'. McMahon stifled his doubts, writing to Hardinge, Permanent Under Secretary at the Foreign Office: 'I think that with a little care we will be able to keep the Mission on the right track and turn it to our own use, but without some care it may easily develop into a most inconvenient heritage. Colonel Brémond strikes me as an able and reasonable man with common-sense views. ... On one point I find that Brémond and I are in complete accord and that is the extreme importance of taking a little risk in regard to this year's pilgrimage'. If the Hajj took place in security under the aegis of the Sharif, his prestige and belief in his independence would grow enormously in the Muslim world.

Brémond was received also by General Sir Archibald Murray, Commander-in-Chief in Egypt, who welcomed him with the remark that it would be nice to have a real soldier in the Hijaz, for Wilson and others were merely civilians in uniform. Brémond tried to persuade him to capture Aqaba and his espousal of this pet project of the Arab Bureau still further enhanced its officials' good opinions of him: they could not have known that he was telling Paris that it would provide a useful springboard for French ambitions in Syria. Murray, as always, clung to the hope that one day he would defeat the Turks in Sinai and that any diversion of effort to the Arabian Peninsula was unnecessary and possibly dangerous.

While Brémond was still in Cairo there were strong fears that the Turks would advance on Mecca to extinguish the revolt before the start of the Hajj; the Arab Bureau indeed thought that the collapse of the Sharif was possible. The British, who were intercepting Turkish signals, knew that there were about 9,000 men available for this task and that such a large force could not march from Medina by the inland route which Burton took, the Darb Sharqi, through Sufayna, at a time when the wells had not been replenished by the autumn rains. It would have, therefore, to go by way of the coast at Rabegh where a base to support Sharif Faysal's operations in the Medina area was being established. At the beginning of September Wingate asked that troops be sent to Rabegh and McMahon agreed, adding that Faysal regarded the situation as so critical that even Christians would be welcomed as reinforcements indicating that such a visible sign of support would encourage his tribesmen. Murray repeated that he had none to spare and the Chief of the Imperial General Staff, Field Marshal Sir William Robertson, was adamant that none could be sent from home. The military view was helped by the Commanders-in-Chief in Egypt and Mesopotamia who, when asked if the recapture of Mecca would cause them concern, replied that it would not; the Viceroy said that it would indeed be preferable to the intervention of European troops in the Hijaz. When the Foreign Office told McMahon that the French were ready to provide Muslim troops, particularly gunners, and that it had 'invited them to proceed at once with the training and dispatch of such units', he replied that this he would 'greatly deplore as it would rob us of the very great political advantages which the Sharif's success will hereafter give us'.

Brémond who disembarked at Jedda on 21 September added his voice to the pleas of the local British officials and a few days later Hardinge told Lord Bertie, Ambassador in Paris, that the French 'keep on bombarding us with urgent demands for an expedition to a place called Rabegh'. Brémond and Wilson were obviously working closely together, for on 2 October they jointly requested that a British brigade be sent and Wingate, supporting this, privately stressed the advantage of getting there before the French were ready, but added that in default of British help he could not advise the Sharif to rebuff the French. Their intervention was becoming a possibility for their main force was starting to assemble at Suez, although its deployment was not complete until mid-November.

The Arabs were clearly desperate and on 18 October their Foreign Minister, Sharif Abdullah, complained to Brémond that the British were letting them down and asking for the dispatch of French troops on their own. Two days later Wilson reported that Abdullah had told him that they really wanted British troops and that the French would only be a last resort. Brémond warned that Mecca might fall and Briand instructed Cambon to continue pressing Whitehall for action. The India Office still opposed the landing of Christians but on 24 October Wingate confirmed that the Sharif had no objection to them and he quoted Brémond as saying that his Muslim gunners could not go alone, as they had not been trained to operate without their French officers. The possibility was mooted of sending two Senegalese battalions available in Jibouti but it was soon found that they included fetishists who were quite unsuitable for service in the Holy Land of Islam.

Wingate reported that the Turks were about to move, sent two Egyptian companies with two British officers to Rabegh and asked for authority to order the French to proceed there from Suez although Brémond still insisted that his gunners must have a British infantry brigade in support. On 2 November the War Committee instructed him to see if the Royal Navy could defend the town but if it could not, authorised him to send any British or French troops available. Murray still refused to release a brigade but he did detach four aircraft and although on 10 November the War Committee decided that British troops should go, Robertson still stubbornly insisted that less than 15,000 men would not suffice and that such numbers simply could not be found.

On 16 November Brémond went to Rabegh and saw that, as there would be a perimeter of six kilometres to defend, a large force would be needed, but the situation became more confused still as Lawrence advised that the presence of Christian troops in the Hijaz would cause the Arab movement to disintegrate. In London, however, Hardinge gloomily felt that it would be necessary to invite French participation although 'I dislike such a policy, as being contrary to our policy of the last hundred years to eliminate French influence from the Red Sea'. He later wrote to McMahon that it was only the result of French pressure that the question of a force for Rabegh had ever been considered: clearly Brémond's advocacy had proved more effective than that of McMahon or Wingate.

A lull of nearly a month followed until on 9 December Wingate stated that now the Turks really meant business and that Rabegh must either be reinforced or evacuated. Brémond's deputy at Jedda reported that morale was so low that when the Sharif came to the port, people thought that he was about to escape to Egypt while Lawrence quoted Faysal as saying that the revolt was about to collapse. The War Cabinet decided that the Arabs must be saved with even Austen Chamberlain, Secretary of State for India, commenting 'I disliked stirring up the Sharif, but since he was egged on by Lord Kitchener and Egypt, I dislike still more the possibility of seeing him go under': it was decided that British troops must go, for the matter could not be left to the French alone. On 11 December the Foreign Office instructed Wingate to send troops 'whenever you receive a request from the Sharif' and in reply he commented 'it is not likely that he will consent to our landing Christian troops until the crisis actually arises and it will be too late'. However the Chief Qadi of Mecca issued a *fatwā* that such allies would be acceptable and the Sharif asked for them to be put on standby.

Brémond went to Khartoūm to co-ordinate activities with Wingate and they agreed that Colonel Cadi with eight officers and 50 men should go to Rabegh where they found 200 British and 960 Egyptian troops already established. Wingate stopped further reinforcements until a written request should be received from the Sharif. At Christmas Wilson and Brémond together visited Rabegh where they found the local Arab authorities extremely worried and begging for more men. Reporting on his inspection to Paris on 1 January 1917 Brémond said that European troops must be sent for the Sharif could not control the tribes, as he was too weak to take hostages, his men were selling their food and arms and could not be taught to use modern weapons. The Turks had declared that they would retake Mecca and if they succeeded, there would be such unrest in Muslim areas ruled by Britain and France that the Allies would have to commit far more troops to keeping order than would ever be needed at Rabegh.

Murray was ordered to prepare a brigade but on 8 January Wilson and Brémond recommended that their embarkation should await a written request from the Sharif and on the same day the War Cabinet decided that one was essential. None was ever received for the Turks remained inactive and the danger passed. The Arabs went over to the offensive and on 23 January occupied Wejh and when in March the Turks launched a half-hearted attack on Rabegh, it was easily beaten off by local forces with some help from British aircraft.

During the prolonged Rabegh crisis much had been happening elsewhere. The military and religious missions had been welcomed at Jedda with what Brémond valiantly called 'acceptable cuisine', although a British guest described the meal as a 'nightmare' with dead flies continually dropping on the food. On 29 September Brémond sent Cadi to Mecca with orders to provide military advice, organise an intelligence system particularly directed at Medina and to cultivate the resident Syrians, teaching them to speak French. He was reminded that the Sharif was an independent prince, that the French had no ambitions in the Hijaz and that he must work with the British.

The North African pilgrims did all that France could hope of them and Brémond reported that their good behaviour and evident prosperity had created a most favourable impression. Ben Ghabrit was invited to participate in the annual cleansing of the Kaaba and on 23 October Brémond reported that the results of his diplomacy had been 'grandiose'. French influence, he boasted, was now preponderant in Mecca. Negotiations for a hostel were successful, although they were not completed until January. Ben Ghabrit returned by way of Paris where he was gratefully received by the President and the Prime Minister.

Brémond had exulted too soon. Twice in the first few days of October Abdullah forwarded to Wilson letters from Brémond with requests on advice on how to reply: on McMahon's instructions he was told to be friendly but guarded. On 5 October Wilson commented that the French 'want to get a foothold in the country but I am, I think, still very much top dog with the Sharif etc.', while as early as 13 October Brémond ruefully told Paris that the British considered Arabia, like Aden or Egypt, to be part of their 'enclave'. It was clear already that whatever the harmony between London and Paris, there was rivalry and competition between their representatives in the Hijaz. On 2 November McMahon forwarded to Grey a copy of the letter from the President of the Republic that Ben Ghabrit had borne to the Sharif with the comment that Wilson had been unable to secure a copy of the reply. His agent in Mecca, Hussein Ruhi, had, however, managed to read and summarise it; presumably Wilson had told him to keep an eye on the French.

Even while they were collaborating over Rabegh, British officers in the area became increasingly suspicious of the political intentions of France. On 30 September Wilson reported a suggestion from Brémond that French officers should go inland and attack Medina, ignoring any objections from the Sharif. McMahon hastily squashed the idea and at his request the Foreign Office asked the Quai for a firm veto. Brémond then apparently felt that if Medina were not taken by the French it would be preferable that it should remain in Turkish hands. On 15 October Wilson told Wingate 'Brémond is a *sahib* and I like him, he is obviously nervous of the Arabs taking Medina in the near future and a revolt in Syria. When Storrs was here he ... told us outright that he did not particularly trust the Sharif or any of his sons and that he thought it possible that they had an understanding with the Turks, a ridiculous idea and shows how little he knows them'.

In November Wilson's distrust deepened. He reported that Brémond was deliberately failing to train Arab soldiers because they might subsequently constitute a hindrance to French ambitions in Syria and a few days later he found that Brémond had sent a 'strictly confidential telegram' to Cadi in Mecca, instructing him to press Abdullah to permit the establishment of a French bank in the Hijaz and that this would be to Cadi's own advantage. Brémond had never mentioned this to his colleague and thereafter Wilson always felt that he was 'not straight'. He wrote later to Clayton 'he does do things behind my back ... all the news that I get of his doings comes from the Sharif'.

Lawrence played his part in fanning suspicions. In November he said that Brémond had told him that the dispatch of European troops to Rabegh would cause the Arab movement to disintegrate and that this was his real reason for urging that they be sent. There is no independent evidence for this statement which is completely at variance with what we have seen of Brémond's own actions and reports and even if it were his policy, it is unlikely that the Colonel would have been so monumentally indiscreet as to confide in Lawrence whose anti-French sentiments were already well known. McMahon, however, passed on the statement to Hardinge with the comment 'it is well to remember this in any proposals that the French may now or hereafter make in regard to our present assistance to the Sharif'. One may also reasonably assume that Lawrence made similar efforts to instil doubts about French motives into his Arab contacts. At any rate, the British and Sharifian authorities deliberately kept Brémond in the dark about the intention to advance on Wejh.

There was certainly some justification for the British attitude. After proposing the attack on Medina on 30 September, on 16 October Brémond warned Paris that if the Sharifians took the Holy City they would press on into Syria so that it was in French interests that they should not have it until the end of the war when it might be ceded in return for help in Syria. It was important, he urged, that the Arabs should not have a complete victory, although it was essential to help them to keep afloat. He repeated these views in a telegram to the Prime Minister two days later. On 24 October he reported that Hussein was so discouraged by the British inactivity that he might sue for peace and a few days later he warned Paris that it was only through using French troops that control of Syria could be gained. On 27 November Briand ordered him not to interfere in the affairs of Syria, adding that, even if a new Arab Empire were impossible, it was not for France to say so.

As Brémond's attitude was already so well known in London, it is ironic to find, on 2 December, Jules Cambon of the Quai warning the Ministère de la Guerre that the Colonel should not allow French opposition to the capture of Medina to become known to the British or the Arabs. A few days later Brémond received a sharp rebuke from the Commander-in-Chief, General Joffre saying that the Allies already knew about it and that the French Government considered that the expulsion of the Turks from the Hijaz would have a useful effect in breaking up the Ottoman Empire.

From his reports it is quite clear that Brémond was spying on his British colleagues, having suborned the Director of Posts and Telegraphs to listen in to their discussions with the Sharif. On 19 January, for example, he reported that the Sharif had spoken to Wilson for 1½ hours complaining about Hussein Ruhi, and five days later he told Paris that his contact had told him of Wilson's demand for the President's letter: he could do nothing officially for fear of compromising his valuable source. A report of 29 June shows that he had agents specially watching Ruhi.

Quite soon these rivalries came to the attention of people outside Arabia. On 30 October Lieutenant Doynel de St. Quentin, Military Attaché in Cairo expressed to Clayton his astonishment at the touchiness of some British officers towards any French activities and Clayton replied that he did not feel any sense of competition and indeed he hoped that the Mission would be increased. The matter, however, soon went higher for on 25 November Hardinge wrote privately to Wingate that 'we are somewhat perturbed by indications that there is not complete harmony between France and England in the Hijaz and it would be desirable to impress on your subordinate the need for the most loyal co-operation with France whom HMG do not suspect of ulterior motives in the Hijaz. I refer particularly to the methods of espionage which Hussein Ruhi appears to have adopted towards the French Mission'. Wingate passed this message on to Wilson, asking for an assurance that he was adhering scrupulously to the official policy of co-operation. The next day Wilson replied in a 'very secret' telegram that 'my personal and official relations with Brémond are and always have been very cordial. As far as I am aware there is complete harmony between us'. Hardinge, he thought, must have got a wrong impression as a result of the difference of opinion over Medina. As for the espionage, he added somewhat ingenuously, 'it occurred at Mecca and was directed at Rashid Rida rather than at the French Mission, against whom I have never employed and have no intention of employing any method of espionage . . . I am well aware of the necessity for loyal co-operation'.

Despite all his reservations, there is no doubt that Brémond worked most sincerely to increase the military strength of the Arabs for numerous telegrams ask for the dispatch of men and munitions. On 6 October, for example, he asked for a battery of 80 mm. guns, repeating on 1 November that the matter was urgent and that they could be sent without crews for there were trained artillerymen who had deserted from the Turkish forces available. (Incidentally Wilson had told Wingate that he thought that the French would never send weapons without men as it would deprive them of an opportunity for infiltration.) On 8 November he asked for two Captains to command machine-gun sections and on 23 November for 20 machine-guns. In April after seeing Faysal he passed on a request for Schneider 75 mm. guns and when this was refused, pleaded for 65 mm. guns instead. A few days later he said that Sharif Ali was in urgent need of two 80 mm. mountain guns. On 22 June he asked for 40 machine-guns with 80 Muslim soldiers and the following month he reported that it was vital to have a wireless set and operator for Yenbo: he was still demanding this in mid-October. On 3 October he lost patience and telegraphed that 'for the twentieth time', Abdullah had asked for 65 mm. guns. Stung, the Ministère de la Guerre asked him to list all these occasions and he testily replied that they were so numerous that he had not passed on them all.

The failure of Paris to provide these relatively small requisitions for material weakened greatly Brémond's levers for influencing Arab policy. He was, however, sometimes successful for on 16 October he was joined by 25 North Africans who had been trained to destroy railways and later another 50 sappers were sent, together with signallers. In May 1917 some 80 mm. guns requested in the previous November arrived and the following month he reported that he had provided Faysal with 300 kgs of explosives.

Brémond's hopes of influencing the training of the Arab army were quickly dashed. As early as 27 September he was worried that the Syrian officers around the Sharif were making difficulties and he complained that Aziz Ali al-Misri, the Chief of Staff, never came to visit him. It was soon obvious that his North African officers lacked the knowledge of Arabic and the general culture to carry weight in Mecca and he was reduced to asking the British to teach them how to ride camels. By the end of 1916 only two remained and in March Brémond admitted that there had been no progress towards establishing a military school, for the Sharif now said that he had sufficient Egyptians available. The Maghrebis were eventually withdrawn and in November 1917, just before he left, Brémond begged Paris to send some Muslims to reside in Mecca for he had nobody there.

Although unsuccessful in this, Brémond's officers and men played an important military role which has not received justice in British accounts. As early as 11 November Captain Raho was attached to Abdullah's column and a year later the French force with this Sharif had grown to five officers, 106 men, two guns, two machine-guns and 15 light machine-guns. Raho proved extremely skilled at attacking the railway from the North to Medina and in the summer he destroyed 39 kms. of track in 40 days. He blew up another train in November. The number of officers with Ali's column varied from two to six, including Colonel Cadi who replaced Nuri al-Said as chief military adviser and they had over 40 men, two guns and six machine-guns. With Faysal there were 140 men, two guns and six machine-guns under Captain Pisani who managed to establish cordial relations with Lawrence, co-operating in attacks on the railway. Despite their achievements, Brémond reported on 23 February that their very presence displeased certain British and Syrian officers around the Sharif.

Brémond's efforts to promote French economic and commercial interests brought him no more success than he gained in the political and military fields. In November he suggested to Paris that the French might demand a banking monopoly in the Hijaz in return for recognition of the Sharif's assumption of a crown, and he pressed for Maghrebis to be brought in to replace Syrians and Indians. He offered doctors, agricultural advisers, dyers and other technicians. In February he complained that the British and Italians were dominating the trade of the Red Sea and he urged that France should do more. In March Cambon told Balfour, now Foreign Secretary, that the King had apparently spontaneously asked Brémond if the French would set up a wireless network for him: the British objected most strongly and doubted if the initiative had indeed not come from the Colonel. In April Wingate reported that he had learned 'from a very reliable source in Mecca' that Brémond had offered to build a railway from Jedda to Mecca and to provide coinage for the kingdom: this writer has not found any trace of these suggestions in the records of the Mission and one cannot dismiss the possibility that someone was deliberately trying to fan the resentment at French activities found in some British circles.

Justifiably or not, British resentment grew. In February the authorities in Cairo tried to block the transfer of money to pay for the pilgrim hostels and at the India Office Hirtzel, Secretary of the Political Department, minuted that all that could be done was to build a more impressive one for British subjects. In March Balfour wrote that that he was 'somewhat perturbed' that Brémond appeared rapidly to be assuming the function of intermediary between the Sharif and the other allies and instructed Wingate to tell the Arabs that they should deal only through the British.

George Lloyd of the Arab Bureau wrote that while the French were perhaps technically correct to treat the Hijaz as outside the Sykes-Picot agreement and therefore a fair area for competition, this was unacceptable. He went on, 'we should never have spent so much and we should not have been justified in incurring the very serious political risks vis-à-vis the Muslim world ... had it not been fully understood that our action was to result in our acquisition of a unique and privileged position in this country'. London agreed and the India Office minuted that it 'regarded French moves in the Hijaz with much misgiving ... it will be necessary for HMG to make counter-moves, and on a scale that must be proportional to their larger interests'. Hardinge instructed Wingate that he should be careful to stop the French from getting undue influence: 'they have recognised our predominant interests and this must be rubbed into them'.

By the end of April 1917 Brémond realised that he was failing for he wrote sadly to Defrance that British influence was practically complete. Khatib, the Sharif's main adviser, was a professor from the Sudan, an Egyptian colonel was in charge of the food supplies, the Royal Navy controlled the port and the RAMC the hospital. No one could leave the Hijaz without permission from Wilson and French doctors and a bank were being kept out by him. The English, he concluded, regarded the Hijaz as merely an extension of the Red Sea Province of the Sudan and wanted only a token allied presence to preserve the fiction that it was independent.

It had already become apparent in Paris that the Mission was not producing the results for which it had hoped. On 2 February Briand signalled to Brémond that in refusing to ask for European troops, the Sharif had doomed every prospect of intervention in the Hijaz and that it was clear that he did not want the French even as instructors. On 27 February he asked Cambon in London if there were any further point in maintaining the Mission unless the Sharif would be upset by its withdrawal. On 6 March the Ministère de la Guerre agreed that the Mission was underused and a few days later Brémond himself confirmed that the Sharif had refused to ask for the services of his nine officers and 49 NCOs and that his effectiveness was further diminished by a fire which had destroyed much of the war material at his Suez base.

Paris considered that the troops could be better used elsewhere and that there was no longer any point in trying to organise the Sharif's forces which anyway should not be allowed to become too strong. The Prime Minister, now Alexandre Ribot, wrote that the winding up of the Mission would please local British officials, if not Whitehall and on 21 April General Bailloud was ordered to visit the area and report. He was told that the Mission had 'lost much of its political importance and that military co-operation was limited by the "reservations" of the British and of the Sharif', although Paris felt that some elements should be left behind to maintain the principle of collaboration. On 29 April Brémond himself suggested a reduction of his strength as he had achieved little due to the 'tenacious, under-hand' opposition of the local British and the hostility of the Egyptians and Syrians who surrounded the Sharif. On 10 May

Georges-Picot, French High Commissioner for the Middle East, wrote to Ribot asking if there were now any point in keeping the Mission: he added that one could never forget Fashoda and had to realise that the British did not really want any foreigners in the Hijaz and were very touchy with regard to Brémond's attempts to infiltrate French Muslims.

While the French were discussing the future of the Mission, the British were moving towards action. On 11 February Wingate wrote privately to Balfour, forwarding a letter from Wilson referring to Brémond's attempts to establish a bank – if successful, it could 'only be a question of time before French influence would be predominant'. Brémond had told Abdullah that Wilson supported his request, although Wilson had not even been informed about it. Wingate enclosed also a letter from Lawrence saying that Brémond had told Faysal that his alliance with Britain would not be permanent and that it was in his interests to establish direct relations with France: as with Lawrence's previous statement impugning the Colonel's good faith, there is no confirmation in the French archives that Brémond had taken this line. Wingate commented 'I cannot but agree that our allies have given some grounds for the suspicion that they are preparing to sacrifice the success of the Hijaz revolt ... in the belief that its success, directly or indirectly, might militate against the full realisation of their territorial claims in Syria'. The British, he continued, had always tried to persuade the Arabs that they were working with the French but 'Brémond has not scrupled to convey to them a contrary impression'. Hirtzel minuted 'we shall be well rid of Brémond' and Austen Chamberlain agreed, 'I thoroughly distrust Colonel Brémond'.

In March George Lloyd saw Sir Mark Sykes and obviously gave him further particulars of Cairo's allegations for Sykes wrote to Wingate 'truly Brémond's performances have been disgusting. I had gathered as much from Picot'. At the end of the following month Sykes and Picot were together in Cairo and on 27 April Sykes telegraphed to the Foreign Office that Picot had promised that 'he would endeavour to get the French Government to bring the French Military Mission to an end, and of their own motion, inform HMG that they regarded the Hijaz as in the British sphere of influence, stipulating for certain rights in regard to supervision of the French pilgrim traffic'. He added that he found this very satisfactory, and largely due to the efforts of Lloyd. As we have seen Picot did this on 10 May.

Sykes arrived in the Hijaz on 4 May and the following day a 'very secret' signal to London gave his conclusions. 'I am convinced that the sooner the French Military Mission is removed from Hijaz the better. The French officers are without exception anti-Arab, and only serve to promote dissension and intrigue. Their line is to crab British operations to the Arabs, throw cold water on all Arab activities to the British, and make light of the King to both. They make no disguise that they desire Arab failure.... My chief difficulty in bringing about a better feeling between the Arabs and the French is owing to the deliberately perverse attitude and policies followed by Colonel Brémond and his staff'. He did not think that Picot would succeed in having the Mission recalled and so he asked Whitehall to make an official request to Paris.

On 12 May, therefore, Balfour instructed Bertie to do this, stressing that it was undesirable that there should be two military missions in the Hijaz with apparently divergent aims, although the French might if they wished attach a Liaison Officer to Wilson's staff. He was to complain that Brémond's talk of railways had been 'premature' and 'disturbing' for the Arabs. The following day Bertie presented a formal note expressing 'the profound desire' of the British Government that Brémond should be recalled now that his task had been accomplished. He followed closely the language of Sykes's telegram which caused the latter to complain that it divulged the fact that some of his own relations with Picot had been behind the back of the French Government.

On 22 May Ribot replied that the recall of the Mission was already under consideration but that France would require a formal undertaking that the British would be able to prevent the Turks from recapturing Mecca. A few Muslim officers would remain as instructors, but Brémond, with whom Paris was 'entirely satisfied', would then be too senior to command such a reduced force which could then be placed under Colonel Cadi. This would maintain the right of France to equality in the Hijaz as had been agreed by Sykes-Picot for, as a great Muslim power, it could not allow any other state to predominate in Mecca. He hoped, he added, that HMG had been misinformed about the attitude of the Mission for nothing in Brémond's reports showed that he had not done his utmost to help the Sharif while his Muslim officers were obviously pro-Arab. Two days later he told the Ministère de la Guerre of his answer, saying that Brémond must stay for the moment for France could not let down her man under British pressure. Diplomats confirmed that the Mission was achieving little for on 4 June Picot stated that only the British were consulted about operations and policy and a replacement for Brémond would probably do nothing more than irritate them: he suggested that France should lie low, and let the British take the odium when things went wrong for it would then be in a position to take over. Defrance from Cairo agreed that Brémond had failed to gain any influence for McMahon had been hostile from the beginning and the local British had intrigued against the Colonel while the latter had played it straight.

On 20 June the Ministère de la Guerre instructed Brémond to consider what should be done to wind up his Mission and General Bailloud suggested that officers should be left with the columns and at Mecca: this would be enough to calm the British while still safeguarding the prestige of France. A few days later Brémond was promoted to the rank of Commandeur of the Légion d'Honneur.

On the ground the situation was soon transformed by Lawrence's capture of Aqaba on 6 July and the subsequent northward thrust of Faysal's men which turned Jedda practically into a backwater. The British never gave the pledge that they would defend Mecca which had been the price for the recall of Brémond and did not pursue the matter. They seem, indeed, to have lost all interest in him and his name practically disappears from their correspondence, except for a formal letter of thanks in September and the award of British decorations to members of the Mission the following month. Brémond reciprocated by recommending Lawrence for the Croix de Guerre.

Bailloud recommended that the French detachments should be withdrawn from Arabia as their small numbers served only to emphasise the feebleness of their resources when compared with those of the British. Wilson tried to convince him that some should be left for they were not easily replaceable and their departure might lead the tribesmen to feel abandoned. On 12 September Paris decided that the role of the Mission should be confined to giving material and in exceptional cases personnel support.

There were a few more flurries of intrigue. The French tried to repeat the success of the previous Hajj by sending a delegation led by an Algerian notable, Mustafa Cherchali who reported on 24 June that he was confident that he could restore French influence in Mecca. In August he promised a lump sum in gold to the Sharif and a worried Wingate asked the Foreign Office 'can you suggest any grounds upon which we could refuse permission?'. Whitehall replied that there was no need to object. Wingate specifically said that Brémond was not involved in this matter but he was involved in one final effort to establish French influence in Syria. On 8 October he reported that he had established contact with a grandson of the Algerian hero Abd al-Kader, also named Abd al-Kader who was resident in Damascus and seemed a useful tool. A month later he signalled that Abd al-Kader had written to him on his return home, declaring that he would support France against Faysal and the British, but as so often before Brémond was doomed to disappointment. A year later when the Arabs entered Damascus Abd al-Kader seems to have tried to seize power but was killed in the attempt, 'murdered by the Anglo-Sharifians' as Brémond bitterly put it in his book.

At the end of October 1917 the Ministère de la Guerre considered raising an Arab legion which would be trained by the Brémond Mission. In fact only a few scallywags enlisted and the Quai thought that any involvement of Brémond would upset the British and the project lapsed.

Brémond by then had had enough. On 26 November he applied for leave, hoping to return to a high command in the Levant. His request was granted and he left Arabia for the last time on 14 December. In February 1918, when his leave expired, the Quai recommended that a post be found for him in Egypt and the Ministère de la Guerre gave him posting orders with instructions not to interfere in Arabia. A few days later this was countermanded and Brémond spent the rest of the war in France. The story of his subsequent clashes with Lawrence are beyond the scope of this article. So, too, is the subsequent activity of this Mission which lingered on in Jedda until August 1920 with little to do except try to pick up scraps of political intelligence.

The Mission never achieved the results that had been intended. It appears that at the highest level in London and Paris there was a genuine desire for military co-operation against the Ottoman Empire and for an amicable division of the subsequent spoils. It seemed as if the Sykes-Picot agreement had achieved this in the spring of 1916 before the start of the Revolt but this was never communicated to the officers in the field, and, as late as January 1917 neither Wilson nor Brémond had been informed. They were both men who had spent their formative years in the period of the intense Anglo-French rivalry over colonies which had culminated in the Fashoda incident and in Morocco until it was brought to an end by the Entente Cordiale: old habits of thought died hard in men who had been involved at first hand in this competition. Each man seems to have liked the other personally but distrusted him politically. Brémond was perhaps the more ready to bury the past but Wilson, having been present at the struggle to keep the French from the Sudan clearly felt that it would be folly to welcome them to the other side of the Red Sea where the British were still striving to establish themselves. Even before the Revolt started, Lawrence was determined to keep the French out of Syria, which was always his main concern, and he saw that if they were once strongly installed in the Hijaz, they would have a base from which to move northwards. Wilson and Lawrence therefore worked to prevent the Mission from becoming a real force and presented its activities in a way that prejudiced their superiors and ultimately the British Government against it. Paris knew that to attain its aims in Syria it would need British acquiescence and did not wish to endanger it by antagonising their allies over the Hijaz so they starved Brémond of the support that might have enabled him to play a dominant role. The experience of a man, intrigued against by his allies and let down by his masters is bitter and Brémond suffered it to the full.

Sources

There are numerous references to Brémond in the biographies of T.E. Lawrence but these are rarely based on archival research. For Lawrence-worshippers like Graves and Liddell Hart, Brémond is a rather sinister buffoon who is outwitted by the hero, while for Aldington he is a dignified and honourable man who proved no match for a crafty charlatan. Brémond himself wrote *Le Hedjaz dans la guerre mondiale* (Paris, 1931) which is most useful, but naturally neither impartial nor complete. Many of his letters and telegrams appear in the officially published *Les Armées Françaises dans la grande guerre*, IX 1, but the most important do not and those that do are often drastically shortened. One is left, therefore, with archives and as it will be obvious which source I have used, I have not given detailed references, particularly as many have unnumbered pages. I consulted: India Office Records, particularly L/P&S/10/615 – the French Mission; L/P&S/10/616 – French and Italian policies; L/MIL/5/858 – Rabegh. Service historique de l'Armée (Vincennes) – Boxes 6 N 191, 7 N 2135–2144, 16 N 2985, 17 N 498 and 499. Wingate Papers in the Sudan Archive at Durham University. Hardinge Papers in Cambridge University Library. Sykes Papers in the Middle East Centre, Oxford University.

Some remarks on the ritual significance of the bull in pre-Islamic South Arabia

Walter Dostal

The essential question dealt with in this paper is whether and, if the answer is in the affirmative, how recourse to ethnographic data for the interpretation of pre-Islamic cultural phenomena might prove fruitful.

In the limited framework of this article, it will not be possible to discuss in detail the wealth of methodological problems. It is certainly incontestable that one may infer from the present to the past only on the basis of relations by which the past is connected to what exists at present. It should, therefore, be understood that the axiom of the existence of such a relationship within the area of South Arabian cultures provides the theoretical basis for the following description, in which I shall discuss, by means of ethnological data, two aspects of the sacrifice of bulls:[1]

1 The bull sacrifice on the occasion of al-ʿĪd al-kabīr;

2 The bull sacrifice in present-day common law.

The selected data have been taken from my field studies in the years 1971 and 1972 in the Yemen Arab Republic.

1 – The Sacrifice of the *Thawr al-ʿĪd*

In the region of ʿIyāl Yazīd, four to six weeks before the 10th Dhū ʾl-Ḥijjah, three to seven men of a village combine in a festival company (*sharika ḥaqq al-ʿĪd*), in order to buy a sacrificial bull (*thawr al-ʿĪd*). This festival company is recruited from men of the same kin or from the local community. They are the heads of the economic units which belong to their extended families, for it is only these heads who have the right of disposal, derived from patrilineality, over the means of production to complete such purchases. The bull is selected according to certain criteria: his colour must be white and he must be free from any physical defect. The bull is put up with a group member who has appropriate accommodation at his disposal, with all members of the festival company providing the fodder in equal proportion.

On the day of the sacrifice, the men of the company assemble before sunrise in front of the house of the man who has looked after the bull. The fattened (*maʿlūf*) bull is led out of the shed and fumigated with incense. Then the women paint him with henna or a green vegetable paint and decorate his horns. The horn adornment (*ʿiqāwah*), which consists of a braid of fragrant plants and flowers, is wound garland-like around the horns. On the forehead, exactly in the middle, a bunch of plants (*mashkūr*) is placed (Plates 2–3). The bull, thus adorned, is led by the men through the settlement; in the past, the procession also proceeded through the fields that belonged to the village (*madār al-'Īd*). All that was said to me, by way of explanation, was that this procession was conducive to the thriving of the crops. After this, the bull is handed over for slaughtering to the butcher, who belongs to the socially inferior class of the Muzāyinīn.[2] With an incense ceremony that follows the slaughter, the sacrifice of the bull comes to an end.[3] The meat is divided between the members of the festival company in equal parts, and to the ensuing feast (*walīmah*), relatives and friends are invited.[4] Nowadays it may possibly happen that redundant meat is sold. The butcher retains the skull and skin of the sacrificial bull.

Two characteristics of this ceremony would seem to be suitable for understanding the deeper meaning of this custom: the ritual procession and the way the head of the sacrificial bull is adorned. In the former, when the fields were included, the relation between the bull and the fertility of the crops is obviously finding expression. The idea of such a relationship has been proved by J. Ryckmans to have existed in the religious conception of the world, as held by the old societies of South Arabia.[5] In the same conceptual connection one must see another custom which is being adhered to in the same region on the first day of the sowing of *dhurah*. At the '*karāmat al-mazra'ah*' ('honouring of the sown land'), after the midday meal, which the farmers partake in the fields, butter is spread on the horns of the bull, that is, stated more precisely, butter is sacrificed to the bull, as may also be inferred from the Arabic passage '*yiḍaḥḥūn qurūn al-thawr bi-zibd*'.[6] This sacrifice of butter on the occasion of the sowing of *dhurah* brings out in full relief the ideological connection between the bull and fertility.

The custom of adorning the bull with plants also may certainly be derived from the ideological connection between bull and fertility. The adornment of the sacrificial bull with a garland in particular should be attributed to the category of manifold fertility symbols to be found in the customs of present day Yemenis.[7] It is certainly no coincidence that, for example, one of the customs accompanying a marriage consists of garlanding the head of the bridegroom with flowers and fragrant plants.

The only question that remains outstanding is whether we have any indications for a clearer understanding of the meaning of the sacrificial bull. A starting point for answering this question may be found in the term *mashkūr* for the bunch of plants that is put between the horns. If we go back to the basic meaning of that term, 'thank', we have a direct indication of a thanksgiving sacrifice.

For the archeology of South Arabia, the above description of the plant adornment of the *thawr al-'Īd* is of interest because, by showing its existence in recent customs, one can postulate a new interpretation of the depiction of bulls with similar adornments – bunches between the horns. The relevant pictures that are available in the literature are shown in Table 1. This head adornment has, until now, been described as a 'thunderbolt', following an interpretation by A. Grohmann.[8] Under the headword 'thunderbolt', M. Höfner writes: 'Most often, it is to be found between the horns of the bull heads, the former having either the form of the crescent moon or of a two-pronged flash of lightning ("lyre-shaped"). For a long time, it (viz. the thunderbolt) has here been taken for a forehead adornment or for a quiff, but Grohmann has identified the object in question as a thunderbolt'.[9] Having pointed out the head adornment of the *thawr al-ʿĪd*, it should be understandable that any re-interpretation of the head adornment described as 'thunderbolt' will only look promising if it can be proved that the head adornments, depicted on those reliefs of bulls, did consist of plant material.[10] In order to make the analysis of the head ornament easier, I have brought together in the following classification scheme all the types of head ornament represented on those reliefs (Table 4).

The results of the analysis are the following: Types I A-D are undoubtedly and unequivocally identifiable as plant ornaments. As for Types I C-D, it is important to emphasise that, as shown by Plates 2–3, they are depicted with horns that are without doubt carrying plant ornaments. Thus we have shown a complete correspondence with the type of head ornament as worn by the *thawr al-ʿĪd*.

The head of the bull depicted in Table 2(3), where the horns end in vine shoots, may probably be interpreted as an artistic rendering of the original horn ornament.

Plant material is also clearly visible in I H from the stylised leaves or buds. Type I E shows a bunch-like headpiece into which the hair of the forehead seems to have been interwoven. The same may be assumed for Types I F and G.

In contrast to these unambiguous indications for the depiction of plant ornaments – except for I F and G – the case for the types included in Group II is less clear. It is likely that they are headpieces that were attached between the horns, but which we cannot identify. For this reason we must leave aside this group from further examination.

If the analysis given here is correct, we may re-define the depictions under discussion as bouquets, that is, that in pre-Islamic South Arabia sacrificial bulls were adorned in a way similar to present custom with the *thawr al-ʿĪd*.[11] In this connection one should not fail to notice the fact that, in the case of two objects (Table 2/1–2), we were able to prove full correspondence with the present way of adornment of the sacrificial bull.

In conclusion, another question remains to be treated that is also of interest from a historico-cultural point of view, i.e., whether the various types of head adornment of Group I are to be evaluated as objects specific to certain regions. Unfortunately, the random spread of the objects and the paucity of indications as to their provenance rule out a satisfactory answer. In so far as exact indications of the provenance of the objects are available, they show at least that we must reckon with a wide scale of variations of the head adornment of the bulls within any region, as is shown by Types I C-G, which all came from the region of Ẓafār. The same phenomenon may be proved of the decoration of the forehead hair on the reliefs of the bulls (Table 3). The adornment of the hair of the forehead also gives rise to the assumption that, similar to recent practices in painting the animals, various parts of the body of sacrificial bulls were also adorned (Plates 2 and 3).

To summarise:

a If our interpretation of the types of old South Arabian head adornments on depictions of bulls is correct, then it follows that Grohmann's interpretation is improbable.

b From the formal correspondence between the recent type of head adornment of the bulls and the old South Arabian types of head adornment on the reliefs of the bulls, no statement can be derived about any correspondence as regards the *content* of the custom that is connected with this way of adornment, for the source material does not allow such a conclusion. The common conceptual content must be seen as limited to the idea of a close connection between bull and fertility.

c The unidentifiable headpieces that are included in Group II may, perhaps, represent special, regionally different forms of the types of head ornament discussed before.

2 – The Sacrifice of the bull in common law practice

In this section I intend to demonstrate, on the basis of data ascertained by me, a completely different aspect of the bull sacrifice, namely as an integral part of common law by way of expiatory sacrifice. From this point of view, we are in a position to add further aspects to the studies on Yemenite law by E. Glaser, C. Rathjens and E. Rossi and to open the way to a better understanding.[12]

This expiatory sacrifice appears in two forms: as a *complex* expiatory sacrifice in which one bull each is sacrificed in each of three different legal stages, and as a *simple* expiatory sacrifice, in which only one bull is immolated. Both mark a certain legal status and are therefore the symbolic and functional expression of defined inter-relations within legal acts. To bring out clearly these inter-relations is the intention of the following description.

For the moment, it may be useful to describe the course of a sacrificial ceremony which I had occasion to observe. It concerned the *khīrah*-sacrifice, the first sacrificial ceremony in the course of the complex expiatory sacrifice ceremony (Plates 1, 4–7). As for the past history: a woman had killed a man in the course of a violent quarrel and had therefore, according to our interpretation of the law, committed manslaughter. On the day following the burial of the slain man, the sacrifice of the *thawr al-khīrah*, 'the bull of propitiation' – a white bull without blemish – was offered at the graveside. To give clarity to the description, I summarise the main phases of the sacrificial ceremony:

1 The men, who belong to the kin of the slain man, assemble at his grave.

2 The husband of the woman perpetrator leads the purchased bull to the grave. He is accompanied by men of his kin and by a sayyid, who has been requested by the husband to act as mediator in this conflict. The husband is also followed by a butcher and his assistant (Plate 1).

3 The bull is examined by the relatives of the slain man and, after they have accepted the bull as the sacrificial animal (*'aqīrah*), the butcher and his assistant make preparations for the slaughter.[13] First the bull's forefeet are tied up, then the butcher leads the rope to its hind feet, as can be seen from the photos, winding the rope so that, on being tugged just once, the animal will lose its equilibrium and fall to the ground. Afterwards the forefeet are closely bound to one hind foot (Plates 4–6).

4 After a short joint prayer, the butcher's assistant bends the head of the bull forcibly backwards to make the slaughter easier. Having said the ritual phrase '*bi-'smi 'llāh*', the bull is sacrificed. As soon as it is bled dry, the butcher separates the head from the trunk and flays the hide (Plate 7).

5 After flaying, the animal is cut up. A quarter each goes to the two groups of relatives who are involved in the case; the other half is reserved for the inhabitants of the settlement of the slain man. The skull and the hide of the bull represent the share of the butcher who, in addition, also receives some payment.

After this necessary digression, let us now return to the problem of the complex expiatory sacrifice. We must now discover its connection to legal acts. To do this, we chose as our starting point the facts of the case described before which was the immediate cause for the performance of the sacrificial ceremony set forth above. As I have already pointed out, we would describe the committed crime as manslaughter, because it was an act of unintentional slaying as against murder, which is defined as intentional killing. Now it is important to know that in Arab common law the two crimes, manslaughter and murder, are considered congruent. This view is derived from the principle of reciprocity, which characterises this legal system. This principle of '*do ut des*' reduces the motivation of an act to insignificance because, from the point of view of retaliation, the act itself that has caused the damage is the only subject matter of the legal action. Therefore this killing, which was done in a violent outburst of temper, is punished as *qatl bi-dūn al-ḥaqq*. It is in this frame of reference that complex expiatory sacrifices play an important role in so far as they give expression to each legal stage in the process of settling the dispute. The sacrifice I have called complex comprises the *khīrah*-sacrifice, the *ṣawāb*-sacrifice, and the *ṣulḥ*-sacrifice.

The sacrifice of the *thawr al-khīrah*, 'the bull of propitiation', is offered at the grave of the slain person; the *thawr al-ṣawāb*, in a figurative sense: 'the bull of the legal status', is sacrificed in front of the slain person's house, after conclusion of the negotiations about blood-money; the *thawr al-ṣulḥ*, 'the bull of appeasement', that is also offered as sacrifice in front of the slain person's house, after the blood-money has been paid.

It is now necessary to emphasise, in more concrete terms, the legal frameworks of those three sacrifices. First of all it is necessary to view the *khīrah*-sacrifice separately from the other two. It is considered as an obligatory action, to be performed by the next of kin independently of whether the crime is expected to be settled by material compensation or by actual vengeance. Directly connected with the legal system are the *ṣawāb*-

sacrifice and the *ṣulḥ*-sacrifice. Their offering becomes obligatory only when the material compensation has become legally binding, that is, after agreement has been reached on the amount of blood-money and the mode of its payment. In this context they secure public sanction of the settlement reached between the two groups of kin involved. With the *ṣulḥ*-sacrifice and the ensuing joint sacrificial feast (*walīmah*), the unlawful slaying is, at least theoretically, considered fully atoned for.[14]

Now to the expiatory sacrifice, where only one bull is offered. Its legal framework is completely different from that of the complex sacrifice, for it comprises any cases of conflict except those of unlawful slaying. By its offering, expression is being given to the intention of settling the conflict, that is, it is an attestation of volition.[15] In this case the sacrificial bull (*ʿaqīrah*) is slaughtered in front of the house of the person with whom one has the dispute. By so doing, the disputing party, who is ready for conciliation, forces the opposing party to a settlement of the dispute.

This becomes an effective means not only in the relations between individuals but also between tribes, on the one hand, and the central government, on the other. Thus I have observed Khawlāni tribesmen sacrificing a bull in front of the Prime Minister's office in Ṣanʿā', to initiate peace negotiations with the government.

Thus the sacrifice of the bull turns out to be an important social means of reconciliation, and the various purposes of the sacrifice are each found to be correlated with a different legal framework which, I hope, I have succeeded in outlining.

Notes

1 As to the significance of the sacrifice of bulls in old South Arabia, cf. Henninger: 1942/45: 305; Ryckmans: 1975a. Regarding the question of survival from pre-Islamic times cf. Ryckmans: 1973c; 1975b; also the various statements in the works by Serjeant: 1949; 1954; 1971; 1976.

2 Cf. Dostal: 1974: 3.

3 Cf. Müller, W. W.: 129 passim.

4 Cf. Ryckmans: 1973a; 1973b: 327 passim; 1974: 132; 1975b: 451; 1975c: 217 passim. In Ḥaḍramawt, the use of the term to designate the wedding celebration has been verified: Serjeant: 1949: 159, note 18.

5 Cf. Ryckmans: 1975a: 366 passim. As for the old South Arabian month of Dhū Thawr, Serjeant: 1976: 68 refers to a recent idiomatic expression in Ḥaḍramawt: '*Al-thawr mā yadkhul fī 'l-thawr*' – 'The bull (presumably for plowing) does not enter (sc. enter the field) in al-Thawr'. Unfortunately, the paper mentioned by Hartmann: 271, written by Ed. Glaser, 'The cult of the bull with the old Sabeans' (Communications 2–6), was not available to me.

6 Cf. Chelhod; Henninger: 1963: 449 passim.

7 With the B. Ḥushaysh in North Yemen, two fertility symbols are prepared for the wedding celebration: one symbol of the tree of life (*mashujab*) and the *tawrāyah*, a bowl with a mixture of earth and sesame, on

to which are strewn barley and wheat. In addition, an egg and a cucumber are put on it, as is a candle.

[8] Cf. Grohmann: 1914: 32 passim.

[9] Höfner: 505 'Am häufigsten findet er sich zwischen den Hörnern der Stierköpfe, die entweder die Form der Mondsichel oder des zweistrahligen Blitzbündels haben ("lyraförmig"). Man hat ihn hier lange für einen Stirnschmuck oder für Stirnlockegehalten, doch hat Grohmann den fraglichen Gegenstand als D. identifiziert.'

[10] Hartmann: 270 already took the head adornment, depicted on our Table 1, No. 6, for a pine cone.

[11] On the existence of this type of horn adornment outside South Arabia, cf. Dostal: 1957: 85 passim, and also pictures 9–12.

[12] Glaser: 1884; Müller-Rhodokanakis: 122–125; Rathjens: 1951; Rossi: 1948.

[13] Cf. Henninger: 1963: 470; Gräf: 20; Serjeant: 1976: 94, note 88; Wellhausen: 181.

[14] Regarding the meaning of the joint meal cf. Müller-Rhodokanakis: 36; Wellhausen: 124.

[15] Cf. Ryckmans: 1975b: 450; Goitein: 35; Serjeant: 1976; 94, note 88; Wellhausen: 128. According to Brauer: 289, Jews who had gone through some heavy punishment were obliged to offer such an expiatory sacrifice. That we are not dealing here with a typically Semitic phenomenon may be seen from Jensen: 455.

Addendum

In this connection I would like to thank Professor Walter W. Müller for the following remark which he communicated to me in a letter dated 4th of August 1980 concerning the dedicatory inscription Ja 669, published in A. Jamme, *Sabaean Inscriptions from Maḥram Bilqîs (Mârib)*, Baltimore 1962 (Publications of the American Foundation for the Study of Man, III), 174f.: 'In this inscription the dedicators promise to the god Almaqah that, if a son were born to them and this son were to remain alive, they, among other things (line 13–14) *yhślnn/ṯny/ṯwrn/bklwnm*; in line 24–25 of the same text we read again: *yhqnynn/wyhślnn/ṯwrn/bklwn*. A. Jamme has translated the above cited passage in line 13–14 as follows: 'and they would drive two bulls to Kalwânum'; this interpretation does not only make no satisfactory sense, but is also hardly supported by the underlying text. The word *klwn* or *klwnm* respectively is certainly not a place-name; since it is, however, a *hapaxlegomenon* it cannot be determined definitely what it means. For that reason it will be left untranslated in the forthcoming Sabaean dictionary, edited by A. F. L. Beeston, Mahmud A. al-Ghul, Jacques Ryckmans and myself. To my opinion, however, *klwn(m)*, with which the bulls destined for sacrifice are provided, is perhaps to be connected with the word for 'bridegroom', widely spread in South Arabia, cf. in Ḥaḍramawt *kulān* (v. R. B. Serjeant, *South Arabian Hunt*, London 1976, 67), likewise in Dathina and Dhofar, Soqoṭri *kelān*, Mahri *kelōn* and

Sḥeri *kulún*. The word designates the bridegroom on the wedding-day, when he is adorned and crowned, and its original meaning is most probably 'the crowned one, the one adorned with a wreath'. Therefore it cannot be excluded that also in the Sabaean text Ja 669 two adorned bulls are mentioned. The two passages cited above may consequently be translated: 'and they would offer two bulls with wreaths' and 'they would dedicate and offer the two bulls with wreaths' respectively.'

Regarding the ethnographic description of the *thawr al-'id* the author would like to refer a similar description of this custom in Goitein: 'Jemenische Geschichten'. In *Zeitschrift für Semitistik und verwandte Gebiete*. Bd.9 (1933/34) p. 36. The bunch of plants is mentioned there as mashqur 'bouquet of flowers' cf. also Landberg, C., *Glossaire Daṯinois* Vol. 3 (1942) p. 2067.

Bibliography

Bowen, Lebaron, R. V., Albright, F. P., 1958. *Archaeological Discoveries in South Arabia*, Baltimore.

Brauer, E., 1934. *Ethnologie der Yementischen Juden*, Kulturgeschichtliche Bibliothek IR/7, Heidelberg.

Chelhod, J., 1952. 'Le sacrifice arabe nommé "ḍaḥiya"', *Revue de l'Histoire des Religions*, Paris, CILII, 206–215.

Costa, P., 1973. 'Antiquities from Ẓafār (Yemen)' *Annali* I (Istituto Orientale di Napoli), XXXIII, 23, 185–206. Pl. I–XXVI.

—— 1976. 'Antiquities from Ẓafār (Yemen) – II' *annali* 445–456, XXXVI, 26, Pl. I–XXX.

Dostal, W., 1957. 'Ein Beitrag zur Frage der religiösen Weltbilder der frühesten Bodenbauern Vorderasiens', *Archiv für Völkerkunde*, Vienna, XII, 54–109.

—— 1974. 'Sozio-ökonomische Aspekte der Stammesdemokratie in Nordost-Yemen' *Soziologus*, XXIV, 1–15.

Garbini, G., 1970. 'Antichità Yemenite' *Annali* (Istituto Orientale di Napoli) XXX, 20, 400–404, Taf. I–XVIII/537–548 Taf. XIX–XLVI.

Glaser, Ed., 1884. 'Meine Reise durch Arhab und Hâschid' *Petermann's Mitteilungen*, Gotha, XXX, 170–183; 204–213.

Goitein, S. D., 1947. *The Land of Sheba. Tales of the Jew of Yemen*, New York.

Gräf, E., 1959. *Jagdbeute und Schlachttier im islamischen Recht*. Eine Untersuchung zur Entwicklung der islamischen Jurisprudenz Bonner Orientalische Studien, Bonn, VII.

Grohmann, Ad., 1914. 'Götter, Symbole und Symboltiere Auf Südarabischen Denkmälern', *Denkschrift der K.Akademie der Wissenschaften in Wien. Phil-Hist.K1.*, LVIII, 1, Vienna.

—— 1963. 'Arabien.' In: *Kulturgeschichte des Alten Orients* III.Abschn. IV.Unterabschn. *Handbuch der Altertumswissenschaft* ed. Müller, I.von, Otto, W., Bengston, H., Munich.

Hartmann, M., 1908. Südarabisches VII, VIII. *Orientalische Literaturzeitung*, Berlin, 11.Jhg.: 174–179; 270–274.

Henninger, J., 1942/45. Das Opfer in den Alt-Südarabischen Hochkulturen. *Anthropos*, XXXVII/XL: 779–810.

—— 1963. 'Deux Etudes Récentes sur l'Arabie pré-islamique', *Anthropos*, Salzburg, LVIII, 437–476.

Höfner, M., 1965. 'Südarabien', *Wörterbuch der Mythologie, Götter und Mythen im Vorderen Orient*, 490–567, Stuttgart.

Jensen, Ad. E., 1960. 'Beziehungen zwischen dem Alten Testament und der Nilotischen Kultur in Afrika', *Culture in History – Essays in Honor of Paul Radin*, 449–464, Columbia Univ. Pub.

Müller, D. H., 1899. *Südarabische Altertümer im Kunsthistorischen Hofmuseum*, Vienna.

Müller, D. H. und Rhodokanakis, N. (ed.), 1913. *Eduard Glasers Reise nach Mârib*. Sammlung Eduard Glaser I, Vienna.

Müller, W. W., 1973. 'Ergebnisse der Deutschen Yemen. Expedition 1970', *Archiv für orientforschung*, Berlin, XXIV, 150–161.

—— 1976. 'Notes on the use of Frankincense in South Arabia', *Proceedings of the Seminar for Arabian Studies*, London, VI, 124–136.

Nielsen, D., 1927. *Handbuch der altarabischen Altertumskunde*. In Verbindung mit Fr. Hommel und N. K. Rhodokanakis herausgegeben. Mit Beiträgen von Adolf Grohmann und Enno Littmann. I. Die altarabische Kultur, Paris – Kopenhagen – Leiden.

Pirenne, J., 1957. 'Le Rinceau dans l'Évolution de l'Art Sud-Arabie'. *Syria*, Paris, XXXIV, 99–127.

Rathjens, C., 1951. 'Tâghût gegen Scherī'a. Gewohnheitsrecht und islamisches Recht bei den Gabilen des yemenitischen Hochlandes', *Jahrbuch des Museums für Länder-und Völkerkunde/Linden-Museum*, Stuttgart, 172–187.

—— 1955. *Sabaeica*. Bericht über die archäologischen Ergebnisse einer zweiten, dritten und vierten Reise nach Südarabien. II Teil. Mitteilungen aus dem Museum für Völkerkunde in Hamburg, XXV/2.

Rossi, E., 1948. 'Il diritto consuetudinaro delle tribu arabe del Yemen,' *Rivista degli Studi Orientali*, Rome, XXIII, 1–36.

Ryckmans, J., 1973a. 'Ritual meals in the ancient South Arabian Religion', *Proceedings of the sixth Seminar for Arabian Studies*, London, 1972, 36–39.

—— 1973b. 'Le Repas Rituel dans la Religion Sud-Arabe', *Symbolae Biblicae et Mesopotamicae Francisco Mario Theodoro de Liagre Bohl Dedicatae*, Leiden, 327–334.

—— 1973c. 'Du Rite d'Istiqâ' au Temple Sabéen de Mârib', *Annuaire de l'Institut de Philosophie et d'Histoire Orientales et Slaves*, XX (1968–72), Brussels, 379–388.

—— 1974. 'Formal Inertia in the South Arabian Inscriptions (Ma'īn and Saba)', *Proceedings of the Seminar for Arabian Studies*, IV, London, 131–139.

—— 1975a. 'Notes sur le Rôle de Taureau dans le Religion sud-arabe', *Mélanges d'Islamologie*, II, *Correspondance d'Orient*, Brussels, 13, 365–373.

—— 1975b. 'Les Inscriptions Sud-Arabes Anciennes et les Etudes Arabes', *annali* (Istituto Orientali di Napoli), XXXV, 25, 443–463.
—— 1975c. 'Himyaritica (5)', *Le Muséon*, Louvain, LXXXVIII, 199–219.
Serjeant, R. B., 1949. 'The Cemetries of Tarīm (Ḥaḍramawt)', *Le Muséon*, Louvain, LXII, 151–160.
—— 1954. 'Hūd, and other pre-islamic Prophets of Ḥaḍramawt, *Le Muséon*, Louvain, LXVII, 121–179.
—— 1971. 'The "White Dune" at Abyan: An Ancient Place of Pilgrimage in Southern Arabia', *Journal of Semitic Studies*, Manchester, XVI, 74–83.
—— 1976. *South Arabian Hunt*, London.
Wellhausen, J., 1897. *Reste arabischen Heidentums*, Berlin.[2]

Illustrations and Plates

Table 1 Table 2 Table 3	Patterns of bull's head adornment
Table 4	Classification Scheme
Plate 1	The setting for the *khīrah* sacrifice
Plate 2 Plate 3	Head adornment of the sacrificial animal
Plate 4 Plate 5 Plate 6 Plate 7	Four stages of the *khīrah* sacrifice

Note on illustrations

TABLE 1

1 Garbini: 1970: Pl.XVII c.p. 404; from Ghaymān.
2 Rathjens: 1955: Nr. 424; p. 253; unknown origin.
3 Nielsen: I. Abb. 62, p. 169; unknown origin.
4 Costa: 1973: Pl.XVIII/6; p. 197; from Ẓafār.
5 Costa: 1973: Pl.XVIII/4; p. 197; from Ẓafār.
6 Müller, D.H.: Taf. IX/Nr. 24; p.45; unknown origin a similar representation c.f. Müller, W. W.: 1973: abb. 12; p.157, from Baynūn.
7 Costa: 1973; Pl.XIV/2; p.195; from Ẓafār.
8 Müller, W. W.: 1973: Abb. 7; p.153; from Yaṣhī.
9 Müller, W. W.: 1973: Abb. 2; p. 151; unknown origin.
10 Costa: 1973: Pl. XV/4; p. 195; from Ẓafār.
11 LeBaron Bowen: Nr. 5; p.279; p.269; from Mārib.
12 Serjeant: 1976: Pl. 5; from Shabwah.
13 Costa: 1973: Pl. XVIII/3; p.196; from Ẓafār.

TABLE 2

1 Costa: 1973: Pl. XX/2; p.198; from Bayt al-Ashwāl, Ẓafār.
2 Garbini: 1970: Pl. XXXIX/a.; p.545; from Bayt al-Ashwāl, Ẓafār.

3 Pirenne: Pl. X/b; p.118; Nielsen: Abb. 62 p.169; Hartmann: 173; Grohmann: 1963: taf.XXVI/2.

TABLE 3

1 Costa: 1973: Pl. XVIII/3; p.196; from Ẓafār.

2 Costa: 1973: Pl. XVIII/4; p.197; from Ẓafār.

3 Costa: 1973: Pl. XV/4; p.195; from Ẓafār.

4 Costa: 1976: Pl. XVII/Nr. 153; P.451; from Ẓafār.

5 Costa: 1976: Pl. XVI/nr. 148; p.451; from Ẓafār.

6 Costa: 1976: Pl. XVI/nr. 143; p.450; from Ẓafār.

TABLE 4

Classification scheme.

TABLE I

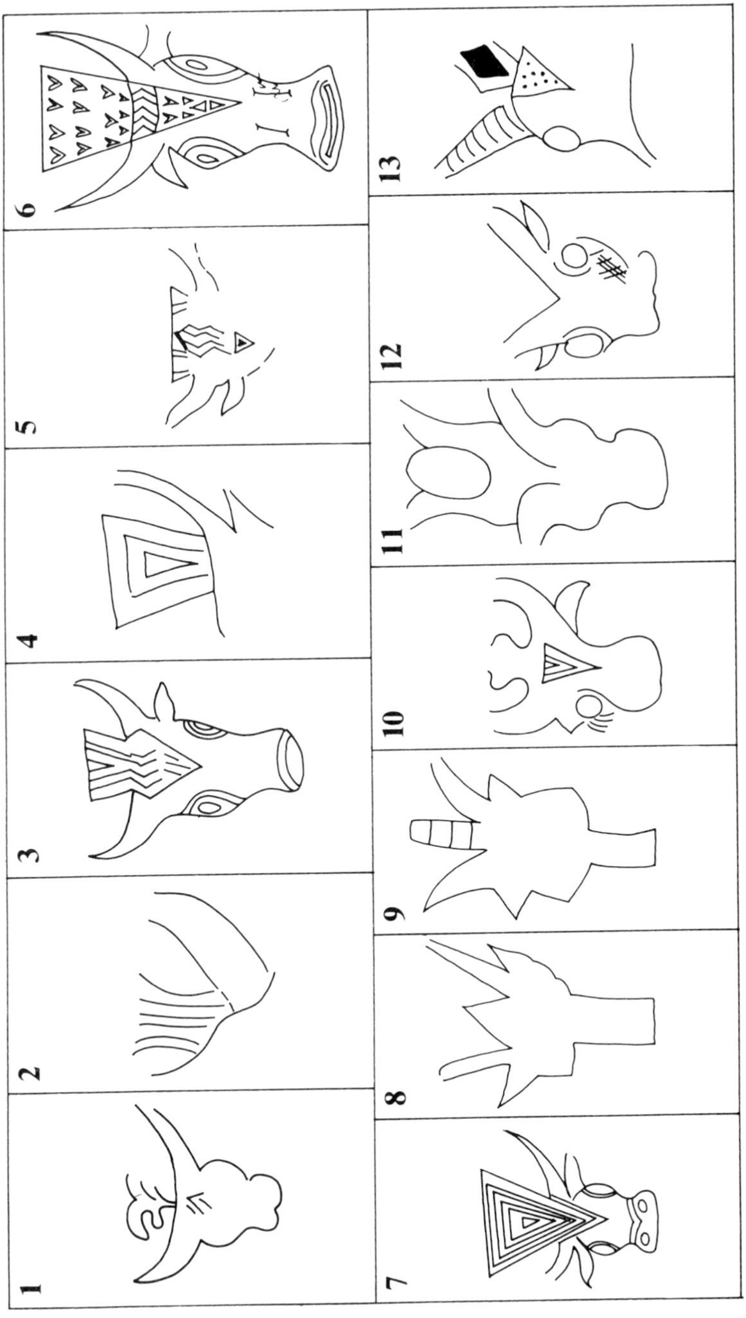

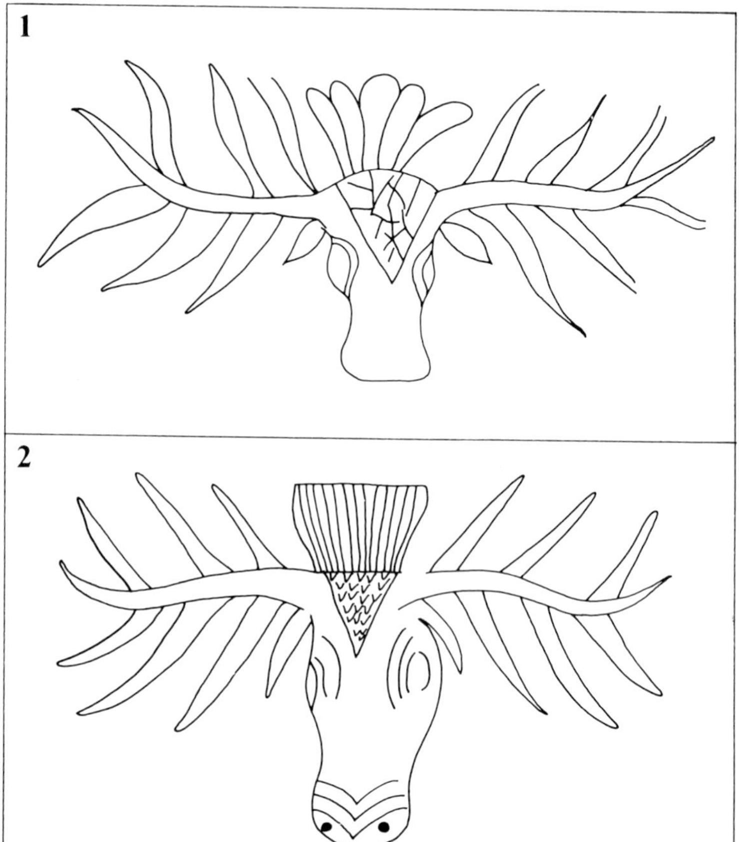

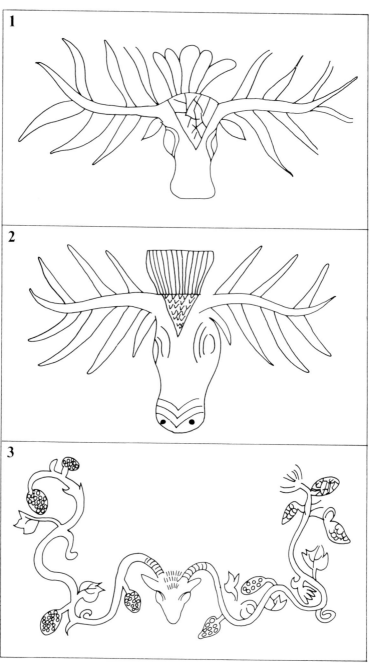

TABLE 2

TABLE 3

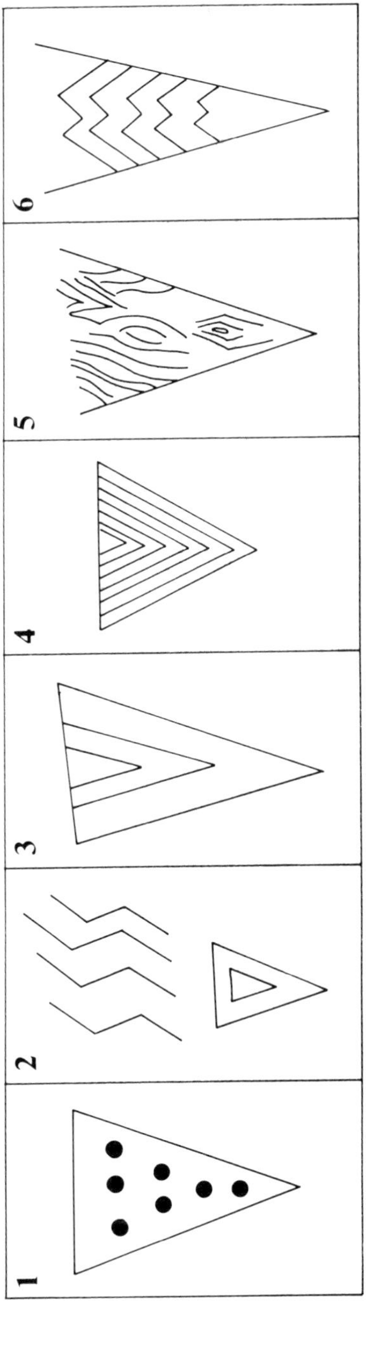

TABLE 4

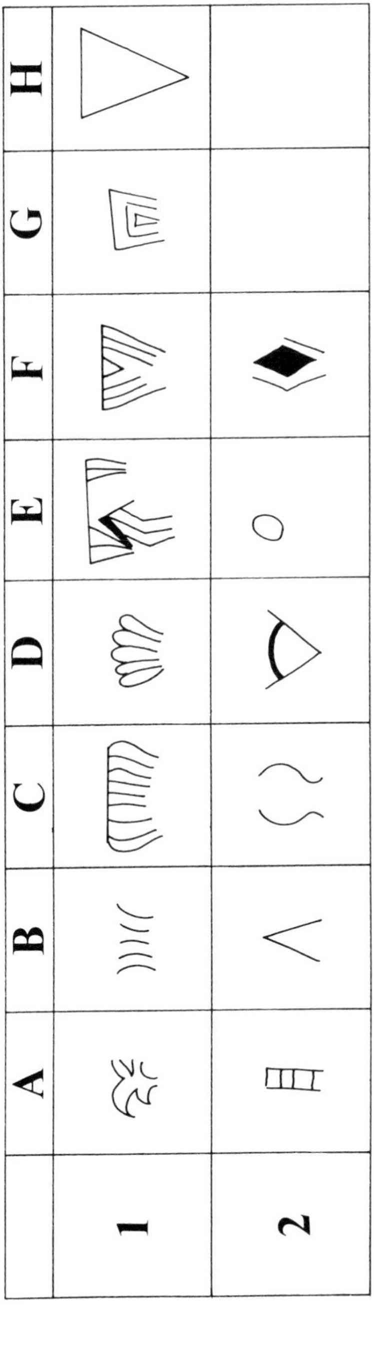

1

2

3 

4

5

6

7

Anglo-Ottoman confrontation in the Yemen: The First Mocha Incident, 1817–22

Caesar E. Farah

Anglo-Ottoman confrontation in the Yemen began with an incident in Mocha in 1817. The significance of Mocha lies in its strategic location at the lower entrance of the Red Sea and before the capture of Aden, it was the main port for British trade linked with Bombay. It served also as the principal supply station for British vessels operating in the Red Sea and as the main outlet for trade with the Yemen.

Trade contacts with Mocha can be traced back to 1628 when the first Factory was established there to deal in the coffee bean that bears its name. It first appears in the trade lists of the East India Company in 1660.[1] Records show that throughout the eighteenth century Mocha provided the greatest revenue of all Yemeni ports.[2] However its fortunes were radically transformed a century later when it was described as 'a dead-alive, mouldering town whose trade as a port for coffee and hides has been killed by excessive taxation in the past and by its proximity to Aden . . . the coffee that bears its name is shipped from Aden or Hodeida'.[3]

British interest first in Mocha and later in Aden was bound to arouse Ottoman concern, particularly following the bombardment of Mocha in 1820. Almost from the start Ottoman authorities viewed British demands in southern Arabia through the Bombay government as part of a broader design to deny them the exercise of full sovereign rights in a land considered sacred to them as Muslims.

Suspicions of British motives coupled with local resentment of the Anglo-Indian trader led to what the British described 'an outrageous attack' on the Factory at Mocha in July 1817. The local Dola, agent of the Imam of Ṣanʿā', was accused of manhandling Lieutenant Dominicetti of the Bombay Marine and Resident of the British East India Company at Mocha together with his companions. The Bombay government decided to take advantage of the crisis to make demands that would have granted them greater extra-territorial rights than hitherto enjoyed. When the local authorities refused, the British responded with a naval bombardment of Mocha on 4 December 1820, eliminating in the process the port's protective gun emplacements at both ends of its semi-circular harbour. The Imam's government yielded and agreed to terms, including dismissal of officials that the British deemed obnoxious. John Richard Lumley, the squadron's commander, sailed back to Bombay on board the 'Topaze' and the four accompanying cruisers.[4]

William Bruce, Bombay's agent at Mocha, was charged with extracting a formal treaty from the Imam embodying the concessions he was compelled to make. Negotiations on his part were carried on by his *wakīl*, Fatḥ Allāh, and members of the Mocha council. Captain Bruce himself served as official agent of the Bombay, and by extension, of the British Government.

The opening clause of the treaty stated that Lieutenant Robson, acting Resident would attend to the Imam's wishes 'regarding the public service'. The Resident would be permitted a guard of thirty men – equal in strength to those allowed British Agents at Baghdad, Basra and Bushire. He was allowed to ride on horseback through all gates of Mocha, and given access to outlying regions as well. The Residency was to have a plot of land on which to raise the British flag, and another to serve as a burial ground for its non-Muslim dependents. More importantly, the treaty recognised the Resident's right to journey to Ṣan 'ā' and communicate directly with the Imam on matters of common interest.

Provisions in the treaty relating to commerce improved the British position. Item 5 exempted British vessels from paying the anchorage charge of 400 Austrian crowns per vessel whether cargo was landed or not. Item 6 extended exemption privileges to all dependents of the British Crown, including Anglo-Indians, the merchants of Surat trading under the British flag, and even Indians themselves. They were to be protected by the Resident, and only the Muslims among them who opted for it were to have their disputes heard according to the provisions of the Islamic *Sharī'a*. The enforcement of decisions, including punishment, was to be the prerogative of the Resident. Item 7 lowered the rate of customs duty levied from $3\frac{1}{2}$ to $2\frac{1}{4}\%$, the amount then being levied on French trade.[5]

Needless to say, neither the Imam nor his agent at Mocha entered into this treaty arrangement voluntarily, and the resentment generated by what they regarded as coercion was discernible in the resistance to British efforts to enforce its provisions.

This exploitation of the incident was the climax of long standing efforts to secure a firm foothold in this strategic port. The Bombay government was determined to obtain from the Imam of Ṣan'ā', 'on whom the Government of India is dependent', a public submission and apology, punishment of offenders, the removal of the 'offending Dola', and indemnification for losses sustained by the East India Company and its personnel in the plundering of the Factory at Mocha. The Governor General had approved all this in Council and authorised the dispatch of the naval squadron under the command of Captain Lumley who set sail on board the 'Topaze' on 19 November 1820. Captain Bruce, the Resident at Bushire was empowered to conduct negotiations with representatives of the Imam on behalf of the Bombay government. Bombardment of Mocha followed the Imam's refusal to submit to their demands.[6]

News of the events at Mocha created 'a strong sensation at Constantinople' and the Company was asked for an explanation.[7] The Sultan's government informed the British Ambassador, Viscount Strangford, that they regarded the assault on Mocha an expression of British designs on the Yemen as a whole. Strangford demanded an explanation of the 'circumstances which may have excited suspicions of the Porte respecting the views of the British Government at Mocha'. In a preliminary response from the Secretary of the India Board he was told that there were complaints that the Mocha government was not able to 'preserve the tranquillity of the country and that the detachment at Mocha had only a few rounds of ammunition', hence the landing of men and additional munitions of war. The Secretary denied that the Board entertained 'aggrandisement in the Arabian Gulf . . . and that we were about to erect facts to promote them'.[8]

Within a week the Board had an explanation for the action taken at Mocha. London, Cairo and Istanbul sought it. The Viceroy of Egypt was first to receive news of what was construed a premeditated course of provocation on the part of the Resident aimed at justifying the action taken.

Objections appeared to relate firstly to the methods employed in provoking Mochan authorities and secondly to the provisions of the treaty extracted as a result thereof. In the first set of complaints the Resident is accused of housing sixty armed men and causing loud music to be played every morning and evening. His obtaining two hundred tents, a number of large chests containing gun powder, bullets and other munitions, unloaded by vessels recently arrived from Bombay aroused suspicion that he planned to close the Bāb al-Mandab. He was accused of attempts to bribe the Imam of Ṣan'ā' with 100,000 piasters annually in order to permit the British to extend their authority over Muslim and non-Muslim subjects. On turning down the offer, the Resident allegedly gathered a force with the intention of journeying to Aden to propose that its ruler join hands with the British against Mocha and the Imām.

The Indian government categorically rejected the accusations and sent word to assure both Muḥammad 'Alī, and the Sultan's government that it entertained no design on the interior of the Yemen, nor did it intend to violate the sacred territory of Mecca as alleged. Furthermore, it had not sought jurisdiction over Mocha by purchase nor to raise the tribes around Aden against either the Imam or the Sultan. The Board then caused a letter to be addressed by the Government of Bombay through the Secret Committee of the East India Company to London for transmission to Cairo and Istanbul explaining the several topics of complaint and assuring the Sublime Porte that the Indian government did not seek aggrandisement nor to encroach upon the authority of the sultan over his dependencies in Yemen.[9]

As concerns terms of the treaty, confusion and suspicion stemmed allegedly from what was left out of the Arabic version of the English original. The Dola had called the Resident's attention to the omissions in August 1821. He also complained of lack of payment in return for a permit to allow the Factory's Hindu broker to return to India.[10] The Resident in turn displayed open anxiety over the Dola's ability to contain bedouins threatening to cut off water supplies from the well and circumscribe 'the insolent behaviour of the authorities'. This is why he asked for more armed men and ammunition. That he should ask for broad powers to adjudicate disputes was due to 'the litigious nature of the natives'. The permanent stationing of a naval cruiser at Mocha was deemed necessary to protect British trade, particularly since the chief of the Yām tribe might attempt to spread 'his depredations' to Mocha.

In addition to the official areas of dispute there were also the personal ones. It appears that the Dola had repeatedly pressured the Resident to arrange loans for him, up to five thousand crowns to liquidate the cost of goods purchased from Surat. In the end he yielded to the Dola's demands and turned over the sum to him without obtaining authorisation from Bombay. Not wishing to act without explicit instructions from Bombay, the Resident wrote for specific answers to questions posed.

Francis Warden, Secretary of the Government of Bombay replied on 6 September 1821 cautioning the Resident against compromising the objectives of the Factory in his transactions with the Imam's government. This was all the more important because already consideration was being given to the eventual transferring of the post to Aden or some other place beyond the Imam's territorial reach. He was asked to minimise complaints by not exempting brokers from the payment of duty if they were not in the immediate service of the Company. All ships visiting Mocha must have their register and passes scrutinised to determine which ones were entitled to exemption from duty charges.

With regard to his role as adjudicator, he was told to exercise judgement and restraint, particularly when complaints were not initiated by British subjects residing at Mocha. Disputes involving natives were to be dealt with by the court of justice at Mocha. If a British subject were involved with a native then the Resident could enforce judgement either through his own guard or through the administration of the Dola. The Governor could not sanction fees for punishment; but if the guilty party happened to be a British subject, the Council could confine him until he was returned to the Residency. A cruiser was authorised to be stationed in the Red Sea both to protect trade and to despatch messages, but not in ordinary duty. The Resident finally was enjoined against making loans to the Dola lest a precedent be set, and particularly when no advantage could be perceived from them.

To improve relations with the Dola's administration, the Resident dismissed the Indian *munshi*, Sayyid Ḥusayn, from the position he had occupied by appointment of Captain Robson and retained under Captain Bruce because of what was interpreted as obnoxious behaviour on his part towards the local authorities and his ignorance of the country and its surrounding states. He was immediately returned to India.

While the Imam took note of the treaty between his government and Bruce as agent of the British Government, he sent a deputy to seek clarification of certain provisions. The Imam was also concerned over the assaults of the Yām tribes and their control of Zabīd after they had plundered al-Luḥayyah. It was twenty days before he learned of the fall of Zabīd, although the town was only a three-day journey from Ṣan'ā'. The letter[11] borne by the deputy informed the Resident that he intended to establish his authority over the entire Tihāmah and of his impending visit to him at Mocha.

After delivering two Arabian horses to the Resident as a gift from the Imam, his Hindu agent handed over another letter to the Broker[12] requesting a loan of 20,000 Yemeni crowns for the purpose of defraying the cost of an expedition which he was about to lead against the Yams still in control of Zabīd. The Broker notified the Resident of the Imam's request stating that he regarded the loan a private matter and wished to refuse it provided the Company would offer him protection against the anticipated wrath of the Imam. Since the Resident had already been instructed by the Company to adhere to matters of commerce only and transmit intelligence of a political nature, he informed the Broker that he would not get involved in the Imam's concerns.[13]

Meanwhile the reactions from Istanbul were reaching London and forwarded on to India. Ottoman authorities were told by agents of Muḥammad ʿAlī in the Yemen that the land of Islam was about to be defiled by the ambitions of foreign intruders. In a secret dispatch to the Governor in Council at Bombay, the Secretary of State for Foreign Affairs conveyed messages contained in Lord Strangford's dispatches from Istanbul regarding the concern of the Sultan's government 'relative to certain proceedings of the Resident at Mocha . . . not less offensive to the religious feelings than injurious to the political rights and interests of the state'.[14]

The indignation of the Porte was fanned by three dispatches from Rustum Āghā, the agent of Muḥammad ʿAlī at Mocha, whom the Viceroy of Egypt described as merely a customs agent. The Reis Efendi summed up the dispatches to state that the Indian government had taken a hostile disposition towards the Sultan's authority and rights of sovereignty in Yemen through their agent at Mocha, the Resident, who was also accused of encouraging tribal Arabs to revolt and offering the Imam 100,000 piasters a year to become a dependency of the Government of India.

In relaying this information to the Marquis of Londonderry, the Foreign Secretary, Strangford informed him that the Sultan's government attached much importance to the country which holds the holiest cities of Islam. He also relayed to him the tenor of a rescript from the *dīvān* (council of ministers) in which the Sultan purportedly described the Indian government to be 'as faithless and as ambitious as that of Russia' insisting he would not yield an inch of the territory 'which has been sanctified by the footsteps of the Prophet'. He enclosed in his dispatch to India a resumé of the letters from Rustum Āghā.

The résumé referred to a host of complaints about offensive conduct on the part of the men housed by the Resident, about arms and ammunition brought in illegally and, in addition, about chains imported from Bombay allegedly for blocking the straits of Bāb al-Mandab. The complaining customs agent suspected the motives and aims of the British at Mocha when they refused inspection of the cargo unloaded followed by the monetary offer to the Imam, and efforts to remove residents from Bombay, Banyans and Ismāʿīlīs from the jurisdiction of the Mocha courts in treating them as British rather than residents subject to Islamic law in spite of repeated assertions by the Imam that he would not tolerate Muslims being subject to non-Islamic law.[15]

It was on the basis of these reports that the Reis Efendi relayed to Strangford the Porte's demand that the British government openly disavow the conduct of their agent in Mocha and formally acknowledge that the country belongs to the Ottoman Empire and is subject in its totality to Ottoman jurisdiction. In the note delivered to the Ambassador by the Reis Efendi, the British government was called upon not to compromise friendly ties with the Sultan's government.[16]

In transmitting this intelligence to London Lord Strangford warned that the Mocha affair could have a most serious effect upon British influence and credit at Constantinople. He stated further that 'the strongest feelings of the Sultan and of his ministers have been called into action by the powerful appeals which have been lately addressed to them by the Turkish authorities, as well religious as political, on the subject of the proceedings at Moka'.[17]

The Sharīf of Mecca, Muḥammad b. ʿAwn was alleged to have also written in a long dispatch to the Mufti at Istanbul alluding similarly to the 'insults' that were reportedly being offered by the English to the '*Sacred Territory*' (sic) in the 'highest colours'. Since the Mufti communicates *directly* (sic) with the Sultan, the latter issued a rescript stating that 'if the English are to range themselves among the enemies of the Ottoman government (he) will yield to the decree of Providence but would not suffer the birth land of the Prophet to be defiled'.[18]

The Sultan's government were of the opinion that deliberately provocative action at Mocha by the British was for the purpose of forcing a change in the terms of the commercial agreements which, at the time of its conclusion, were satisfactory to both sides. The note embodying this opinion went on to state that British traffic with the Imam of Ṣanʿāʾ, offering him tents and a pavilion for gifts, illicitly importing guns and ammunition for use in arousing tribesmen against Ottoman authority, and deliberately being rowdy, all of which 'suggest a line of conduct not presently understood, and so near to the land of the Kaaba . . . an insult to our religion and to all Moslems'.[19]

Lord Strangford's dispatches stated also that Muḥammad ʿAlī had decided to take up the affair as a political question and that he was protesting strongly, viewing it as an affront to the Sultan's sovereign rights and authority in the Yemen. Strangford was not convinced on the other hand that the Viceroy was venting meaningless indignation to ward off suspicion from himself by seizing upon this opportunity to demonstrate his loyalty 'at so cheap a rate . . . knowing that his allegiance is suspect by the Sultan'.[20]

The Ambassador himself was not fully informed about what had transpired at Mocha. He requested background information from Consul General Henry Salt stationed at Alexandria and details of Rustum Āghā's three letters that caused a major stir in both Cairo and Istanbul. In his reply of 16 August 1822 Salt stated that following the bombardment of Mocha a treaty was concluded with the Imam of Ṣanʿāʾ recognising, among other things, the Resident's right to a guard of up to forty sipahis similar to concessions made to other British consular officials and agents at Baghdad and Bushire. The sounding of drums at sunrise, dinner and sunset, which offended the Muslims of the town, was in accord with the practice of the guard everywhere. The tents were offered as gifts, but only one to the Imam; the other was for his Wazīr. The large base which Rustum alleged housed canon actually housed wine and other provisions, including furniture for the Residency. Captain Hutchinson, then Resident, had them inspected at his own house according to Salt's report and agents of the Imam were reportedly satisfied. He did not deny that three to four guns were unloaded and housed in the Residency's Magazine; indeed, so was the steel cable alluded to earlier; but the latter was not for the purpose of blocking the straights at Bāb al-Mandab as alleged, a ridiculous feat considering the distance, rather it was for the cruiser 'Antelope' when it returned from Cosseir.

The above information was based primarily on oral reports made to Salt by Captain Thompson of the 17th Light Dragoons and 'another gentleman lately from Moka'. But at the heart of the disagreement between the Resident and the native administration at Mocha was the issue relating to jurisdiction. The Imam's representative insisted on trying all disputes involving non-British subjects, dependents of the Factory and the Banyans according to Islamic law while the Resident was demanding they be judged in all matters by the Resident himself according to the capitulations respected by the Ottoman government.

Judging by Captain Hutchinson's impression of the Imam and his administration, one can scarcely anticipate a cordial resolution of differences. He accused the government of 'bad faith and rapacity'; the Dola in his opinion 'was too engaged in the debauchery of his own harem to attend to the business of government'. Yet by his own confession much of the difficulty was occasioned by the confusion over interpretation of the last article of the treaty.

On the other points of the accusations levelled against him, the Resident admitted that he did go to Aden and make offer of presents to the 'sultan of that petty kingdom', but that was by order of his own government. He saw no fault in that, for the Sultan was regarded as 'a perfectly independent prince, long united in the strictest friendship with the English'. Hutchinson argued moreover that, when he first called upon the sultan of Laḥj in 1810, the latter urged the British to establish a commercial factory at Aden. Now, in view of the difficulties encountered in their relationships with the Imam's government at Mocha it was very probable that 'if the Imam's government does not fulfill its engagements the Factory will be removed from Moka and established in Aden'. This was the main reason for his journeying to Aden, arousing thereby the suspicions of the Porte.

As far as Hutchinson was concerned both the Imam of Ṣanʿā' and the 'chief of Aden' are independent princes 'so it is not necessary to have the consent of the Porte to any arrangements that the Indian Government may please to establish with these countries'. This was also the position of the Governor-General the Marquis Hastings and Mountstuart Elphinstone,

Governor of Bombay, who was the one to authorise the blockade of Mocha in revenge for what was termed 'the atrocious conduct of the Dola': imprisoning and beating the Resident, digging up the corpse of the British surgeon and giving it to the dogs, and other acts of maltreatment.

Such conduct called for exemplary retribution, and the Government of India argued this had been done with the utmost delicacy towards the Sublime Porte. Hastings allegedly informed Muḥammad ʿAlī of his intention to blockade Mocha and assured him at the same time of his pacific intentions, regretting later the extremities engaged in by the expeditionary force sent to Mocha. Assuming it was a mistake, he submitted, still it could be explained in terms of the unexplicit orders to Elphinstone who was allegedly absent from Bombay when the harsh orders were issued to the commander of the expedition. Hutchinson also registered his annoyance with Muḥammad ʿAlī for sending on to Istanbul the letters of Rustum Āghā in view of what he termed good relations which had hitherto existed between the Egyptian Viceroy and the British. He blamed it on 'a certain Effendi of considerable talent from Constantinople who has been in the service of the Pasha for a year and a half' without naming the person.[21]

Consul General Salt took up the matter with Muḥammed ʿAlī in person and was assured by him that the originator of the reports from Mocha (Rustum Āghā) was not his agent in the Yemen, but rather the Custom House master at Jedda who ostensibly transmitted the remarks of 'unspecified' agents at Mocha. The Viceroy seized upon this opportunity to inform Salt that the Sultan's government for some time had been urging him to take control of the ports along the Red Sea as far south as Aden and that he might have to do so yet. In reply Salt voiced the opinion that the Indian government might be happier to see the Ottoman government take direct control of these ports rather than see them 'fall into the hands of local Barbarians'. However, in his dispatch to Strangford, Salt stated 'I don't believe that the India govt. (sic) would want them (Ottomans) to take over Aden though; it is too strong a post, and too near Bombay to leave in the hands of any first-rate Power (Egypt), that might hereafter join with, or become our Enemy . . .'[22]

The explanations ultimately forwarded to Istanbul by the Indian government via London and Alexandria did not appear to alleviate the Porte's concern over the motives of the Bombay government and their ambition in that strategic corner of the Arabian Peninsula. The reaction of the ministers was communicated to Strangford by the Reis Efendi who hinted rather strongly that the Ambassador himself might have been misled by the information he had received from agents at Mocha and the Bombay government, which he singled out as the proper defendant in this instance. The note he delivered on behalf of the Sultan's government stated, among other things, 'we could not for a moment entertain the supposition that you have sanctioned any measures which could justly subject the British government in India to the suspicion of entertaining any project of territorial aggrandizement in the Arabian Gulf, but we are anxious nevertheless for details from you concerning every proceeding that has taken place at Moka since the establishment of the Residency at that Port'.[23]

The Secretary of State for Foreign Affairs relayed the communications received from Strangford concerning the happenings at Mocha, and which embodied the views of the Sultan's government to all appropriate quarters at Bombay and Mocha. He was particularly perturbed over the Porte's interpretation of the affair as 'not less offensive to the religious feelings than injurious to the political rights and interests of the state'. He requested the Bombay government to submit information that would remove 'the bad implications' thereof, together with a cogent full explanation of the hostilities prevailing at Mocha between the British agent and the Imam's administrative representatives there. He also wanted a detailed account of the arrangements concluded with them. He asked that the explanations be submitted by the Bombay government should be forwarded directly to him.[24]

In India the Board acknowledged all communications forwarded by London and promised to conduct a full inquiry into the circumstances occasioning the Sublime Porte's concern over happenings at Mocha. The explanations submitted subsequently were less than convincing. Most of the blame for misunderstanding was placed on omissions in the translation of the original treaty from English into Arabic rather than on commissions of improprieties by the British Resident. The Indian government admitted that it did insist on the provision stipulated in article 6, only to learn later that Captain Bruce had ostensibly gained the concession they wished independently. The Imam of Ṣanʿāʾ himself allegedly made that concession. It seems rather strange indeed that the concession should appear in English but not in Arabic, the Imam's only language. This was attributed to an oversight, not to any attempt deliberately to prevent the Imam's government from realising what it had agreed to.

Other explanations proffered indicated that the provision relating to the payment of duty would apply only to British merchants not to others trading under the British flag. The Arabic version of the treaty was blamed for making it appear that all those under the jurisdiction of the Resident would be governed by its terms. As a matter of fact, the Bombay government had indeed insisted that only dependents of the Factory, English and Hindu, were to enjoy the same consideration and immunity.[25]

With regard to the rest of the complaints, the Bombay government was at a loss to provide adequate answers. Nor did they address the key inquiry: how do you explain those happenings 'which may have excited the suspicions of the Porte respecting the views of the British government at Mocha?'[26]

Weak as they might have seemed, the Foreign Office forwarded Bombay's explanations to Constantinople with necessary copies to Alexandria for the enlightenment of the Egyptian Viceroy who demonstrated open concern for what had transpired and equal interest in learning the results of the inquiry. Needless to say, the Porte's suspicions and scepticism were not alleviated by Bombay's arguments but it was prepared to accept assurances from the British government that they did not entertain any territorial aggrandisement in southern Arabia. The matter thus was allowed to settle. Sultan Maḥmūd was about to embark on full-scale plans for modernisation, particularly of his armed forces, and in this he needed the good will of Europe. The episode was attributed to misunderstanding; the whole 'unpleasant business' was blamed on wrong information conveyed by Rustum Āghā to Muḥammad ʿAlī and thence to Constantinople by an unnamed zealot who excited unduly the concern of the Ottoman Sultan and his government.[27]

Thus ended the first phase of Anglo-Ottoman confrontation in Yemen.

Notes

1 For additional information see Peter Boxhall, 'The Diary of a Mocha Coffee Agent', *Arabian Studies*, I, 1974, 102–15.

2 George W. Bury, *Arabia Infelix or the Turks in Yemen*, London, 1915, 119.

3 Ibid., 24.

4 See dispatch from William Bruce to Henry Salt, Mocha, 16 January, 1821. F.O. 78/103.

5 The treaty was dated 15 January 1821 and purported to be a 'true copy' of the terms agreed on. See Incl., Bruce to Salt, 16 January 1821. F.O. 78/103.

6 Details in a copy of a Memorandum prepared 5 September 1822. Incl. in B. S. Jones (secretary of the India Board) to Joseph Planta, with a copy to Lord Strangford. F.O. 78/112.

7 Jones to Planta of 5 September 1822. F.O. 78/112.

8 B. S. Jones of the India Board to Joseph Planta of 7 September 1822 transmitting a report by Culloch of 6 September. F.O. 78/112.

9 Jones to Planta of 13 September 1822. F.O. 78/112.

10 He wanted 600 crowns, a much larger sum than that previously agreed.

11 Copy of the letter from the Imam, dated July, 1821. F.O. 78/112.

12 This was the current appelation of Bhemjee in partnership with Nānjee Shaishkand et al., a company headquartered in India.

13 See extract of a letter from Warden, Secretary to the Government of Bombay to the Resident at Mocha, 26 September 1821. F.O. 78/109.

14 Dated 10 September 1822. F.O. 78/112.

15 See No. 106 from Constantinople of 10 July 1822. F.O. 78/109.

16 See Strangford's No. 117 to the Marquis of Londonderry, dated 25 July 1822 from Constantinople. F.O. 78/109.

17 See No. 120 from Constantinople of 10 August 1822. F.O. 78/109.

18 Ibid.

19 See English translation of the Porte's note of 25 July 1822 in Strangford's dispatch No. 117. F.O. 78/109.

20 Strangford's dispatch No. 117 of 25 July 1822.

21 See extract of a letter from Consul General Salt to Ambassador Strangford, Alexandria, 16 August 1822. Incl. in Hamilton's dispatch to Canning from Constantinople of 25 October 1822. F.O. 78/111.

[22] Extract of a letter from Salt to Strangford of 17 August. Incl. No. 2 in Hamilton's dispatch to Canning of 25 October. F.O. 78/111.
[23] Note of 10 September, translated by Chabert 19 November 1822. No. 19 in Strangford's dispatch to the Foreign Office (with copies to Bombay and Mocha). F.O. 78/111.
[24] See incl., *Secret*, dispatch of 10 September 1822 to the Governor in Council at Bombay with copies to Strangford and the Resident at Mocha. F.O. 78/112.
[25] B. S. Jones of the India Board to Planta, 2 October 1822. F.O. 78/112.
[26] See Incl., copy of report from Culloch to B. S. Jones of 6 September 1822. F.O. 78/112.
[27] Hamilton to George Canning of 25 October 1822. F.O. 78/111.

The system of enumeration in the South Arabian Languages

T. M. Johnstone

The numbers in the Modern South Arabian (MSA) languages are of considerable interest for comparative Semitics, if only because they show substantial differences from Arabic in their phonology, morphology and syntax. At the same time many centuries of symbiosis with a culturally dominant language have brought with them large-scale borrowings from Arabic, to produce in these languages to a greater or lesser degree mixed systems. This is most noticeable in the numbers above ten, and in this way MSA resembles other minority languages such as, for example, Welsh and Gaelic, which have a rather clumsy system for the higher numbers based on scores (twenties) and which as a result are disfigured by borrowings from English.

In terms of radicals the Epigraphic South Arabian (ESA) numbers 1–10 compare well with MSA, but it is interesting to note that ESA shows, in certain of its later forms, a closer correlation with Arabic (Ar.) than do the MSA languages. Thus (giving masc. forms with fem. forms following after a comma, and bracketing variants) compare:

	ESA[1]	MSA[2]
1	’ḥd, ’ḥt (ṭd, ṭt; ʿs^{1}t(nm))	ṭd, ṭ(y)t
2	ṯny (ṯnw), ṯty (ṯnty)	ṯrw, ṯryt
3	s^{2}lṯ, s^{2}lṯt (ṯlṯ, -t; s^{2}lwṯ(?); s^{2}ls^{3}t)	śhlṯ (ślṯ, ślś), ślṯt (śṯt, śft, śġṯt)
4	’rbʿ, ’rbʿt	’rbʿ (rbʿ), ’rbʿt (rbʿt)
5	xms^1, xms^{1}t	xmš, *m. and f.*
6	s^{1}dṯ, s^{1}dṯt (s^{1}ṯ, s^{1}ṯt; s^{1}t)	št (šʿt), štt (šdt, šdṯt)
7	s^{1}bʿ, s^{1}bʿt	šbʿ, šbʿt
8	ṯmny, ṯmnyt (ṯmn, ṯmnt; ṯhmny)	ṯmny (ṯmn), ṯmnyt (ṯmnt)
9	ts^{1}ʿ, ts^{1}ʿt	sʿ (tsʿ), sʿt
10	ʿs^{2}r, ʿs^{2}rt	ʿśr, ʿśr

Most of the ESA numerals set out above correlate well with the MSA equivalents. However some detailed comment is necessary. Although *’ḥd* occurs in MSA it is not a number, thus compare Mahrī (M) *’əḥād*, ‘somebody’. The equivalents to Qatabanian *ṭd*, *ṭt* are M *ṭāṭ* (with assimilation), *ṭayt*; J[3] *ṭad*, *ṭit*; S *ṭad*, *ṭəyh*.[4]

The ESA *ṯny* is closer to Arabic than to MSA in regard to the second radical (cf. also ESA *bn*, MSA *br* ‘son’). The Qatabanian *ṯnw* would seem to agree with MSA in regard to the final radical, however: thus M *ṯrō(h)*, *ṯrayt*; J *ṯro(h)*, *ṯrut*; S *tro*, *trih*.

In MSA the syntax of the numerals 3–10 is as in ESA and Arabic, viz. fem. nouns are qualified by masc. numbers and vice versa. MSA, however (except apparently Socotri for which no examples have been recorded), has a series of numerals which are confined to enumerating days, the noun *ywm* being feminine in all the MSA languages. These numbers, which are of the pattern fīʿəl in M and féʿəl in J, often show a different root from the basic numeral, and these will be referred to hereafter in square brackets. It is possible that there was a similar series in ESA.[5]

The older Sabaean form for 3, viz. *s*^{2}*lṯ*(*t*) shows the best correlation with the MSA: thus M *śhəlīṯ, śāṯáyt* [*śīləṯ*]; J *śhəléṯ, śɔṯét* [*śélṯ*]; S *śéleh, śáʿteh*. Both M and J have an 'intrusive' *h* in the masc. form and vocalisation of the *l* in the fem. form. In S earlier -*ṯ*> -*t*> -*h*; the fem. form is odd, but it is supported by a (Southern) M fem. form *śaġatīt* recorded by Jahn.[6] Ḥ(arsūsī) has *śəláyś, śāfáyt*, and B(aṭḥarī) a f. sing. form *tawṯēt*. The masc. Ḥ form is perhaps comparable with ESA (Ḥaḍramī) *s*^{2}*ls*^{3}*t*, and the B form with late Sabaean *ṯlṯt*. It is interesting that the MSA forms in general correlate better with early Sabaean *s*^{2}*lṯ-t* than with later forms.

The ESA and MSA forms for the number 4 all have the radicals *ʾrbʿ* or *rbʿ*: thus cf. M[7] *ʾarbaʾ, rəbōt* [*rība*], J *ʾórbaʿ, ɛrbəʿɔt* [*rīʿ*]; S *ʾórbəʿ, ʾərbaʿah*; Ḥ *ʾōrba, rəbōt* [*rība*].

The MSA numbers for 5 correspond in radicals to ESA, but are interesting in that the fem. numerals have no final ṯ element and show gender by a difference in internal vocalisation. Thus cf. M *xáyməh, xəmmōh* [*xayməh*] (in which *h* < *š*); J *xīš, xōš* [*xīš*] (in which intervocalic *m* is replaced by nasalisation); S *ḥémih* and *ḥéimih, ḥámoh* and *ḥámɔy* (in which *ḥ* < *x*, and -*h*, -*y* < *š*).

The Minaean, Qatabanian and early Sabaean numeral *s*^{1}*dṯ-t* has parallels only in M, but the Ḥaḍramī *s*^{1}*t* and Middle Sabaean *s*^{1}*ṯ-t* have parallels in all the MSA languages. Thus M *hēt, yətīt* [*šīdət*] (in which h-, *y*- < *š*); J *šɛt, štət* [*šɛt*]; S (m.) *hyat, yhaʿt* and *yaʿt*, (f.) *hyéʿtəh, hítəh*[8] (in which the pharyngal radical is intrusive); Ḥ *hāttəh, yətēt*. Although the M ordinal *sōdəs* is borrowed from Ar. (as is *xōməs*, 5th), the fem. *šədṯīt* has preserved the much earlier root.

The ESA root (*sʿbʿ*) occurs in all the MSA languages, *mutatis mutandis*, thus: M *hōba, yəbáyt* [*šība*] (where the day-enumerator does not show the sound-change *š* > *h*, *y*); J *šōʿ, šəbʿə́t* (the m. numeral showing the replacement of intervocalic *b* by a long vowel); S *yhóbəʿ, (h)yə́bʿah*; Ḥ *hōba, həbáyt*; B (f.) *həbaʿēt*.[9]

The MSA numeral 8 has the roots *ṯmny* and in fem. forms *ṯmnt*, but also *ṯmnyt*. In ESA *ṯmny-t* is early Sabaean and Harami, and *ṯmn-t* middle and late Sabaean and Qatabanian. Minaean *ṯhmny* has an 'intrusive' *h* of a kind fairly commonly occurring in MSA, but not in this root. Thus compare M *ṯəmōni, ṯəmənyīt* [*ṯīmən*]; Ḥ *ṯəmōni, ṯəmənīt*; J *ṯōni, ṯīnét*; S *tə́məni, tə́mənəh*.

The MSA number 9 lacks, except for the M day-enumerator, the initial ṯ of ESA and of the other Semitic languages. South Semitic shows some variation in regard to this number, however,[10] and Tigre has a form like MSA, namely *səʿ*. The MSA forms are: M *sā, sāt* [*tīsa*] (but ESA *ts*^{1}*ʿ*); J *sɔʿ, saʿét* [*tésʿ*]; S *saʿ, sə́ʿəh*.

The number 10 has the radicals *'śr* in both ESA and MSA, thus: M *'ōśər, 'āśərīt* [*'áyśər*]; J *'ɔ́śər, 'əsirét* [*'έśər*]; S *'áśər, 'əśírəh*.

In the numbers 11–19, though often replaced by the colloquial Ar. equivalents (especially in Ḥarsūsī and Baṭḥarī), the elements are put together in a different way in ESA, MSA and Arabic. ESA and MSA agree, however, in that the numbers of this series are ordinarily followed by a plural.[11]

In ESA the units precede the ten without *w*, and the 10 element of the compound is always *'s²r*. The unit is masc. when a fem. noun is qualified and vice versa, and in this respect ESA and MSA are in agreement.

The MSA system can be illustrated by considering the following M numbers: *'ōśər wə-śhəlīṯ*, 13 women, and *'āśərīt wə-śāṯáyt ġəyōg*, 13 men.

The MSA numbers 20 and 30 show some interesting similarities to ESA, though, except in Socotri, the other decads are borrowed from Arabic, as, e.g., J *εrbə'ín* (40), *xamsīn* (50), etc.; M *ərbə'áyn* (40), *xəmsáyn* (50) and also *'āšráyn* (20).

Interesting, however, are J *'έśəri*, and S *'áśərə* (*-i*?) (in which the *-i* is the same as the MSA nominal dual ending) as against ESA *'s²ry*.[12]

The other examples are more complex to interpret, namely J *śhεlɔ́ṯ*, S *səlóh* (< *-ṯ*), 30. This pattern could denote a broken plural. The difference between the forms for 20 and 30 suggests that the former are dual and the latter plural.[13] Socotri has a complete series of decads, moreover, in which an external plural of *'áśər* is the second element, as, e.g. *śə́lεh 'əśárhən* (30), *'órbə' 'əśárhən* (40), *ḥémih 'əśárhən* (50), etc.

The number 100 shows good correlation between ESA and MSA. Thus compare ESA *m't* and M *myīt*, J *mut*, and S *muwyέnoh* (a diminutive: the more usual word is *maḥbir*). ESA has a number of plurals: early Sabaean *m'*, Minaean and Ḥaḍrami *m'h*, middle Sabaean *m'n* and late Sabaean *m't*. With early Sabaean, cf. M *myī* (*mī*) and with middle Sabaean, cf. J *mun*.

The remaining kinds of numerals, ordinals and fractions, are a very mixed bag in MSA. In J there are virtually no ordinals, though *'έnfí, 'έnfε̄t* can mean 1st (as well as 'preceding', etc.). The same seems to be true of S. In M and even more in Ḥ there are heavy Arabic borrowings. Thus cf. M *ṯōni, ṯənyīt*, 2nd; *śōləṯ, śəwṯīt*, 3rd; *rōbə', ərbáyt*, 4th; *xōməs* (borrowed), *xəmhīt*, 5th; *sōdəs* (borrowed), *šədṯīt*, 6th, etc. Cf. Ḥ *xāməh, xəmhēt*, 5th; *hētt, hēttət*, 6th, etc.

The fraction $\frac{1}{2}$ is always of the root *fkh in MSA but the other fractions seem to be borrowed. Compare M faḳh*, pl. *fáḳhi*; J *fɔḳh*, pl. *fuṣḥi* (where the pl. is in fact a dual); S *fákaḥ*; Ḥ *fōḳəh*. The ESA are of the pattern *f'l*, pl. *'f'l*, and can be presumed to be something like Ar. *fu'l*/*'af'āl*. Compare M *śəlēṯ*, pl. *śəlwōṯ*; J *śélṯét*, $\frac{1}{3}$: M *rəba't* and *rəbáyt*; J *rī'át*, pl. *rīá'*; Ḥ *rəbáyt*, pl. *rəbēya*; B *rəb'āt*, $\frac{1}{4}$: M *xúmus*, J *xmus*, $\frac{1}{5}$, etc.

The comparison between ESA and MSA, therefore, has many points of interest, not least that the MSA numbers frequently correspond to the earlier rather than the later ESA numerals.

Notes

1 The source of all the printed ESA material quoted is A. F. L. Beeston, *A descriptive grammar of Epigraphic South Arabian*, London, 1962, 40 seqq. In this table regularly (but not invariably) ESA s^1 ~ MSA *š*, and s^2 ~ *ś* (a lateral).

2 The MSA radicals given are based on common features and bracketed roots show only major differences. For a general discussion of the MSA numbers, see also Johnstone, *The Modern South Arabian Language*, a monograph in *Afro-Asiatic Linguistics*, 1, 5, 1975.

3 Namely the central dialect of Jibbālī. Most of my earlier work was in Eastern Coastal Jibbālī.

4 In Socotri the final *h* of fem. forms corresponds to MSA *ṯ*, and *-ṯ* > *-t* > *-h*: also MSA *ḏ*, *ṯ* > *d*, *t*; *ġ*, *x* > ʿ, *ḥ*; and *š* (often) > *yh* (*hy*, *h*, *y*).

5 Cf. Beeston, *Grammar*, 41 (35:11).

6 Jahn, *Grammatik der Mehri-Sprache in Südarabien*, Vienna, 1905, 74. On S *ġ* > ʿ see the note above.

7 In M (and Ḥ) *ʿayn* seldom occurs explicitly but affects the syllabication of forms in which it occurs as a radical: see, on Ḥ, Johnstone, *Ḥarsūsi Lexicon*, Oxford, 1977.

8 Leslau, *Lexique Soqoṭri*, Paris, 1938, only *híte*, *'íte*, *yíte*, f. *hyat*. On the initial *hy*, *yh*, *y*, *h* (< *š*) see note above.

9 And (from the field-notes of Miranda Morris) *həbəʿēt*.

10 E. Ullendorff, *The Semitic languages of Ethiopia*, London, 1955, 134. The Tigrinya *təšʿattɛ* is prob. not to be relevantly compared to ESA $ts^{1ʿ}$ (sc. *tšʿ*) for the reasons Ullendorff discusses, namely a generalised (but incompletely realised) tendency for *š* < *s* in the numbers 3–10.

11 Beeston, *Grammar*, 42 (35:18). All MSA and ESA numbers above 3 are (or may be) followed by a plural.

12 Ethiopic (and Akkadian) *-ā*. See Dillman, *Ethiopic Grammar* (trans. Bezold), London, 1907, 368.

13 Professor Beeston (personal communication) now considers it possible that the status absolutus ending *-y* and emphaticus *-nhn* may be external m. plurals rather than duals as he believed in his grammar.

Fishing in Bahrain: Some Techniques and Technical Terms

A. M. al-Khalifa

A number of methods of fishing are used in Bahrain and it is the aim of this article to describe some of them and to list the relevant technical terms employed on the island in connection with them.

Line fishing

Ḥadag or *ḥadāg* is the term indicating line fishing, cf. CA *ḥadaja* 'he looked with piercing eyes'. The bait (*yīm*) is pierced by the hook and line (*khēṭ*) and weight (*bild*) are also required. The bait may be pieces of cuttle-fish, prawns or any small fish (fig. 1). Line fishing may be performed in two ways. Firstly the line may be cast, using the weight (fig. 2), if one is fishing from the shore or in shallow water; secondly in the case of deep sea fishing by casting, again using the weight, from the side of the fishing boat (fig. 3). Line fishing from the boat is termed *sumār*. In both types of line-fishing it is imperative to take into account the tide and the direction of the wind. For line fishing from the shore or from shallow water, the start of high tide is the ideal time, especially if this coincides with the time just before sun-set or sun-rise. It seems that the movement of the fish in search of food at those times is just right for the fisherman. In deep sea fishing, carried out in summer, the tide and direction of the wind are extremely important and both have direct impact on conditions in the fishing boat. If, for example, the wind is blowing with the tide, this helps to steady the boat and enables the fisherman to keep the line straight with the result that the fish can spot the bait, follow it and take it up.

The main catch of shore fishing is *sbēṭī* and *shi'm*, though occasionally other species are caught. In shallow water line fishing, which takes place near reefs (*fshūt*), *shi'rī* and *hāmūr* are caught. The main catch in deep sea fishing is also *shi'rī* and *hāmūr*, on occasion others as well. In the latter type of fishing it is important to fish where the bottom of the sea is rocky (*gū'*). *Ṭīna*, a muddy bottom, and *ma'shūra*, a weedy bottom, should be avoided, as the favourite fish like *shi'rī* and *hāmūr* frequent the *gū'*, while less popular fish like *chimm* (cat fish) and *bāsay* are found elsewhere. The rocky bottom is located by throwing down a lead weight (*bild*) attached to a rope (fig. 4). When hauled in, red fragments of the coral formations of the *gū'* would show on the weight – in which case the expression is *nagal al-bild*, 'the lead has brought up [the indications of a rocky bottom]'. If the bottom is muddy or weedy, the weight will show nothing when hauled in. Another method of ascertaining the type of sea bottom is by dragging the weight along the bottom (*shār*, or with *imālah*, *shēr*) and by noting how the weight behaves as it is dragged along.

Line fishing in Bahrain is as much a hobby as a profession and as more amateurs take up the sport, the building of dhows in the island has revived over the last few years to cater for their needs. The sale of fishing equipment and accessories is flourishing too. Fishing with traps and nets is, however, carried out mostly on a professional basis.

Fishing with traps

The largest fish trap employed in Bahrain is called *ḥaḏra*[1] (plur. *ḥḏūr*) (fig. 5). This is a permanent structure made of palm-*jarīd* from the local plantations,[2] held together with rope. Special importance is attached to the choice of site (*saṭwa*) for the *ḥaḏra*, which, although renewed every few years, remains the same. Some *ḥḏūr* are passed on from generation to generation in the same family. The *ḥaḏra* is built near the shore and facing it. With the movement of the tide away from the shore, the fish are led along the walls of the *ḥaḏra* into the middle area (*ḥawsh*), then into the *sirr*,[3] from where they would be unable to find their way out. A large variety of fish are trapped in the *ḥaḏra*, the species varying with the seasons.

Collecting fish or prawns from the *ḥaḏra* is called *mbārāh*. This task must be carried out at low tide when the fisherman can approach the *ḥaḏra* on foot. He carries a matting basket (fig. 6) attached to a rod over his shoulder in which are kept his small net (*sālyah*) and spear (*ḥarba*).[4]

Another type of fish-trap is the *gargūr* (fig. 7) (plur. *garāgīr*). They come in different shapes and sizes and are made of either wire or palm-*jarīd*. The smaller ones are used for catching smaller fish like the *ṣāfī* and the *yanam* close to the shore. In some places it is necessary to protect the *garāgīr* against sharks and dolphins, in which case they are protected with a fence of palm-*jarīd*.

The larger traps (*duwābī*, sing. *dābwī*) are for use in deep water to catch larger fish or greater quantities of fish. They are made only of wire. *Duwābī* are set in rocky areas (*gūʿ*) near *lḥūf* (sing. *liḥif*), *kharāyib* or *ḥawādd* (sing. *ḥāddah*) which are all places of rock and coral formations. The *duwābī* are identified on the surface by means of floating objects like branches (*karab*) or pieces of white fibre glass. These signs are called *chiyābīl* (sing. *chībāl*) and are attached to the *duwābi* by means of ropes.

Fishing with nets

The nets naturally vary greatly in size from the small *sālyah*, handled by one man, to the large *sharkh* or *yārūf*, which would require several men to manipulate it. The smaller nets are used in shallow water, near the shore, the latter to fish for shoals of fish, also in shallow water.

Some nets are used differently and are more permanent. They are left in slightly deeper water in a vertical position, weighted with lead weights at the bottom and held also by floating material attached to the top, thus the net is held in the appropriate position. These nets are circular in shape and are called *manāṣib* (sing. *manṣab*) and are used mainly for catching *chan'ad* (king mackerel) when the latter fish is in season.

Other types of fishing

Spear fishing, both the modern sophisticated variety and the old, traditional method, is still practised in Bahrain, though it is uncommon. Some fishing is still carried on too by using a bright light at night and catching the fish by hand.

To finish this brief account of fishing in Bahrain, the *zarga* can be mentioned. This is used by children to catch small fish, *'afāṭī*, near the shore. It is a vessel covered with a tightly bound cloth with bait inside and a small opening in the cloth. In no time at all the vessel is full of *'afāṭī*!

Notes

[1] For a detailed discussion and illustration of the *ḥaḍra*, cf. R. B. Serjeant, 'Fisherfolk and fish-traps in al-Baḥrain', *BSOAS*, XXXI, 486–514, especially 489 ff.
[2] Serjeant, 491.
[3] [Shaykh 'Abd al-'Azīz appears here to be describing a *ḥaḍra* similar to that shown in Serjeant, 497, fig. 7. The *sirr* is the small end compartment of the *ḥaḍra*.] (editorial note.)
[4] cf. Serjeant, 493.

Illustrations

Fig. 1 Line, weight and bait
Fig. 2 Casting the line
Fig. 3 Deep sea fishing
Fig. 4 Lead weight (*bild*)
Fig. 5 Fishing trap (*ḥaḍra*)
Fig. 6 Fisherman with net (*sālyah*), and spear (*ḥarba*)
Fig. 7 Fishing traps (*gargūr*)

1

2

3

4

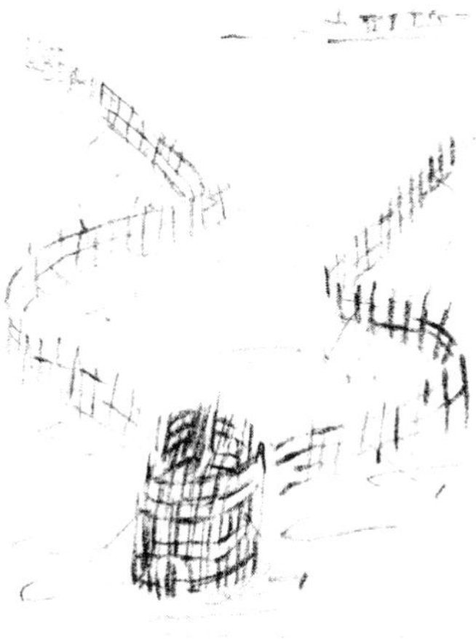

5

6

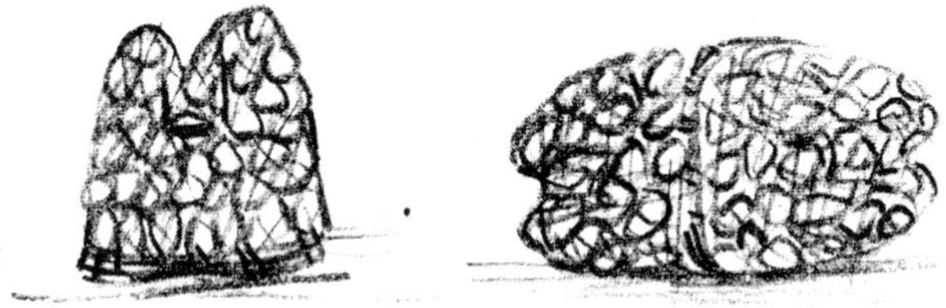

7

Notes on some ordinances, decrees & laws of the Kathīrī Sultanate 1942–64

Abdulla M. A. Maktari

I

In the summer of 1965, I had the opportunity of spending a little over a month in Say'ūn, then the capital town of the Kathīrī Sultanate. At that time, I was working for an American oil exploration company which was partly operating within Kathīrī territory. My presence was at the request of the Kathīrī Sultan, Ḥusayn b. 'Alī b. Manṣūr al-Kathīrī, who had approached my employer and asked if I could be attached to his government for several weeks to function as a secretary to a high committee formed to review constitutional matters, submit suggestions and a draft on constitutional improvements to the Sultanate.

My presence in the State Office had led me to investigate the Laws of the Kathīrī State. At that time, I had in mind a research programme leading to a Ph.D. degree. My investigation, though resented by some officials, was assisted by most, particularly Mr. 'Alī b. Ṣāmit, the then State Secretary. Events which I do not propose to detail here prevented me from completing my collection or from using it later as the subject of my Ph.D. research.

Ten years later, I met a Ḥaḍramī scholar and historian in Ṣana'ā' who was, I believe, knowledgeable in the modern affairs of Ḥaḍramawt. I had then asked him to review the list of my collection of Kathīrī legislation consisting of twenty-nine titles including two printed and published booklets. Having reviewed them, he assured me that my collection was not far from being complete but was unable to recollect the titles which I had missed. I then tried to get in touch with Ibn Ṣāmit, but my efforts failed and investigations elsewhere were fruitless.

The history of modern legislation in the now defunct Kathīrī State in Ḥaḍramawt can not go back further than to the year when the British colonial government in Aden began to take an interest in the running of proper government in what was then termed the Eastern Protectorate. British colonial sources indicate that interest in this area commenced before the first World War, but the actual presence of British colonial officers did not take place until 1938–39 when the Governor of the Colony of Aden decided that the time was ripe for the British to become more involved in the Eastern Protectorate. British colonial sources rarely mention the reason behind this move, but Arab and other sources suggest that perhaps the true reason may be related to (a) the discovery of oil in Saudi Arabia; and (b) the activity of some European powers in the Red Sea and Indian Ocean territories.

Harold Ingrams, who had first taken charge of advising the Kathīrī Sultan, was indirectly, but greatly, assisted in this task by Sayyid Abū Bakr Āl Kāff, a merchant of Tarīm whose early life in Singapore and travels in British India had convinced him that the real salvation of his poor and disorderly place of birth lay in the hands of the British government in Aden which had signed with his country a Treaty of Protection as early as 1882.

The objectives of these two gentlemen were to establish government and to restore to the Sultan of Say'ūn his authority and then extend it where possible beyond his traditional boundaries. The wealth of Sayyid Abū Bakr Āl Kāff, his personality and standing among other sayyids in the towns of Ḥaḍramawt and beyond among overseas Ḥaḍramī communities, brought a general acceptance from the sayyids and their followers who, up to that time, had rejected the authority of the Kathīrī chiefs. On the other hand, the power and authority coupled with drive, gift of government and genuine understanding of Arab character on the part of Harold Ingrams had led to his success among the weak, isolated and starving population of the Ḥaḍramī towns.[1]

Thus, the road was paved for the establishment of a government in Say'ūn headed by a Sultan, a member of the Kathīrī tribe. This done, the second step was to organise the business of government which of course led to the issue of Sultanic orders and laws.

II

The list below shows the titles of the collected copies of decrees in chronological order. Most have the precise *hijrah* date with the corresponding Gregorian calendar. With the exception of two decrees as indicated below in (20) and (21), all decrees are in Arabic typescript. Few of these, however, bear the original signature of the Kathīrī Sultan, Ḥusayn b. ʿAlī Manṣūr (Plate I).

1 Date-palm Taxation (*al-ḍarā'ib ʿalā 'l-nakhīl*) Law, no. 1, 1361/1942.
2 Law providing for the control of goods (*murāqabat al-baḍā'iʿ*), no. 4, 20 Jumād al-Ākhar [sic] 1362/20 June 1942.
3 Law for the issue of passports to Kathīrī subjects, no. 2, Dhū 'l-Ḥijjah 1361/10 September 1942.
4 Law on the payment of customs duties (*ḍarībah*) on all goods imported into or entering our state, no. 3, 4 Jumād Awwal [sic] 1361/8 May 1943.
5 Sharīʿah court fees (*rusūm*) Law (no number), 17 Dhū 'l-Qaʿdah 1362/15 November 1943.
6 Law providing for the Protection of Public Health (*li-'l-muḥāfaẓah ʿalā 'l-ṣiḥḥah*), no. 1, 24 Rabiʿ Awwal [sic] 1365/26 February 1946.
7 Slavery law (*Qānūn al-ʿabīd*), 1 Rabīʿ al-Thānī 1365/5 March 1946.
8 Clubs Registration (*tasjīl al-nawādī*) Law, no. 3, 20 Shaʿbān 1366/7 February 1947.
9 Regulation (*lā'iḥah*) for the preparation of prohibiting the carrying of mail by means other than the postal services, no. 2, 1 Rabīʿ Awwal [sic] 1367/11 January 1948.

10 Law relating to the currency (*nuqūd*) currently circulating in our Sultanate, no. 5, 17 Jumādā 'l-Thānī [sic] 1367/7 April 1948.
11 Control of Weapons and Ammunition Law, no. 7, 17 Jumādā 'l-Thānī [sic] 1367/27 April 1948.
12 Motor Car Tax (*ḍarībat al-mawātir*) Law (no number), 17 Jumādā 'l-Thānī [sic] 1367/27 April 1948.
13 Law providing for the replacement of the Indian Rupee by the East African Shilling in the Kathīrī State, no. 1/28/12, 19 February 1951.
14 Law providing for the levy of taxation on houses and building permits (*rukhaṣ al-bināyāt*), no. 15, 20 October 1951.
15 Law providing for the extension (*tawsī'*) of agricultural lands for the purpose of improving the state of agriculture in the Kathīrī State, 27 Jumād al-Ākhar [sic] 1371/23 March 1952.
16 Departmental Order, no. 16, for 1952, concerning the regulation of sub-committees, 6 December 1952.
17 Law providing for the establishment of Local Council Courts (*maḥākim al-majālis al-maḥalliyyah*), no. 2, 18 Rabī' Awwal [sic] 1372/6 December 1952.
18 Law providing for the destruction of records, no. 22, 15 Rabī' al-Thānī 1373/24 December 1953.
19 Law amending the law concerning Medical Treatment, no. 26, 29 Shawwāl 1374/20 June 1955.
20 Sharī'ah Criminal Law, no. 27, 21 Jumādā 'l-Ākhar [sic] 1377/12 January 1958.
N.B. Published by al-Jamāhīr Printing House, Aden, 22 al-Muḥarram 1381/5 July 1961.
21 Sultanic Order: collection of twelve Sultanic Orders published 9 Sha'bān 1377/28 February 1958, printed at Dār al-Janūb, Aden.
22 Law for the protection of irrigation canals (*ṣiyānat al-masāqī*) to improve flood water systems (*li-taḥsīn majārī 'l-suyūl*) in the Kathīrī State (no number), 12 Rabī' al-Thānī 1378/25 October 1958.
23 Law for the control and unification of the rentals of shops (*li-tawḥīd niẓām ījār al-ḥawānīt*) within the Kathīrī State (no number), 12 Rabī' al-Thānī 1378/25 October 1958.
24 Law providing for loans to government employees (*al-muwaẓẓafīn*) (no number), 17 Dhū 'l-Ḥijjah 1379/10 June 1960.
25 Amendment to the State Council Law (no number), 23 Dhū 'l-Ḥijjah 1380/7 June 1961.
N.B. This law amends the State Council Law no. 1, issued 25 Rajab 1366/25 May 1947.
26 Law providing for the protection of antiquities (*ḥifẓ al-āthār al-qadīmah*) (no number), 23 Dhū 'l-Ḥijjah 1380/7 June 1961.
27 Press and Printed Matter Law (no number), 30 Safar 1383/22 July 1963.
28 Appendix to law governing passports and immigration matters (no number), 1384/1964.
29 Law of Pensions (*ma'āshāt*), End of Service Benefits (*mukāfa'āt*) and

Other Allowances granted for services rendered by government employees, no. 2, 16 Rabīʿ al-Awwal 1384/26 July 1964.

III

The Decree I have selected for translation is one that serves as a good example of the social and economic development of the isolated Kathīrī State after some fourteen years of exposure to the influence of the British Colonial Administration in Aden. Compared with earlier recorded decrees, it is also an excellent example of the penetration of modern legal thought into this little desert community. The form, and to a great extent the contents of this decree bears the 'finger prints' of a British political officer, but the language and legal terminology remains to a great extent Islamic, though it shows an increasing tendency to adopt modern Arab legal expressions, particularly Egyptian.

> 'The reasons we succeeded in building up an indigenous administration . . .' said Harold Ingrams recollecting his 'thoughts at a journey's end', is because 'these Arabs knew we believed them inherently capable of doing the job and had no measure to think ourselves superior'.[2]

For myself and at least in so far as it concerns the Kathīrī State, I have no reason to question the honesty of this statement by Ingrams or to doubt its validity. After many years now of trying to examine, or at least understand my country's colonial past, I have found research, or just mere thoughtful reflection, leads one to a totally different conception of events and developments, historical or otherwise, from that recently projected by various authoritative assessments by Arab or western writers.

Perhaps it is because of this uncommon view of events and developments in colonial Aden and its Eastern and Western protectorates that I venture to write these notes presenting these legal records. Such material and similar simple sources will, I am certain, contribute greatly in reconstructing a true picture of life and events in that part of the world. Briefly the following may perhaps demonstrate what is meant by what I have called 'my uncommon view of events and developments': 'In the Eastern areas', says Sir Tom Hickinbotham, 'the main progress has been made in the centre wherein the Quaiti and Kathiri States administrations have been firmly established and even Town Councils are functioning with reasonable efficiency'. He then goes on to attribute this to the fact that 'these States have been lucky in having rulers who had the good sense to pay heed to their able advisers'.[3]

While I agree with the first part of this statement, I would, however, suggest that the success should rightly be attributed to the Ḥaḍramī community of sayyids and merchants, for these were men who had come back home after years of toil and patient work in places such as East Africa, India and South-East Asia where colonial powers had transformed the government administration and effected change in the economic and domestic lives of societies. These people are 'the astute and hardest businessmen in the world',[4] which the author himself described early in his book.

The Ḥaḍramī Kathīrī State

We assent
Ḥusayn b. ʿAlī b. al-Manṣūr
Sultan of the Ḥaḍramī Kathīrī State
18 Rabīʿ I 1372
Corresponding to 6 December 1952

In the Name of the Merciful, the Compassionate:
A Law for the Establishment of Local Council Courts Law No. (2) 1372/1952.

Decreed by His Highness the Sultan of the Ḥaḍramī Kathīrī State

Article 1

Short Title — This law shall be referred to as the Law of Local Councils.

Article 2

Application — This law shall be applied to all parts of our kingdom.

Article 3

Definition — The following terms and expressions shall in this law, unless otherwise stated, impart the meaning given opposite:

al-Nā'ib: includes a person deputising for the Deputy and the person acting on behalf of the *Ra'īs*.

al-Ra'īs: means the person who presides over any court of the Local Council as established under this law.

Government Officials: means civil and military personnel of Her Majesty's Government of the states of the Aden Eastern protectorates.

Article 4

Establishment of Courts (1) — The Secretary of the State is authorised to establish local courts in locations where he feels fit.

Local Councils (2) — The establishment of a Local Council Court shall be by means of an order bearing the signature of the Secretary of the State.

(3) — The order that shall establish the Local Council Court shall include definition of jurisdiction, the names of members of the council qualified to sit as judges in the court, and it may also state the names of 'ʿāqils' in the area of the council who are qualified to sit as members of the law court together with the other members of the council.

Article 5
Establishment of the Council Court

The members mentioned below will sit together with the President of the Council in order to form a court:

a) The president or the Deputy of the Council as President of the Court.
b) Not less than three members of the Council or "*āqils*' in the area of the Council only.

Article 6
The law in application

The Local Council Courts shall apply the following:

a) Prevailing customs in the area within the authority of the court, provided that such customs shall be consonant with justice, morality and order.
b) The clauses of the Local Courts Decree of 1952 and the text that should be applied under that law such as Local Orders or Orders or Regulations the authority of which is vested in the court which is required to apply them; provided that the local court shall have the authority to levy fines not exceeding the sum of 35 shillings.

Article 7
Execution

The Deputy has power to execute any court order or resolutions issued by the Local Council Court whenever the President of the Court requires execution and such order shall be regarded as if issued by any ordinary court.

Article 8
Regulations

I The Deputy has the right to issue regulations which are not contrary to the clauses of this law or those of the Local Council for the following [purposes]:

a) Defining the authority of the local court in so far as concerns its relation with individuals and offense which the court has the right to look into and apply against penalties. Also any other definition which the Deputy deems necessary.
b) The court fees to be applied in the Local Council Court.
c) Auditing and applying revenue from fines and fees received by Local Council Courts.
d) The procedure followed by the Local Council Court.
e) Application of the provisions of this law in general.

II All regulation shall be subject to the approval of the Secretary of the State and in the instance of regulations devised for fees or revenues and expenditures other than those mentioned in the budget such regulation shall be subject to the approval of the Secretary of the State or the Inspector of Treasury.

Article 9

The Record of the Court

There shall be a Register of all cases reviewed under this law and such Register shall consist of the following:

a) Name of the President and the members of the Court.
b) Date and place of the hearing of the case.
c) Names of disputants in the case.
d) Names of witnesses which the court had listened to.
e) A brief statement of the facts of the case.
f) The decision of the court which must be endorsed by the President and the Members.

Article 10

The required majority for making a decision legally binding

All members shall constitute the court and the President should endorse the decision, or the decision should be endorsed by the Deputy who shall not endorse it unless a majority of the court has done so.

Article 11

Appeal

The decisions of the Local Council Courts are appealable to the court of the Deputy.[5]

Article 12

Imprisonment in instances where a person fails to pay the fine

Where the decision of the Local Council Court is supported by the Deputy, the Deputy may, in instances where the fine is not paid, imprison the person who fails to do so for a term of a single day in lieu of each one shilling of the sum of the fine or any part thereof.

Article 13

Competence

Each Local Council Court shall have full competence and authority within the definition laid down in this law provided the Local Council Court shall not entertain the following:

a) Any civil case in which the disputed sum exceeds 100 shillings.

Conditions

b) Any civil case in which the parties to the dispute do not fall within the competence of the court unless otherwise the party accepts to be adjudged by the court.

c) Any civil case in which only one party falls within the competence of the court unless otherwise the other party falling the outside competence of the court accepts to be adjudged so.
d) Any case in which the defendant is a government employee.
e) Any offense or dispute other than the following:
   1) Disputes specified by the Local Council Law of 1952.
   2) Agricultural disputes normally settled in accordance with the customs of the area regardless of the value of the amount of dispute.
   3) Disputes concerning customs of Quarters.
   4) Damage resulting from agricultural animals.
   5) Slight quarrels.

Article 14

This law shall be effective from 18 Rabīʿ al-Awwal 1372/6 December 1952.

Notes

[1] Sir Tom Hickinbotham in his book *Aden*, London, 1958, 157, demonstrated how Sayyid Abū Bakr Āl-Kāff 'that great Philanthropist' was interested in the development of his part of the world. The author writes, '[He,] at his own expense to the tune of more than £1,000,000.00, constructed the first motor road from the Wadi Hadramawt to Mukalla, thus, linking the Wadi with the sea for the first time'.
[2] Harold Ingrams, *Arabia and the Isles*, 2nd Ed., London, 1952, 385.
[3] Hickinbotham, op. cit., 159.
[4] Ibid, 158.
[5] The term Deputy in this section translates the Arabic *Nā'ib* (Deputy Governor) of the Sultan in the District.

الدولة الكثيرية الحضرمية

نوافق حسين بن علي بن المنصور
سلطان الدولة الكثيرية الحضرمية
التاريخ ١٨ ربيع الأول سنة ١٣٧٢ هجرية
موافق ٦ ديسمبر سنة ١٩٥٢ ميلادية

بسم الله الرحمن الرحيم

قانون يؤسس محاكم المجالس المحلية
قانون نمرة (٢) لسنة ١٣٧٢ هجرية
١٩٥٢ ميلادية

سنّه صاحب العظمة سلطان الدولة الكثيرية الحضرمية

عنوان مختصر (١) يسمى هذا القانون بقانون المجالس المحلية .

التطبيق (٢) يطبّق هذا القانون في كافة نواحي مملكتنا .

التحديد (٣) سوف تحمل الكلمات والعبارات الآتية في هذا القانون مالم يظهر من الموضوع أو العبارة قصد آخر .

(النائب) يتضمن النائب بالنيابة و (القائم) أو القائم بالنيابة

(الرئيس) يعني الشخص الذي يترأس أي محكمة من محاكم المجالس المحلية المؤسسة تحت هذا القانون .

(موظف حكومي) يعني الرجال المدنيين والعسكريين التابعين لحكومة صاحبة الجلالة أو دول محمية عدن الشرقية .

القانون المعمول به (٦) سوف تعمل محكمة المجلس المحلية بما يأتي:-

-١- العادة السائدة في المنطقة التي تقع ضمن دائرة اختصاص المحكمة على شرط الأمتثال في تلك العادة مع العدالة والأخلاق والنظام .

-٢- نصوص قانون المحاكم المحلية لعام ١٩٥٢ ميلادية ونصوص ما يعمل تحت ذلك القانون من أوامر محلية ونصوص أي أوامر أو أنظمة تفوض المحكمة لتطبيقها من وقت لآخر .

شـرط بشـرط

أن يكون لمحكمة المجلس المحّلي الصلاحية أن تعاقب بغرامة لا تتجاوز ٣٥ عن خمسة وثلاثين شلناً .

التنفيذ (٧) يجوز للنائب أن ينفذ أي أمر حكم وقرار تصدره محكمة المجلس المحلّـي عندما يطلب التنفيذ رئيس المحكمة هذه وكأنه صادر من محكمة قانونية اعتيادية .

الأنظمـة (٨) يجوز للنائب أن يعمل أنظمة لا تتنافى مع نصوص هذا القانون أو مع نصوص المجالس البلدية وذلك للأغراض التالية :

(أ) تحديد صلاحيات محكمة المجلس فيما يتعلق باختصاصها مع الأفراد والمخالفات لها حق النظر فيها والعقوبات وأي تحديدات أخرى يرى النائب أجرائها .

تأسيس محاكم المجالس المحلية (٤) -١- يجوز لسكرتير الدولة أن يؤسس محاكم محلية في المحلات التي يراها مناسبا .

-٢- يكون تأسيس محكمة المجلس المحلي بواسطة أمر يحمل أمضاء سكرتير الدولة .

-٣- يتضمن الأمر الذي يتم تأسيس محكمة المجلس المحلي بمقتضاه حدود الأختصاص وأسماء أعضاء المجلس المتأهلين للجلوس على مقاعد الحكم كأعضاء في المحكمة ويجوز أن يبين أسماء العقلاء في منطقة المجلس المتأهلين للجلوس على مقاعد الحكم في المحكمة مع أعضاء المجلس .

تأسيس محكمة المجلس (٥) سيعقد مع رئيس المجلس الأعضاء الآتية ذكرهم وفيهم رئيس المجلس ليشكلوا محكمة .

(أ) رئيس أو نائب رئيس المجلس كرئيس للمحكمة .

(ب) لا أقل عن ثلاثة أما من الأعضاء بالمجلس أو منهم أو من عقلاء منطقة المجلس فقط .

(ب) الرسوم التي تأخذها محكمة المجلس المحلي .

(ج) النظر وتطبيق الغرامات والرسوم التي تستلمها محاكم المجلس المحلية .

(د) اجراءات محكمة المجلس المحلي .

(هـ) تنفيذ نصوص هذا القانون بصورة عامة .

أن تكون الأنظمة عرضة لموافقة سكرتير الدولة وفي حالة علاقة تلك الأنظمة بتعيين الرسوم أو مواد الايراد والمصروفات الأخرى الغير منصوص عليها في الميزانية فأن تلك الأنظمة تكون عرضة لموافقة سكرتير الدولة أو ناظر المالية .

سجل المحكمة (٩) سيفتح سجل بجميع القضايا التي تم النظر فيها بمقتضى هذا القانون ويشمل السجل النقط الآتية :-

(أ) اسم رئيس المحكمة وأعضاءها .

(ب) تاريخ ومكان سماع تلك القضية .

(ج) أسماء الأشخاص المتنازعين في القضية .

(د) أسماء الشهود الذين سمعت المحكمة أقوالهم .

(هـ) بيان مختصر عن حقائق القضية .

(و) حكم المحكمة ـ وهذا يجب أن يمضي عليه الرئيس والأعضاء .

الأكثرية المطلوبة لجعل الحكم قانونياً (١٠) الأشخاص الذين يشكلون المحكمة أي الرئيس والأعضاء أو صادق عليه النائب ويجب على النائب ألا يصادق على حكم ألا إذا مضته أغلبية المحكمة .

الاستئناف (١١) حكم أو قرار محكمة المجلس المحلي قابل للاستئناف إلى محكمة النائب .

السجن في حالة العجز عن دافع الغرامة (١٢) في حالة تأييد حكم محكمة المجلس المحلي من قبل النائب يجوز للنائب في حالة العجز عن دفع الغرامة المحكوم بها أن يحكم بسجن يوم عن كل خمسة شلن محكوم بها أو جزء منها .

الاختصاص (١٣) سيكون لكل محكمة مجلس محلي اختصاص تام وصلاحية إلى الحد المنصوص عليه في هذا القانون .

شرط بشرط أن محكمة المجلس المحلي لن تكون لها صلاحية أن :

(أ) تسمع أي قضية مدنية تتجاوز ثمن مادة النزاع فيها مائة شلناً .

(ب) تسمع أي قضية مدنية طرفا النزاع فيها لا يشمله اختصاص المحكمة ألاّ برضى الطرفين أو :

(ج) تسمع أي قضية مدنية أحد طرفي النزاع فيها يشمله اختصاص المحكمة ألا في حالة رضى الطرفين الغير داخل تحت اختصاص المحكمة .

(د) تنظر أي قضية المتهم فيها موظف حكومي .

(هـ) تنظر أي مخالفة أو تعالج أي نزاع ماعدى المخالفات والمنازعات الآتية ذكرها :

(١) المخالفات تحت قانون المجلس المحلي لعام ١٩٥٢ ميلادية .

(٢) المنازعات الزراعية التي تحل حسب عوائد المنطقة بصرف النظر عن قيمة موضوع النزاع .

(٣) المنازعات حول عوائد الحويف .

(٤) الأضرار التي تحدثها البهائم في الزراعة .

(٥) المخاصمات الطفيفة .

(١٤) يصبح هذا القانون ساري المفعول اعتباراً من تاريخ

١٨ ربيع الأول سنة ١٣٧٢ هجرية

موافق ٦ ديسمبر سنة ١٩٥٢ ميلادية

The signature of Sultan Ḥusayn b. 'Ali b. Manṣūr al-Kathīrī.

An Assessment of Gibran

Mahmoud Samra

What shall I write about Gibran, now that the times have changed and I am no longer young enough to be able to appreciate him as I used to? In the 1930s the younger generation read him avidly and responded to him romantically. But the younger generation of these days hardly ever read him, and I do not think that those among them who do read him are likely to admire him. Here, perhaps, lies the major difference between ephemeral and lasting literature.

On the one hand, Gibran was the product of the Arab, more specifically Lebanese, soil of the latter part of the nineteenth century and the early decades of the twentieth, with all the injustice and poverty that prevailed then, and, on the other, of industrialised America, which failed to provide the salvation he had hoped for. Out of these two conflicting backgrounds came Gibran the romantic dreamer, the idealist thinker, whose ideas strike us now as rather frothy and incapable of withstanding close scrutiny and rigorous logic.

Studies on Gibran are by no means wanting. The enthusiastic among his critics have created an immortal saint out of him;[1] others, less enthusiastic and fewer in number, have seen nothing in him except an immoral renegade whose influence on society is pernicious.[2] And a few others have studied him as a writer and artist conditioned by a particular milieu.[3] Michael Naimy's study, however, remains our best guide to the real Gibran.[4]

Fortunately, too, the late Tawfīq Ṣāyigh was able to publish his *New light on Gibran* (1966), based on the collection of letters, now deposited in the library of North Carolina University, written by Gibran and Mary Haskell, his American friend and patron. Everybody knows that that lady helped Gibran and stood by him at a time when hardly anybody knew he existed. She provided him with a monthly grant in aid of $75 and urged him to go to Paris to study art at her own expense. When he asked her to marry him, she refused because she knew their marriage would not last. Naimy is of the opinion that Gibran's offer of marriage was motivated by self-interest: 'She had her own school, which secured her a handsome income. Why not marry her, Gibran thought, and legalise his relationship with her? Let her stay in her school until he was able to do work for both; meanwhile, he would devote himself to his art'.[5] Mary Haskell, as we know, was also the woman to whom Gibran bequeathed all his paintings, books, and other remains.

The North Carolina University collection includes 325 letters written by Gibran to Mary and about 300 written by Mary to Gibran between 1908 and 1931. The last letter was written by Mary only four days before Gibran's death. The letters are extremely important because they shed new light on his life and dispose of many 'facts' propagated in earlier studies.

The collection also includes a large amount of manuscripts and documents related to Mary and Gibran, most important of which, perhaps, is Mary's diary.[6]

A comprehensive assessment of Gibran's life, writings, and art is obviously beyond the scope of the present study. All that will be attempted here is a consideration of what seems to shed new light on selected aspects of Gibran. My remarks will be based on a fresh reading of incontestably established facts and of Gibran's own writings. The topics to be discussed are: Gibran's views on man, life, and the universe; Gibran, language, and literature; and, finally, Gibran and politics.

To start with, I believe that Gibran suffered from two problems that shaped not only his life but also his writings and art. These are his Oedipus complex and his poverty and ambition. Gibran's Oedipus complex will be easy to understand if we remember his markedly close attachment to his mother. There are in Naimy's book a number of revealing dramatised descriptions of the attachment:

> 'Gibran, enough studying for today, son.'
> 'What have you prepared for dinner, mother?'
> 'Potted crushed wheat, dear. You like potted crushed wheat, don't you?'
> 'Everything you cook is delicious, mother. All you do is good. May God bless your hands!'
> 'Your father would not agree with you. Your brothers complain of my cooking all the time.'
> 'Never mind my father and brothers. Think only of Gibran!'[7]

Some critics think that such scenes in Naimy's book are imaginary, and therefore do not reflect the reality of the situation.[8] The fact remains, however, that Gibran's attachment to his mother was so strong that it developed into a complex. Evidence for this may be found in Gibran's letters to Mary, which make it clear that he loved only such women as resembled his mother in one way or another. He tells Mary (1914) about the woman who 'seduced' him, and describes her as having a magnetic personality because 'she had much of the mother in her'. In 1921 he tells her that she, Mary, was the only woman in the world with whom he felt like a child, like a son. In 1922 he writes: 'I always enjoyed your cooking, Mary, and you always filled my plate and glass. But now . . . I no longer feel that I am a loved guest but a child in my mother's home'. In the autumn of 1928 he writes about New York's cold weather and about his need for warmth, saying that 'only a mother's heart can give (him) such warmth. There is such a heart. May God bless that heart, the mother's heart'.[9]

Khalīl Ḥāwī's study recognises this aspect of Gibran's life and cites a number of quotations from Gibran's writings as evidence. Gibran's love for Ḥalah Ẓāhir, two years his senior,[10] and his relationships with Mary Haskell and other married women (e.g., Mary Qahwajī and Mary Khoūrī) seem to be conclusive evidence.

The second problem, that of poverty and ambition, exerted a profound influence on Gibran's life, for his ingrained romanticism made him create a world of his own that had nothing to do with reality. This explains, in my view, those unbelievable exaggerations of his (or shall we call them delusions, perhaps even lies?) which at first may seem rather puzzling.

Gibran was born on 6 December 1883 to a poor family living in a backward environment where Maronite Christians were not allowed to buy oil from Orthodox Christians. His father was an inveterate drunkard whose business was to count sheep and goats on inventory days for taxation purposes while seated on his own horse, with nothing else to do during the rest of the year. Gibran's mother was Kāmilah, daughter of Stefan ʿAbd al-Qādir Rahmah, a priest. The mother, together with Gibran, his elder brother Butros, and his two sisters, Marian and Sulṭānah, emigrated to Boston in 1885 in order to 'bury their poverty', and took residence in the Chinese quarter, one of the filthiest quarters of that American city.

But Gibran severed all ties with this past and began to think of himself as somebody else. In his letters he tells Mary that he belongs to a noble family whose known history extends several centuries back. His forefathers, he claims, came to Damascus in the ninth century and became its rulers. Three of them were hanged, and in the twelfth century some of them went to Lebanon, which they ruled tyrannically. During the Crusades a crusading bishop saw one of the kings of the Gibran dynasty riding a horse and clad in white. On hearing his name the bishop said he, King Gibran, might have been the angel Gabriel himself, so grand was he. . . .

Gibran's paternal grandfather, the fantasy continues, was a great aristocrat, while his maternal grandfather was a well-known bishop whose wife was the daughter of the richest man in Lebanon. The family residence in Bisharrī was a grand palace sumptuously furnished and elegantly decked with antiques. Gibran's mother, who, according to Ḥāwī, was an illiterate woman, was transformed into a highly cultured lady who spoke French, Italian, Spanish, and English, in addition to Arabic.[12]

Such stories as we find in Gibran's letters to Mary clearly exculpate Michael Naimy of all feelings of jealousy levelled against him because he has recorded some of Gibran's fabrications. One such fabrication involves Gibran's feelings towards his native village Bisharrī in Lebanon. According to Naimy, Gibran felt that a man of his stature must have a more mysterious birthplace. Is there any place in the world more exotic and mysterious than India? Thus, when Nasīb ʿArīdah asked him for a short biography to be published in *Funūn*, Gibran said that he was born in Bombay, India, and that he did not mind if the 'secret' were to be made public. It would even be quite all right if the secret were to be placed within parentheses, for that would be the best way to draw attention to it.

And so it was. The short biography did appear in *Funūn*, saying that Gibran 'was born in 1883 in Bisharrī, Lebanon (or, as other reports have it, in Bombay). . . .'[13] These details were quoted *verbatim* by the publisher of *Al-Badāʾiʿ wa-ʾl-ṭarāʾif* (*A Collection of gems*) in the prefatory note, which says further that 'Gibran obtained a *licence* from the French Beaux Arts, that he was a member of the French Fine Arts Society, and that he was an honorary member of the British Society of Painters'. In all probability, Gibran obtained none of these honours; he only wished he had. Gibran the misanthrope, the malcontent, and the despiser of people's littleness and servility to tradition was, in fact, more servile to tradition than they.

If, now, we add to these two aspects of Gibran (his Oedipus complex and his poverty and ambition) that he was genuinely talented, that he was insufficiently educated (of which more below), and that he deliberately cultivated ambiguity ('What good would it do him to address them if he did not want them to understand him lest he should be degraded to their level – for if they understood him, he would hate himself, and if they did not, he would hate them')[14] and if we recall the environment in which he was brought up, we will be in a much better position to understand Gibran the writer as well as the artist.

Gibran was torn between two forces: his weaknesses as a man and his aspirations as an artist. The man in him craved for wealth, glory, and pleasure; the artist despised all this worldly dross and hankered after an ideal world. Michael Naimy reports that 'whenever Gibran got acquainted with any man, woman, or family celebrated for some artistic, financial, political, or social distinction, he told me about it with an air of seeming indifference, but with a secret sense of self-importance for being close to those considered by the world to be great. Dreading the possibility of my pointing out to him the contradiction between his critical attitude towards accepted traditions and his pride in those very traditions, Gibran used to shroud his relationships with others with an air of secrecy'.[15]

Gibran's views on man, life, and the universe seem to revolve round three concentric circles: the smallest is that of the jungle (nature or simple life away from cities); the middle one is his belief in metempsychosis; and the largest involves pantheism and the rejection of dualism as a guiding principle in this world.

Gibran rebelled against the authority and privileges of the feudal lords, the plutocrats, the oligarchs, the theocrats, and against the traditional values of his society. His writings are full of such rebellious tendencies. His 'Mad John', for example, a parable in his *Brides of the meadows*, is the story of a young shepherd whose absorption in the New Testament, which he reads in secret, makes him neglect his cows, which graze part of the monastery's crops. The priests are infuriated and they end up by throwing him and his cows in prison. At this point the writer gives vent to his rancour against 'Christ's apostles', and, addressing Jesus, he says: 'Come again, O Jesus alive, and cast those who trade in religion out of your temples; they have turned them into caves rife with the writhing serpents of their tricks and deception'.[16]

In his 'Flower of the Blessed' in *Rebellious spirits* we read about a proud maiden forcibly married to an old husband. Gibran uses this familiar situation as a springboard to attack social customs and praise the spirits that rebel against such commercial arrangements. 'Conflict of the Graves' in the same collection tells how a tyrannical prince sentences three criminals (two men and one woman) to be hanged without witnesses or investigation. The first man is accused of having killed one of the prince's military commanders in self-protection. The second is accused of having stolen a basketful of flour from the monastery to feed his hungry children. The woman is accused of having been unfaithful to her husband, to whom she was given in marriage without her consent. In this story Gibran attacks the laws that the powerful have legislated to subdue the weak: 'To shed blood is sinful, but who has permitted the prince to shed it? Stealing money is criminal, but who has turned stealing souls into a virtue? Adultery is ugly, but who has made stoning human bodies beautiful? Should we counter evil with greater evil and say: this is the law? Should we combat corruption with worse corruption and say: this is the norm? Should we fight crime with more heinous crime and say: this is justice?'[17]

This rebellion against man and his bleak reality made Gibran seek salvation in withdrawal into the world of the jungle, where simplicity and innocence prevail, and where the duality of ruler and ruled does not exist. It also made him seek compensation for life lost here and now in life to be lived somewhere else and at some other time; in other words, it led him to believe in metempsychosis. In his story 'The Ashes of generations and immortal fire' we read about a priest who lives in Baalbek in 116 B.C. When his mistress dies, he begins to roam aimlessly in the desert. His love, however, does not die, and so the lovers are re-incarnated and they meet each other in A.D. 1890. Gibran became acquainted with the metempsychosis theory through translated Indian books, then very popular.

This belief in metempsychosis is also found in Gibran's *Sand and foam*, where life is described as a 'handful of sand and another of foam, and man is only a passer-by walking on the shore: the waves soon erase his footsteps and the wind takes away the foam. But the sea and the shore (the symbol of life) remain forever, and the elements of nature pass through perpetual transformations: the fog becomes a worm, the worm a bird, the bird a man, the man fog again'.[18]

Gibran's belief in metempsychosis enriched his imagination. In his letters to Mary Haskell, for example, he insists that he was conscious of having lived in the past twice in Syria (two short periods), once in Italy (for twenty-five years), once in Greece (for twenty-two years), once in Egypt (well into old age), six or seven times in Chaldea, once in Persia, and once in India. He adds that in all these lives he lived as a human being. In answer to a question Mary asked about how far in the past or the future he was able to see he says that he was able to see future events for about five hundred years to come, 'but I don't feel I can foresee events for more than one thousand years'. As for the past it was possible for him to relive in the Renaissance quite easily, but the easiest period for him to relive was that of two thousand years ago.[19]

Gibran's rebellion against bleak reality led him to pantheism and pantheism led him to the rejection of dualism, which he viewed as the source of all evil in this world. This aspect of Gibran's thought appears at its clearest in his *Mad man*, his first book to be written in English, in his poem 'The Pageants', and, supremely, in 'The Prophet'.

Gibran's 'Mad man' is akin to Colin Wilson's *Outsider*.[20] He is a man who lives among those who do not understand him. He alone knows the truth. But Gibran's truth is not Colin Wilson's. Gibran's mad hero sees in man, God, and the universe an indivisible unity; still, he is a stranger in his own country: 'Why am I here, O God of lost souls?'

Gibran's ideas mature somewhat in 'The Pageants', a long poem of 203 lines, which, untypical of Gibran, follows classical form. There are two voices in the poem, indicating an internal dialogue. The first voice, following one metre (*basīṭ*), stresses the reality of human life as it is. The second, following another (dimetric *ramal*), depicts the world the poet dreams of.[21] The poem deals with the pageants of humanity as they are led astray in their search for happiness, freedom, and immortality in places other than the jungle. These misguided pageants have lost the real meaning of happiness and immortality because they have accepted to be shackled by existing laws, which divide the world into warring dualities such as good and evil, justice and injustice, happiness and unhappiness. Man, however, will never recover his freedom and happiness until these dualities are destroyed. Only by returning to the jungle can man achieve happiness, for it is in the jungle that the unity of man, God, and the universe is manifested.

Gibran's rejection of dualism complements his rebellion against those religions which have divided the world into good and evil, and man into body and soul, and promised punishments and rewards to be meted out in the next world. These ideas are clearly a continuation of tendencies popularised by the romantics, who glorified nature and rejected established codes. We need only refer to Rousseau and Diderot to remember the sources of Gibran's views on the dualism and the jungle.

'The Pageants' opens by talking about corruption and inequality in the world as we know it. Then the poet depicts the world he dreams of, the world of the jungle, from which the duality of ruler and ruled, for instance, has disappeared. This dream world is simple; even its music, which is played on the flute, is simple:

> In the jungle there is no shepherd, nor is there a flock. . . .
> In the jungle there is no sadness, nor are there worries. . . .
> In the jungle you do not get intoxicated by wine or dreams. . . .
> In the jungle there is no religion, nor is there infidelity. . . .

Not only do these lines reject dualism and invite us to the world of the jungle, but they also express Gibran's belief in the unity of man, God, and the universe:

> In the jungle there is no difference between body and soul.
> The air is flowing water, and dew is water stilled.
> Fragrance is flower etherealised; earth is flower materialised.
> In the jungle there is no death, nor are there graves.
> When we cease to forget, we do not cease to rejoice.
> Fear of death is delusion enfolded in the heart.
> He who has lived for one spring has lived forever.

Gibran's description of the jungle is given in concrete terms to make it vividly present in the minds of the readers:

> Have you chosen the jungle to live in rather than palaces, as I have?
> Have you followed the streams and climbed up the cliffs, as I have?
> Have you bathed in perfume and used light for a towel?
> Have you drunk the light of the sun at sunrise, served in ethereal cups?
> Have you sat in the afternoon among the vines, with the bunches of grapes dangling like chandeliers, as I have?
> Have you used grass for a mattress? Have you used the sky for a quilt?
> Have you been as indifferent about the future and as forgetful of the past as I have?

The jungle, then, is Gibran's version of nature which Coleridge, Wordsworth, and the other romantic poets glorified. The conclusion of the poem, however, is significant. In the last three lines Gibran admits that the world of the jungle is far from realisable; it is merely a dream:

> Were it in my power to change the course of time, I would have made the world of the jungle prevail.
> But time merely uses me for its own purposes: whenever I wish for something, it only gives me regrets.
> Fate has its own inscrutable ways, and man constantly falls short of realising his dreams.[22]

Gibran said his last word on the subject in 'The Prophet', which is a mature summation of ideas scattered in his other books. The Prophet's views on religion are similar to those expressed in 'Mad John' and 'Unbelieving Khalīl'. His pantheism may be found in *A Tear and a smile*. His ideas on love and marriage are identical with those expressed in *Broken Wings*. And his belief in metempsychosis and pantheism informs all of Gibran's other writings.[23]

We come now to Gibran's position with regard to language and literature. A number of critics have already dealt with Gibran's stylistic and grammatical errors, reporting how he used to misread even his own writings and to mis-scan his own verses. Others have retorted that since Gibran has enriched the language so much and freed it from traditional forms, his errors are inconsequential; after all, such errors may be found even in some pre-Islamic poets.[24] Gibran defends himself by saying that the best, if not only, means of renovating the language is to let it filter through the poet's heart, lips, and fingers. The poet is the intermediary between creativity and humanity. 'If the poet is language's father and mother, the imitator is the weaver of its shroud and the digger of its grave'.[25] 'Of your language', Gibran adds, 'you take the dictionaries and the long unmanageable poems of old; I will take what the ear has sifted and what the memory has preserved, what is familiar and current, what people actually use to express their happiness and sorrow. You have your language and I have mine. You have prosody and grammatical rules about the permissible and the impermissible, and I have that linguistic stream which runs towards the sea, mindless of whether accurate metre consists of the rocks along the way or good rimes of the autumn leaves that dance upon its rippling waters. . . .'[26]

There is no doubt that renovation is desirable, that language is an ever-developing living phenomenon, and that fixity can lead only to death in language as well as in life. But renovation must not amount to destruction, and it must not be based on ignorance. Michael Naimy, Gibran's close friend, reports the following story: 'Gibran used to make so many mistakes while reading that, were he to be heard by someone who does not know him or of him, he would scarcely be taken to be the composer of what he was reading. However, I used to admire his native ability to preserve the metrical pattern of what he was reading despite his grammatical errors. Once I pointed out an irregularity in one of his lines to him, but he refused to accept my scansion of it, for he did not know how to scan even though he had studied prosody in school. He kept repeating the line without noticing the irregularity until I changed the troublesome word with another. Only then was he convinced. I also pointed out some of his grammatical mistakes, as in the line

Fa-sāriqu 'l-zahri madhmūmun wa-muḥtaqaru; wa-sāriqu 'l-ḥaqli yudʿā 'l-bāsila 'l-khaṭira.

(He who steals the flowers is blamed and despised, but he who steals the whole farm is said to be a valiant hero.) Gibran, however, would be convinced neither by logical nor grammatical analysis. Naimy adds in a footnote that 'the line remained as it was in the New York edition, but I have seen it corrected in an Egyptian edition to read:

wa-sāriqu 'l-ḥaqli fa-hwa 'l-bāsilu 'l-khaṭiru.

(where the last word is no longer in the accusative case as it should be in the original version)'.[27]

Gibran's letters to Mary make it clear that he did not like to read lest acquired culture should harm his native genius and individuality. In one of his letters he tells her that 'his friends used to advise him not study too much for fear of spoiling his talent, and he was content with what he was doing'.[28] The letters also make it clear that Gibran never developed a coherent theory of literature or art. In his observations on writers and artists he never gives a carefully considered opinion or an original idea. He merely advances generalised judgements similar to the comments reported from the pre-Islamic and early Islamic periods to the effect that this or that line is the most poetic of its kind or this or that poet is the greatest of all poets. Of Gibran's own pronouncements of this sort we may cite the following:

> Any Arab shepherd has more poetic sensitivity than the best French poet.[29]
> Arab music is by far the greatest of all.[30]
> The Song of Songs is the greatest lyrical composition in the world, but I doubt if Solomon actually wrote it.[31]

The letters are full of such sweeping generalisations.[32]

But if Gibran did not formulate a theory of art, what *was* art to him? In a letter to Mary from Paris (1909) he writes: 'Art to me, dear Mary, is beyond what we see. Nature is the body of God, the form of God, and God is what I sing and what I desire to know'.[33] Only Gibran will be able to say what this means.

The troubles of Gibran's home country do have a place in his letters to Mary, but they do so only because the pressure of contemporary events in Lebanon and the Arab East in general was too great to be ignored. Gibran hated the Turks heartily: 'Anything that might cause the Syrians to hate the Turks must be a good thing'.[34]

Sometimes Gibran imagined himself a new Christ sacrificing himself to save others. He tells Mary about an 'Open Letter to Islam,' 'which might turn the whole world against me. But I am ready for it. I am now accustomed to being nailed on a cross'.[35] When the idea of autonomy began to be voiced by the Syrians in 1913, Gibran wrote that it was he who had initiated it.[36] In her diary for late 1917 Mary writes that Gibran showed her a scar on his arm, saying it had been caused by a bullet shot at him while speaking in Paris against the Turks, that it was the Turks who had attempted to assassinate him, and that the bullet was fired from short range.[37]

The Paris Conference, however, was not attended by Gibran, who had been invited, for he thought that the Conference was doomed to failure because the participants 'talked like poets and acted like dreamers, and the result was a poem – a dream'. This verdict is rather puzzling, coming from Gibran, one of the most prominent of poets.

In 1914 he again mentions his 'Open Letter to Islam'. He says that his friends in his home country predicted that by publishing it he was signing his death warrant in his own hand. But 'I do not care', he comments. 'If I am barred from returning to my country, I can go to another'. He describes the letter as 'a simple message to all Muslims, explaining in prophetic manner how the Turkish government is socially and politically destructive to Islam'.

Gibran's political dreams were boundless. On 30 August 1914 he writes to Mary about his dream of establishing an Arab empire: 'You know that one of my dreams, and one of the things I want to achieve, is to establish an Arab empire. I expect the dream to require several years of my life. It would have been helpful for me to be more qualified for this, for the Arab World believes in me as a writer. Even my enemies believe in me. It would have been great for me to know about military tactics'.

In a letter written on 7 November 1928, after Mary had married someone else, Gibran's tendency to dream reaches its climax: 'I have informed the Lebanese that I have no wish to go back to assume their leadership. They want me to do so, and you know, Mary, that I am homesick and that I yearn to see the hills and valleys of my country. But it is better for me to stay and work here'. In another letter (8 November 1929) he relieves his imagination of all things political and says: 'My responsibilities in the East are over'.[38]

These were responsibilities that Gibran undertook only in his imagination. He kept dreaming about them until they became real to him. He never changed. We have seen him as a man; we have seen him as a writer. We have tried to grasp his ideas, but was there anything to grasp? What is it that has remained of him today? What is it that will remain tomorrow?

Notes

[1] One of the books that treat Gibran as a saint is Barbara Young's *This Man from Lebanon*, 8th printing New York, 1956; Arabic version by Sa'īd 'Afīf Bābā, São Paolo, 1953. See also Ḥabīb Mas'ūd's *Jibrān ḥayyan wa-mayyitan* [Gibran Dead and Alive], São Paolo, 1932, which consists of selections from Gibran's writings and drawings and of pieces written on him by others.
[2] See Amīn Khālid, *Muḥāwalāt_ fī dars Jibrān* [Approaches to Gibran] Beirut, 1933 and Father Elias Zughbi, *Gibrān Khalīl Gibrān*, Ḥreiṣa, Lebanon, 1939.
[3] Chief among such studies is *Al-Shi'r al-'arabī fī 'al-Mahjar: Amrīka al-shimāliyyah* [Arabic Poetry in North America] by Iḥsān 'Abbās and Muḥammad Yūsuf Najm, Beirut, 1957. The following are also useful: Jamīl Jabr, *Jibrān: sīratuhu, adabuhu, falsafatuhu, wa-rasmuh* [Gibran: His Life, Writings, Philosophy, and Art], Beirut, 1958; George Ṣaydaḥ, *Adabunā wa-'udabā'unā fī 'al-Mahājir al-Amrīkiyyah* [Our Literature and Writers in the Americas], Beirut, 1957; Wadī' Dīb, *Al-Shi'r al-'arabi fī 'al-Mahjar al-Amrīkī* [Arabic Poetry in America], Beirut, 1955; 'Īsā Nā'ūrī, *Adab al-Mahjar* [Arabic Literature in America], 2nd ed. Cairo, 1967; Nādirah Jamīl Sarrāj, *Shu'arā' al-Rābiṭah al-Qalamiyyah* [Poets of the Rābiṭah Qalamiyyah], Cairo, 1957; 'Abd al-Karīm al-Ashtar, *Al-Nathr al-Mahjarī: Kuttāb al-Rābiṭah al-Qalamiyyah* [Arabic Prose in America: The Rabiṭah Qalamiyyah Writers], 2 vols., Cairo, 1961.
[4] Michael Naimy, *Gibrān Khalīl Gibrān: hayātuhu, mawtuhu, adabuhu, fannuh* [G.K.G.: His Life, Death, Writings, and Art], 5th ed., Beirut, 1964.
[5] Naimy, 118.
[6] Ṣāyigh, 10–11.
[7] Naimy, 39.
[8] Ṣāyigh, 13.
[9] Ibid., 100–101.
[10] Some critics believe that Ḥalah Ẓāhir, Gibran's youthful sweetheart, is the same as Salmā Karāmah, the heroine of his *Broken Wings*. But this widely held idea is denied by Gibran in one of his letters to Mary Haskell: 'Not a single experience in the book was based on my own. Not a single character was based on a real person. And not a single episode was taken from real life. Authors often build their novels on their own experiences, but I have not. Characters and events are my own creation because I believe that writers should create something new, something that enriches life. I say this because the book treats of a young man awakening to life and

narrates his love story and is likely , therefore, to be called autobiographical. In fact, it has already been called so. I have had love affairs, of course, and I have awakened to life, but the book has nothing personal in it, and I have never encountered any of its characters'. Cf. Ṣāyigh, 221–22.

[11] Khalīl Ḥāwī, *Khalīl Gibran*, Beirut, 1963, 94, 96, 103, 104, 108, 183.

[12] For more details see Ṣāyigh, 45–47, and Young, 179–81.

[13] Naimy, 147–48.

[14] Ibid., 159.

[15] Ibid., 156.

[16] Gibrān Khalīl Gibrān, *Al-Majmū'ah al-Kāmilah* [Complete Works], Beirut, n.d., 78.

[17] Ibid., 104. See also the story entitled 'Unbelieving Khalīl'.

[18] Jamīl Jabr, 165.

[19] Ṣāyigh, 47–48.

[20] Colin Wilson, *The Outsider*, London, 1956.

[21] Nasīb 'Arīḏah misreads the poem when he says in his introduction to it that the first voice is that of an old man and the second that of a young man, and that the two voices are in conflict.

[22] See the excellent analysis of 'The Pageants' in Iḥsān 'Abbās and Muḥammad Yūsuf Najm, *Al-Shi'r al-'arabī fī al-Mahjar*, 41–50, 71–75, 89–91.

[23] Of the many comments on 'The Prophet' one may cite Jamīl Jabr's Gibrān, 152–58; Ṣāyigh's *New Light*, 227–28; and Barbara Young's *This Man from Lebanon*, 87–100.

[24] For details see the books by Jamīl Jabr, 186–92; George Ṣaydaḥ, 71–75; Wadī' Dīb, 21–30; and Khalīl Ḥāwī, 244–77. One of Gibran's most ardent defenders was Michael Naimy in his *Al-Ghirbāl* [The Sieve], 7th ed., Beirut, n.d., 90–106. Muḥammad Mandūr was also among those who defended the Arab writers of America against such accusations. See his *Fī 'al-Mīzān al-jadīd* [The New Criterion], 3rd ed., Cairo, n.d., 69–85.

[25] *Al-Majmū'ah al-kāmilah*, p. 560.

[26] See the whole essay entitled 'You have your language, I have mine' in Ḥabīb Mas'ūd's *Gibrān ḥayyan wa-mayyitan*, 95–97.

[27] Naimy, *Gibrān*, 163–64.

[28] Ṣāyigh, 216.

[29] Ibid., 180–81.

[30] Ibid., 211.

[31] Ibid., 193.

[32] Ibid., 159–236.

[33] Ibid., 216.

[34] Ibid., 116.

[35] Ibid., 117.

[36] Ibid., 57.

[37] Ibid., 57.

[38] For more details see Ṣāyigh, 109–56.

Fayṣal b. ʿAbd al-ʿAzīz: a personal reminiscence

Bayly Winder

To the best of my belief Robert Serjeant never met His Late Majesty King Fayṣal b. ʿAbd al-ʿAzīz, but I take particular pleasure and some honour in offering, as it were, a joint homage to each of them. Had they met, King Fayṣal would have immediately recognised and applauded the deep knowledge and sincere interest of Bob Serjeant in everything Arabian. For his part Professor Serjeant, with his almost instinctive insight into Arabians, would have appreciated the commanding force of Fayṣal's intelligence and personality with particular savour.

I would like to emphasise at the very beginning that this personal reminiscence is not a scholarly study. It lays no claim to some self-assertive objectivity (if that exists anywhere?) and it is not based on 'research', the combing of books (though God knows a good one on King Fayṣal is needed), learned journals, or newspaper analyses. I also lay no claim to intimate friendship. Rather, what I intend to do is make some very personal remarks about a man who at once over-awed me while putting me at my ease, and whom I admired and respected over a period of three decades and more.

My method will be to present, in more or less instinctive categories, a series of vignettes which are quite personal, not only as far as King Fayṣal is concerned, but also in regard to my wife, Viola, but for whom I would never have met Fayṣal in the first place and, having met him, would not have got to know him. Permit me to digress slightly. Viola could paint at least as vivid a picture of Fayṣal as I can and probably much more so. She may be in fact the earliest American writer in English about him. When she accompanied her father, Philip K. Hitti, to the San Francisco Conference in 1945, she was on assignment from a local paper, *The Princeton Herald*, and she sent back to Princeton insightful portraits of the conference as a whole and of the Arab delegates particularly – amongst whom her overwhelmingly favourite subject was the then Amīr Fayṣal.

Our subject is Fayṣal b. ʿAbd al-ʿAzīz b. ʿAbd al-Raḥmān b. Fayṣal b. Turkī Āl Suʿūd. That is a lineage that carries a large historical freight on which I shall not dwell, but I would like to take just a moment to comment on *our* Fayṣal's great-grandfather, Fayṣal, and on our Fayṣal's father, His Late Majesty King ʿAbd al-ʿAzīz. Perhaps I am attracted to the Imām Fayṣal, who ruled the Saudi State from 1834 to 1865 only because of the fact that *our* subject bears his great-grandfather's name and because of the fact that I have written on the Imām Fayṣal; but there are certain meaningful parallels between the two Fayṣals. Both took over the reins of government against a background of chaos or near chaos; both had the astuteness and the intelligence to put the Saudi state on its feet and, relative to their times, to conduct themselves with dignity and effectiveness both at home and *vis-à-vis* foreign officials and powers; both were constant in their devotion and duty to Islam as a culture and as an unshakable personal faith. Colonel Lewis Pelly, the British Political Resident in the Gulf during much of the first Fayṣal's imamate, wrote, in 1866 the following:

> ... I could not but observe that all parties admitted Ameer Fysul ben Saood to be a just and stern ruler who had been unprecedentedly successful in curbing the predatory habits of his tribes; and who was desirous of inculating among them more settled habits, and of turning their minds toward agriculture and trade.[1]

Move down a century, and the words are remarkably apt. But the most striking statement reported by Pelly is the following: 'We dare say you wonder how we can remain here [in Riyadh] thus cut off from the rest of the world. Yet we are content. We are princes according to our degree. We feel ourselves every inch a king'.[2] Fayṣal b. ʿAbd al-ʿAzīz was in that mould.

A still briefer word on King ʿAbd al-ʿAzīz. As a youngster interested in Arabia, I longed mightily for a chance to meet the mighty founder of modern Saudi Arabia (who also took over at a time of chaos and restored the Saudi state), to visit the still-walled and crenelated Riyadh, a visit which then required ʿAbd al-ʿAzīz' personal approval. The chance never came, and I was disappointed. Yet, there is solace. For me, Fayṣal was enough: I felt him every inch a king.

What then are those qualities which my experience with this human being, Fayṣal b. ʿAbd al-ʿAzīz, highlighted for me over a period of some thirty years? Let me start with his sense of humour – especially because it relates to the first occasion on which I met him. The time was, I believe, in 1947. The occasion was a glittering reception offered by His Royal Highness Prince Fayṣal, the Saudi Arabian Minister for Foreign Affairs, in the Grand Ballroom of the Waldorf Astoria in New York. I, in effect, tagged along with Professor and Mrs Hitti and Viola, my new bride. It was the first time Viola had seen him since the San Francisco Conference. In the rather formal receiving line, Professor Hitti started to introduce me to His Highness, but hardly had he started when Viola indicated that she would introduce me and although, as is well known, Fayṣal actually spoke English with some facility, public matters were always in Arabic. My wife was born and bred in America, had grown up in an English-speaking home, and had never had any reason to pursue the intricacies that constitute *lisān al-malāʾikā* – the tongue of the angels, Arabic – and consequently, naturally, she had a somewhat deficient knowledge of the intricacies of its inflection. She upturned her face to His Highness and in a quiver of enthusiasm said, '*Yā Amīr Fayṣal, hādhā marʾatī*!' Fayṣal roared with laughter as Viola blushed. The real point is, however, that he never forgot that incident. Usually, when I saw him, he would not ask me, '*Kayf* Viola?' rather, he would say, '*Kayf hādhā marʾatī*?' and once again smile broadly.

Another example of this sense of humour comes from an even earlier period, that of Fayṣal's first visit to the United States in 1943. In the course of that trip, on which Prince Fayṣal was accompanied by Prince Khālid b. ʿAbd al-ʿAzīz, later his successor as the ruler of the Kingdom of Saudi Arabia,[3] the royal party passed through Princeton to visit what was then called the Department of Oriental Languages and Literatures and which was under Professor Hitti's chairmanship. Incidentally, *The Princeton Herald*,[4] in the caption of an interesting photograph showing the royal party in the Hitti's front yard identifies the long-time Saudi Ambassador to the United Nations as 'Janeal (*sic*) Baroody, Instructor of Arabic in the Area and Language Program at Princeton University'. Jamīl Bārūdī had known King Fayṣal 'in the thirties when I lived in London and was involved in Arab affairs . . . When then Prince Faisel saw me in New York, he was happy I was no longer in London during the war, and when he told me he had received an invitation to visit Princeton, I encouraged him to accept and accompanied him to the University where. . . . I taught Arabic in 1943'.[5] Clearly, the visit of the Saudi princes to Princeton was no small thing. The *Herald* indicates that a number of Near Eastern diplomats made the 200-mile trip to Princeton from Washington for the occasion. Part of the trip included a visit to the University's Palmer Stadium to watch a game of American football. I do not know who won the game, but Fayṣal was subsequently asked by a *Herald* reporter how he had liked football: 'Prince Faysal said that the gridiron struggle reminded him of the year 1934 when he led 40,000 Arab troops in the battle against al-Yemen'![6]

A second quality which stands out in my mind is best characterised by the Arabic word, *ṣabr*. The word is usually and inadequately translated as *patience*, but patience is only part of the meaning of *ṣabr*, the rest is *steadiness*, *calm*, *endurance*, *tenacity*. Perhaps we should think of it as *self-control*. Two incidents in my personal experience, quite different in type, indicate the profound degree to which Fayṣal b. ʿAbd al-ʿAzīz had internalised *ṣabr*. The first of these was in June, 1966 when he came to the United States for a state visit at the invitation of Lyndon Johnson. There were two successive nights: the first was a State Dinner at the White House, the second a dinner in New York to be hosted by Mayor Lindsay. The first was, not at Fayṣal's request I am confident, a stag affair; the second, mixed. I had the honour to be invited to the White House, and also Viola and I were invited to the mayor's dinner which was to be in the Metropolitan Museum of Art. The day after the White House affair, where King Fayṣal had returned most graciously President Johnson's after-dinner remarks, I was driving from Washington to New York listening to the car radio. What I heard was a crescendo of vitriolic political reaction to a remark that King Fayṣal had made in a press conference about Zionism and the State of Israel. My alarm grew until it was finally reported that Mayor Lindsay had cancelled his dinner. As an aside, I may indicate that I stopped at the next public telephone and called Viola up, thinking that she might be unaware of this development. She said that they had called her from the mayor's office and that anyway she had heard it on the radio. Finally, she said that she was sending Mayor Lindsay a bill for a new dress she had bought! However, to return to *ṣabr*, I did see His Majesty the next day in the Waldorf. We had a long conversation about a variety of subjects, one of which was the Lindsay snub, which had been featured in headlines around the world. Fayṣal brushed it aside in a manner which displayed neither rancour nor concern, but which rather suggested the dismissal of a matter of no significance – in short with *ṣabr*. My own instinct was to interpret his remarks as reflecting a certain gratification at what had happened. At the time, President ʿAbd al-Nāṣir of Egypt was busily portraying Fayṣal as soft on imperialism and Zionism and as insufficiently Arab. The politically motivated snub may have served King Fayṣal as well as it did – perhaps – Mayor Lindsay. It should not, however, be thought that Fayṣal did not care about such matters. I know for a fact that, in the wake of this incident, he firmly declined an invitation which would have insured a completely insulated private meeting with Governor Nelson Rockefeller, of New York State, with the comment that if Governor Rockefeller did not want to meet him publicly, then he (Fayṣal) did not want to meet Governor Rockefeller privately.

The second incident illustrating self-control was much more dramatic. It occurred shortly before Fayṣal's assassination on an occasion when I had the privilege of an audience with him in Riyadh. The occasion was simply to pay my respects, and the Royal Protocol had arranged for me to call on him in *majlis* on a day that Saudi petitioners occupied most of the time. I went into the *majlis* as the last petitioners were in line handing their petitions to an aide and greeting their monarch. When the king saw me, he motioned for me to sit down, and we both sat down. The protocol interpreters backed off to a respectful distance since their services were, in my case, more or less unnecessary. Suddenly a bedouin with a real or imagined grievance of great seriousness turned back from the group of his fellows who were now exiting the audience hall and stood in front of the seated King Fayṣal. The man began in a rather agitated way to reiterate his grievance. At first, neither I nor anyone paid much attention to this incident, for we assumed that he would say whatever he was going to say and then go his way. In fact, however, instead of politely passing on, he became increasingly agitated shouting more and more loudly and pressing his face closer and closer to the king's. In the end he leaned forward so far that his face was no more than an inch or two from the king's. In the twinkling of an eye, his voice rose to a level of extreme anger and near loss of control. My first instinct was to stand up and try to back him off before some violence should ensue. But I then thought that I might rather trigger the violence and that the best thing would be to sit quietly. Of course, in a matter of seconds, several other people from the protocol, from the guard, and from the *khulūwī* had rushed up. Quietly they took the man by the arms and backed him off so that no harm came from it all. But, what was remarkable was how Fayṣal conducted himself. His face at no time displayed the slightest emotion, and for the most part, he simply sat silently as this not-far-from demented man raged at him. Occasionally, he said in a relatively low voice, '*ṭayyib, ṭayyib*'. When the man was led off, Fayṣal turned to me and in the blandest way possible, welcomed me to Riyadh. A sensitive observer of the Arabian ethos noted that handling all conceivable situations in a *majlis* was instilled in senior members of the Saudi royal family from childhood. No doubt the observation is just, but there can be few men who could have gone through an experience as searing as that one without displaying the quiver of an eyelash. It took *me* several hours to recover!

Another characteristic which might be construed as the reverse of my point about *ṣabr* is what I could simply dub *frankness*. Occasionally, outsiders get the impression that Arabians are wooden people because of the dignified facade which is normally exposed, but they are real people, and King Fayṣal was a very real person. On occasion, he could be frank in the extreme, and I will now relate an incident which still surprises me today. The account is absolutely accurate. I saw him in a private audience on an occasion in Jedda in 1962. On the next day, or even perhaps that same evening, he was proceeding to Alexandria, for a summit conference with President ʿAbd al-Nāṣir. The situation in the Middle East was at its usual level of intensity at that time, and as I began to take my leave, I expressed to King Fayṣal in a kind of formal way my hope that the summit conference would produce positive results for peace in the Middle East and in the world, or something like that. He looked me straight in the eye and said something like, '*Fa-kayf tantaẓir natā'ij ijābiyyah min mu'tamar maʿ kadhdhāb*?' ('How can you expect positive results from a conference with a liar?') Possibly the remark was out of character, but it certainly was frank!

Related to the frankness is another set of characteristics which always struck me in King Fayṣal: *informality* and *modesty*. These characteristics represent the Najdī way, and there are many today who still follow them, but one has the impression that today something like a conscious decision is made. With Fayṣal, they were so natural that he surely never gave any thought to them. One should have known, but, nevertheless, when one day in 1973 he looked at me and said, 'Yes, that is an interesting idea. Why don't you go and talk to Fahd about it', I was momentarily puzzled. He referred, I quickly understood, to His Royal Highness Prince Fahd b. ʿAbd al-ʿAzīz, now the king, who was, even then, Minister of Interior and one of the most senior officers of the realm; it was enough to make one draw his breath.

Gentlemanliness is another characteristic which I believe moved the mind of Fayṣal, even if he could sometimes be cold and efficient. Note the following two reactions on two separate occasions during the 1943 visit to Princeton. The first was in response to an American soldier, who on behalf of a group of his fellows in the U.S. Army Specialized Training Program, read to the prince in the noble language of the Qur'ān a brief address welcoming him to Princeton, and, *inter alia*, asking Fayṣal to convey the *salāms* of the American soldiers to their Arab counterparts. Prince Fayṣal responded as follows:

> 'I thank you and your comrades from the bottom of my heart for this expression of sincere and cordial welcome through the Arabic language. I marvel at the progress you have made and trust that each one of you may

become a messenger of Arab culture and good will to the American Army. I shall surely convey your *salāms* to your comrades in arms in the Arab world'.

It is a routine ceremonial remark, but has the sure touch of a born gentleman. The second response was in answer to a question from a local reporter about America and Princeton. First, Prince Fayṣal expressed his admiration for America and then in language reminiscent of a famous remark about Dartmouth University, said of Princeton, 'It is a charming place. While it is a small town, its size does not indicate its importance'.

Finally, in this category of ordinary human gentlemanliness and warmth, I might mention the occasion on which he turned to me, wanting to contrast me with some of my countrymen with whom he was less than sympathetic and said, '*Lākin inta rajul muḥtaram*' ('but you are a respected man'). His tone of voice led me to think that his comment represented a fact known to all and thus to conclude that I might be the only respected man in the whole wide world; but it did embody that quality of gentlemanliness and warmth that I am trying to capture.

Switching to a different vein, I cannot refrain from reporting a couple of personal conversations which involve one or another aspect of King Fayṣal's statecraft. The most important of these, one perfectly in accord with the strict Wahhābī tradition, grew out of a conversation about the House of Suʿūd and its stewardship. King Fayṣal was certainly a man born to rule as much as any other in history, and one does not imagine that he was inflicted with much self-doubt on that score. On this occasion, however, he said to me that, 'We of Āl Suʿūd were not given by God a special right to rule these people, and if we do not shepherd them faithfully, they will, with justification, find others to do so'.

Another example shows him in a mood more serious than some to which I have alluded. Once, when I was in Riyadh and feeling somewhat frustrated because of the over-exaggerated support which the senior senator from the state of Washington was displaying for Israel, I asked, half-jestingly, if His Majesty had ever considered buying the Boeing Corporation and then inviting Senator Jackson to Riyadh to discuss Middle Eastern policy. Fayṣal startled me by taking my suggestion with deadly seriousness. 'Yes, we have considered it, but we can't do it'. Not knowing quite where the conversation was heading, I inquired hesitantly, 'Why not?' He said, 'We would be put under great pressure, both internally, and in the Arab world beyond, by leftists and radicals'. I still failed to grasp the drift of what he was getting at and asked something like, 'How so?' He said, 'Well, they would accuse us of putting our money in to support the American economy, and since America does not take a very friendly attitude toward some matters which are of great interest to the Arab world, they would resent it'. Since I had approached the whole question from a kind of a reverse point of view, I was startled by the response, but it did indicate both that King Fayṣal was thinking far ahead and that he had to worry about considerations that had not occurred to me.

This point leads me to ask a question or make an observation more relevant to Western, especially American, government officials and influential citizens than to King Fayṣal. As long as I knew him, I seldom had a conversation which did not touch on the Palestine problem. The 'Twin Evils'[7] speech aside, it was clear to me and presumably to others that Fayṣal felt very strongly about Palestine and Israel. And yet it was equally clear to me from many conversations with officials of the Department of State and with involved businessmen and academic colleagues that they dismissed what he said. The implication of their reaction was usually: 'Well, the Saudis, after all, are only paying lip service to this cause. They are ultraconservatives unlikely ever to take any effective action on the matter', etc., etc. The following considerations may contribute to an understanding of why people in various walks of life did not take Saudi Arabia or King Fayṣal seriously. Firstly, the orientation of the Middle East 'establishment', whether academic, governmental or even business has until recently been toward the Arab countries of the eastern Mediterranean. Baghdad, Beirut, Cairo and Damascus were where and what they had studied and where mediaeval and early modern Arab history had unfolded. Arabia was a backwater of little interest. Secondly, because Saudi Arabia *was* a conservative region, and 'we' all considered ourselves progressive, there was a stereotyping which ended up in 'our' viewing Saudis as feudal, corrupt and, hence, not serious. Thirdly, most of those who heard King Fayṣal and others of his countrymen speak about the problems of the world had no knowledge of the depth of Saudi and Wahhābī history – of the strength of purpose of that twin-engined machine. Finally, it is my impression that those who dismissed Fayṣal in a cavalier way had either never read, or worse, had misread the man's character, strength of will, subtlety, and high intelligence. It is always tempting to dismiss what people in authority say when one's own interest runs counter to their view, but my own hope is that some lesson will have been learned by the issues and events of 1973–74 and that in the future at least all opinions will be treated as serious ones deserving serious consideration. After all, King Fayṣal financed a war, imposed an embargo, and significantly changed the world by raising the price of oil. If his oft-repeated words had been taken seriously, the world would at least have made realistic calculations.

The last major point I would like to stress and possibly the most revealing aspect of King Fayṣal as a man, as a monarch, and as a Muslim has to do with his attitude toward *education*. Islam is an intellectual culture. Its adherents are 'People of the Book'. Its genius, aside from theology, has been its intellectual attainment. The Prophetic *ḥadīth* or Tradition, *Uṭlub al-'ilm wa-law fī 'l-Ṣīn* ('seek knowledge even in China') is a Leitmotif of the drive of Muslims to educate themselves, their families, and their people through the centuries.

Two concrete aspects stick in my mind. The first is the opening of the first regular[8] girls' school in 'Unayzah. The story is familiar. The school was opened. There was a conservative outcry against it. The school was closed and stayed closed for about a year, as I remember it. Then, following quiet pressure from those who wanted their daughters educated, the school was reopened without a murmur from the conservatives. Several quick lessons are implicit in these bare facts. Fayṣal wanted to have the school opened, or put in other words, he favoured the education of girls at a time when probably a majority were, if not hostile to the idea, at least not strongly in favour of it. Secondly, we also observe the patient way that he went about achieving what he wanted without tearing at the social fabric. It represented in one area Fayṣal's virtue of *ḫilm*, a quality related to *ṣabr*, but emphasising clemency and forbearance toward others.

At a much more personal level, I would like to illustrate Fayṣal's attitude toward the education of his own sons. I refer to his sons after his oldest son, ʿAbd Allāh. As I understand it, his next eldest son, Muḥammad, accompanied his father to the United States in 1948 and fell in love with the country. During the course of the next year, a considerable dialogue of the kind with which all parents and children are familiar took place between Muḥammad and his father. The gist of it was that Muḥammad wanted to come to the United States to study, but that Fayṣal was not much in favour of that course. He wanted Muḥammad to study in England. In time, Fayṣal, who had by now established confidence in Jamīl Bārūdī, asked Jamīl to prepare for him a plan for the education of his children. Jamīl prepared an initial plan which involved a choice between a secondary school in Beirut or one in Cairo. 'After which I told ... Prince Faisel it would be appropriate to send them to British or American Universities. He told me that they might be spoiled by courtiers in Beirut or Cairo, and both he and his wife asked me if I had any objection to supervise their high school education in America. This is how it happened that I took charge of them'.[9] Jamīl evolved a plan for Prince Fayṣal's sons to attend the Hun School in Princeton. The advantage was that they would be close enough for the Hittis in Princeton and Ambassador Bārūdī in New York to exercise over them a certain amount of supervision *in loco parentis*, but on their own enough to grow up, and perhaps more importantly, in a learning environment which would minimise the princelings' background. The plan had an additional feature designed to safeguard against the possibility of loss of knowledge of the native language and culture, a possibility which could happen all too easily given the sustained absences in the United States that would be required of the boys. The solution found to this problem was to arrange for them to take regular instruction in Arabic and Arab history and culture from Professor Hitti.

Fayṣal accepted this plan not only because of its objective advantages but also no doubt because its managers were Jamīl Bārūdī and Philip Hitti, both of whom he knew and trusted. It went forward in a steady way. The boys attended Hun School and once or twice a week, as the case may have been, Mrs Hitti would get in her car, drive over to the Hun School, collect the boys and deliver them to 144 Prospect Avenue for a couple of hours of that peculiar form of punishment, from which all of Professor Hitti's graduate students had also benefitted, namely, learning the intricacies of the grammar of the 'tongue of the angels' and of the history of those who spoke with the *ḍād – i.e.*, the Arabs. Jamīl also came frequently to Princeton to either encourage his charges or, occasionally, to put in a good word for them with either a disciplinary or an academic dean. In due course the boys grew into young men and went off to pursue higher education whether in California, in Princeton, at Oxford and Cambridge, Sandhurst, or elsewhere, and today this band of brothers has risen to very high places in the Kingdom, whether in government or in the private sector.

It is no insult to Saudi Arabia to note that as far as I am aware the first Saudi subject to receive advanced Western education was as late as the time of Shaykh ʿAbd Allāh Bālkhayr, who attended the American University of Beirut in the early 1940s and who, as a result of having English, served as translator, especially of war-time news broadcasts, for King ʿAbd al-ʿAzīz and subsequently as Minister of Information under King Suʿūd. When Fayṣal's sons, Prince Muḥammad, Prince Khālid, Prince Suʿūd, Prince Saʿd, Prince Bandar, Prince ʿAbd al-Raḥmān, and Prince Turkī began to return to the Kingdom a decade and a half after ʿAbd Allāh Bālkhayr's time, they were better qualified and more competent than most of their fellow subjects. This result was no doubt what Fayṣal had in mind. Fayṣal's decision to send his sons abroad was at once innovative and farsighted, not only for his sons, but also for his country. He was certainly the first highly placed person in Saudi Arabia who deliberately set out to educate his sons *en masse* in a way which combined not only knowledge of traditional learning, but also the most modern education, and it cannot have been easy for a traditionally raised Najdī to separate himself from his male children in such a mass way. However, starting with his youthful travels to London and Europe, including Moscow, Fayṣal b. ʿAbd al-ʿAzīz had learned that there was a horizon beyond that of the desert which his great grandfather described to Louis Pelly. He understood that to function in the world of television, supersonic planes and earth-girdling satellites, not only his own children, but all the subjects of the kingdom would have to have a training relevant to the world into which Saudi Arabia was rapidly emerging. It is fortunate for all that he set a pattern and established a leadership in education which served as a persuasive model for his fellow Arabians.

Let me start my conclusion by switching attention from the categories I have been using, such as sense of humour, frankness, gentlemanliness, sincerity and the like to certain other characteristics which Arabians, Arabs, and Muslims have throughout the ages held in the highest regard as the measure of a man. Let us summarily measure Fayṣal b. ʿAbd al-ʿAzīz on this scale as well: *ḍiyāfah* (hospitality) is a characteristic that Fayṣal had. There is no need for me to elaborate on it here beyond reiterating that I personally had the good fortune to enjoy his gracious hospitality, as, indeed, did most people who knew him. *Ḥamāsah* (fortitude and enthusiasm) is evident in his military campaigns, whether directly, as when he led those 40,000 troops into the Yemen, or indirectly, as when he gave his blessing to the undoubtedly highly risky operations which constituted the Ramaḍān War of 1973. *Murūʾah* (manliness) is a more inclusive term than those above and one which his life exemplified *par excellence*. *Mulk* (kingship) is an ambiguous term in Islamic history. The Umayyads were charged with introducing this foreign concept into the purely Islamic polity which had informed the early decades of Islam. But that is an issue settled long ago, and if Imam Fayṣal b. Turkī speaking to Pelly in 1866 could say, 'We feel ourselves a king every inch', how much more could King Fayṣal b. 'Abd al-'Azīz have said the same thing? But his *mulk* was always tempered by his *ḥilm*, by that lack of vengeance seeking and that willingness to forgive which enabled him to achieve the respect and, more difficult, the love of the vast majority of his subjects. Of *ṣabr* (tenacity or endurance) I have already spoken at length. Here one should perhaps only stress that the incidents I cited were mere examples. Fayṣal surely dealt with numerous other problems, including his personal medical problems in the same stoic, dignified manner. The ancient Arabian virtue, *'aṣabiyyah* (tribalness, clannishness), is a quality which today has come to have the negative sense of extreme chauvinism or exclusive clannishness, but if one defines the term differently, stressing loyalty to one's own, it still takes on a positive value. Whether one thinks of Fayṣal's immediate family, the House of Su'ūd broadly conceived, Arabs in general, or Muslims in general, Fayṣal spent his life inculcating that kind of *'aṣabiyyah*. *Nasab* (noble ancestry) is another characteristic held in high esteem in the Near East as elsewhere. The Āl Su'ūd have ruled in Arabia since well before the establishment of the United States of America. Back beyond that, the Saudi *nasab* is as impeccable as any. In terms of these Arabian qualities, Fayṣal rated about as high on the scale as a man could.

Whatever his rating on these scales, as King Fayṣal grew older and his mortality became more evident, I am sure that he thought more in terms other than those I have introduced above. I feel confident that what was most important to this man was *Islām*. I here use the word somewhat in its lower case sense of 'full submission to God,' being the chief characteristic of a Muslim, rather than in the formalistic sense of adherence to a religion. It would be highly pretentious for me to examine the degree to which this man-made Muslim monarch carried out the personal requirements of his faith whether in terms of *praxis* or *doxis*, but I state my conviction that, no matter how great his achievements were in regard to *al-dunyā* (this world), they were not greater than those he achieved in regard to what for him would have been the most important thing, *al-ākhirah* (the other world).

In closing, I would like to submit the following quotation:

> 'In [him] the sense of finesse politique was developed to a degree, probably higher than in any other [ruler] . . . . his supreme virtue was his *ḥilm*, that unusual ability to resort to force only when force was absolutely necessary and to use peaceful measures in all other instances. His prudent mildness by which he tried to disarm the enemy and shame the opposition, his slowness to anger and his absolute self-control left him under all circumstances master of the situation. "I apply not my sword," he is reported to have declared, "where my lash suffices, nor my

lash where my tongue is enough. And even if there be one hair binding me to my fellowmen, I do not let it break: when they pull, I loosen, if they loosen, I pull"'.

There is hardly a person to whom this quotation is more appropriate than Fayṣal b. 'Abd al-'Azīz b. 'Abd al-Raḥmān b. Fayṣal b. Turkī Āl Su'ūd unless it be his father. The actual quotation was written by Philip Hitti about Mu'āwiyah b. Abī Sufyān.[10]

Finally, I cannot refrain from calling to mind the lines of Hamlet, speaking of his slain father:

He was a man, take him for all and all.
I shall not look upon his like again.

Raḥimahu Allāh ta'ālā.

Notes

[1] Pelly, *Report on a journey to the Wahabee Capital* . . . ., Bombay, 1866, 7.
[2] Op. cit.
[3] Others in the Saudi party were Shaykh 'Abd Allāh Bālkhayr, then secretary to Fayṣal and Shaykh Ḥāfiẓ Wahbah, Ambassador to the Court of St. James.
[4] 12 November, 1943.
[5] Jamīl Bārūdī, personal communication.
[6] *The Princeton Herald*, 12 November, 1943.
[7] Towards the end of Fayṣal's life, his oft-repeated remarks that Zionism and Communism constituted the major dangers confronting the world were so dubbed by those who had heard them a number of times.
[8] The very first school for girls was privately established through the encouragement and generosity of Queen 'Iffat and was for orphan girls.
[9] Jamīl Bārūdī, personal communication.
[10] *History of the Arabs*, 197. We can *almost* apply the rest of Professor Hitti's paragraph, which concerns a presumed letter to al-Ḥasan from Mu'āwiyah after the latter had taken power, to the situation when Fayṣal took power from his brother: 'I admit that because of thy blood relationship, thou art more entitled to this high office than I. And if I were sure of thy greater ability to fulfil the duties involved, I would unhesitatingly swear allegiance to thee. Now then, ask what thou wilt'. Enclosed was a blank for al-Ḥasan to fill in, already signed by Mu'āwiyah.

Published works of Robert Bertram Serjeant

J. D. Pearson

What follows is a catalogue, as complete as I could make it, of the published writings of R. B. Serjeant, in the form of books, articles in periodicals, *Sammelbände*, reference books and an encyclopaedia. This is followed by a list of his book reviews submitted to the Bulletin of the School of Oriental and African Studies and the Journal of the Royal Asiatic Society. A great deal more of his work is embodied in the dissertations presented by his students for doctoral degrees in London and Cambridge, which it has not been possible to enumerate.

Books and Articles

Abbreviations

BSOAS	Bulletin of the School of Oriental and African Studies
IC	Islamic culture
IQ	Islamic quarterly
JNES	Journal of Near Eastern Studies
JRAS	Journal of the Royal Asiatic Society
JSS	Journal of Semitic Studies
RSO	Rivista degli studi orientali

1942

'The dhows of Aden'. *Geog. mag.* 14 (1942), 296–301.

A handlist of the Arabic, Persian and Hindustani MSS. of New College, Edinburgh. London: Luzac, 1942.

'Material for a history of Islamic textiles up to the Mongol conquest.' *Ars Islamica*, 9 (1942), 54–92; 10 (1943), 71–104; 11 (1946), 98–135; 13–14 (1948), 75–117.

'The mountain tribes of the Yemen'. *Geog. mag.* 15 (1942), 66–72.

1944

'Al-adab al-ʿaṣrī fī'l-janūb al-gharbī li-shibh jazīrat al-ʿarab?' *Al-Adab wa'l-fann* 2 ii (1944), 22–34; 2 iii (1944), 13–24.

'Al-mansūjāt fī ʿahd al-khilāfa al-islāmiyya.' *Al-Adab wa'l-fann* 2 i (1944), 2–11.

'A rare Ottoman MS. with two contemporary portraits of Murad III.' *IC* 18 (1944), 15–18.

'Yemeni Arabs in Britain'. *Geog. mag.* 17 (1944), 143–147.

1944 or 1945

Translation of the Charter of the Arab League for the Ministry of Information.

1945

'Al-ʿālam al-islāmī fī ʿahdihi 'l-awwal wa'l-khazaf al-ṣīnī.' *Al-Adab wa'l fann* 3 i (1945), 14–26.

1946

'The ʿAudhali treaty'. *Western Arabia and the Red Sea*, Naval Intelligence Division, pr. Oxford 1946 (BR 527 Geographical handbook series), 587–589.

1947

The Arabs. Harmondsworth: Penguin Books, 1947. (A Puffin book, 61).

1948

(With A. Lane.) 'Pottery and glass fragments from the Aden littoral, with historical notes.' *JRAS*, 1948, 108–133 (reprinted in Aden, *Dept. of Antiquities Bull.* no. 5, 1965).

'"Cant" in contemporary South-Arabic dialect.' *Trans. Philol. Soc.*, 1948, 121–126.

1949

'Building and builders in Ḥaḍramawt'. *Muséon*, 62 (1949), 275–284.

'The cemeteries of Tarīm (Ḥaḍramawt). (With notes on sepulture.)' *Muséon* 62 (1949), 151–160.

'Hunger in Hadramawt. Problems of overcrowding in Southern Arabia.' *The Times*, 16 Sept. 1949.

'Two Yemenite *djinn*.' *BSOAS* 13 (1949), 4–6.

(With G. M. Wickens.) 'The Wahhabis in Western Arabia in 1803–04 A.D.' *IC* 23 (1949), 308–311.

1950

(With C. F. Beckingham.) 'A journey by two Jesuits from Dhufār to Sanʿā in 1590.' *Geog. J.* 115 (1950), 194–207.

'Materials for South Arabian history. Notes on new MSS. from Ḥaḍramawt.' *BSOAS* 13 (1950) 281–307, 581–601.

'The quarters of Tarīm and their tanṣūrahs.' *Muséon* 63 (1950), 277–284.

1951

South Arabian poetry, I: Prose and poetry from Ḥaḍramawt. Edited, collated and corrected with an introductory preface. London: Taylor's Foreign Press, 1951.

'Two tribal law cases (documents). (Wāḥidī Sultanate, South-west Arabia.)' *JRAS* 1951, 33–47, 156–169.

1953

'A battle axe from Ḥabbān, Wāḥidī Sultanate, Aden Protectorate.' *Man* 53 (1953), 120–121.

'A Judeo-Arab house-deed from Ḥabbān (with notes on the former Jewish communities of the Wāḥidī Sultanate).' *JRAS*, 1953, 117–131.

'Notes on Ṣubaiḥi territory, West of Aden.' *Muséon* 66 (1953), 123–131.

'A Zaidi manual of ḥisbah of the 3rd century (H).' *RSO* 28 (1953), 1–34.

1954

'Hūd and other pre-Islamic prophets of Ḥaḍramawt.' *Muséon* 67 (1954), 121–179.

'Star-calendars and an almanac from South-West Arabia.' *Anthropos* 49 (1954), 433–459.

1955

'Forms of plea, a Šāfiʿī manual from Al-Šihr.' *RSO* 30 (1955), 1–15.

'What's wrong in the Aden Protectorate.' *Spectator* 195 (15 July 1955), 90.

1956

'Folk-remedies from Ḥaḍramawt.' *BSOAS* 18 (1956), 5–8.

1957

(With Cl. Cahen.) 'A fiscal survey of the medieval Yemen. Notes preparatory to an edition of the *Mulaḫḫaṣ al-fitan* of Al-Ḥasan b. ʿAlī al-Šarīf al-Ḥusaynī.' *Arabica* 4 (1957), 23–33.

'Majmūʿ khaṭṭī fī Ḥaḍramawt.' *Majallat Maʿhad al-Makhṭūṭāt al-ʿArabiyya* 3 (1957), 341–342.

The Saiyids of Ḥaḍramawt. An inaugural lecture delivered on 5 June 1956. London: School of Oriental and African Studies, 1957.

1958

'Professor A. Guillaume's translation of the Sīrah.' *BSOAS* 21 (1958), 1–14.

'Two sixteenth-century Arabian geographical works.' *BSOAS* 21 (1958), 254–275.

'A new map of Southern Arabia, 2: The problem of the place-names.' *Geog. J.* 124 (1958), 167–171.

1959

'A metal padlock and keys from Southern Arabia.' *Man* 59 (1959), 49.

'*Miḥrāb*.' *BSOAS* 22 (1959), 439–453.

'Saint Sergius.' *BSOAS* 22 (1959), 574–575.

(With E. Wagner.) 'A sixteenth-century reference to Shaḥrī dialect at Ẓufār.' *BSOAS* 22 (1959), 128–132.

'Tribes of the Eastern Protectorate. Arab nationalism and anti-colonialism are growing influences in politics.' *The Times British Colonies R.* 33 (1st qr., 1959), 11.

'Ukhdūd.' *BSOAS* 22 (1959), 572–573.

1961

'The Maʿn "gypsies" of the West Aden Protectorate.' *Anthropos* 56 (1961), 737–749.

1962

'Ḥaram and Ḥawṭah, the sacred enclave in Arabia.' *Mélanges Taha Husain*, Le Caire, 1962, 41–58.

'Historians and historiography of Ḥaḍramawt.' *BSOAS* 25 (1962), 239–261.

'A note on rock drawings from Wādī Hirjāb, reported by G. F. Walford, Esq.' *BSOAS* 25 (1962), 149.

'Recent marriage legislation from al-Mukallā, with notes on marriage customs.' *BSOAS* 25 (1962), 472–498.

'Sex, birth, circumcision: some notes from South-west Arabia.' *Hermann von Wissmann-Festschrift*, Tübingen, 1962, 193–208.

1963

The Portuguese off the South Arabian coast. Ḥaḍramī chronicles. Oxford: Clarendon Press, 1963.

1964

'The "Constitution of Medina".' *IQ* 8 (1964), 3–16.

'Heiligenverehrung in Südwestarabien.' *Bustan*, 1964, ii, 16–23.

'Some irrigation systems in Ḥaḍramawt.' *BSOAS* 27 (1964), 33–76.

'Yemen letter: the king's story.' *New society* 100 (27 August 1964), 24–25.

1965

'Arabic poetry.' *Encyclopaedia of poetry and poetics*, ed. A. Preminger, Princeton 1965, 42–47.

'Notices on the "Frankish chancre" (syphilis) in Yemen, Egypt, and Persia.' *JSS* 10 (1965), 241–252.

1966

'South Arabia and Ethiopia – African elements in the South Arabian population'. *Proc. 3rd Int. conf. Ethiopian studies*, 1966, 25–33.

1967

'Kinship terms in Wādī Ḥaḍramawt.' *Der Orient in der Forschung. Festschrift für O. Spies*, Wiesbaden, 1967, 626–633.

'Société et gouvernement en Arabie du Sud.' *Arabica* 14 (1967), 284–297.

'Yemen inside out.' *Guardian*, 26 Jan. 1967, 8.

1968

'Fisher-folk and fish-traps in al-Baḥrain.' *BSOAS* 31 (1968), 486–514.

1969

'Historical review'. *Religion in the Middle East*, General editor: A. J. Arberry, Cambridge, 1969, vol. 2, 3–30; bibliography, 671–672.

'In memoriam: Professor Charles Ambrose Storey.' *IC* 43 (1969), i–ii.

'The Zaydis.' *Religion in the Middle East*, General editor: A. J. Arberry, Cambridge, 1969, vol. 2, 285–301; bibliography, 682–683.

1970

'Maritime customary law off the Arabian coasts.' *Sociétés et compagnies de commerce en Orient et dans l'Océan indien*, Paris, 1970, 195–207.

'Obituary: Professor Arthur John Arberry.' *JRAS* 1970, 96–98.

1971

'Agriculture and horticulture: some cultural interchanges of the medieval Arabs and Europe.' *Oriente e Occidente nel medioevo*, 1971, 535–548.

'Arabic literature.' *The Middle East; a handbook*, ed. by Michael Adams, London, 1971, 535–542.

'The "White Dune" at Abyan: an ancient place of pilgrimage in Southern Arabia.' *JSS* 16 (1971), 74–83.

'The Republic of South Yemen.' *The Middle East; a handbook*, ed. by Michael Adams, London, 1971, 91–94; bibliography, 263–270.

'Yemen.' *The Middle East; a handbook*, ed. by Michael Adams, London, 1971, 130–132; bibliography, 335–341.

1973

'The two Yemens: historical perspectives and present attitudes.' *Asian affairs* NS 4 (1973), 3–16.

1974

(With M.A.G[hul].) 'Arabia, history of.' *Enc. Brit.*, 15th ed., 1974, vol. 1, 1043–1051.

'The cultivation of cereals in mediaeval Yemen. A translation of the *Bughyat al-fallāḥīn* of the Rasūlid Sultan, al-Malik al-Afḍal al-ʿAbbās b. ʿAlī, composed circa 1370 A.D.' *Arabian studies* 1 (1974), 25–74.

'Porcupines in the Yemen,' *Arabian studies* 1 (1974), 180.

'The ports of Aden and Shihr (medieval period).' *Recueils Société Jean Bodin* 32 (1974), 207–224.

1975

(With B. Doe.) 'A fortified tower-house in Wādī Jirdān (Wāḥidī Sultanate).' *BSOAS* 38 (1975), 1–23, 276–295.

1976

'Introduction' [and contributions to] *City of Sanʿā*, ed. J. Kirkman, London, 1976, 7–17.

'Notes on some aspects of Arab business practices in Aden.' *Al-Bahit, Festschrift J. Henninger*, St. Augustin bei Bonn, 1976, 309–315.

South Arabian hunt. London: Luzac, 1976.

1977

'Customary law documents as a source of history.' *Studies in the history of Arabia.* Proc. 1st Int. Symp. Studies Hist. Arabia, 1977, vol. 1, pt. 2, 1979, 99–103.

'South Arabia.' *Commoners, climbers and notables*, ed. C. A. O. van Nieuwenhuijze, Leiden, 1977, 226–247.

1978

'Historical sketch of the Gulf in the Islamic era from the seventh to the eighteenth century A.D., *Qatar archaeological report, excavations 1973*, ed. B. de Cardi, London, 1978, 147–163.

'The *Sunnah Jāmiʿah*, pacts with the Yat͟hrib Jews and the *Taḥrīm* of Yat͟hrib: analysis and translation of the documents comprised in the so-called "Constitution of Medina".' *BSOAS* 41 (1978), 1–42.

'Wards and quarters of towns in South-West Arabia.' *Storia della città* 7 (1978), 43–48.

1979

'Perilous politics in two Yemen states.' *Geog. Mag.* 51 (1979), 769–774.

'The Yemeni poet Al-Zubayrī and his polemic against the Zaydī Imāms.' *Arabian studies* 5 (1979), 87–130.

1980

'Introduction.' *Le Coran : traduction et notes de M. Kazimirski*, Paris: Haso Ebeling, 7–20.

'Customary law among the fishermen of al-Shiḥr.' *Middle East studies and libraries : a felicitation volume for J. D. Pearson*, 1980, 193–203.

(ed.) *The Islamic city.* Selected papers from the colloquium held at the Middle East Centre, Faculty of Oriental Studies, Cambridge . . . from 19 to 23 July 1976. Paris: Unesco, 1980.

'Social stratification in Arabia.' *The Islamic city*, ed. by R. B. Serjeant, Paris, Unesco, 1980, 126–147.

1981

(With Ḥusayn al-ʿAmrī.) 'A Yemenite agricultural poem.' *Studia Arabica et Islamica, Festschrift for Iḥsān ʿAbbās*, Beirut, 1981, 407–427.

'Islam.' *Divination and oracles*, ed. M. Loewe and C. Blacker, London; Allen & Unwin, 1981, 215–232.

Studies in Arabian history and civilisation, London: Variorum Reprints, 1981.

'A maqāma on palm protection (shirāḥa).' *JNES* 40 (Nabia Abbot Festschrift volume, Chicago, 1981) pp. 307–322.

1982

(ed. with Ronald Lewcock) *Ṣan'ā': an Arabian Islamic city*, London: Scorpion Press for World of Islam Festival Trust, 1982.

'Ḥaḍramawt to Zanzibar: the pilot-poem of Nākhudhā Sa'īd Bā Ṭāyi' of al-Ḥāmī.' *Festschrift for James Kirkman*, (*Paideum* 28).

Periodically

(ed. with Robin Bidwell) *Arabian studies*

Annually

'Islam.' *The Middle East and North Africa*, London: Europa Publications.

Book Reviews

1949–51

J. Spencer Trimingham: *Islam in the Sudan*. London, 1949. *BSOAS* 13 (1949–51), 779–80.

1952

Oscar Löfgren: *Arabische Texte zur Kenntnis der Stadt Aden im Mittelalter, II: Biographien, Zweite Hälfte, Glossar*. Uppsala, 1950. *BSOAS* 14 (1952), 181–183.

1955

Jacques Ryckmans: *L'institution monarchique en Arabie méridionale avant l'Islam (Ma'în et Sabâ)*. Louvain, 1951. *BSOAS* 17 (1955), 167–168.

1956

R. Bayly Winder and Farhat J. Ziadeh: *An introduction to modern Arabic*. Princeton, 1955. *BSOAS* 18 (1956), 377.

1957

H. T. Norris and F. W. Penhey: *An archaeological and historical survey of the Aden Tanks*. London, 1955. *BSOAS* 19 (1957), 174–175.

Wendell Phillips: *Qataban and Sheba: exploring ancient kingdoms on the Biblical spice routes of Arabia*. London, 1955. *BSOAS* 19 (1957), 175–177.

Ṣalāh al-Dīn al-Munajjid (ed.): *Ṣalāh al-Dīn al-Ṣafadī, Umarā' Dimashq fi'l-Islām*. Damascus, 1955. *JRAS*, 1957, 242–243.

1958

W. Montgomery Watt: *Muḥammad at Medina*. Oxford, 1956. *BSOAS* 21 (1958), 187–188.

Wilhelm Hoenerbach (ed.): *Die vulgärarabische Poetik al-Kitāb al-'Āṭil al-ḥālī wal-muraḥḥaṣ al-gālī des Ṣafīyaddīn Ḥillī*. Wiesbaden, 1956. *BSOAS* 21 (1958), 405–407.

Pierre Cachia: *Ṭahā Ḥusayn: his place in the Egyptian literary renaissance*. London, 1956. *BSOAS* 21 (1958), 411–412.

C. J. Edmonds: *Kurds, Turks and Arabs: politics, travel and research in north-eastern Iraq, 1919–1925*. Oxford U.P., 1957. *BSOAS* 21 (1958), 414–415.

Philippe Lippens: *Expédition en Arabie centrale*. Paris, 1956. *BSOAS* 21 (1958), 629–630.

A. S. Tritton: *Materials on Muslim education in the Middle Ages*. London, 1957. *JRAS*, 1958, 192–193.

1959

H. A. R. Gibb: *The travels of Ibn Baṭṭūṭa, A.D. 1325–1354, translated with revisions and notes from the Arabic text edited by C. Defrémery and B. R. Sanguinetti, Vol. 1*. Cambridge, 1958. *BSOAS* 22 (1959), 145–146.

P. M. Holt: *The Mahdist state in the Sudan, 1881–1898: a study of its origins, development and overthrow*. Oxford, 1958. *BSOAS* 22 (1959), 146–147.

Hans Wehr (ed.): *Das Buch der wunderbaren Erzählungen und seltsamen Geschichten, mit Benutzung der Vorarbeiten von A. von Bulmerincq*. Wiesbaden, 1956. *BSOAS* 22 (1959), 188.

Farhat J. Ziadeh and R. Bayly Winder: *An introduction to modern Arabic*. Princeton, N.J., 1957. *BSOAS* 22 (1959), 582.

Hans Wehr (ed.): *Arabisches Wörterbuch für die Schriftsprache der Gegenwart. Dritte, unveränderte Auflage*. Wiesbaden, 1958. – *Supplement*, 1959. *BSOAS* 22 (1959), 582–583.

Wadie Jwaideh (tr.): *The introductory chapters of Yāqūt's Mu'jam al-buldān*. Leiden, 1959. *BSOAS* 22 (1959), 583–584.

J. Spencer Trimingham: *Islam in West Africa*. Oxford, 1959. *BSOAS* 22 (1959), 607–608.

1960

Richard LeBaron Bowen, Jr. and Frank P. Albright: *Archaeological discoveries in South Arabia*. Baltimore [1958]. *BSOAS* 23 (1960), 582–585.

1961

Franz Rosenthal (tr.): *Ibn Khaldūn: the Muqaddimah: an introduction to history*. 3 vols. *BSOAS* 24 (1961), 143–144.

1962

'Abdullāh al-Ṭaiyib: *Muḥādarāt fī'l-ittijāhāt al-ḥadīthah fī'l-nathr al-'arabī fī'l-Sūdān*. Cairo, 1959. *BSOAS* 25 (1962), 413.

Jörg Kraemer and Helmut Gätje: *Wörterbuch der klassischen arabischen Sprache auf Grund der Sammlungen von August Fischer, Theodor Nöldeke, Hermann Reckendorf und anderer Quellen herausgegeben durch die Deutsche Morgenländische Gesellschaft*. 1–2 Lieferung[en]. Wiesbaden, 1957, 1960. *BSOAS* 25 (1962), 341.

Hans Wehr: *A dictionary of modern written Arabic*. Edited by J. Milton Cowan. Wiesbaden, 1961. *BSOAS* 25 (1962) 341–342.

M. C. Lyons (comp.): *An elementary classical Arabic reader*. Cambridge, 1962. *BSOAS* 25 (1962), 342–343.

George T. Scanlon (ed. and tr.): *A Muslim manual of war: being Tafrīj al-kurūb fī tadbīr al-ḥurūb, by 'Umar ibn Ibrāhīm al-Awsī al-Anṣārī*. Cairo, 1961. *BSOAS* 25 (1962), 348.

Leon Zolondek: *Di'bil b. 'Alī: the life & writings of an early 'Abbāsid poet.* Lexington, Ky [1961]. *BSOAS* 25 (1962), 349–350.

Lein Oebele Schumann: *Political history of the Yemen at the beginning of the 16th century: Abū Makhrama's account of the years 906–927 H. (1500–1521 A.D.) with annotations.* Groningen [1960]. *BSOAS* 25 (1962), 350–351.

1963

Alfred Guillaume: *New light on the life of Muḥammad.* Manchester [1960]. *BSOAS* 26 (1963), 427–428.

J. M. S. Baljon: *Modern Muslim Koran interpretation (1880–1960).* Leiden, 1961. *BSOAS* 26 (1963), 428.

H. A. R. Gibb (tr.): *The travels of Ibn Baṭṭūṭa, A.D. 1325–1354, translated with revisions and notes from the Arabic text edited by C. Defrémery and B.R. Sanguinetti, Vol. II.* Cambridge, 1962. *BSOAS* 26 (1963), 655–657.

J. Spencer Trimingham: *A history of Islam in West Africa.* Oxford U.P., 1962. *BSOAS* 26 (1963), 678–679.

1964

Nada Tomiche (ed. & tr.): *Ibn Ḥazm: épitre morale (Kitāb al-aḥlāq wa-l-siyar).* Beyrouth: Commission Internationale pour la Traduction des Chefs-d'Ouevre, 1961. *BSOAS* 27 (1964), 168–169.

Mohammed Mostafa (ed.): *Die Chronik des Ibn Ijās. Vierter Teil, A.H. 906–921/A.D. 1501–1515.* 2.Aufl. Wiesbaden, 1960. *BSOAS* 27 (1964), 169.

Salāma Mūsā: *The education of Salāma Mūsā (Tarbīyat Salāma Mūsā), translated from the Arabic by L. O. Schuman.* Leiden, 1961. *BSOAS* 27 (1964), 169–170.

1965

M. J. L. Hardy: *Blood feuds and the payment of blood money in the Middle East.* Beirut, 1963. *BSOAS* 28 (1965), 395–396.

J. Kritzeck (ed.): *Anthology of Islamic literature.* London, 1964. *JRAS*, 1965, 92–93.

1966

G. S. P. Freeman-Grenville: *The French at Kilwa island: an episode in eighteenth-century East African history.* *BSOAS* 29 (1966), 433–434.

1968

J. H. Kramers and G. Wiet (tr.): *Ibn Hauqal: Configuration de la terre (Kitāb ṣūrat al-'ard).* Beyrouth, Paris [1965]. *BSOAS* 31 (1968), 149–150.

Walter J. Fischel: *Ibn Khaldūn in Egypt, his public function and his historical research (1382–1406): a study in Islamic historiography.* Berkeley & Los Angeles, 1967. *BSOAS* 31 (1968), 150–151.

P. J. Vatikiotis: *Politics and the military in Jordan: a study of the Arab Legion, 1921–1957.* London, 1967. *BSOAS* 31 (1968), 155–156.

Werner Caskel: *Gamharat an-nasab: das generalogische Werk des Hišam ibn Muḥammad al-Kalbī.* 2 vols. Leiden, 1966. *BSOAS* 31 (1968), 616–617.

Ewald Wagner: *Abū Nuwās: eine Studie zur arabischen Literatur der frühen*

'Abbāsidenzeit. Wiesbaden, 1965. *BSOAS* 31 (1968), 617–618.

Fazlur Rahman. *Islam*. London, 1966. *JRAS*, 1968, 76–77.

1969

Francesco Gabrieli: *Muḥammad and the conquests of Islam*. Transl. by Virginia Luling and Rosamund Linell. London, 1968. *JRAS*, 1969, 172–173.

H. T. Norris: *Shinqīṭī folk literature and song*. Oxford, 1968. *JRAS*, 1969, 177–179.

1970

Manfred W. Wenner: *Modern Yemen, 1918–1966*. Baltimore [1967]. *BSOAS* 33 (1970), 211–214.

Hubert Daunicht: *Der Osten nach der Erdkarte al-Ḥuwārizmīs: Beiträge zur historischen Geographie und Geschichte Asiens. Bd.1 : Rekonstruktion der Karte, Interpretation der Karte : Südasien*. Bonn, 1968. *BSOAS* 33 (1970), 617–618.

1971

Isma'īl Qurbān Ḥusain [I. K. Poonawala] (ed.): *al-Sulṭān al-Khaṭṭāb: ḥayātuhu wa-shi'ru-hu*. Cairo [1969]. *BSOAS* 34 (1971), 146–147.

Walter Dostal: *Die Beduinen in Südarabien : eine ethnologische Studie zur Entwicklung der Kamelhirtenkultur in Arabien*. Wien, 1967. *JRAS*, 1971, 65–66.

Donald Foster: *Landscape with Arabs : travels in Aden and South Arabia*. Brighton, 1969. *JRAS*, 1971, 66.

1972

J. D. Latham and W. F. Paterson: *Saracen archery : an English version and exposition of a Mameluke work on archery (ca. A.D. 1368)*. London [1970]. *BSOAS* 35 (1972), 146–147.

H. A. R. Gibb (tr.): *The travels of Ibn Baṭṭūṭa, A.D. 1325–1354*. Vol. III. Cambridge, 1971. *BSOAS* 35 (1972), 628–629.

Franz Rosenthal: *The herb : hashish versus medieval Muslim society*. Leiden, 1971. *BSOAS* 35 (1972), 633–636.

Wahib Atallah (ed. & tr.): *Les idoles de Hicham ibn al-Kalbi*. Paris, 1969. *JRAS*, 1972, 150–151.

1974

Max Schoessinger (ed.): *The Ansāb al-ashrāf of al-Balādhurī. Vol. 4A*. Revised and annotated by M. J. Kister. Jerusalem, 1971. *BSOAS* 37 (1974), 227–228.

Ewald Wagner (ed.): *Der Diwan des Abū Nuwās. Teil II*. Wiesbaden, 1972. *BSOAS* 37 (1974), 229–230.

J. D. Pearson: *Index Islamicus, third supplement 1966–1970; fourth supplement (Part i) 1971–2*. London. *JRAS*, 1974, 180.

Sami A. Hanna (ed.): *Medieval and Middle Eastern studies in honour of Aziz Suryal Atiya*. Leiden, 1972. *JRAS*, 1974, 180–181.

1975

A. J. Cameron: *Abû Dharr al Ghiffârî : an examination of his image in the hagiography of Islam*. London, 1973. *BSOAS* 38 (1975), 143–144.

Ursula Sezgin: *Abū Miḥnaf : ein Beitrag zur Historiographie der umayadischen Zeit*. Leiden, 1971. *BSOAS* 38 (1975), 144–145.

Daniel S. Lev: *Islamic courts in Indonesia: a study in the political bases of legal institutions*. Berkeley, &c., 1972. *BSOAS* 38 (1975), 196–197.

1976

Fuat Sezgin: *Geschichte des arabischen Schrifttums. Bd.II: Poesie bis ca. 430 H.* Leiden, 1975. *BSOAS* 39 (1976), 656–657.

Richard W. Bulliet: *The camel and the wheel*. Cambridge, Mass., 1975. *BSOAS* 39 (1976), 662–664.

1977

Jean-Pierre Greenlaw: *The coral buildings of Suakin*. Stocksfield, &c., 1976. *BSOAS* 40 (1977), 204–206.

Oscar Löfgren and Renato Traini: *Catalogue of the Arabic manuscripts in the Biblioteca Ambrosiana. Vol.1: Antico Fondo and Medio Fondo*. Vicenza, 1975. *BSOAS* 40 (1977), 147–148.

André Miquel: *La géographie humaine du monde musulman jusqu'au milieu du 11e siècle.* [*II*:] *Géographie arabe et représentation du monde: la terre et l'étranger*. Paris, La Haye [1975]. *BSOAS* 40 (1977), 148–149.

Franz Rosenthal: *Gambling in Islam*. Leiden, 1975. *BSOAS* 40 (1977), 617.

J. Sadan: *Le mobilier au Proche-Orient médiéval*. Leiden, 1976. *BSOAS* 40 (1977), 616–617.

1978

Clifford Edmund Bosworth: *The medieval Islamic underworld: the Banū Sāsān in Arabic society and literature. Part 1: The Banū Sāsān in Arabic life and lore*. Leiden, 1976. *BSOAS* 41 (1978), 157–158.

Hortense Reintjens: *Die soziale Stellung der Frau bei den nordarabischen Beduinen unter besonderer Berücksichtigung ihrer Ehe- und Familienverhältnisse*. Bonn, 1975. *BSOAS* 41 (1978), 381.

Manfred Ullmann: *Wörterbuch der klassischen arabischen Sprache. Bd.II, 2–4 Lief*. Wiesbaden, 1973–6. *BSOAS* 41 (1978), 422–423.

J.D. Pearson: *Index Islamicus: fourth supplement (part II)*. London, 1972–3. *JRAS*, 1978, 60–61.

T.M. Johnstone: *Harsūsi lexicon and English-Harsūsi index*. London, 1977. *JRAS*, 1978, 74–76.

J. Wansbrough: *Quranic studies: sources and methods of scriptural interpretation*. Oxford U.P., 1977. *JRAS*, 1978, 76–78.

Patricia Crone and Michael Cook: *Hagarism, the making of the Islamic world*. Cambridge U.P., 1977. *JRAS*, 1978, 76–78.

1979

G.R. Smith and M.A.S. Abdel-Haleem (ed. & tr.): *The book of the superiority of dogs over many of those who wear clothes, by Ibn al-Marzubān*. Warminster, 1978. *BSOAS* 42 (1979), 414–415.

J.C. Wilkinson: *Water and tribal settlement in south-east Arabia: a study of the aflāj of Oman*. *BSOAS* 42 (1979), 378–380.

Clifford Edmund Bosworth: *The medieval Islamic underworld: the Banū Sāsān in Arabic society and literature. Part 2: The Arabic jargon texts: the Qaṣīda sāsāniyyas of Abū Dulāf and Ṣafī d-Dīn*. Leiden, 1976 [publ.

1978]. *BSOAS* 42 (1979), 381–382.

J. D. Pearson: *Index Islamicus: fourth supplement 1971–1975*. London, 1977. *JRAS*, 1979, 56–57.

1981

Dominique Sourdel: *L'Islam médiéval*. Paris, 1979. *BSOAS* 44 (1981), 166.

Carla Makhlouf: *Changing veils: women and modernisation in north Yemen*. London, 1979. *BSOAS* 44 (1981), 166–167.

Sheila A. Scoville: *Gazetteer of Arabia: a geographical and tribal history of the Arabian Peninsula. Vol. 1: A–B*. Graz, 1979. *BSOAS* 44 (1981), 372–373.

Notes on Contributors

Professor A. F. L. Beeston, F.B.A., started his career in the Oriental Books Department of the Bodleian Library. In 1956 he was appointed Laudian Professor of Arabic at Oxford, a post that he held until his retirement in 1978. During his tenure of the Chair he normally met RBS several times a term. They are both members of the Editorial Board of the *Cambridge History of Arabic Literature* and of the Steering Committee of the Arabian Seminar Society.

Professor Jacques Ryckmans is Dean of the Oriental Institute at the Catholic University of Louvain. Although RBS had long known his uncle, the distinguished epigrapher Canon Gonzague Ryckmans, it was not until an early Arabian Seminar that he first met Jacques Ryckmans. Since then they have been together at several conferences in Europe and Arabia.

Hussein Abdullah al-Amri was born in Sanaa, the son of the Chief Adviser of the Imam Yahya of the Yemen, who was murdered with him in 1948. He joined the YAR diplomatic service and while in the Embassy at Damascus, took a degree in the University there. He has also been Foreign Minister of the YAR. He first met RBS in Sanaa about 1974 and subsequently helped with the Exhibition of the City of Sanaa in the World of Islam Festival in 1976. He is at present at Durham University preparing a dissertation on the Yemeni scholar al-Shawkānī for a doctorate. He has written a book on Yemeni foreign policy.

Professor Claude Cahen has held Chairs at the University of Strasbourg and the Sorbonne. He has also been President of the Société Asiatique of Paris. He and RBS share an interest in mediaeval Arab commerce about which they have been corresponding for nearly forty years. They hope to publish an edition of *Mulakhkhaṣ al-Fitan*.

Dr. Paolo M. Costa took his doctorate at Turin and subsequently worked with the Italian Archaeological Mission in Iraq. In 1970 he was lent by the Italian Government as Museums Adviser to the Government of the YAR. He is now Archaeological Adviser to the Ministry of the National Heritage and Culture in the Sultanate of Oman. It was during his Ṣanʿāʾ days that he first met RBS and they have since often worked together. There is a proposal that they should jointly edit the proceedings of the Conference on Oman Studies that was held in Muscat in November, 1980. Dr. Costa has recently published *Yemen, land of builders*.

Professor A. J. Drewes holds the Chair in South Semitic Languages in the University of Leiden. He first met RBS at the Ethiopian Congress in Addis Ababa in 1966, and subsequently they travelled together to Harar to search for Arabic MSS.

Professor C. L. Geddes took a Ph.D. in SOAS in 1959 when he was helped and subsequently examined by RBS. He has held University posts in Cairo and Katmandu. Since 1966 he has been Resident Director of the Institute of Islamic Studies in Denver and has held a Chair of History there since 1968.

Professor J. Derek Latham, recently appointed Professor of Arabic at Edinburgh University, had been at Manchester University since 1958 as Lecturer, Senior Lecturer and Reader in Arabic. He has been in frequent touch with RBS, whom he succeeded as Chairman of the Middle East Libraries Committee. He has been Editor of the *Islamic Quarterly* and is a J.P. for Manchester. He is also a member of the Editorial Committee of CHAL.

Dr. Ronald Lewcock studied architecture at the University of Cape Town and subsequently taught at the University of Natal. He came to Cambridge in 1970 and since then has been one of the closest collaborators of RBS. They played the leading roles in organising the Exhibition of Ṣan'ā' as part of the World of Islam Festival and are joint Editors of a major work on the city of Ṣan'ā', recently published.

Sami al-Sakkar took a degree at the American University of Beirut and then joined the Iraqi diplomatic service. In the 1960s he was Ambassador to Yugoslavia and Bulgaria. During this period he met RBS in Beirut and decided to come to Cambridge to be supervised by him for a Ph.D. His dissertation has been published as *Tārīkh Irbil* (Baghdad, 1980). He now holds a Chair in the History Department in the University of Riyadh.

G. Rex Smith was taught by RBS as an undergraduate at SOAS, 1958–61. After spending the years 1961–65 as Aden Student Liaison Officer in London and Assistant Adviser in the Western Aden Protectorate, he came to Cambridge to take his doctorate under the supervision of RBS. His thesis was later expanded and published in the Gibb Memorial Series, *The Ayyubids and early Rasulids in the Yemen* (2 vols., 1974–8). He is Lecturer in Arabic in the University of Durham and Executive Editor of CHAL.

Dr. Al-Tayib Zein al-Abdin is a lecturer in Middle Eastern politics and Islamic political thought at the University of Khartoum. He was the head of department of Afro-Asian studies at the Institute of African and Asian Studies. Currently he is the director of the Islamic African Centre in Khartoum.

Leila Ahmed was born and educated in Cairo. She was engaged in research at Cambridge from 1966 to 1971, in which RBS and the late Professor Arberry were her supervisors. She was awarded a Ph.D. for a dissertation on Edward Lane which has subsequently been published. She has taught at the University of Ain Shams and al-Azhar in Cairo and al-Ain in the UAE. She has also been Inspector of English Language Teaching in the UAE. She is at present in the USA, lecturing at various Universities.

Professor C. F. Beckingham started his career in the Department of Printed Books in the British Museum. From 1946 until 1965 he was firstly Lecturer and then Professor of Islamic Studies at Manchester University. In 1965 he succeeded RBS at SOAS with the title of Professor of Islamic Studies. He retired from this position in 1981. He has been President of both the Hakluyt Society and the Royal Asiatic Society. He first met RBS during the war, when they collaborated on the Admiralty *Handbook of Arabia*. Subsequently they have worked closely together, sharing an interest in Portuguese activities in Arabia in the sixteenth and seventeenth centuries.

Robin Bidwell first met RBS when he was serving as a Political Officer in the WAP in 1958. Subsequently he did a Ph.D. at Cambridge with RBS as his supervisor. This was published as *Morocco under Colonial Rule*. In 1968 he was appointed Secretary/Librarian of the Middle East Centre, Cambridge, of which RBS was Director until his retirement in September 1982. They jointly founded and still edit *Arabian Studies*. He has a book *The Two Yemens* recently published.

Professor Walter Dostal has held Chairs of Ethnology in Bern and in Vienna where he is also Director of the Institut für Völkerkunde. He first met RBS in the 1950s, when he came to consult him before his first visit to Arabia. They have since been together in Hadhramawt, the UAE and Yemen, sharing the same interests in tribal customs, urban organisation etc.

Professor Caesar E. Farah has held the Chair of Middle East Studies at Minnesota University since 1969. Previously he had held posts in the US Information Service. He spent the academic year 1973/4 in Cambridge where he was made an Associate Member of the Middle East Centre.

Professor T. M. Johnstone was appointed a Lecturer in Arabic at SOAS in 1957. He took his Ph.D. there, supervised and examined by RBS in 1962. He held the Chair of Arabic there from 1970 until his retirement in 1982. He and RBS were both on the Expedition to Socotra in 1967 and had subsequently been together in other parts of the Peninsula. With RBS he was a member of the Editorial Committee of the *CHAL* and of the Steering Committee of the Arabian Seminar Society. He died in January 1983.

Shaykh Abd al-Aziz b. Muhammad al-Khalifa, who died in the summer of 1981, was a member of the ruling family of Bahrain. He had studied in Cairo and at SOAS. There he was supervised by RBS and they often worked together on matters concerning fishing techniques, technical terms and fishermen's songs (*mawwāl*). He made his career in the Bahrain Education Service and was Minister of Education from 1973 until his death.

Abdullah M. A. Maktari was born in Aden of a leading family of Yemeni origin. He was a student at SOAS where he was supervised by RBS. As an undergraduate he shared the interests of RBS in tribal law and they collaborated. Subsequently he took an MA at the University of California at Berkeley and in 1965 came to Cambridge to do a Ph.D. with RBS as his supervisor. This was subsequently published as *Water rights and irrigation practices in Lahej* (C.U.P. 1975). Later he held a University post in Malaya and was then Vice-Principal of the recently founded University of Sanaa. He is now a legal consultant in that city.

Professor Mahmoud Samra took a degree in Cairo and then came to SOAS where he was supervised by RBS. He took a Ph.D. in 1958 with a dissertation on modern Syrian literature. From 1958–1962 he was in Kuwait as Deputy Editor-in-Chief of the magazine *al-Arabi*. Since 1966 he has been at the University of Jordan in Amman as Professor, Dean of the Faculty of Arts and since 1973 as Vice-President.

Professor Bayly Winder took a Ph.D. at Princeton where he taught from 1949–1971. He is now a Professor of History and Near Eastern Languages in New York University where he has been Dean of the Faculty of Arts. He first met RBS in Beirut in the early 1960s.

Professor J. D. Pearson, then on the staff of Cambridge University Library, studied Persian together with RBS, under Reuben Levy before the war. Since then they have been in constant touch, serving on numerous committees and attending several conferences together. They were the joint founders of MELCOM. He was Librarian of SOAS from 1950 to 1972 when he was appointed Professor of Bibliography. He created *Index Islamicus* and his outstanding services to bibliographical scholarship were marked by the publication in 1980 of a felicitation volume to celebrate his 'jubilee' as a librarian.

تقديم وإهــداء

يعتبر البروفسور روبرت بيرترام سرجنت المولود في إدنبرة في مارس ١٩١٥م أحد أعلام الاستشراق الحديث في بريطانيا وأوربة، فمنذ أن نال درجة الدكتوراه في الدراسات الاسلامية من جامعة كمبردج عام ١٩٣٩ حتى تسلمه كرسي الأستاذية في نفس الجامعة وهو منهمك ومكرس وقته وجهده في خدمة الثقافة العربية والتاريخ الاسلامي دارساً وباحثاً ومحاضراً، وما زال كذلك أمد الله في عمره.

لقد كانت الزيارة الأولى التي قام بها الأستاذ سرجنت للمشرق العربي عام ١٩٣٥ حيث زار سورية. ثم ساقته مقادير الحرب العالمية الثانية عام ١٩٤٠ ليعمل عامين في جنوب اليمن. فكان لذلك أبلغ الأثر في زيادة اهتمامه بتاريخ اليمن وتراثه الحضاري والاجتماعي الرفيع. وظهر ذلك الاهتمام واضحاً في معظم أبحاثه ودراساته المكرس معظمها لليمن وحضارة جنوب الجزيرة العربية. وبعد عودته من اليمن قام في هيئة الاذاعة البريطانية بتحرير مجلة الاذاعة العربية الذائعة الصيت «المستمع العربي». ثم مع نهاية الحرب عين محاضراً في جامعة لندن في مدرسة الدراسات الشرقية والافريقية، وتدرج في مناصب التدريس حتى استحدث خصيصاً من أجله كرسي الدراسات العربية الحديثة عام ١٩٥٥ وشغله حتى عام ١٩٦٤ حين استقال منه ليتفرغ للتدريس والمزيد من البحث في جامعة كمبردج التي رأس فيها مركز الدراسات للشرق الأوسط. وبوفاة البروفسور آربري A.J.Arberry عام ١٩٦٩ خلفه في منصب الأستاذية حتى تقاعده في ديسمبر ١٩٨١.

لقد عرف البروفسور سرجنت مغرب العالم العربي ومشرقه ولم تقتصر زياراته على العواصم أو المدن الكبيرة بل زار الأرياف والقرى التي أحبها وكتب عنها، ويعتبر كتابه الضخم الذي صدر حديثاً عن مدينة صنعاء أكبر دليل على ذلك الحب وعلى بالغ الجهد وعميق البحث.

والمحرران إذ يقدمان هذا الكتاب إلى الأستاذ الكبير إجلالا وتقديراً ليشكران كل المساهمين فيه من زملاء وأصدقاء وتلاميذ البروفسور سرجنت ومنهم باحثون من بعض أصدقائه وتلاميذه العرب، فلهم التقدير جميعاً.

المحرران

دراسات

عربية وإسلامية

دراسات عربية وإسلامية

مهداة إلى البرفسور سيرجنت

بمناسبة تقاعده من مركز الاستاذية

في جامعة كمبردج

تحرير: الدكتور روبن بدول

والدكتور ركس سميث